CSS Mastery

Advanced Web Standards Solutions

Third Edition

Andy Budd

Emil Björklund

Apress®

CSS Mastery: Advanced Web Standards Solutions, Third Edition

Andy Budd
Brighton, United Kingdom

Emil Björklund
Malmo, Sweden

ISBN-13 (pbk): 978-1-4302-5863-6

ISBN-13 (electronic): 978-1-4302-5864-3

DOI 10.1007/978-1-4302-5864-3

Library of Congress Control Number: 2016944612

Managing Director: Welmoed Spahr
Acquisitions Editor: Ben Renow-Clarke
Development Editor: Matthew Moodie
Technical Reviewers: Anna Debenham and Andy Hume
Editorial Board: Steve Anglin, Pramila Balen, Louise Corrigan, James DeWolf, Jonathan Gennick,
    Robert Hutchinson, Celestin Suresh John, Nikhil Karkal, James Markham, Susan McDermott,
    Matthew Moodie, Douglas Pundick, Ben Renow-Clarke, Gwenan Spearing
Coordinating Editor: Nancy Chen
Copy Editor: Bill McManus
Compositor: SPi Global
Indexer: SPi Global

Distributed to the book trade worldwide by Springer Science+Business Media New York, 233 Spring Street, 6th Floor, New York, NY 10013. Phone 1-800-SPRINGER, fax (201) 348-4505, e-mail orders-ny@springer-sbm.com, or visit www.springer.com. Apress Media, LLC is a California LLC and the sole member (owner) is Springer Science + Business Media Finance Inc (SSBM Finance Inc). SSBM Finance Inc is a Delaware corporation.

For information on translations, please e-mail rights@apress.com, or visit www.apress.com.

Apress and friends of ED books may be purchased in bulk for academic, corporate, or promotional use. eBook versions and licenses are also available for most titles. For more information, reference our Special Bulk Sales–eBook Licensing web page at www.apress.com/bulk-sales.

Any source code or other supplementary materials referenced by the author in this text is available to readers at www.apress.com. For detailed information about how to locate your book's source code, go to www.apress.com/source-code/.

This book is dedicated to all my colleagues at Clearleft—both past and present. Were it not for their support and wisdom, this book would never have happened.

—Andy Budd

Dedicated to the memory of my grandfather: the engineer, artist, and life-long tinkerer Sven Forsberg (1919–2016).

—Emil Björklund

Contents at a Glance

Contents

About the Authors

Andy Budd is one of the founding partners at digital design consultancy, Clearleft. An early champion of web standards in the UK, the first edition of this book played a small but important role in the eventual adoption of CSS. These days, Andy is primarily focused on advancing the field of user experience design. He does this by consulting with clients, writing articles, mentoring new designers, and speaking at events like SXSW, An Event Apart, and The Next Web. Andy founded the long running dConstruct conference, and currently curates the popular UX London conference. In 2011 Andy co-founded the Brighton Digital Festival, which now sees 40,000 visitors attend 190 events in the city of Brighton each September.

As an active member of the design community, Andy has helped judge a number of international design awards, and is a mentor at Seedcamp. He is also the driving force behind Silverback, a low-cost usability-testing tool for the Mac. An avid Twitter user, Andy occasionally finds time to blog at andybudd.com.

Never happier than when he's diving in some remote tropical atoll, Andy is a qualified PADI dive instructor and retired shark wrangler.

Emil Björklund is the Technical Director at digital design consultancy inUse, where he's usually busy building websites—or helping clients and co-workers better their craft. Emil created his first HTML page on Geocities in 1997, but got confused by the mess of table tags. Coming back to the Web in 2001, he found this magical thing called CSS and has been fascinated by it ever since.

For the last decade, Emil has been building websites professionally, hacking on anything from client-side JavaScript to server-side Python, but always with a special place in his heart for good old HTML and CSS. Emil's writing and advice on CSS has been published in Net Magazine and on CSS Tricks. He also writes about (mostly) web-related stuff on his blog at thatemil.com.

Emil lives with his girlfriend and their cat in Malmö, Sweden, far from any sharks.

About the Technical Reviewers

Andrew Hume is a web developer from Brighton in the UK. He's spent the last fifteen years leading front-end teams for websites like Twitter, Bing, and The Guardian. As a consultant for Clearleft, he helped figure out large, scalable CSS systems for clients like the BBC, eBay, and Mozilla.

Anna Debenham is a Freelance Front-end Developer living and working in London in the UK. In 2013, she was awarded Netmag's Young Developer of the Year award. She's the author of Front-end Style Guides, a Technical Editor for A List Apart, and every December, she co-produces 24 Ways.

Acknowledgments

We would like to thank the tireless work of Jeffrey Zeldman, Eric Meyer, and Tantek Çelik, without whom the web standards movement would never have happened. We'd like to thank those who followed. People like John Allsopp, Rachel Andrew, Mark Boulton, Doug Bowman, Dan Cederholm, Andy Clarke, Simon Collison, Jon Hicks, Molly E. Holzschlag, Aaron Gustafson, Shaun Inman, Jeremy Keith, Peter-Paul Koch, Ethan Marcotte, Drew McLellan, Cameron Moll, Dave Shea, Nicole Sullivan, and Jason Santa-Maria, who answered the challenge and helped take CSS mainstream. Finally, we'd like to thank all those tireless designers and developers who have subsequently picked up the baton, and have helped turn CSS into the modern design language we know today. There are too many to list everybody, but some of the people who have made the biggest impact on our practice in later years include Chris Coyier, Vasilis van Gemert, Stephen Hay, Val Head, Paul Lewis, Rachel Nabors, Harry Roberts, Lea Verou, Ryan Seddon, Jen Simmons, Sara Soueidan, Trent Walton, and Estelle Weyl. We'd also like to thank all the designers and developers who constantly help and inspire us by bouncing ideas about CSS on Twitter and various Slack teams.

We want to thank everybody who helped get this book over the finish line, including inUse who sponsored part of the work. A special thanks to technical editor Anna Debenham—if there are any errors in the book, it's more than likely we put them in there when she was looking the other way. We'd also like to thank Andy Hume, who contributed his expertise during the early phases of writing, setting the direction for this new edition. Furthermore, we'd like to thank Charlotte Jackson, Peter-Paul Koch, Paul Lloyd, Mark Perkins, and Richard Rutter for reading early drafts, bouncing ideas, and giving invaluable feedback.

Photos in the book or in examples are in most instances taken by us or gathered from Public Domain sources. The following images are licensed via the Creative Commons Attribution 2.0 license (`https://creativecommons.org/licenses/by/2.0/`): "Portrait" by Jeremy Keith (`https://flic.kr/p/dwFRgH`) and "A Long Night Falls on Saturn's Rings" by NASA Goddard Space Flight Center (`https://flic.kr/p/7ayNkz`).

Finally, we'd both like to thank our partners for patience and support during the considerable time it took to produce these pages.

Introduction

When I started writing the first edition of *CSS Mastery* way back in 2004, there were already two CSS books in the market, so I wasn't sure the world needed a third. After all, CSS was still a relatively niche subject back then; largely the preserve of bloggers and web standards enthusiasts. The majority of sites were still being built using tables and frames, and the folks on my local developer mailing list thought I was mad, and CSS was just a pipe dream. Little did they know we were on the verge of a web standards revolution and the field exploded around the time the book was published, pushing the book to the top of my publisher's bestselling chart for years to come.

By the time the second edition came out, CSS was now firmly established. The role of the book changed from exposing new people to the power of CSS, to helping make them more efficient and effective. So we scoured the Web for the latest techniques, workarounds, and hacks, and created a book we hoped would become the definitive guide for web designers and front-end developers everywhere. It felt like we'd reached a stable point in the development of the language, and the book would remain relevant for a long time. How wrong we were.

Rather than becoming stagnant, CSS of recent years feels like it has finally started to live up to its original promise. We entered the golden age of web standards; an age where browser support was good enough for us to finally move focus away from hacks, instead putting our efforts into writing elegant, well-crafted, and highly maintainable code for the largest and most complicated sites around.

So it was time to write a third edition; to bring together all these new tools, techniques, and ways of thinking into a single reference. To help in this task I drew upon the skills of my good friend, Emil Björklund, a developer of rare skill and ability. What Emil brings to the book is a deep understanding of modern CSS practices; how to craft highly flexible code using the latest techniques that works across the widest range of browsers, screens, and platforms, in the most elegant way possible.

Together we've almost completely rewritten the book from the ground up, adding new chapters on web typography, animation, layout, responsive design, how to structure your code, and much more. This new edition follows in the footsteps of previous editions, offering a mix of practical examples, language reference, and cross-browser workarounds for tricky techniques. The sign of CSS mastery is no longer about knowing all the arcane hacks to make CSS work at all, or knowing all properties by heart. CSS today consists of several dozen specifications, encompassing hundreds of properties—there's probably no one who knows it all! Instead, this book emphasizes flexibility and robustness, making sure your code works in the ever-changing landscape of different browsers, devices, and usage situations. We won't cover every single language feature, but you will find a good overview of what's available, some lesser-known old-school tricks, and the occasional glimpse into the future of CSS.

To enjoy the book fully, you should have at least some small grasp of how CSS works—maybe you have played with it for a while, or even worked on a website or two. The book starts with three short introductory chapters on the very foundations of creating and styling web pages, so even if you're rusty, you'll get a recap. After that, each chapter introduces new features of the language and progressively more complex examples. Even if you're a seasoned CSS practitioner, you should find plenty of interesting and useful techniques for solving common web design problems, in which case you should feel free to jump to the chapters that pique your interest.

Regardless of your previous understanding of the language, we hope the resulting book will help you unlock some of the secrets of CSS and become a true CSS Master.

CHAPTER 1

■ ■ ■

Setting the Foundations

The human race is a naturally inquisitive species. We just love tinkering with things. When we got our new Parrot AR Drone at the office, we had it in pieces before we'd even looked at the instructions. We enjoy working things out ourselves and creating our own mental models of how we think things behave. We muddle through and only turn to the manual when something goes wrong or defies our expectations.

One of the best ways to learn Cascading Style Sheets (CSS) is to jump right in and start tinkering. In fact, this is likely how many of you learned to code; by picking up tips from blogs, viewing source to see how your favorite designers had achieved a particular effect, and by browsing open source repositories for snippets of code. You almost certainly didn't start out by reading the full specification, which is enough to put anyone to sleep.

Tinkering is a great way to start, but if you're not careful, you may end up misunderstanding a crucial concept or building in problems for later on. We know; we've done so several times. In this chapter, we're going to review some basic but often misunderstood concepts and show you how to keep your HTML and CSS clear and well structured.

In this chapter you will learn about:

- The importance of maintainability

- Different versions of HTML and CSS

- Strategies for future-friendly and backward-compatible code

- Adding meaning to your HTML and using newer HTML5 elements

- Adding appropriate styling hooks to HTML

- Extending HTML semantics with ARIA, microformats, and microdata

- Browser engine modes and validation

Structuring your Code

Most people don't think about the foundations of a building. However, without solid foundations the majority of buildings wouldn't stay standing. While this book is about CSS techniques and concepts, much of what you are about to learn would not be possible (or at least would be very difficult) without a well-structured and valid HTML document to work with.

In this section you will learn why well-structured and meaningful HTML is vital to standards-based development. You will learn how you can add more meaning and flexibility to your documents, and by doing so, make your job as a developer easier. But first up is a topic of the utmost importance no matter what language we happen to be working in.

Electronic supplementary material The online version of this chapter (doi:10.1007/978-1-4302-5864-3_1) contains supplementary material, which is available to authorized users.

© Andy Budd and Emil Björklund 2016
A. Budd and E. Björklund, *CSS Mastery*, DOI 10.1007/978-1-4302-5864-3_1

Maintainability

Maintainability is arguably the most important characteristic of any good code base. If your code begins to lose structure and becomes hard to read, then lots of things become difficult. Adding new features, fixing bugs, and improving performance all become more complicated and frustrating if you're struggling with unreadable and brittle code. In some cases it gets so bad that developers will resist making changes altogether, because nearly every time they do, something breaks. This can lead to a situation where no one enjoys working on the website or, in very bad circumstances, to a strict change control process where releases can only be carried out once a week or even once a month!

If you are building websites that are to be handed off to a client or another development team, maintainability is even more important. It's critical that you provide code that is easy to read, explicit in its intent, and *optimized for change*. "The only constant is change" is a particularly appropriate cliché to invoke here, because whose project doesn't have continually changing requirements, along with constant feature requests and bug fixes?

CSS is one of the hardest languages to keep maintainable as a codebase grows, and the style sheets for even a relatively small site can get out of hand quickly. Other modern programming languages have features like variables, functions, and namespaces built in; all features which help keep code structured and modular by default. CSS doesn't have these features, so we need to build them into the way that we use the language and structure our code. As we discuss different topics throughout the book, you'll see the theme of maintainability evident across nearly all of them.

A Brief History of Markup

> *The power of the Web is in its universality. Access by everyone regardless of disability is an essential aspect.*
>
> —Tim Berners-Lee

Tim Berners-Lee created HTML in 1990, for the purpose of formatting scientific research documents. It was a simple markup language that enabled text to be given basic structure and meaning, such as headings, lists, and definitions. These documents were typically presented with little or no visual embellishment, and could be easily indexed by computers and read by people using a text-only terminal, a web browser, or screen reader if necessary.

However, humans are very visual creatures, and as the World Wide Web gained in popularity, HTML started to acquire features for creating presentational effects. Instead of using heading elements for page headlines, people would use a combination of font and bold tags to create a specific visual effect. Tables got co-opted as a layout tool rather than a way of displaying data, and people would use blockquote elements to indent text rather than to indicate quotations. Very quickly HTML lost its primary purpose of giving structure and meaning to content, and became a jumble of font and table tags. Web designers came up with a name for this kind of markup; they called it *tag soup* (see Figure 1-1).

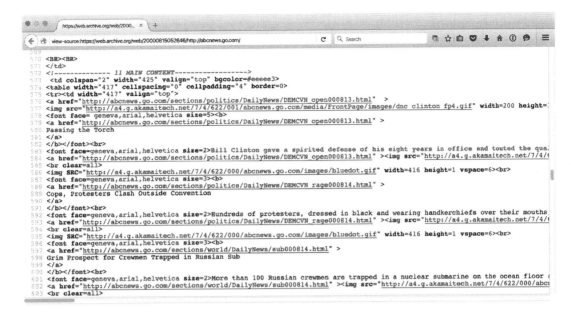

Figure 1-1. *The markup for the lead story from abcnews.com on August 14, 2000, uses tables for layout and large, bold text for headings. The code lacks structure and is difficult to understand*

The Web had become a mess, and CSS was created to help tidy things up. The primary purpose of CSS was to allow the presentational rules that had found their way into HTML to be extracted and put into their own system; to *separate content and presentation*. This encouraged meaning and semantics to creep back into HTML documents. Presentational tags like the font tag could be ditched, and layout tables could be slowly replaced. This was a boon for the accessibility and speed of much of the Web, but CSS also provides a number of benefits for web designers and developers:

- A language specifically designed to control visual style and layout

- Styles that can be more easily reused across one site

- Improved code structure through separation of concerns

SEPARATION OF CONCERNS

The concept of separation of concerns is common in software development. On the Web, it can be applied not only to the separation of markup and style, but also to how the styles are written. In fact, it's one of the main methods for ensuring maintainable code.

There's a phrase common in the Unix development community that expresses this concept through the mantra "Small pieces, loosely joined." A "small piece" is a focused module of code that does one thing really well. And because it is "loosely joined" to other components, that module can be easily reused in other parts of the system. A "small piece" in Unix could be a word count function, which will work with any piece of text you feed into it. In web development, a "small piece" could be a product-list component, which if loosely coupled will be reusable across multiple pages of a site, or in different parts of the layout.

You could think of these small pieces of code as LEGO bricks. Each brick is incredibly simple, but they can be joined together in numerous ways to create objects of immense complexity. Towards the end of the book, in Chapter 12, we will return to this topic, and examine how to use this strategy in a structured way.

Different Versions of HTML and CSS

CSS comes in various versions, or "levels", and it's good to have some historical context around what these versions mean and how they impact what features of CSS you should or shouldn't use. The World Wide Web Consortium (W3C) is the organization that looks after standardizing web technology, and each of its specifications goes through a number of phases of development before it finally becomes a W3C recommendation. CSS 1 became a W3C recommendation at the end of 1996 and contains very basic properties such as fonts, colors, and margins. CSS 2 became a recommendation in 1998 and added advanced concepts such as floating and positioning, as well as new selectors like the child, adjacent sibling, and universal selectors.

CSS 3 is a slightly different beast. In fact, there *is* no CSS 3 as such, but a collection of modules each *leveled* independently. When a module specification continues to improve an existing concept, it starts at level 3. If it's an entirely new technology it starts at level 1. When the term CSS 3 is used, it usually refers to anything new enough to be part of a module specification. Examples of modules include "CSS Backgrounds and Borders Level 3," "Selectors Level 4," and "CSS Grid Layout Level 1." This modular approach allows different specifications to move at different speeds, and some level 3 specifications, such as "CSS Color Level 3", have already been published as recommendations. Others are in candidate recommendation status, and many are still in working draft status.

Although work began on CSS 3 at about the time CSS 2 was published, progress on these new specifications was initially slow. For that reason, in 2002, the W3C published CSS 2 Revision 1. CSS 2.1 fixes errors in CSS 2, removes features that were poorly supported or nonexistent in browsers, and generally cleans things up to provide a more accurate picture of browser implementations. CSS 2.1 reached recommendation status in June 2011, over a decade after work on CSS 3 had started. That gives you an idea of how long it can take for standards bodies and browser makers to nail down exactly how these technologies work. That being said, browsers often ship experimental support for features when the features are in the draft stage, and at the candidate recommendation stage things are usually quite stable. The date when something becomes a usable technology is usually much earlier than the date when it becomes a recommendation.

The history of HTML is no less complex. HTML 4.01 became a recommendation in 1999, at which point the W3C switched its attention to XHTML 1.0. XHTML 1.1 was meant to follow, but the level of strictness it imposed proved impractical and it fell out of favor among members of the web development community. Essentially, progress on the main language of the Web stalled.

In 2004, a group of companies formed the Web Hypertext Application Technology Working Group (WHATWG) and started working on a new set of specifications. The W3C acknowledged the need for this work in 2006, and joined in on the fun. In 2009, the W3C gave up on XHTML completely, and formally embraced the new standard from the WHATWG that had become known as HTML5. Initially, both the WHATWG and the W3C harmonized their work on the standards, but somewhere along the line, their relationship status turned complicated. Today, they edit two separate standards, the one from the WHATWG being known as just HTML, and the one from the W3C known as HTML5. Yes, we know, it's all a bit nuts. Fortunately, the two standards are very close to each other, so speaking of HTML5 as a single thing still makes sense.

What Version Should I Use?

Designers and developers often ask which version of HTML or CSS they should use, but there's no simple answer to this. Although the specifications provide a focal point for standards and the work that goes on in developing web technology, they are largely irrelevant to designers and developers on a day-to-day basis. What *is* important is knowing what parts of HTML and CSS have been implemented in browsers, and how robust and bug-free those implementations are. Are they experimental features that should be used with caution? Or are they robust and well tested, with matching implementations across a large number of browsers?

Understanding the state of browser support is one of the trickiest parts of writing CSS and HTML today. Sometimes it can seem like things move very fast, and you have to work hard to keep up. At other times it can feel frustratingly slow. Throughout this book you will see browser support notes for various features of HTML and CSS, along with tips as to how and when you should consider using them. Inevitably the information printed here will become outdated, so it is important to keep up with this information yourself.

There are several good places to start learning about browser support. For CSS properties, the "Can I use" website (http://caniuse.com) allows you to search for a property or suite of properties, complete with statistics on what percent of browsers support it, across both desktop and mobile browsers. Another ambitious initiative is http://webplatform.org, a collaboration between the W3C and several browser makers and industry giants, attempting to collect and merge all their respective documents on support for CSS, HTML, JavaScript APIs, and so forth. However, as large projects are prone to do, putting together this canonical web technology documentation is taking a lot of time. While that's happening, Mozilla's developer documentation, MDN (http://developer.mozilla.org), is generally considered the gold standard.

When discussing browser support, it's important to accept that not all browsers are created equal; and they never will be. Some CSS 3 features are supported by very few browsers today. For example, Flexible Box Layout (or *flexbox* for short) was not correctly supported in Internet Explorer until version 11 and in Safari until version 6.1. Even if you need to support legacy browsers, it does not mean that flexbox is of no use at all. You might avoid using flexbox for the core layout of your site, but you could still choose to use it in a specific component where its powerful features are extremely useful, and make sure that there is an acceptable fallback in browsers that don't understand the properties. The ability to make judgment calls on backward compatibility vs. future-friendly code is part of what defines the true CSS Master.

Progressive Enhancement

The ability to balance backward compatibility with the latest HTML and CSS features involves a strategy known as *progressive enhancement*. What this stands for is basically "start by making it work well for the lowest common denominator, but feel free to take things further where they are supported." Using progressive enhancement means you'll write your code in "layers," where each successive enhancement is only applied if it's supported or deemed appropriate. This may sound complicated, but the good news is that both HTML and CSS partly have this built in.

For HTML, this means that unknown elements or attributes generally cause no trouble for the browser; it will gobble them up without complaining but might not apply the resulting changes to how the page works. As an example, you could use the new types of input elements that are defined in HTML5. Say you have a form field for an e-mail address that's marked up like this:

```
<input type="text" id="field-email" name="field-email">
```

You could change the value of the type attribute like this:

```
<input type="email" id="field-email" name="field-email">
```

Browsers that haven't implemented the new field types will simply respond "I have no idea what that means" and fall back to the default type value, which is "text", just like in the first example. Newer browsers that do understand the "email" type will know what kind of data the user is supposed to enter into this field. On many mobile devices, the software keyboard will adjust to show a view optimized for inputting e-mail addresses, and if you're using the built-in support for form validation in newer browsers, this will pick up on that too. We have *progressively enhanced* the page, with no downside for users on older browsers.

Another simple change is to update the document type declaration to the new, shorter version from the HTML5 standard. The document type, or doctype for short, is the bit at the top of an HTML document that's supposed to be a machine-readable hint about the version of the markup language used in the document. It used to be a long and complicated affair in older versions of HTML and XHTML, but in HTML5 it's been simplified down to just this:

```
<!DOCTYPE html>
```

You can safely switch to writing your HTML documents with this doctype because the HTML5 syntax and doctype are backward compatible. We'll have a closer look at some of the new elements available in HTML5 in upcoming sections, but if you need more in-depth information on how to start writing HTML5 markup today, check out Jeremy Keith's *HTML5 for Web Designers* at http://html5forwebdesigners.com.

Progressive enhancement in CSS works in a similar manner when it comes to how the browser interprets new properties. Any property or value that the browser doesn't recognize causes it to discard that declaration, so adding new properties has no ill effects as long as you provide a sensible fallback.

As an example, many modern browsers support the rgba functional notation for color values. It allows you to specify colors using separate values for the red, green, and blue channels as well as a transparency value, called the alpha channel. We can use it like this:

```
.overlay {
    background-color: #000;
    background-color: rgba(0, 0, 0, 0.8);
}
```

This rule states that elements with the overlay class name should have a black background color, but then immediately redeclares the background color to be a slightly transparent black using rgba. For browsers that don't understand the rgba notation, the second statement will be ignored, and the element will have a solid black background color. For browsers that *do* understand the rgba notation, the second statement overwrites the first. So even if rgba notation isn't supported everywhere, we can still use it, provided we use a fallback declaration that comes first.

Vendor Prefixes

Browser makers use the same principle to introduce experimental features into their browsers. They do this by prefixing the property name or value with a special string, so that only their own browser engine will apply it and other browsers will ignore it. This allows browser makers to introduce new features while the specifications are missing or immature. Style sheet authors can try them out without risk of breaking their pages if the different browsers interpret new features differently. For example:

```
.myThing {
  -webkit-transform: translate(0, 10px);
  -moz-transform: translate(0, 10px);
  -ms-transform: translate(0, 10px);
  transform: translate(0, 10px);
}
```

This applies a transformation to the element (something we will look at in Chapter 10) with a couple of different prefixes. Those starting with -webkit- apply to the WebKit-based browsers such as Safari. Google Chrome and Opera are based on the Blink engine, which in turn was initially based on WebKit, so the -webkit-prefix often works for them as well. The -moz- prefix applies to Mozilla-based browsers like Firefox, and the -ms- prefix applies to Microsoft's Internet Explorer.

Finally, we've added the unprefixed version, so that browsers that support the standardized version of the property don't miss out. Historically, developers have been sloppy with adding the standardized versions. This has gone so far that some browser makers have started supporting the prefixes of competing engines, just to make sure popular sites work on their browser. As a consequence of this confusion, most browser makers are turning away from vendor prefixes. Experimental features are instead hidden behind preference flags, or in special preview releases.

Examples in the book will mostly use only the standardized properties without prefixes, so you are advised to check with websites like `http://caniuse.com` to make sure how the current support situation looks.

Conditional Rules and Detection Scripts

For more advanced cases where we'd want completely different solutions based on the CSS support available, there's the `@supports`-block. This special block, known as a conditional rule, checks the declaration inside the parentheses, and only applies the rules inside this block if the declaration is supported:

```
@supports (display: grid) {
  /* rules for when grid layout is supported go here */
}
```

The problem with this is that this rule is fairly new in itself, so we can only use it for bleeding-edge features not implemented in any legacy browser (for example, we'll look at grid layout in Chapter 7). For other cases, we can use JavaScript to figure out if something is supported. This type of feature test is available in several JavaScript libraries, the most popular being Modernizr (`http://modernizr.com`). It works by appending support hints to the HTML, which you can then base your CSS on.

We'll look more closely at strategies and tools like this in upcoming chapters, but the important takeaway is that progressive enhancement can help us break free from worrying about version numbers and specifications too much. With careful application, we can use the new shiny toys where they're appropriate, without leaving behind users on older browsers.

Creating Structurally and Semantically Rich HTML

Semantic markup is the foundation of any good HTML document. *Semantics* is the scientific study of meaning. In the context of a made-up language with a formal set of symbols, such as HTML and its elements and attributes, semantics refers to what we mean by using a certain symbol. Put simply, *semantic markup* is the practice of using the right element in the right place, resulting in meaningful documents.

Meaningful documents help ensure that content is accessible to the greatest number of people possible, whether they're using the latest version of Google Chrome, running a text-only browser like Lynx, or relying on assistive technology such as a screen reader or braille display. Whatever fancy graphics or interactions might be required later in the project, the fundamental semantics of the document should never, and need never, be compromised.

Good structural markup also means that your content is more easily consumed by machines— specifically, search engine spiders such as Googlebot, which indexes and ranks pages for inclusion in Google's search results. The more rich data Googlebot can get from your pages, the better chance it has of indexing and ranking them correctly. As a result, you will most likely benefit by higher positions in the search rankings.

More importantly in the context of CSS, meaningful markup provides you with a simple way of targeting the elements you wish to style. It adds structure to a document and creates an underlying framework for you to build on.

In fact, many modern approaches to crafting CSS suggest starting with a set of "base" styles for your site. The style guide page by Paul Lloyd shown in Figure 1-2 contains every plausible element he is likely to need on his personal blog. It describes how and when to use them, and his style sheet ensures that whatever element he adds to his pages over time will be appropriately styled without having to do further work.

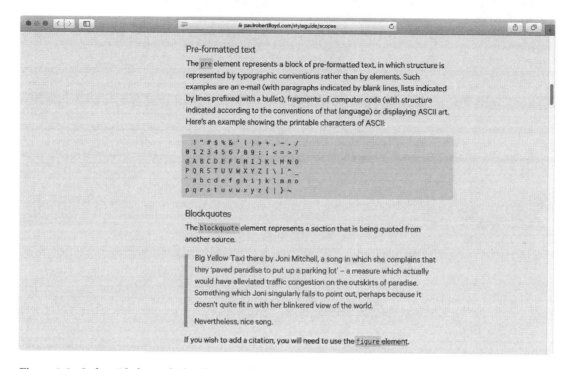

Figure 1-2. *Style guide for paulrobertlloyd.com, found at http://paulrobertlloyd.com/about/styleguide/*

Paul's style guide contains all the obvious meaningful elements such as:

- h1, h2, and so on
- p, ul, ol, and dl
- strong and em
- blockquote and cite
- pre and code
- time, figcaption, and caption

It also includes base styles for forms and tables with their associated elements, including:

- fieldset, legend, and label
- caption, thead, tbody, and tfoot

The value of having this base set of styles cannot be overstated. Clearly you'll need to begin inheriting and overriding them pretty soon in the design and development process, but having a solid foundation of element styles to build on sets you up very nicely for future work. It can also serve as a proof sheet. As you make changes to the CSS, you can scan the components in your style guide and verify that you haven't unintentionally overridden certain styles as you work on others.

Class and ID Attributes

Meaningful elements provide an excellent foundation, but they won't provide you with all the "hooks" you'll need to apply every visual effect. Nine times out of ten you'll want to adjust the styles of your base elements depending on their context. We need a way of providing other styling "hooks" into our document, and one common approach is to use ID and class attributes.

Adding an ID or class attribute doesn't *inherently* add meaning or structure to your document. Adding these attributes is a general-purpose way of allowing other things to interact with and parse your document, and CSS is one thing that can take advantage of them. The value of these attributes is that they can contain names that you define.

It sounds trivial, but naming something is one of the most important (and often most difficult) parts of writing code. Choosing a name allows you to state what something *is*, and hint at its purpose or how it should be used. When you are writing code, clarity and explicitness is absolutely critical. So let's take a simple list of links and give it a class attribute with a nice readable and useful value:

```
<ul class="product-list">
  <li><a href="/product/1">Product 1</a></li>
  <li><a href="/product/2">Product 2</a></li>
  <li><a href="/product/3">Product 3</a></li>
</ul>
```

Here we've used the class attribute to create a product-list module in our document. In CSS we think of class names as a way of defining what a thing is. The product-list class name gives us a way of designating any list we'd like to be of this type. Once we've created the CSS to style our product list, we can use it not only here, but in any other context in the website—like a blueprint, or template.

Even if we're adding a class name as an explicit hook for styling, we should normally avoid using a name that indicates what it will look like visually (we'll cover if and when to break this rule in Chapter 12). Instead, we should choose a name that indicates what type of component it is. For example, here we've chosen product-list rather than a generic name such as large-centered-list.

You'll notice that we've chosen to use a class attribute rather than an ID attribute in the previous example. There are some important differences between ID and class attributes when used for styling, but the most applicable at this point is that a single ID name can be applied to only one element on a page. This means it can't be used as easily to define a reusable "template" for a module such as our product-list. If we had used an ID attribute, we wouldn't be able to reuse product-list more than once per page.

We prefer to use an ID attribute to identify a *single instance* of a particular module. For example, one instance of our product-list module might appear as follows:

```
<ul id="primary-product-list" class="product-list">
  <li><a href="/product/1">Product 1</a></li>
  <li><a href="/product/2">Product 2</a></li>
  <li><a href="/product/3">Product 3</a></li>
</ul>
```

This is another instance of our product-list that picks up its styles due to the class attribute, but here it has also been defined as the *primary* product-list. It seems reasonable that you can have only one primary product-list per page, and so the ID attribute might be an appropriate choice. The ID could then be used to add extra overriding styles to the module, or it could be used to add some interaction to it with JavaScript, or serve as an in-page anchor for navigation.

In reality, using the ID attribute as a hook for CSS often isn't particularly valuable. You'll usually create simpler and more maintainable code if you favour classes for styling, and only use IDs to identify elements in your document for purposes other than styling. We'll cover this topic in more detail in Chapter 12.

Structural Elements

HTML5 introduced a whole new family of structural elements:

```
section
header
footer
nav
article
aside
main
```

These elements were introduced to create logical sections of an HTML document. You can use them to denote sections containing stand-alone content (article), navigation components (nav), headers for a particular section (header), and so forth. The main element is the newest addition of the bunch, highlighting the area that holds the main content for the page. A good resource where you can dive into the correct use of all these new elements is http://html5doctor.com.

All of these new elements except the main element can be used multiple times in a document, giving it a better chance of being interpreted correctly by machine and human alike. Before these new elements arrived you would often see div elements with similar class names, for example when marking up a blog post:

```
<div class="article">
  <div class="header">
    <h1>How I became a CSS Master</h1>
  </div>
  <p>Ten-thousand hours.</p>
</div>
```

Those div elements don't provide any real semantic value to the document; they were likely included simply as styling hooks, using the class names. The only part of the preceding fragment with any real meaning is the h1 and the p, but with our newfound HTML5 elements we can improve things:

```
<article>
  <header>
    <h1>How I became a CSS Master</h1>
  </header>
  <p>Ten-thousand hours.</p>
</article>
```

We've improved the semantics of our HTML with this change, but with unexpected side effects. The only hooks we have for styling are now the article and header elements. CSS selectors for styling them could look something like this:

```
article {
  /* styles here */
}
article header {
  /* other styles here */
}
```

Both the `article` and `header` elements could be reused elsewhere in the page, for other purposes than showing a blog post. If they *were* reused now, and we attached the styles directly to the elements in the selector, they would pick up the styling rules that we'd intended for the blog post, whether they were appropriate for the new situation or not. A more flexible and forward-thinking approach would be to combine the two examples:

```
<article class="post">
  <header class="post-header">
    <h1>How I became a CSS Master</h1>
  </header>
  <p>Ten-thousand hours.</p>
</article>
```

The associated CSS rule could then use the class names to hook into this structure:

```
.post {
  /* styles here */
}
.post-header {
  /* other styles here */
}
```

With that simple change we've actually demonstrated quite an important concept. We've decoupled the semantics of our document from the way that it is styled, making it more portable, clearer in purpose, and therefore more maintainable. If we now decide that an `article` isn't the most appropriate element to contain this content, or we find that our content management system (CMS) constrains us to using a `div` for some reason, we don't need to make any further changes. The styles that we've hooked to the `class` attributes will work perfectly well whatever elements we choose (or are forced) to use.

OLD INTERNET EXPLORERS AND NEW ELEMENTS

In most browsers, using these new elements works fine, but Internet Explorer 8 and older doesn't apply styles to elements it doesn't know about. Luckily, this can be remedied using a snippet of JavaScript known as a "shim" or "polyfill" script.

You can find one version of such a script at `https://github.com/aFarkas/html5shiv`.

It is also included in the previously mentioned Modernizr library, which we'll be coming back to in upcoming chapters.

If you expect that a significant part of your users are on very old browsers, you should be careful in relying heavily on these new elements, since it results in an additional JavaScript dependency to make things work as intended.

Using Divs and Spans

All these fancy new semantic elements don't mean that our old workhorse the `div` element is redundant just yet. A `div` is an appropriate element to use for grouping content when there is no other more semantically correct element that suits your purpose. Sometimes you need to add an extra element to your document purely for styling purposes, such as a wrapper around the entire page to assist with creating a centered layout.

If you can use one of the more semantic elements to structure your content, then always do so, and give it an appropriate class attribute if it needs styling. But if you need a nonsemantic element as an extra styling hook, use a div. There's an old term known as "divitis" which refers to HTML authors' inclination to litter their markup with divs, or use divs for everything, regardless of whether there's a more appropriate element. Only add divs where they are necessary to provide simple and clear styling hooks, but don't feel embarrassed or ashamed that you've had to add a few. We'll look at some specific examples in later chapters where some extra nonsemantic divs become extremely valuable in creating clean, maintainable code.

An associate of the div element is the span. Like div, it has no semantic meaning and can be used purely for adding presentational hooks to your document. span is distinct from div in that it is a *text-level element*, and is used to provide structure within the flow of a piece of text. Again, before using the nonsemantic span, always ensure that there is not a richly semantic HTML element that can be used in its place. For example, time should be used for marking up times and dates, q for quotations, and the usual suspects em for stress emphasis and strong for strong importance:

```
<p>At <time datetime="20:07">7 minutes past eight</time> Harry shouted, <q>Can we just end
this, now!</q> He was <strong>very</strong> angry.</p>
```

Presentational Text Elements, Redefined

The <b> and <i> elements, remnants of the days of presentational markup, are used to stand for bold and italicized text, respectively. You'd think that they would have been culled from the new HTML5 specification, but they're actually still in there. Since they are widely occurring in older content around the Web, or content created via subpar WYSIWYG editors, the editors of the HTML5 specification decided to leave them in there, and instead update their definition.

Today, the <i> element stands for content that is different from its surrounding context, and would generally be typographically styled as italic. Examples from the HTML5 specification include expressions in a different language or the name of a ship.

The <b> element has almost the exact same definition, but for content that traditionally would be boldface. Examples here include a product name or category.

It all sounds a bit fuzzy, but the important takeaway is that these two elements are different from their cousins <em> and <strong> in that they don't say anything about the emphasis of the content within them. Most of the time you'd want <em> or <strong>, since they are the semantically correct choices for emphasis and strong emphasis in a piece of text.

Extending the Semantics of HTML

For a long time web developers have been exploring ways of adding new semantics and structure to the limited vocabulary of HTML. Richer expression of meaning within content opens up all sorts of possibilities for the Web and the tools built around it. Although progress toward the Nirvana of a Semantic Web hasn't been blindingly fast, there have been some positive steps in allowing authors of HTML to add more granular and expressive semantics to their documents.

ARIA Role Attributes

Many of the new HTML5 elements open up the possibility for accessibility benefits. For instance, if assistive technologies such as screen readers can understand what and where a nav element is in a page, they can help users to skip this navigation to get to the content, or return to the navigation when needed.

Another way to achieve this is to make use of Accessible Rich Internet Applications (ARIA), which acts as a complementary specification to HTML. ARIA allows you to provide even more semantic meaning for assistive technology, by specifying what different elements of a document contain or what functionality they provide. For example, `role="navigation"` is what's known as a "landmark role" attribute and declares an element to have a navigational role. Other landmark roles include:

- banner

- form

- main

- search

- complementary

- contentinfo

- application

A full list of ARIA roles and their definitions can be found in the ARIA specification `http://www.w3.org/TR/wai-aria/roles#role_definitions`.

If you need a short breakdown of when to use landmark roles, Steve Faulkner of the Paciello Group has published an overview of how and when to use them at `http://blog.paciellogroup.com/2013/02/using-wai-aria-landmarks-2013/`.

ARIA also allows developers to specify more complex pieces of content or interface elements. For example, when recreating a volume control slider widget in HTML, it would contain a `role` attribute with a value of `slider`:

```
<div id="volume-label">Volume</div>
<div class="volume-rail">
  <a href="#" class="volume-handle" role="slider" aria-labelledby="volume-label"
  aria-valuemin="1" aria-valuemax="100" aria-valuenow="67"></a>
</div>
```

The extra attributes `aria-labelledby`, `aria-valuemin`, `aria-valuemax`, and `aria-valuenow` all provide extra information that assistive technology can use to help users with visual impairments, motor deficiencies, or differing abilities that could prevent them using a slider widget.

Adding extra semantic information about what role the various components of an HTML page play is also a great way to provide hooks for scripting and styling, so it's a classic win-win.

Microformats

The most widely adopted way of extending the semantics of HTML so far is *microformats*, a set of standardized naming conventions and markup patterns to represent specific types of data. These naming conventions are based on existing data formats such as vCard and iCalendar. For example, here are some contact details, marked up in the hCard format:

```
<section class="h-card">
  <p><a class="u-url p-name" href="http://andybudd.com/">Andy Budd</a>
    <span class="p-org">Clearleft Ltd</span>
    <a class="u-email" href="mailto:info@andybudd.com">info@andybudd.com</a>
  </p>
```

```
  <p class="p-adr">
    <span class="p-locality">Brighton</span>,
    <span class="p-country-name">England</span>
  </p>
</section>
```

Contact details marked up with microformats make it easier for developers to write tools that extract this data. For example, a browser plug-in could find microformats in pages you are browsing and allow you to download contacts into your address book or add events to your calendar application. There are microformats for a range of data types: contact details, events, recipes, blog posts, resumés and so forth. Microformats can also be used to express relationships between for example a piece of content and another URL that the content links to.

Microformats gained traction partly because of their ease of implementation, and have since been adopted by publishers including Yahoo! and Facebook as well as added directly into publishing tools such as WordPress and Drupal. A study of structured data implementations in 2012 (`http://microformats.org/2012/06/25/microformats-org-at-7`) found that microformats have the greatest adoption across the Web, but there are alternatives that have started making significant inroads in more recent times, such as microdata.

Microdata

Microdata was introduced with HTML5, and provides another way of adding structured data to HTML. Its purpose and goals are very similar to microformats, but the details of embedding microdata into content are somewhat different. Let's look at how we might mark up the same type of contact details from the previous section using microdata:

```
<section itemscope itemtype="http://schema.org/Person">
  <p><a itemprop="name" href="http://thatemil.com/">Emil Björklund</a></p>
    <span itemprop="affiliation" itemscope
    itemtype="http://schema.org/Organization">
      <span itemprop="name">inUse Experience AB</span>
    </span>
    <a itemprop="email" href="mailto:emil@thatemil.com">emil@thatemil.com</a>
  </p>
  <p itemprop="address" itemscope itemtype="http://schema.org/PostalAddress">
    <span class="addressLocality">Malmö</span>,
    <span class="addressCountry">Sweden</span>
  </p>
</section>
```

As this example shows, the microdata syntax is a little more verbose than the corresponding microformat; but there's a good reason for that. Microdata is designed to be extensible so that it can represent any type of data required. It simply provides some syntax for expressing data structures, but doesn't define any particular vocabularies itself. This is in contrast to microformats, which define specific types of structured data, such as hCard or hCalendar.

Microdata leaves it to others to define and document particular formats. The format we've used in the previous example is one of the vocabularies defined by `http://schema.org`, which was created by representatives of Bing, Google, and Yahoo! These search engines use it to help them index and rank pages, meaning these vocabularies are another way of helping the search spiders index your content richly and efficiently.

Validation

Even if the core of your markup is well thought-out and semantically sound, there's still the risk that a typo or formatting mistake can cause you unforeseen trouble up ahead. This is where validation comes in.

Most HTML documents in the real world are not in fact valid HTML. To use the parlance of the spec writers, they are *nonconformant*. These documents have elements that are incorrectly nested, contain unencoded ampersands, and are missing required attributes. Browsers deal with these kinds of errors extremely gracefully and always attempt to guess the intent of the author. In fact, rules for dealing with invalid HTML are included in the HTML specification to ensure browser makers deal with error handling in a consistent way.

The fact that browsers are so good at dealing with our mistakes is a blessing for the Web as a whole, but does not abdicate us from responsibility in this area. As much as possible, we should attempt to create valid documents. Doing so will help us catch bugs more quickly, or stop them being introduced altogether. If you have a rendering or layout bug that doesn't have an immediate and obvious fix, a good first step is to validate the HTML, to ensure you are attempting to style a correctly formatted document.

Many tools exist to help you validate HTML. You can use the HTML validator on the W3C site itself (`http://validator.w3.org/`), or one of the many browser plug-ins that communicate with it. The Web Developer extension (`http://chrispederick.com/work/web-developer/`), for instance, is available for Mozilla Firefox, Opera, and Google Chrome, and has options for validating both publicly available sites and local sites (as well as other really useful features!). Alternatively, if your projects have any kind of automated build or test process, you can include HTML validation as a step here.

CSS validation is also possible. The W3C has a CSS validator available at `http://jigsaw.w3.org/css-validator/`. One could argue that validating CSS files is not as important as validating HTML—errors in your CSS are perhaps not as likely to cause JavaScript to fail or make your page inaccessible for people using assistive technology such as screen readers. Still, you should make sure that you check your CSS now and again, to ensure you're not making any simple mistakes like forgetting to add a unit to a measurement.

Depending on the settings you choose in the CSS validator, you will get a lot of warnings or errors about using vendor prefixes in your code. These are nonstandard properties or values that browser makers allow you to set as stand-ins for the real thing when they implement experimental support for a CSS feature. For example, the `-webkit-flex` value for the `display` property is the experimental version for the `flex` property in WebKit-based browsers. This is likely flagged by the validator as a warning or an error, but your file works fine even if the validator yells at you a bit. You just have to make sure you understand why it flags things as problematic.

Validation isn't an end unto itself, and many otherwise good pages fail to validate due to content from third parties, unwieldy CMS systems, or experimental CSS features that you might want to use. There's also the risk that the validator hasn't actually kept up with the standards and browser implementations. So don't be militant about validation, but use it as a means to catch errors that are simple to fix before they cause too many knock-on effects.

Summary

In this chapter we looked at some of the ways you can make sure you have a solid foundation to build on, both in terms of HTML and CSS. You learned a little bit about the history of HTML and CSS, how to keep up with changes, and how you can make your code both backward compatible and future friendly. You now know the importance of writing maintainable code, as well as some methods for structuring HTML so that it is easily and consistently styled with CSS.

In the next chapter, we will recap some of the basic CSS selectors and then move on to a host of more advanced selectors from the Level 3 and Level 4 Selectors specification. You'll learn about specificity, inheritance, and the cascade, and how to put them to use in creating efficient style sheets.

CHAPTER 2

▦ ▦ ▦

Getting Your Styles to Hit the Target

A valid and well-structured document provides the foundation to which your styles are applied. You may already have added appropriate styling "hooks" to your HTML, or you may return to add more as the design requirements for a page evolve. In this chapter we will look at the range of *selectors* we have available to target that HTML and the extra hooks we can use to gain more control. We'll cover:

- Common selectors

- Bleeding-edge selectors for now and the future

- The wonderful world of specificity and the cascade

- Applying styles to your pages

CSS Selectors

The most basic selectors are *type* and *descendant* selectors. *Type* selectors are used to target a particular type of element, such as a paragraph (as shown next) or a heading element. You do this by simply specifying the name of the element you wish to style. *Type* selectors are sometimes also referred to as *element* selectors.

```
p {
  color: black;
}
```

Descendant selectors allow you to target the descendants of a particular element or group of elements. A descendant selector is indicated by a space between two other selectors. In this example, only paragraph elements that are descendants of a block quote will be indented, while all other paragraphs will remain unchanged:

```
blockquote p {
  padding-left: 2em;
}
```

These two selectors are great for applying base styles across the board. To be more specific and target selected elements, you can use *ID* and *class* selectors. As the names suggest, these selectors will target elements with the corresponding ID attribute or class name value. ID selectors are identified using a hash character; class selectors are identified with a period. The first rule in this example will make the text in the introductory paragraph bold, and the second rule will make the date gray:

```
#intro {
  font-weight: bold;
```

© Andy Budd and Emil Björklund 2016

A. Budd and E. Björklund, *CSS Mastery*, DOI 10.1007/978-1-4302-5864-3_2

```
}
.date-posted {
  color: #ccc;
}
<p id="intro">Happy Birthday, Andy</p>
<p class="date-posted">20/1/2013</p>
```

Sometimes, rather than adding ID or class attributes to every element you want to target, it's useful to combine ID and class selectors with type and descendant selectors:

```
#latest h1 {
  font-size: 1.8em;
}
#latest .date-posted {
  font-weight: bold;
}
<article id="latest">
<h1>Happy Birthday, Andy</h1>
<p class="date-posted"><time datetime="2013-01-20">20/1/2013</time></p>
</article>
```

These are all very simple and obvious examples. However, you will be surprised by how many elements you can successfully target using just the four selectors discussed so far. Often, these are the real workhorses of a maintainable CSS system. Other advanced selectors can be extremely useful, but they're not as flexible and powerful as these more simple and common selectors.

Child and Sibling Selectors

On top of these basic selectors, CSS contains a number of more advanced selectors. The first of these advanced selectors is the *child* selector. Whereas a *descendant* selector will select all the descendants of an element, a *child* selector only targets the element's immediate descendants, or children. In the following example, the list items in the outer list will be given a custom icon while list items in the nested list will remain unaffected (see Figure 2-1).

```
#nav > li {
  background: url(folder.png) no-repeat left top;
  padding-left: 20px;
}
<ul id="nav">
  <li><a href="/home/">Home</a></li>
  <li><a href="/services/">Services</a>
  <ul>
      <li><a href="/services/design/">Design</a></li>
      <li><a href="/services/development/">Development</a></li>
      <li><a href="/services/consultancy/">Consultancy</a></li>
    </ul>
  </li>
  <li><a href="/contact/">Contact Us</a></li>
</ul>
```

■ Home
■ Services
    Design
    Development
    Consultancy
■ Contact Us

Figure 2-1. *The child selector styles the children of the list but not its grandchildren*

Sometimes, you may want to style an element based on its proximity to another element. The *adjacent sibling selector* allows you to target an element that is preceded by another element that shares the same parent. Using the *adjacent sibling selector*, you could make the first paragraph following a top-level heading bold, gray, and slightly larger than the subsequent paragraphs (see Figure 2-2):

```
h2 + p {
  font-size: 1.4em;
  font-weight: bold;
  color: #777;
}
```

Peru Celebrates Guinea Pig festival

The guinea pig festival in Peru is a one day event to celebrate these cute local animals. The festival included a fashon show where animals are dressed up in various amusing costumes.

Guinea pigs can be fried, roasted or served in a casserole. Around 65 million guinea pigs are eaten in Peru each year.

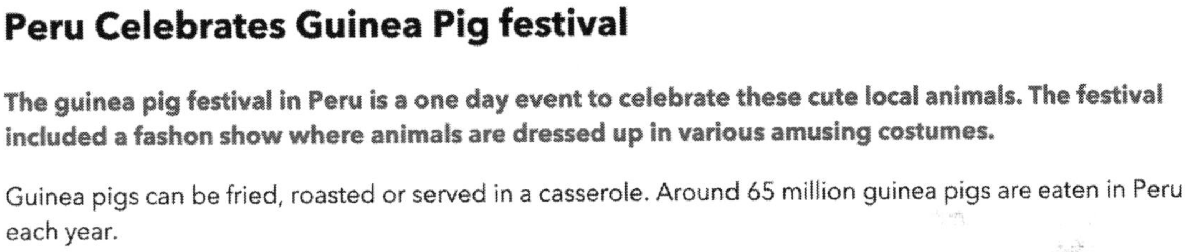

Figure 2-2. *The first paragraph following an h2 is styled differently*

This can be a useful technique, but bear in mind that styling the opening paragraph with its own class value, such as intro-text, might lead to simpler and more flexible CSS. This intro-text class could then be used to style other paragraphs that don't immediately follow an h2.

The > and + tokens are known as *combinators*, because they characterize the way that the two sides of the rule combine. We've seen examples of the *child combinator* (>) and the *adjacent sibling combinator* (+), but there is a third combinator that we should look at—the *general sibling combinator* (~). Going back to the previous example, you could use the *general sibling combinator* to target every paragraph element that has a preceding sibling h2.

```
h2 ~ p {
  font-size: 1.4em;
  font-weight: bold;
  color: #777;
}
```

■ **Note**   You might have noticed that the *adjacent sibling* and *general sibling* combinators don't allow you to select a *previous* sibling—e.g., not a paragraph that is followed by an h2. The reason why there is resistance against such a useful selector is a bit complex, but has to do with page rendering performance.

Generally, the browser styles elements as they come into existence on the page, and at the time the paragraph is supposed to be styled, the h2, which is further along in the HTML source, might not exist yet. A previous sibling combinator would mean that the browser would have to keep track of these selectors, and then perform additional passes of applying styles when processing the document.

There is, however, a proposed version of the previous sibling selector that is being considered for standardization, but so far the idea is to restrict its validity to special uses of CSS selectors, like when they are being evaluated in JavaScript, so even when that standard is shipped in browsers, it might not work the way you hope.

The Universal Selector

The *universal* selector acts like a wildcard, matching any element. Like wildcards in other languages, the universal selector is denoted by an asterisk. Used by itself, the universal selector matches every element in the page. It could be tempting to use it to remove the default browser padding and margin on every element using the following rule:

```
* {
  padding: 0;
  margin: 0;
}
```

This can have a number of unforeseen circumstances, particularly in the formatting of form UI elements such as the button and select elements. It is better to be more explicit about what you are resetting, as in this example:

```
h1, h2, h3, h4, h5, h5, h6,
ul, ol, li, dl, p {
  padding: 0;
  margin: 0;
}
```

Fortunately, there are a number of small, open source libraries that can deal with this for you. Good examples are Eric Meyer's CSS Reset (http://meyerweb.com/eric/tools/css/reset/) and Nicolas Gallagher's Normalize.css (http://necolas.github.com/normalize.css/). The latter takes a slightly different approach: rather than resetting margins and padding to 0, Normalize.css ensures that all elements start off with a consistent styling across browsers. We consider this to be a slightly safer set of defaults than simply resetting everything to 0.

Of course, you don't have to use the universal selector only for setting properties on every element in the document. You can also use it together with combinators where you want to target specific nesting levels, where the nesting level is important but not the type of element. As an example:

```
.product-section > * {
  /* ... */
}
```

This would target any elements that are direct descendants of elements with the product-section class name, but without caring about the type or attributes of the descendants of product-section. This technique is useful when you want to target these elements without increasing specificity—we will address specificity further ahead in this chapter.

Attribute Selectors

As the name suggests, the *attribute* selector allows you to target an element based on the existence of an attribute or the attribute's value. This allows you to do some very interesting and powerful things.

For example, when you hover over an element with a title attribute, most browsers will display a tooltip. You can use this behavior to expand the meaning of things such as acronyms and abbreviations, represented by the <abbr> element:

```
<p>The term <abbr title="self-contained underwater breathing apparatus">SCUBA</abbr> is an
acronym rather than an abbreviation as it is pronounced as a word.</p>
```

However, there is no way to tell that this extra information exists without hovering over the element. To get around this problem, you can use the *attribute* selector to style abbr elements with titles differently from other elements—in this case, by giving them a dotted bottom border. You can provide more contextual information by changing the cursor from a pointer to a question mark when the cursor hovers over the element, indicating that this element is different from most.

```
abbr[title] {
  border-bottom: 1px dotted #999;
}

abbr[title]:hover {
  cursor: help;
}
```

In addition to styling an element based on the existence of an attribute, you can apply styles based on a particular value. For instance, this could be used to fix an inconsistency in which cursor browsers display when hovering on a submit button. With the following rule in place, all input elements with a type attribute value of submit will display a hand pointer when the mouse is over them:

```
input[type="submit"] {
  cursor: pointer;
}
```

Since we might be interested in patterns in the values of the attribute rather than the exact value, the attribute selector allows for more granular ways of matching these attributes. By adding a special character before the equals-sign, we can indicate what type of matching we are interested in.

To match a value at the beginning of an attribute, use a caret character (^) before the equals-sign.

```
a[href^="http:"]
```

To match a value at the end of an attribute, use a dollar-sign ($).

```
img[src$=".jpg"]
```

To match a value anywhere in an attribute, use an asterisk (*).

```
a[href*="/about/"]
```

To match a value in a space-separated list of strings (such as values in `rel` attributes), use a tilde-character (~).

```
a[rel~=next]
```

There's also an attribute selector that selects elements where the start of the value matches, either by itself or immediately followed by a dash. For this kind of matching, use a pipe-character (|).

```
a[hreflang|=en]
```

This example will match both attribute values `en` and `en-us` and hints at the intention with this selector: it's handy for selecting elements with a specific language code in the attribute value, since these are dash-separated. Technically, you could use it with the `class` attribute to match class names, such as `message` and `message-error` respectively, but that wouldn't be very portable: if you put another class before the `message` class in your HTML, like `class="box message"`, the selector wouldn't work.

Pseudo-Elements

There are times when you would like to target a part of the page that is not represented by an element, but you don't want to litter your page with extra markup. CSS provides a short list of ways to do this, for some of the most common cases. These are known as *pseudo-elements*.

To start with, you can target the first letter of a piece of text by using the `::first-letter` pseudo-element. The first line of each piece of text can be targeted with the `::first-line` version.

There are also pseudo-elements corresponding to a hypothetical element that exists at the beginning and end of a piece of content, using the `::before` and `::after` pseudo-elements respectively. This is extremely useful for inserting small symbols and typographic embellishments, and generally acts as a hook for creating visual effects that you'd otherwise attach to a real element. One way of doing this is to insert content in the form of text with the `content` property, but feel free to style the pseudo-element just as you would style any other element, using backgrounds, borders, etc.

■ **Caution**   Be careful when using pseudo-elements to inject content! Don't use them for adding any form of text content that your users couldn't do without, in case your CSS doesn't load correctly. Also be aware that screen readers don't have a standard way to interpret the content of pseudo-elements: some ignore it, others read it.

Putting these pseudo-elements together into an example can give us something like Figure 2-3 with a minimum of markup.

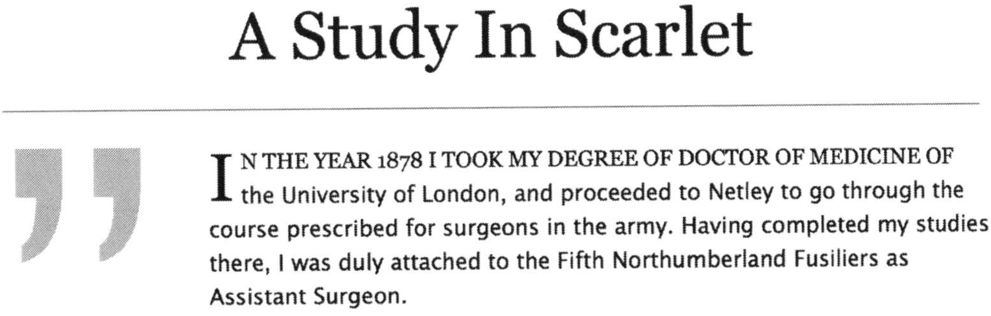

A Study In Scarlet

I N THE YEAR 1878 I TOOK MY DEGREE OF DOCTOR OF MEDICINE OF the University of London, and proceeded to Netley to go through the course prescribed for surgeons in the army. Having completed my studies there, I was duly attached to the Fifth Northumberland Fusiliers as Assistant Surgeon.

Figure 2-3. *The opening paragraph from the Sherlock Holmes novel A Study in Scarlet, given some typographic treatment with the help of pseudo-elements*

Here's an abbreviated version of the HTML and CSS to achieve this.
HTML:

```
<h1>A Study In Scarlet</h1>
<section class="chapter">
    <p>In the year 1878 I took my degree of Doctor of Medicine of the University of London,
and proceeded to Netley to go through the course prescribed for surgeons in the army. Having
completed my studies there, I was duly attached to the Fifth Northumberland Fusiliers as
Assistant Surgeon.</p>
</section>
```

CSS:

```
.chapter::before {
    content: '"';
    font-size: 15em;
}
.chapter p::first-letter {
    float: left;
    font-size: 3em;
    font-family: Georgia, Times, "Times New Roman", serif;
}

.chapter p::first-line {
    font-family: Georgia, Times, "Times New Roman", serif;
    text-transform: uppercase;
}
```

As you can see, we've used the ::first-letter pseudo-element to create a drop-cap letter in a different font at the beginning of the paragraph. The first line is transformed into uppercase and is also using a different font with the ::first-line pseudo-element. We've also added a decorative quote mark inside the chapter container, using the ::before pseudo-element. All of this without having to add a single superfluous element! Handy indeed.

We'll take a closer look at more typographic techniques in Chapter 4.

■ **Tip**   Pseudo-elements are supposed to use the double-colon syntax that we've seen so far, to distinguish them from pseudo-classes, which you will see in the next section use a single colon. However, pseudo-elements were introduced with single-colon syntax in older browsers, and still work written that way. So for compatibility's sake, you can still use the single-colon syntax for some pseudo-elements, and we have done so where appropriate for the examples in this book.

Pseudo-Classes

There are instances where you may want to style an element based on something other than the structure of the document—for instance, the state of a hyperlink or form element. This can be done using a *pseudo-class* selector. These selectors, starting with a colon character (:) are used to target a specific state or relationship found in the element you apply them to.

Some of the most common *pseudo-class* selectors can be used for styling links, as follows, and should always be included in your basic set of styles targeting the most common HTML elements:

```
/* makes all unvisited links blue */
a:link {
  color: blue;
}
/* makes all visited links green */
a:visited {
  color: green;
}
/* makes links red on mouse hover, keyboard focus */
a:hover,
a:focus {
  color: red;
}
/*...and purple when activated. */
a:active {
  color: purple;
}
```

The order of these pseudo-class selectors is important. The :link and :visited rules need to come first, followed by those related to a user's interaction. The :hover and :focus selectors will override :link and :visited as the user hovers over or gives keyboard focus to the links, finally followed by :active as they click or select the link with a keyboard. Links are interactive content, and can be focused and activated by default. There are plenty of other elements that are interactive by default, like form fields and buttons, so these pseudo-classes work for them too. You can also make other elements interactive by using JavaScript.

Finally, you can use the :hover pseudo-class for pretty much any element, but keep in mind that input methods like touchscreens and keyboards don't really have hover states—so don't use :hover for essential functionality.

Targets and Negations

Another useful pseudo-class is `:target`, which matches any element that has an ID attribute that is currently represented in the URL hash of the page. If we were to go to `http://example.com/blog/1/#comment-3` and find a comment on that page marked up as `<article class="comment" id="comment-3">...</article>`, we could highlight that comment with a pale yellow background using the following rule:

```
.comment:target {
  background-color: #fffec4;
}
```

Now, what if we wanted to highlight that comment, but only if it's not one of those grayed-out, downvoted comments whose contents are hidden? Well, there's a selector for excluding certain selectors as well. Meet the negation pseudo-class, or `:not()` selector! Provided we have a special class name on comments that are marked as "downvoted," we could change our rule to this:

```
.comment:target:not(.comment-downvoted) {
  background-color: #fffec4;
}
```

The negation pseudo-class works with pretty much any type of selector you throw into the parentheses, except for pseudo-elements and itself.

Structural Pseudo-Classes

CSS 3 introduced a host of new pseudo-classes relating to document structure. The most common of these is the *nth-child* selector, which could be used to style alternate rows of a table:

```
tr:nth-child(odd) {
  background: yellow;
}
```

This would style the first and then every alternate row in a table with a yellow background. The nth-child selector acts as a function that can accept a number of different expressions as arguments. It will accept the keywords odd and even, as indicated in the preceding example. It can also be a number representing the ordinal position of the targeted elements, such as in the following example, which will set the third row of all tables in a bold font:

```
tr:nth-child(3) {
  font-weight: bold;
}
```

Things start to get a little more complex at this point when we look at the support for number expressions; for example:

```
tr:nth-child(3n+4) {
  background:  #ddd;
}
```

The number 4 in the previous expression relates to the ordinal position of the first element we want to target, in this case the fourth table row. The number 3 relates to the ordinal position of every element to target after the first. So in the previous example the *nth-child* selector would match the fourth, seventh, tenth, and so on rows in the table, as shown in Figure 2-4. To get a little bit into the math here, the n inside the parentheses in the expression is replaced with a number, starting with zero and then increasing by 1 until there are no more elements to match.

Row №.	Result
1	Not matched
2	Not matched
3	Not matched
4	$3 \times 0 = 0$. Add 4 and get a match for row № 4!
5	Not matched
6	Not matched
7	$3 \times 1 = 3$. Add 4 and get a match for row № 7!
8	Not matched
9	Not matched
10	$3 \times 2 = 6$. Add 4 and get a match for row № 10!

Figure 2-4. *A table where the rows are styled using* `:nth-child(3n+4)`. *The expression is evaluated with n as a number, starting with 0 and then increasing by 1 as long as there are matches*

You can do all sorts of crazy stuff with these expressions. For example, instead of adding a number, you could subtract a number—so we could do `:nth-child(3n-4)` and get a different result. The same goes for the number before the n, or n itself—changing that to negative can give you some interesting results. For example, the expression `:nth-child(-n+3)` would select only the first three elements!

There are other pseudo-class selectors that support these types of expressions, such as the following:

`:nth-last-child(N)`

The `:nth-last-child` selector operates in a very similar way to the `:nth-child` selector, except that it counts back from the last child element, rather than counting up from the first.

Back in CSS 2.1 there was a pseudo-element for the first child, sensibly named `:first-child`, so `:nth-child(1)` can be written more simply using that. The Level 3 selectors specification adds a corresponding one for the last child, named (you guessed it) `:last-child`, corresponding to `:nth-last-child(1)`. There's also `:only-child` and `:only-of-type`. The `:only-of-type` selector applies to an element if it is the only child element that is of a particular element type. We can get more advanced with targeting elements of a certain type by using these pseudo-class selectors:

`:nth-of-type(N)`
`:nth-last-of-type(N)`

These two pseudo-class selectors behave in the same way as the `:nth-child` selectors, except they ignore (and do not count) any element that is not of the element type they have been applied to. This gives us opportunities to create some incredibly efficient patterns, without tying the selectors too hard to the markup.

Getting Clever with Structural Pseudo-Classes

You can do a lot using just the structural pseudo-classes: they give you a great deal of precision when selecting elements based on their position in the document and their environment. For example, it's possible to select items based on how many child elements of a certain type there are, which makes it possible to style things like grid columns based on the total number of items. This is achieved by using a combination of the :nth-last-of-type pseudo-selector and the :first-child selector. Here's an example that matches when something contains four "columns", providing the columns have the same element type:

```
.column:nth-last-of-type(4):first-child,
.column:nth-last-of-type(4):first-child  ~ .column {
  /* Rules for when there is exactly four .column elements */
}
```

When this selector matches, it means that the fourth element from the end is also the first element, ergo there are four elements of the same type with the .column class. We also include the adjacent sibling selector to make sure we select all of the rest of the columns. Pretty neat, huh?

Note that the numbered matching does not count only elements with the class name column: it selects all elements with that class name, and then counts items based on them having the same element *type*. In the Selectors Level 4 spec, there is a proposal for filtering matches, using the of keyword followed by a selector inside the parentheses:

```
:nth-child(2 of .column):first-child {}
```

Sadly, this arguably more useful flavor of the structural pseudo-classes is not widely available in browsers yet.

Structural selectors in general have wide support, but are missing in Internet Explorer 8 and earlier. If you need to support these legacy browsers, you may want to restrict this technique to small enhancements, and instead use markup hooks to target elements for overall layout patterns.

For some further inspiration on styling based on element count, see Heydon Pickering's article "Quantity Queries for CSS" (http://alistapart.com/article/quantity-queries-for-css).

Form Pseudo-Classes

There are a number of pseudo-classes specifically for targeting elements within forms. These can be used to reflect the state of certain form inputs depending on how the user interacts with them.

For instance, HTML5 introduced several new attributes for form inputs, some of which we looked at in Chapter 1. One of these new attributes is the required attribute:

```
<label for="field-name">Name: </label>
<input type="text" name="field-name" id="field-name" required>
```

If you wanted to visually highlight the required field to make it more obvious to users, you could use the :required pseudo-class to target form elements with the required attribute, and make the border of the input a different color (see Figure 2-5):

```
input:required {
  outline: 2px solid #000;
}
```

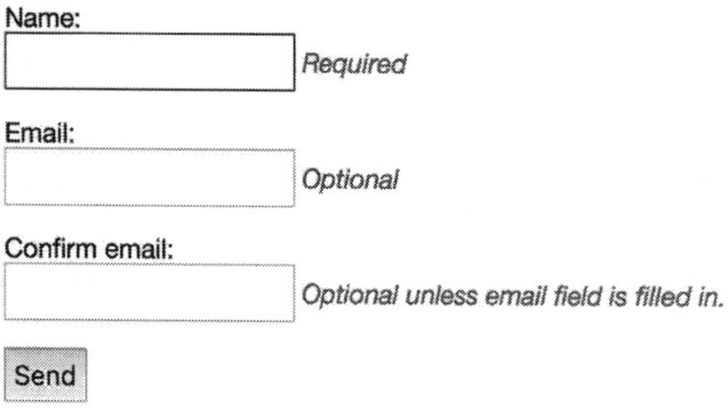

Name:

[   ] *Required*

Email:

[   ] *Optional*

Confirm email:

[   ] *Optional unless email field is filled in.*

[Send]

Figure 2-5. *Using the* `:required` *pseudo-class to give required fields a darker border*

Similarly, we can style inputs that *don't* have the `required` attribute using

```
input:optional {
  border-color: #ccc;
}
```

We also have pseudo-classes to help style valid and invalid fields. If an `input` element requires a specific valid type such as an e-mail address, there are a range of different input types defined in HTML5 that we can use in the type attribute:

```
<input type="email" />
```

This element can then be styled based on the validity of the current value of the input using the following styles (Figure 2-6 shows an example of invalid input):

```
/* When the field contains a valid email address: */
input[type="email"]:valid {
  border-color: green;
}
/* When the contents are not a valid email address: */
input[type="email"]:invalid {
  border-color: red;
}
```

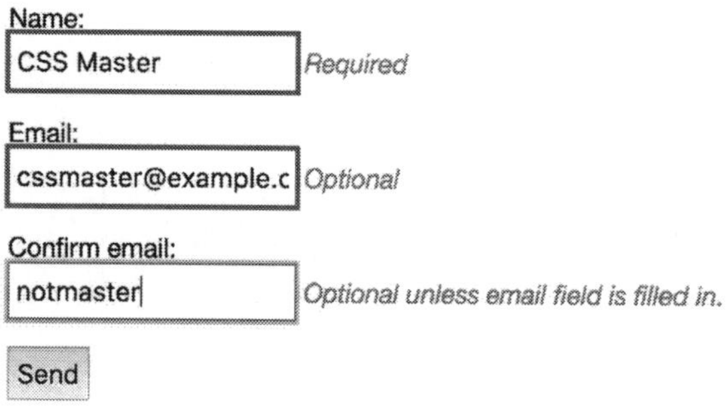

Name:

[CSS Master   ] *Required*

Email:

[cssmaster@example.c] *Optional*

Confirm email:

[notmaster   ] *Optional unless email field is filled in.*

[Send]

Figure 2-6. *The last field is not a valid e-mail address and is given a distinctly different outline with the* `:invalid` *pseudo-class. On screen you will see this invalid e-mail address outlined in red*

There are also numerous other pseudo-classes for forms, such as `:in-range` and `:out-of-range` for targeting inputs with a `type` of `number`, `:read-only` for inputs with a `readonly` attribute, and `:read-write` for inputs with no `readonly` attribute. To learn more about these pseudo-classes, you can get the goods from MDN at `https://developer.mozilla.org/docs/Web/CSS/Pseudo-classes`.

The Cascade

With even a moderately complicated style sheet, it is likely that two or more rules will target the same element. CSS handles such conflicts through a process known as the *cascade*, a concept important enough that it's right there in the name—Cascading Style Sheets. The cascade works by assigning an importance to each rule. Author style sheets are those written by the site developers and are considered the most important. Users can apply their own styles via the browser settings, and these styles are considered the next most important. Finally, the default style sheets used by your browser or user agent are given the least importance, so you can always override them. To give users more control, they can override any rule by specifying it as `!important`, even a rule flagged as `!important` by the author. The `!important` annotation is added to the end of a property declaration, and looks like this when used in a rule:

```
p {
  font-size: 1.5em !important;
  color: #666 !important;
}
```

The reason for letting users override rules using `!important` is to support specific accessibility needs, such as allowing users with certain forms of dyslexia to use a medium-contrast user style sheet.

So the cascade works in the following order of importance:

- User styles flagged as `!important`

- Author styles flagged as `!important`

- Author styles

- User styles

- Styles applied by the browser/user agent

Rules are then ordered by how specific the selector is. Rules with more specific selectors override those with less specific ones. If two rules are equally specific, the last one defined takes precedence.

Specificity

To calculate how specific a rule is, each type of selector is assigned a numeric value. The specificity of a rule is then calculated by adding up the value of each of its selectors. Unfortunately, specificity is not calculated in base 10 but a high, unspecified, base number, meaning that ten `class` selectors (or forty-three, for that matter) is not equal or greater in specificity than one ID selector. This is to ensure that a highly specific selector, such as an ID, is never overridden by lots of less specific selectors, such as type selectors. However, if you have fewer than ten selectors in a specific rule, you can calculate specificity in base 10 for simplicity's sake.

The specificity of a selector is broken down into four constituent levels: a, b, c and d.

- If the style is an inline style, a equals 1.

- b equals the total number of ID selectors.

- • c equals the number of class, pseudo-class, and attribute selectors.

- • d equals the number of type selectors and pseudo-element selectors.

Using these rules, it is possible to calculate the specificity of any CSS selector. Table 2-1 shows a series of selectors, along with their associated specificity.

Table 2-1. *Specificity examples*

Selector	Specificity	Specificity in Base 10
Style=""	1,0,0,0	1000
#wrapper #content {}	0,2,0,0	200
#content .datePosted {}	0,1,1,0	110
div#content {}	0,1,0,1	101
#content {}	0,1,0,0	100
p.comment .datePosted {}	0,0,2,1	21
p.comment{}	0,0,1,1	11
div p {}	0,0,0,2	2
p {}	0,0,0,1	1

At first glance, all this talk of specificity and high but undefined based numbers may seem a little confusing, so here's what you need to know. Essentially, a rule written in a style attribute will always be more specific than any other rule. A rule with an ID will be more specific than one without an ID, and a rule with a class selector will be more specific than a rule with just type selectors. Finally, if two rules have the same specificity, the last one defined prevails, due to the cascade coming into effect.

■ **Note**   The universal selector (*) always has a specificity of 0, regardless of how many times or where it appears in a chain of selectors. We will show an example of how this can produce some unexpected results in the "Inheritance" section a bit later.

Order of Rules when Resolving the Cascade

The fact that the last rule defined takes precedent when two rules have the same specificity is an important one. It means that you have to consider where to place your rules in your style sheets, and the order of your selectors.

A good example of the cascade in action is when using pseudo-classes on the link element as described earlier. Because each of the selectors has the same specificity, the order in which they are declared becomes important. If you had the a:visited selector after the a:hover selector, once you had visited the link, the hover style would not show up again due to it being overridden by the :visited style. This does not seem intuitive until you understand the details of specificity and the cascade. A handy mnemonic to remember the order in which link pseudo-classes should go is "Lord Vader Hates Furry Animals." So you should start with the :link pseudo-class, followed by :visited, :hover, :focus, and finally :active.

Managing Specificity

Understanding specificity is crucial to writing good CSS, and it's one of the most difficult aspects to control and manage on larger sites. Specificity allows you to set general styles for common elements and then override them for more specific elements. In the following example we've set some rules for different types of introductory text. We have a basic introductory text color of gray, overriding the default of black on the body. On the homepage, the intro text is black with a light-gray background, and links inside it are green.

```
body {
  color: black;
}
.intro {
  padding: 1em;
  font-size: 1.2em;
  color: gray;
}
#home .intro {
  color: black;
  background: lightgray;
}
#home .intro a {
  color: green;
}
```

This has introduced a number of rules with a wide range of specificity to them. This isn't likely to cause any problems on a smaller site, but as a codebase grows and more and more styles effect a page, these kind of rules can get difficult to manage, because to apply any further rules to the homepage intro text requires a selector with at least one ID and a class.

For example, let's say we have another component with a call-to-action link that is styled to look a bit more like a button, simply by using a background color and some padding:

```
a.call-to-action {
    text-decoration: none;
    background-color: green;
    color: white;
    padding: 0.25em;
}
```

What happens if we want to add a call-to-action link inside the homepage intro? Well, it would look bad, to put it mildly, since the text wouldn't be visible: the selector for links in the homepage intro would override our "button" styles and create green text on a green background (see Figure 2-7).

Home page

Lorem ipsum dolor sit amet, consectetur adipisicing elit. Mollitia, quam earum aut dignissimos sunt vitae qui doloremque illo obcaecati asperiores! Maiores, nobis officia velit nam consequatur sed sint alias nisi.

Figure 2-7. *The call-to-action component inside the home page intro. The link styling for the intro (#home .intro a) is more specific than the styling for the component (a.call-to-action), giving us green text on a green background*

To mitigate this, we would need to increase the specificity in some way, possibly with another, more powerful selector on the call-to-action component:

```
a.call-to-action,
#home .intro a.call-to-action {
    text-decoration: none;
    background-color: green;
    color: white;
    padding: 10px;
}
```

Having to one-up your rules like this as a style sheet grows can result in a specificity arms race that ends up overcomplicating your code.

A better approach would be to simplify your selectors and reduce their specificity:

```
body {
    color: black;
}
.intro {
    font-size: 1.2em;
    color: gray;
}

.intro-highlighted {
    color: black;
    background: lightgray;
}
.intro-highlighted a {
    color: green;
}
a.call-to-action {
    text-decoration: none;
    background-color: green;
    color: white;
    padding: 10px;
}
```

We've done two things by rewriting the previous code. First, we've removed the ID selector, which reduces the specificity of these selectors to a minimum. We've also removed any reference to the *context* of an intro. Instead of talking about an intro on the homepage, we've made the homepage intro (renamed to "highlighted intro") a more specific version of the original intro. You'd now use those intro classes like this:

```
<p class="intro">A general intro</p>
<p class="intro intro-highlighted">We might need to use this on the homepage, or in the
future, on a <a href="/promo-page" class="call-to-action">promo page</a>.</p>
```

This simpler and more targeted approach gives authors fine-grained control over their styles. The intro-highlighted links no longer override the call-to-action link color, and you have the added benefit of being able to reuse the intro-highlighted component on other pages without changing the CSS.

Specificity and Debugging

Specificity can be extremely important when fixing bugs, as you need to know which rules take precedence and why. For instance, say you had the following set of rules. What color do you think the two headlines would be, at a quick glance?

```
#content #main h2 {
    color: gray;
}

div > #main > h2 {
    color: green;
}

#content > [id="main"] .news-story:nth-of-type(1) h2.first {
    color: hotpink;
}
:root [id="content"]:first-child > #main  h2:nth-last-child(3) {
    color: gold;
}
```

The HTML:

```
<div id="content">
  <main id="main">
    <h2>Strange Times</h2>
    <p>Here you can read bizarre news stories from around the globe.</p>
    <div class="news-story">
      <h2 class="first">Bog Snorkeling Champion Announced Today</h2>
      <p>The 2008 Bog Snorkeling Championship was won by Conor Murphy
    with an impressive time of 1 minute 38 seconds.</p>
    </div>
  </main>
</div>
```

The answer, surprisingly, is that both headlines are gray. The first selector has the highest specificity because it's made up of two ID selectors. Some of the later selectors may look more complicated, but because they contain only one ID, they will always lose out against the more specific selectors. It's worth noting that even if some of the selectors contain references to the ID *attribute* of the HTML, they are still only attribute selectors, and have a lower specificity. This can be a useful tool if you only have ID attributes to hook your styles into, and don't want to give your rules a specificity that is too high.

Debugging specificity issues can be a tricky business, but fortunately there are tools that can help you out. All modern browsers have developer tools built into them that make it very clear how specificity is being applied to a particular element. In Chrome, the Developer Tools (DevTools) allow you to "inspect an element" and will list all of the CSS selectors and rules that match it, including browser defaults. Figure 2-8 shows the second h2 from the previous example code, proving that the second heading is in fact gray due to the very first most specific selector.

Figure 2-8. *Taking a look at what rules actually get applied, via the Google Chrome Developer Tools*

Inheritance

People often confuse inheritance with the cascade. Although they seem related at first glance, the two concepts are actually quite different. Luckily, inheritance is a much easier concept to grasp. Certain properties, such as color or font size, are inherited by the descendants of the elements those styles are applied to. For instance, if you were to give the body element a text color of black, all the descendants of the body element would also have black text. The same would be true of font sizes.

If you set the font size on the body, you will notice that this style is not picked up by any headings on the page. You may assume that headings do not inherit text size. But it is actually the browser default style sheet that sets the heading size. Any style applied directly to an element will always override an inherited style. This is because inherited styles have a null specificity.

Inheritance is very useful, as it lets you avoid having to add the same style to every descendant of an element. If the property you are trying to set is an inherited property, you may as well apply it to the parent element. After all, what is the point of writing:

```
p, div, h1, h2, h3, ul, ol, dl, li {color: black;}
```

when you can just write the following?

```
body {color: black;}
```

Inherited property values have no specificity at all, not even zero. This means that properties set via the universal selector, which has a specificity of zero, will override inherited properties. This gives us the perhaps unexpected situation shown in Figure 2-9, where the color set by the universal selector overrides the color inherited from the heading:

```
* {
  color: black;
}
h2 {
  color: red;
}

<h2>The emphasized text will be <em>black</em></h2>
```

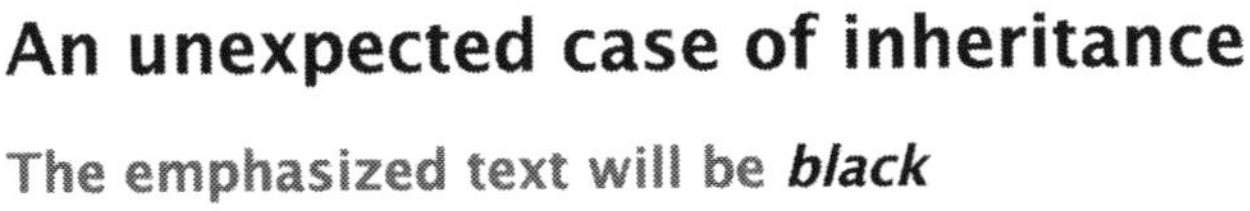

An unexpected case of inheritance

The emphasized text will be *black*

Figure 2-9. *The universal selector has a specificity of 0, but it still beats inherited properties*

Setting a basic color on the body element instead would have been a better choice for this situation, so that color was *inherited* rather than *set* for all other elements.

Just as sensible use of the cascade can help simplify your CSS, good use of inheritance can help to reduce the number and complexity of the selectors in your code. It you have lots of elements inheriting various styles, though, determining where the styles originate can become confusing.

Applying Styles to your Document

As you are writing CSS you need to know how to apply those styles to a given HTML document. There are various methods of doing this, each with its own advantages and disadvantages.

The Link and Style Elements

You can add styles directly to the head of a document by placing them in a `style` element:

```
<style>
  body {
    font-family: Avenir Next, SegoeUI, sans-serif;
    color: grey;
  }
</style>
```

Sometimes this is useful if you have a small number of styles that you want applied to the page immediately, and you don't want the overhead of the browser downloading a separate file. However, you'll typically want to apply styles from an external style sheet that can be easily reused across other pages. There are two ways to attach external style sheets to a web page. The most common approach is to use the `link` element:

```
<link href="/c/base.css" rel="stylesheet" />
```

35

This directs the browser to download the base.css file and apply any styles it contains to the page. You can add this to as many HTML pages as you wish, so it is a good way of reusing a set of styles across multiple pages, and even across multiple sites.

You can also use the @import directive to load an external CSS file:

```
<style>
  @import url("/c/modules.css");
</style>
```

The @import directive can be used in a style block in the head of your HTML document, or alternatively it can be used inside an external style sheet itself. The latter use means including one external CSS file on your page might result in subsequent CSS files being loaded in by the browser.

Using the link element or the @import directive achieves much the same result on the face of it, but there are some important considerations that make link preferable to @import that we'll discuss in the upcoming section on performance.

When adding styles to your page, don't forget that order matters for the cascade: when two or more rules with the same specificity compete over setting properties on an element, the one declared last wins.

When you add several link elements referencing style sheets to your HTML, or add style elements, their place in terms of declaration order is determined by their order in the HTML source. Consider the following snippet from the head of an HTML element, where all of the referenced style sheets and style elements declare a different color for the h1 element, with the same specificity:

```
<link rel="stylesheet" href="css/sheet1.css">
<style>
    @import 'css/sheet3.css';

    h1 {
        color: fuchsia;
    }
</style>
<link rel="stylesheet" href="css/sheet2.css">
```

In this scenario, the order of declarations would be like this:

1. Declaration from sheet1.css

2. Declaration from sheet3.css, imported inside the style element

3. Declaration from inside the style element

4. Declaration from sheet2.css

The winning declaration would be the one in sheet2.css, since it's the last one in the list.

Performance

Which way you choose to load CSS into the page is the single biggest option you have for controlling how quickly your page will be displayed by browsers (assuming the HTML page itself loads fast!).

An important metric in web performance is the time it takes for content to begin being displayed on the screen. This is sometimes called "time to render" or "time to glass."

Modern browsers need a minimum of two things before they start rendering content on the screen: HTML and CSS. This means that getting the browser to download the HTML and *all* the CSS as quickly as possible is extremely important.

Don't be tempted to delay CSS loading by putting it in the body or near the footer. Browsers respond best when they have up front all the CSS information they need to lay out a page. That way they can start to understand what the page will look like and render the page to the screen in one go, rather than constantly having to readjust as new styles are loaded in.

Reducing HTTP Requests

It is important when linking to external style sheets that you keep the number of files to a minimum. Each additional file results in an extra HTTP request, and the act of requesting a file from the server adds significant overhead to the time it takes for the browser to download and apply all the styles. An extra HTTP request means extra data being sent from the browser, such as cookies and request headers. The server then has to send back response headers for each request. Two files will always result in more data being sent between the browser and the server than one file with the same actual CSS content.

Always try and keep the number of CSS files you deliver in a live website to just one or two. Using just one link element to load a CSS file and then using @import inside that one does not mean that the browser only uses one request: on the contrary, it means it needs one request for the linked file, and then subsequent requests to fetch all the imported files. So avoid using @import (at least on a live site).

Compressing and Caching Content

It's also very important that any files you use on a live site are compressed using GZIP. CSS compresses very effectively because it has many repeated patterns such as property names and values. In many cases it's possible to reduce the size of a CSS file by 70–80%, and that can lead to significant reductions in bandwidth and load time for users. Most web servers have a mechanism for enabling automatic compression of content to browsers that support it.

Similarly, it's important that you direct your web server to set appropriate cache times for your CSS files. Ideally you want users' browsers to download a CSS file once, and never again until it changes. The strategies for this involve setting various HTTP headers that instruct the browser to cache the files for a very long time, and then "cache busting" by updating the name of the file if anything changes.

The details of how this works is somewhat outside of the scope of this book. You may need the support of your hosting provider or your company's system administrators to help configure servers, but compressing and correctly caching content are the two most important things you can do to improve performance for your sites.

Avoid Render-Blocking JavaScript

When you add a <script> element in the <head> element of your HTML document, the browser has to download that file before it can start showing your HTML content to the user. As the evaluation of HTML and CSS is completely stopped until the script is downloaded and executed; this is known as "render-blocking". This can considerably slow down how fast your site appears to load.

This has led to the recommendation of loading JavaScript at the bottom of the HTML page immediately before the closing </body> tag:

```
  <!-- Load scripts last -->
  <script src="/scripts/core.js"></script>
</body>
```

A more modern approach is to use the <script> tag inside of <head> together with the async and defer attributes. A <script> tag that has the async attribute set will download the source file while the HTML continues to be evaluated, but stops HTML evaluation to execute the script once it's downloaded. The defer attribute will have a similar effect, but waits until the HTML evaluation is completely done until it executes the downloaded script. Which one is right depends on what the script itself does.

```
<head>
  <!-- will load asynchronously, but execute immediately when downloaded -->
  <script src="/scripts/core.js" async></script>
  <!-- will load asynchronously, but execute after HTML is done-->
  <script src="/scripts/deferred.js" defer></script>
</head>
```

By using either of these methods to load JavaScript, you ensure that both the HTML content and the CSS can be parsed and displayed by the browser without being delayed by requests for JavaScript files. Which method you choose is mostly a matter of browser support: the async and defer attributes are part of the HTML5 standard, and thus newer. Most notably, Internet Explorer prior to version 10 has missing or partial support.

Summary

In this chapter you have reacquainted yourself with the common CSS selectors as well as learned about some powerful new selectors you may not have come across before. You now have a better understanding of how specificity works and how you can use the cascade to structure your CSS rules and help them hit the target. We had a first look at how you can avoid getting into a specificity arms race, and how to use your understanding of specificity, the cascade, and inheritance to your advantage. You have also learned about how to apply CSS to a document and some of the ways this can impact the performance of your web pages.

In the next chapter, you will learn about the CSS box model, how and why margins collapse, and how floating and positioning really work.

CHAPTER 3

■ ■ ■

Visual Formatting Model Overview

Some of the most important CSS concepts to grasp are floating, positioning, and the box model. These concepts control the way elements are arranged and displayed on a page and form the basis of many layout techniques. More recently, new standards specifically designed to control layout have been introduced, and we will look at these individually in forthcoming chapters. However, the concepts that you learn in this chapter will help you fully grasp the intricacies of the box model, the difference between absolute and relative positioning, and how floating and clearing actually work. Once you have a firm grasp of these fundamentals, developing sites using CSS becomes that much easier.

In this chapter you will learn about:

- The intricacies of the box model

- How and why margins collapse

- The different positioning properties and values

- How floating and clearing work

- What a formatting context is

Box Model Recap

The box model is one of the cornerstones of CSS and dictates how elements are displayed and, to a certain extent, how they interact with each other. Every element on the page is considered to be a rectangular box made up of the element's content, padding, border, and margin (see Figure 3-1).

© Andy Budd and Emil Björklund 2016
A. Budd and E. Björklund, *CSS Mastery*, DOI 10.1007/978-1-4302-5864-3_3

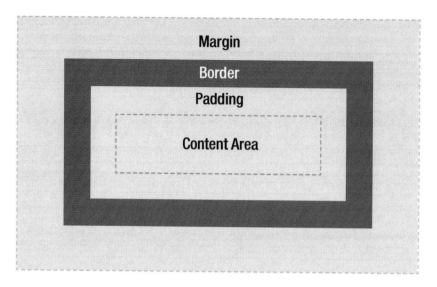

Figure 3-1. *An illustration of the box model*

Padding is applied around the content area. If you add a background to an element, it will be applied to the area formed by the content and padding. As such, padding is often used to create a gutter around content so that it does not appear flush to the side of the background. Adding a border applies a line to the outside of the padded area. These lines come in various styles such as solid, dashed, or dotted. Outside the border is a margin. Margins are the transparent space outside of the visible parts of the box, allowing you to control the distance between elements in the page.

Another property that can be applied to boxes, but does not affect their layout, is the outline property, which draws a line around an element's border box. It does not affect the box's width or height, and can be useful when debugging complex layouts or demonstrating a layout effect.

Padding, borders, and margins are optional and default to zero. However, many elements will be given margins and padding by the user-agent style sheet. For example, headings always receive some margins by default, although these vary depending on the browser. You can of course override these browser styles in your own style sheets, either on specific elements or by employing a reset style sheet, as discussed in Chapter 2.

Box-Sizing

By default, the width and height properties of a box refer to the width and height of the *content box*—the rectangle formed by the edges of an element's rendered content. Adding borders and padding will not affect the size of the content box but will increase the *overall* size of an element's box. If you wanted a box with a 5-pixel border and a 5-pixel padding on each side to be 100 pixels total width, you would need to set the width of the content to be 80 pixels, as shown next. If the box also has a margin around it of 10 pixels, it would occupy a space that is 120 pixels wide in total (see Figure 3-2).

```
.mybox {
  width: 80px;
  padding: 5px;
  border: 5px solid;
  margin: 10px;
}
```

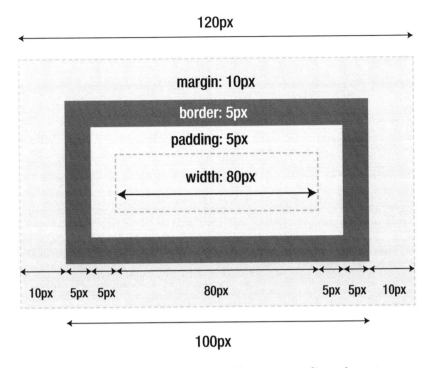

Figure 3-2. *The default box model. The width property applies to the content area*

You can change the way the width of a box is calculated using the box-sizing property. The default value for box-sizing is content-box and applies the behavior described so far. However, it is very useful to be able to have the width and height properties affect more than just the content box, particularly in responsive layouts.

■ **Note** some form control elements (like input) may have different box-sizing default values in some browsers. This is due to compatibility with legacy behavior where it wasn't possible to change things like padding or borders.

If you set the box-sizing property to a value of border-box, as shown next, then the width and height properties will include the space required for the padding and borders of the box (see Figure 3-3). The margin still affects the overall size the element occupies on the page, but is still not included in the measurement given by the width. You could achieve the same overall layout show in Figure 3-2 with these rules:

```
.mybox {
  box-sizing: border-box;
  width: 100px;
  padding: 5px;
  border: 5px;
  margin: 10px;
}
```

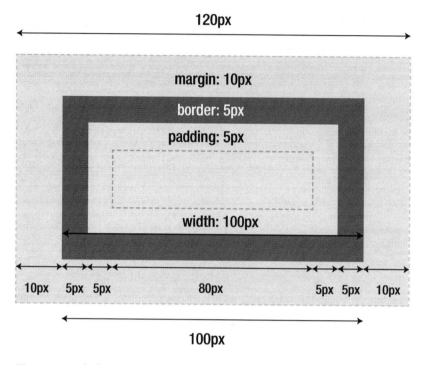

Figure 3-3. *The box model when the box-sizing property is set to border-box. The width property now corresponds to the entire width of the visible parts of the element*

So why is this useful? Well, in many ways this is a much more intuitive way of dealing with boxes, and in fact was the way that the box model worked in old versions of Internet Explorer before IE6. It is "intuitive" because, when you think about it, this is how boxes work in the real world.

Imagine a CSS box as being like a packing crate. The walls of the box act as a border and provide visual definition, while the padding goes on the inside to protect the contents. If the box needs to be a specific width, adding more padding or increasing the thickness of the walls eats into the available content space. Now if you need to space the boxes out before you stack them, the space between each box (effectively the margin) has no effect on the width of the box itself, or indeed the amount of available content space. This feels like a more logical solution, so it's a shame that the browser developers, including Microsoft in subsequent versions of IE, decided to go in a different direction.

Fortunately, the box-sizing property allows us to override the default behavior and simplify some common patterns in CSS layout. Take the following example:

```
<div class="group">
  <article class="block">
  </article>
</div>
```

If we want to ensure that the width of any .block inside our .group is always one-third of the width of its containing column, we could apply the following rule:

```
.group .block {
  width: 33.3333%;
}
```

This would work fine, until we start adding gutters using `padding` on the sides of our `.block` so that its content stands away from the visible edges. Now our `.block` element is one-third of the parent `.group` element's width plus the padding, which could potentially break our intended layout. Figure 3-4 illustrates the difference.

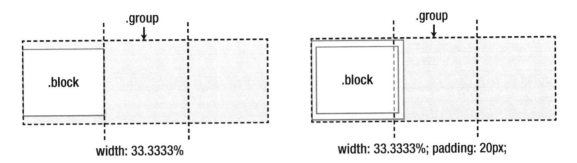

Figure 3-4. *Assuming we want the .block element to be one-third of the .group element, we might get unexpected results when we add padding to it*

We could solve this problem, for example, by adding an extra inner element to which we add our padding—or we could choose a different `box-sizing` property to alter how the `width` is calculated (see Figure 3-5):

```
.group .block {
  width: 33.3333%;
  box-sizing: border-box;
  padding: 20px;
}
```

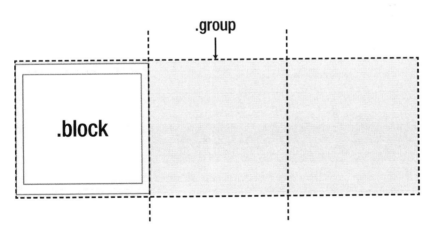

Figure 3-5. *Adding box-sizing: border-box keeps our box at 33.3333% width, even if padding is added*

Now our .block element is exactly one-third of the width of the parent element, just as we declared, no matter how much padding or borders we add to it.

Padding, borders, and margins can be applied to all sides of an element or to individual sides. Margins can also be given a negative value. This can be used in a number of interesting ways to pull elements in and out of positions of the page. We'll explore some of these techniques in later chapters.

You can use any measurement of length (like pixels, ems, and percentages) from the CSS specification to add padding and margins to an element. Using percentage values has some peculiarities that deserve mentioning. Assuming the markup is the same as in the previous example, what does the 5% actually represent in this example?

```
.block {
  margin-left: 5%;
}
```

The answer is that in this case, it's 5% of the width of the parent .group element. If we assume that our .group element is 100 pixels wide, it would have a 5-pixel margin to the left.

When it comes to using these measurements for padding or margins on the top and bottom sides of an element, you'd be forgiven for guessing that the percentage is derived from the parent element's *height*. That seems only logical at first—however, since the height is normally not declared, and can vary wildly with the height of the content, the CSS specification states that the top and bottom values for padding and margins also take their values from the *width* of the *containing block*. In this instance, the containing block is the parent, but this can change—we'll sort out what that means a little bit further ahead in the chapter.

Minimum and Maximum Values

Sometimes it may be useful to apply the min-width and max-width properties to an element. Doing so can be especially helpful when practicing responsive design, as it allows a block-level box to automatically fill the width of its parent element by default, but not shrink smaller than the value specified in min-width or grow larger than the value specified in max-width. (We will come back to responsive web design and how it relates to CSS in Chapter 8.)

Similarly, min-height and max-height properties also exist, although you should be cautious when applying any height values in CSS, because elements are nearly always better off left deriving their height implicitly from the content they contain. Otherwise, if the amount of content grows, or the text size changes, the content could flow out of the fixed-height box. If you do need to set a default height measurement for some reason, using min-height is usually better, since it lets your boxes expand with their content.

The Visual Formatting Model

With an understanding of the box model, we can start to explore some of the visual formatting and positioning models.

People often refer to elements such as p, h1, and article as block-level elements. This means they are elements that are visually displayed as blocks of content, or *block boxes*. Conversely, elements such as strong, span, and time are described as inline-level elements because their content is displayed within lines as *inline boxes*.

It is possible to change the type of box generated by using the display property. This means you can make an inline-level element such as span behave like a block-level element by setting its display property to block. It is also possible to cause an element to generate no box at all by setting its display property to none. The box, and thus all the content, is no longer displayed and takes up no space in the document.

There are a number of different positioning models in CSS, including floats, absolute positioning and relative positioning. Unless specified, all boxes start life being positioned in the normal flow and have the default property of `static`. As the name suggests, the position of an element's box in the normal flow will be dictated by the element's position in the HTML.

Block-level boxes will appear vertically one after the other; the vertical distance between boxes is calculated by the boxes' vertical margins.

Inline boxes are laid out in a line horizontally, following the text flow and wrapping to a new line when the text wraps. Their horizontal spacing can be adjusted using horizontal padding, borders, and margins (see Figure 3-6). However, vertical padding, borders, and margins will have no effect on the height of an inline box. Similarly, setting an explicit `height` or `width` on an inline box will have no effect either.

The horizontal box formed by one line of text is called a *line box*, and a line box will always be tall enough for all the inline boxes it may contain. The only way you can alter the dimensions of a line box is by changing the line height, or setting horizontal borders, padding, or margins on any inline boxes inside it. Figure 3-6 shows the block box of a paragraph with two lines of text, where one of the words is inside a `<strong>` element displayed inline.

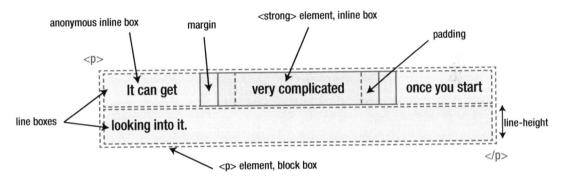

Figure 3-6. *The inline components inside a paragraph block box*

You can also set the `display` property of an element to be `inline-block`. As the name suggests, this declaration makes the element line up horizontally as if it were an inline box. However, the inside of the box behaves as though the box were block level, including being able to explicitly set width, height, vertical margins, and padding.

When you use table markup (the `table`, `tr`, `th` and `td` elements, and so forth), the table itself behaves as a block, but the contents of the table will line up according to the generated rows and columns. It is also possible to set the `display` property of other elements so that they adopt the layout behavior of tables. By applying the values `table`, `table-row`, and `table-cell` in the correct way, you can achieve some of the properties of an HTML table without using tables in the markup.

Modules like Flexible Box Layout (also known as *flexbox*) and Grid Layout, which we will cover in later chapters, have further extended the `display` property. Often, these new layout modes create boxes that act as blocks in their outer context, but create new rules for how the content inside the box is treated.

This division between outer and inner display modes (seen across both `inline-block`, `table` and new values like `flex` or `grid`) is now being standardized in the Display Level 3 module. There, the existing properties and keywords for display modes are being expanded, to allow for more granular control. The important takeaway is that inline-level boxes and block-level boxes are still fundamental to the default behavior of HTML elements, but the reality is slightly more nuanced.

Anonymous Boxes

In the same way that HTML elements can be nested, boxes can contain other boxes. Most boxes are formed from explicitly defined elements. However, there is one situation where a block-level element is created even if it has not been explicitly defined—when you add some text at the start of a block-level element such as a section, as shown next. Even though you have not defined the "some text" bit as a block-level element, it is treated as such.

```
<section>
  some text
  <p>Some more text</p>
</section>
```

In this situation, the box is described as an *anonymous block box*, since it is not associated with a specifically defined element.

A similar thing happens with the line boxes of text inside a block-level element. Say you have a paragraph that contains three lines of text. Each line of text forms an *anonymous line box*. You cannot style anonymous block boxes or line boxes directly, except through the use of the :first-line pseudo-element, which obviously has limited use and only allows you to change certain properties related to typography and color. However, it is useful to understand that everything you see on your screen creates some form of box.

Margin Collapsing

When it comes to normal block boxes, there have a behavior known as *margin collapsing*. Margin collapsing is a relatively simple concept. In practice, however, it can cause a lot of confusion when you're laying out a web page. Put simply, when two or more vertical margins meet, they will collapse to form a single margin. The height of this margin will equal the height of the larger of the two collapsed margins.

When two elements are above one another, the bottom margin of the first element will collapse with the top margin of the second element (see Figure 3-7).

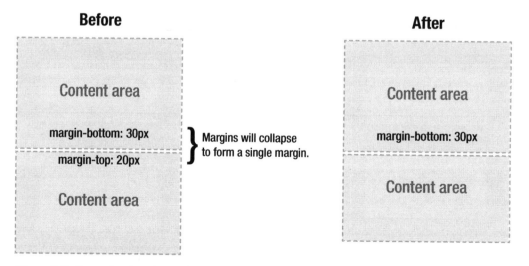

Figure 3-7. *Example of an element's top margin collapsing with the bottom margin of the preceding element*

When one element is contained within another element, assuming there is no padding or border separating margins, their top and/or bottom margins will also collapse together (see Figure 3-8).

Figure 3-8. *Example of an element's top margin collapsing with the top margin of its parent element*

It may seem strange at first, but margins can even collapse on themselves. Say you have an empty element with a margin but no border or padding. In this situation, the top margin is touching the bottom margin, and they collapse together (see Figure 3-9).

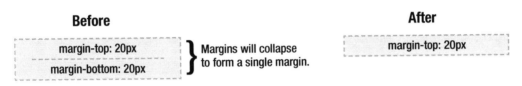

Figure 3-9. *Example of an element's top margin collapsing with its bottom margin*

If this margin is touching the margin of another element, it will collapse itself (see Figure 3-10).

Figure 3-10. *Example of an empty element's collapsed margin collapsing with another empty element's margins*

This is why a series of empty paragraph elements take up very little space, as all their margins collapse together to form a single small margin.

Margin collapsing may seem strange at first, but it actually makes a lot of sense. Take a typical page of text made up of several paragraphs (see Figure 3-11). The space above the first paragraph will equal the paragraph's top margin. Without margin collapsing, the space between all subsequent paragraphs will be the sum of their two adjoining top and bottom margins. This means that the space between paragraphs will be double the space at the top of the page. With margin collapsing, the top and bottom margins between each paragraph collapse, leaving the spacing the same as everywhere else.

Without Margin Collapsing

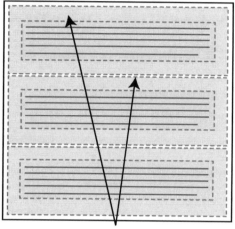

The space between paragraphs is double the space at the top.

With Margin Collapsing

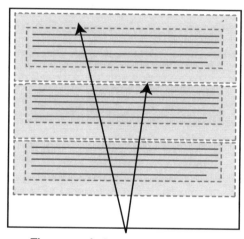

The space between paragraphs is the same as the space at the top.

Figure 3-11. *Margins collapse to maintain consistent spacing between elements*

Margin collapsing only happens with the vertical margins of block boxes in the normal flow of the document. Margins between things like inline boxes, floated boxes, or absolutely positioned boxes never collapse.

Containing Blocks

The concept of what gives an element its *containing block* is important because it decides how various properties are interpreted, like the case with padding and margin set in percentages that we saw earlier.

The containing block of an element depends on how the element is positioned. If the element has a static position (same as no position property declared) or a relative position, its containing block is calculated to the edges of its nearest parent that has a display property set to something that causes a block-like context, including block, inline-block, table-cell, list-item and so forth.

By default, declarations of width, height, margin, and padding are calculated from the dimensions of this parent element when set in percentages. This changes when you change the element to have a positioning model of absolute or fixed. Next up we'll go through the different models and how they interact with the concept of a containing block.

Relative Positioning

When you set the position property of an element to relative, it will initially stay exactly where it is. You can then shift the element relative to its starting point by setting a vertical or horizontal position, using the top, right, bottom, and left properties. If you set the top position to be 20 pixels, the box will appear 20 pixels below the top of its original position. Setting the left position to 20 pixels, as shown next, will create a 20-pixel space on the left of the element, moving the element to the right (see Figure 3-12).

```
.mybox {
  position: relative;
  left: 20px;
  top: 20px;
}
```

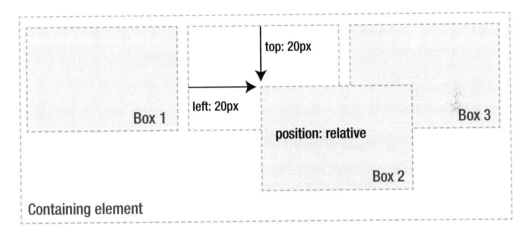

Figure 3-12. *Relatively positioning an element*

With relative positioning, the element continues to occupy the original space in the flow of the page, whether or not it is offset. As such, offsetting the element can cause it to overlap other boxes.

Absolute Positioning

Relative positioning is actually considered part of the normal-flow positioning model, as the element is relative to its position in the normal flow. By contrast, absolute positioning takes the element out of the flow of the document, thus taking up no space. Other elements in the normal flow of the document will act as though the absolutely positioned element was never there (see Figure 3-13).

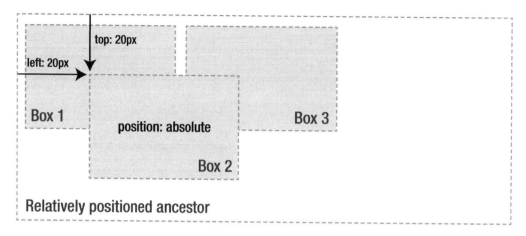

Figure 3-13. *Absolutely positioning an element*

An absolutely positioned element's containing block is its nearest positioned ancestor, meaning any ancestor element that has the position property set to anything other than static. If the element has no positioned ancestors, it will be positioned in relation to the root element of the document, the html element. This is also known as the *initial containing block*.

As with relatively positioned boxes, an absolutely positioned box can be offset from the top, bottom, left, or right of its containing block. This gives you a great deal of flexibility. You can literally position an element anywhere on the page.

Because absolutely positioned boxes are taken out of the flow of the document, they can overlap other elements on the page. You can control the stacking order of these boxes by setting a numeric property called z-index. The higher the z-index, the higher up the box appears in the stack. There are various intricacies to take into account when stacking items with z-index: we will sort those out in Chapter 6.

Although absolute positioning can be a useful tool for laying out elements of your pages, it is rarely used for creating high-level layouts anymore. The fact that absolutely positioned boxes don't participate in the flow of the document makes it quite the hassle to create layouts that adapt and respond to the viewport at various widths and varying lengths of content. The nature of the Web just doesn't easily allow us to specify exact measurements as to where on the page our elements sit. As we have become more proficient with other layout techniques in CSS, the use of absolute positioning has become quite uncommon for page layout.

Fixed Positioning

Fixed positioning is a subcategory of absolute positioning. The difference is that a fixed element's containing block is the viewport. This allows you to create floating elements that always stay at the same position in the window. Many sites use this technique to keep parts of their navigation in view at all times, by fixing them in position in a side column or top bar (Figure 3-14). This can help improve usability because the user never has to look far to get back to an important part of the interface.

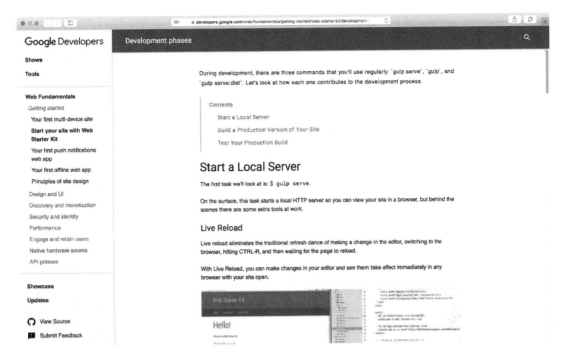

Figure 3-14. *The top bar and side navigation on the Google Developer documentation stays fixed as you scroll down*

Floating

Another important visual model is the float model. A floated box can be shifted either to the left or the right until its outer edge touches the edge of its containing block or another floated box. Because floated boxes aren't in the normal flow of the document, block boxes in the regular flow of the document behave almost as if the floated box wasn't there. We'll explain the "almost" in a minute.

As shown in Figure 3-15, when you float Box 1 to the right, it's taken out of the flow of the document and moved to the right until its right edge touches the right edge of the containing block. Its width will also shrink to the smallest width needed to contain its content, unless you've explicitly told it otherwise by setting a particular `width` or `min-width`/`max-width`.

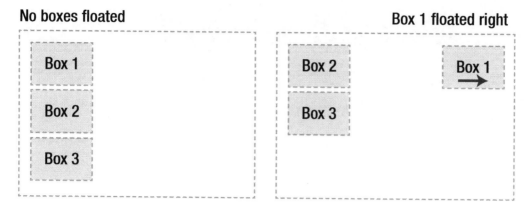

Figure 3-15. *Example of an element being floated right*

In Figure 3-16, when you float Box 1 to the left, it is taken out of the flow of the document and moved left until its left edge touches the left edge of the containing block. Because it is no longer in the flow, it takes up no space and actually sits on top of Box 2, obscuring it from view. If you float all three boxes to the left, Box 1 is shifted left until it touches its containing block, and the other two boxes are shifted left until they touch the preceding floated box.

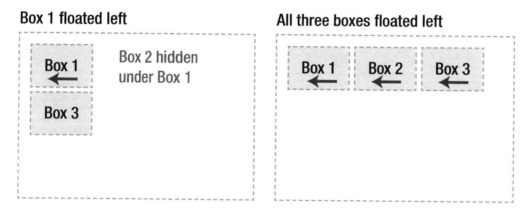

Figure 3-16. *Example of elements being floated left*

If the containing element is too narrow for all the floated elements to fit horizontally, the remaining floats will drop down until there is sufficient space (see Figure 3-17). If the floated elements have different heights, it is possible for floats to get "stuck" on other floats when they drop down.

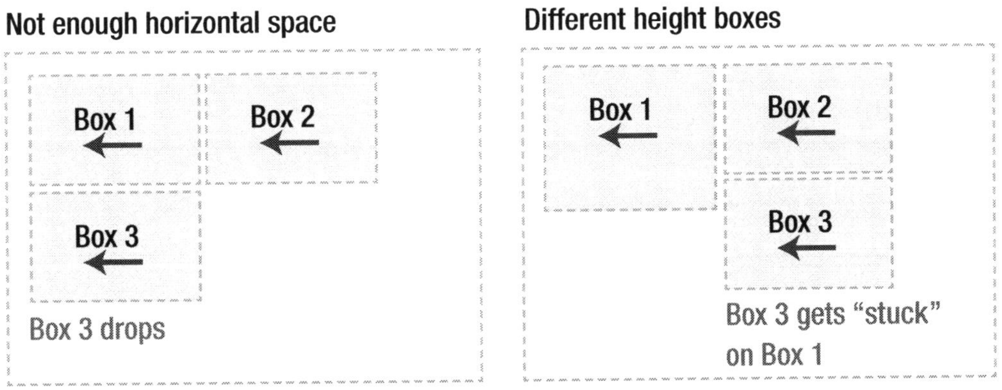

Not enough horizontal space

Box 1 ← Box 2 ←

Box 3 ←

Box 3 drops

Different height boxes

Box 1 ← Box 2 ←

Box 3 ←

Box 3 gets "stuck"
on Box 1

Figure 3-17. *If there is not enough available horizontal space, floated elements will drop down until there is*

Line Boxes and Clearing

You learned in the previous section that floating an element takes it out of the flow of the document where it no longer exerts an effect on non-floated items. Actually, this isn't strictly true. If a floated element is followed by an element in the flow of the document, the element's box will behave as if the float didn't exist. However, the textual content of the box retains some memory of the floated element and moves out of the way to make room. In technical terms, a line box next to a floated element is shortened to make room for the floated element, thereby flowing around the floated box. In fact, floats were created to allow text to flow around images (see Figure 3-18).

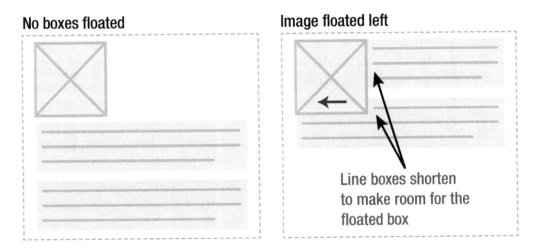

No boxes floated

Image floated left

Line boxes shorten
to make room for the
floated box

Figure 3-18. *Line boxes shorten when next to a float*

To stop line boxes from flowing around the outside of a floated box, you need to apply a clear property to the element that contains those line boxes. The clear property can be left, right, both, or none, and it indicates which side of the box should not be next to a floated box. Many people think the clear property simply removes some flag that negates the previous float. However, the reality is much more interesting. When you clear an element, the browser adds enough margin to the top of the element to push the element's top border edge vertically down, past the float (see Figure 3-19). This can sometimes be confusing when you try and apply your own margin to "cleared" elements, because the value will have no effect until it reaches and goes beyond the value added automatically by the browser.

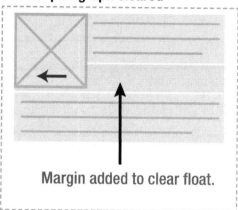

Figure 3-19. *Clearing an element's top margin to create enough vertical space for the preceding float*

As you've seen, floated elements are taken out of the flow of the document and have no effect on surrounding elements apart from shortening line boxes enough to make space for the floated box. However, clearing an element essentially clears a vertical space for all the preceding floated elements. This can be useful when using floats as a layout tool, as it allows surrounding elements to make space for floated elements.

Let's look at how you might create a simple component layout using floats. Say you have a picture that you want to float to the left of a title and a small block of text to the right, often called a "media object" because of the common pattern of having a piece of media (such as a figure, image, or video) and a piece of accompanying text. You want this picture and text to be contained in another element with a background color and border. You could probably try something like this:

```
.media-block {
  background-color: gray;
  border: solid 1px black;
}
.media-fig {
  float: left;
  width: 30%; /* leaves 70% for the text */
}
.media-body {
  float: right;
  width: 65%; /* a bit of "air" left on the side */
}
```

```html
<div class="media-block">
  <img class="media-fig" src="/img/pic.jpg" alt="The pic" />
  <div class="media-body">
    <h3>Title of this</h3>
    <p>Brief description of this</p>
  </div>
</div>
```

However, because the floated elements are taken out of the flow of the document, the wrapper div with a class of .media-block takes no space—it has only floating content, and thus nothing to give it a height in the document flow. How do you visually get the wrapper to enclose the floated element? You need to apply a clear somewhere inside that element, which as we saw earlier creates enough vertical margin on the cleared element to allow room for the floated elements (see Figure 3-20). Unfortunately, as there are no existing elements in the example to clear, you could add an empty element before the closing div tag, and clear that:

```css
/* Added CSS: */
.clear {
    clear: both;
}
```
```html
<div class="media-block">
      <img class="media-fig" src="/img/pic.jpg " alt="The pic" />
      <div class="media-body">
        <h3>Title of this</h3>
        <p>Brief description of this</p>
      </div>
      <div class="clear"></div><!-- added extra empty div -->
</div>
```

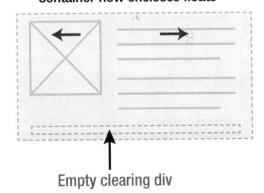

Container does not enclose floats

Container now encloses floats

Floats take up no space

Empty clearing div

Figure 3-20. Adding a clearing div forces the container to enclose floats

This gets the result we want, but at the expense of adding extraneous code to our markup. Often there will be an existing element you can apply the clear to, but sometimes you may have to bite the bullet and add meaningless markup for the purpose of layout. In this case, however, we can do better.

The way we can do this is to simulate the extra clearing element using the :after pseudo-element, as shown next. By applying this to the containing element of your floated elements, an extra box will be created that you can apply the clear rule to.

```
.media-block:after {
  content: " ";
  display: block;
  clear: both;
}
```

This approach and some variations of it are best demonstrated in a small code snippet by Nicholas Gallagher known as the micro clearfix, presented at http://nicolasgallagher.com/micro-clearfix-hack/.

Formatting Contexts

CSS has a number of different sets of rules that apply to how elements interact with each other as they flow horizontally or vertically across the page. The technical name for one of these sets of rules is a *formatting context*. We have already seen some of the rules for the *inline formatting context*—for example, the fact that vertical margins have no effect on inline boxes. Similarly, certain rules apply to how block boxes stack up, like we saw in the section on collapsing margins.

Other rules define how the page must automatically contain any floats sticking out at the end (otherwise the contents inside the floated element might end up outside of the scrollable area) and all block boxes by default have their edge aligned with the left edge of the containing block (or the right edge, depending on the text direction). This set of rules is called the *block formatting context*.

Some rules allow elements to establish their own, internal block formatting contexts. These include the following:

- Elements whose display property is set to a value that creates a block-like context for the contents of the element, like inline-block or table-cell.

- Elements whose float property is anything but none.

- Elements that are absolutely positioned.

- Elements that have the overflow property set to anything but visible.

As we discussed previously, the rule that says that the edge of a block touches the edge of its containing block applies even for content that is preceded by a float. The float is removed from the page flow, and creates the visual effect of making room for itself by triggering the line boxes in elements following it to shorten. The element itself still stretches underneath the float as far as it needs to.

When an element has rules that trigger a new block formatting context *and* is next to a float, it will ignore the rule that says that it has to have its edge up against the side of its containing block. Instead, it will shrink to fit—and not just the line boxes, but the whole thing. This can be used to re-create the .media-block example in the previous section but with simpler rules:

```
.media-block {
  background-color: gray;
  border: solid 1px black;
}
```

```
.media-fig {
  float: left
  margin-right: 5%;
}
.media-block, .media-body {
  overflow: auto;
}
<div class="media-block">
  <img class="media-fig" src="/img/pic.jpg" alt="The pic" />
  <div class="media-body">
    <h3>Title of this</h3>
    <p>Brief description of this</p>
  </div>
</div>
```

In setting overflow: auto; on both the containing .media-block and our .media-body elements, we established new block formatting contexts for them. This has a couple of effects (see comparison in Figure 3-21):

- It contains the floated image inside the .media-block component without the need for clearing rules, since block formatting contexts also automatically contain floats.

- As an added bonus, it allows us to ditch the rules for width as well as the float on our .media-body element if we want—it will simply adjust to the remaining space next to the float and still keep a nice straight edge next to the image. If there wasn't a new formatting context and the text was a bit longer, any line boxes that were beneath the floated .media-fig would stretch beneath it, ending up flush to the left beneath the image.

No block formatting context

.media-fig floated left

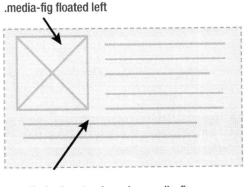

.media-body extends under .media-fig

With block formatting context

.media-body shrinks to fit

Figure 3-21. *If only the .media-fig element is floated and the text is long enough, some lines will wrap under the float and end up to the left. Creating a new block formatting context forces .media-body to shrink*

Creating layouts with as predictable and simple behavior as possible reduces the complexity of your code and increases the robustness of your layouts, so knowing when to apply tricks like this to avoid complicated interaction between floats and clearing elements is A Good Thing. Luckily, even better techniques for doing layout are gaining ground fast.

Intrinsic and Extrinsic Sizing

The CSS module "Intrinsic and Extrinsic Sizing Level 3" defines a list of keywords that can be applied to the (min- and max-) width and height properties, instead of lengths in pixels or percentages, etc. These represent explicit lengths that are derived from either the surrounding context (extrinsic) or the content of the element (intrinsic), but letting the browser figure out the final value—as opposed to the implicit values of either setting the property to auto or using floats or block formatting contexts to create shrink-to-fit scenarios without setting a width at all.

We won't go into the details of the different keywords here, but it's interesting to note that among them we find contain-floats. This keyword should do pretty much what you'd expect; for example, you could make an element contain any floats by using this code:

```
.myThing {
  min-height: contain-floats;
}
```

So far, support for the various keywords in this module is weak—most notably, no versions of IE support any of them at the time of writing. Still, it's something that could be potentially very useful in the future for creating robust sizing without resorting to more involved techniques.

Other CSS Layout Modules

We've covered the fundamentals and most common parts of the CSS visual formatting model, but there are some other areas to briefly mention.

You would imagine that a robust and flexible layout model would be a key part of a visual presentation tool like CSS. You'd be right; but unfortunately it has taken us a very long time to get one. Historically we've used whatever features are available in the language to achieve our goals, even if they are far from the ideal tool for the job. Initially this included adopting data tables because of their useful layout characteristics—despite their bloated markup and inappropriate semantics. More recently we've been coercing floats and absolute positioning to achieve most of our complex page layout, but again, neither of these features is designed for laying out web pages. Both have serious constraints, most of which we just trained ourselves to live with.

Thankfully, more recent CSS modules have introduced new content models specifically designed for creating flexible and robust page layouts. At the time of writing, these modules are all in different states of readiness, and some don't have interoperable cross-browser implementations. We'll look at some of these in detail and some of the more useful techniques they enable in upcoming chapters, but this is a quick summary of the kind of functionality they offer.

Flexible Box Layout

The Flexible Box Layout Module, or *flexbox*, that we've touched on previously is a model of layout introduced in CSS 3. Flexbox allows you to lay out children of a box either horizontally or vertically and determine the size, spacing and distribution of those children. It also allows you to change the order of elements as rendered on the page, regardless of their place in the HTML source. Flexbox acts as an upgrade of the normal flow model (inline and block), offering a balance of precise control and flexibility with regards to the content itself and how it affects sizing.

Flexbox is widely implemented, but support is most notably missing or incomplete in older versions of Internet Explorer. The good news is that it is constructed in such a way that you can combine it with other methods, like floats, to create very robust layouts. We will take a closer look at flexbox in Chapter 6.

Grid Layout

Grid layout is the first fully fledged high-level layout tool for CSS, with a goal of replacing complex page layouts that have historically been created with floats and positioned elements. It offers complete separation of layout from source order, and abstracts the idea of a grid system away from the structure of content and presentation of individual modules. Where flexbox is "micro", grid layout is "macro", so these two methods complement each other well.

Grid layout is not yet widely supported, but browser makers are racing to implement it at the time this book is being written. We will get acquainted with this powerful new module in Chapter 7.

Multi-Column Layout

The Multi-column Layout Module is a fairly straightforward way of allowing content to flow into separate columns; for example, creating a newspaper-like layout where the text of its paragraphs flow into a number of vertical columns. This module allows you to choose either a set number of columns or a preferred width, leaving the number of columns to follow based on available space. You can also control the space of the gaps between columns and apply border-like visual effects to these gaps. As multi-column layout is more a tool for typography than general layout, we will work with it in Chapter 4.

Regions

CSS Regions allows you to specify how content flows between elements on a page. One element acts as a source of content, but instead of the normal block flow, this content can flow into other placeholder elements elsewhere on the page. This means layouts are no longer impacted by the source order of HTML, and again, the layout presentation becomes decoupled from the structure of the content.

CSS Regions allow for layouts that have previously been impossible using CSS alone, and may drive adoption of certain print-based layout patterns in the future. However, few browser makers have shown any love for CSS Regions, and there is a risk that this type of layout won't be mature enough to use for some time. For that reason, we will not cover Regions in any further detail in this book.

Summary

In this chapter, you learned about the box model and how padding, margin, width, and height affect the dimensions of a box. You also learned about the concept of margin collapsing and how this can affect layout. You were introduced to the various formatting models of CSS, such as normal flow, absolute positioning, and floating. You learned the difference between inline and block boxes, how to absolutely position an element within a relatively positioned ancestor, and how clearing really works.

Now that you are armed with these fundamentals, let's start putting them to good use. In the following chapters of this book, you will be introduced to a number of core CSS concepts and you'll see how they can be used in a variety of useful and practical techniques. So launch your favorite editor and let's get coding.

■ ■ ■

CHAPTER 4

Web Typography

Typography has been a fundamental part of graphic design since the invention of the printing press, so you'd expect it to play a central role in the field of web design. Some have gone as far as to say that web design is 95% typography. As such, it is surprising that browsers have only recently allowed us to fully embrace typography and typesetting on the Web. This opens up the possibility for us to learn from hundreds of years of typographic history, and create richly styled content that is a delight to read.

Previous editions of CSS Mastery did not contain a separate chapter on web typography, so perhaps that gives you some indication of the advancement in this area over the last few years. There are a number of areas we will cover in this chapter:

- How to apply solid typographic rules, using the basic CSS font and text properties

- Controlling measure, multi-column text, and hyphenation

- Working with custom web fonts and advanced font features

- Text effects using shadows and other tricks

Basic Typesetting in CSS

One of the first things most designers will do is add the basic typographic styles. Starting with the body element and working down into more and more specific rules, we set the basics for readability, clarity, and tone. As our first example in this chapter, we'll do just that: take an example page and apply a basic typographic treatment.

Figure 4-1 shows a very simple HTML document (a text about the Moon, reproduced from Wikipedia) displayed in the browser with no added styles. The fact that it still renders as a readable document is due to the default style sheet in the browser, where a few relatively sane typographic rules are set.

© Andy Budd and Emil Björklund 2016
A. Budd and E. Björklund, *CSS Mastery*, DOI 10.1007/978-1-4302-5864-3_4

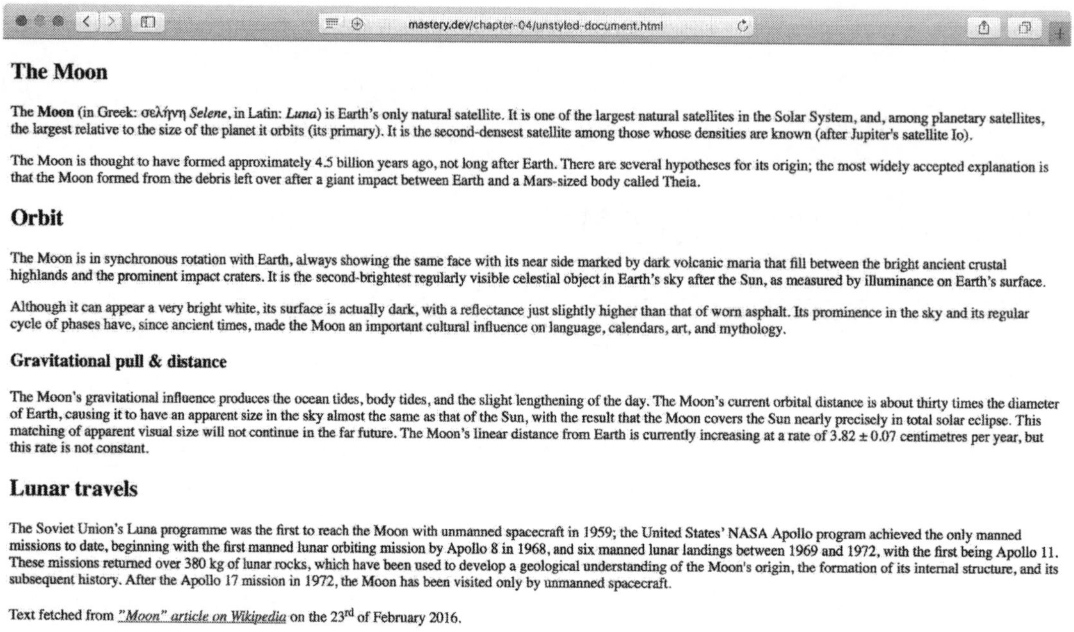

The Moon

The **Moon** (in Greek: σελήνη *Selene*, in Latin: *Luna*) is Earth's only natural satellite. It is one of the largest natural satellites in the Solar System, and, among planetary satellites, the largest relative to the size of the planet it orbits (its primary). It is the second-densest satellite among those whose densities are known (after Jupiter's satellite Io).

The Moon is thought to have formed approximately 4.5 billion years ago, not long after Earth. There are several hypotheses for its origin; the most widely accepted explanation is that the Moon formed from the debris left over after a giant impact between Earth and a Mars-sized body called Theia.

Orbit

The Moon is in synchronous rotation with Earth, always showing the same face with its near side marked by dark volcanic maria that fill between the bright ancient crustal highlands and the prominent impact craters. It is the second-brightest regularly visible celestial object in Earth's sky after the Sun, as measured by illuminance on Earth's surface.

Although it can appear a very bright white, its surface is actually dark, with a reflectance just slightly higher than that of worn asphalt. Its prominence in the sky and its regular cycle of phases have, since ancient times, made the Moon an important cultural influence on language, calendars, art, and mythology.

Gravitational pull & distance

The Moon's gravitational influence produces the ocean tides, body tides, and the slight lengthening of the day. The Moon's current orbital distance is about thirty times the diameter of Earth, causing it to have an apparent size in the sky almost the same as that of the Sun, with the result that the Moon covers the Sun nearly precisely in total solar eclipse. This matching of apparent visual size will not continue in the far future. The Moon's linear distance from Earth is currently increasing at a rate of 3.82 ± 0.07 centimetres per year, but this rate is not constant.

Lunar travels

The Soviet Union's Luna programme was the first to reach the Moon with unmanned spacecraft in 1959; the United States' NASA Apollo program achieved the only manned missions to date, beginning with the first manned lunar orbiting mission by Apollo 8 in 1968, and six manned lunar landings between 1969 and 1972, with the first being Apollo 11. These missions returned over 380 kg of lunar rocks, which have been used to develop a geological understanding of the Moon's origin, the formation of its internal structure, and its subsequent history. After the Apollo 17 mission in 1972, the Moon has been visited only by unmanned spacecraft.

Text fetched from *"Moon" article on Wikipedia* on the 23rd of February 2016.

Figure 4-1. *A simple HTML document with no styles yet applied*

Our simple document contains a couple of headings and some paragraphs of text (with some inline elements to enhance the text where applicable), sitting in an `article` element:

```
<article>
  <h1>The Moon</h1>
  <p> The <strong>Moon</strong> (in Greek: σελήνη...</p>
  ...
  <h2>Orbit</h2>
  <p>The Moon is in synchronous…</p>
  ...
  <h3>Gravitational pull &amp; distance</h3>
  <p>The Moon's gravitational...</p>
  <h2>Lunar travels</h2>
  <p>The Soviet Union's Luna programme...</p>
  <p class="source">Text fetched from...</p>
</article>
```

While the unstyled document is readable, it's far from ideal. Our goal is to create a relatively short style sheet to help improve the legibility and aesthetics of the page. In Figure 4-2 we see the final result we're aiming at.

Figure 4-2. *Our document with the new font properties applied*

Let's go through each rule, breaking down the terminology, why the rule was made, and how the CSS mechanics behind the basic typesetting properties work.

Text Color

Text color is perhaps one of the most basic things we set for a document, but it's easy to overlook its effects. By default, the browser renders most text as black (except for links, of course; those are a vibrant blue), which is a very high contrast against the white background. Sufficient contrast is crucial for accessibility, but can also go too far in the other direction. In fact, screens are so high-contrast that black-on-white text can be overly intensive for longer runs of text, affecting the readability.

We'll leave our headings as the default black, and set paragraphs to display as a very dark blue-gray shade. Links will also still be blue, but we'll dial down the vibrancy a bit.

```
p {
    color: #3b4348;
}
a {
    color: #235ea7;
}
```

Font-Family

The font-family property allows you to list which typefaces you would like to use, in order of preference:

```
body {
  font-family: 'Georgia Pro', Georgia, Times, 'Times New Roman', serif;
}
h1, h2, h3, h4, h5, h6 {
  font-family: Avenir Next, SegoeUI, arial, sans-serif;
}
```

The body element (and thus almost every other element, as font-family is inherited) has a font stack of 'Georgia Pro', Georgia, Times, 'Times New Roman', serif. Georgia is a nearly universally available serif typeface, where the newer Georgia Pro variant is installed on some versions of Windows 10. If neither version of Georgia is available, the Times and Times New Roman fallbacks exist on many systems as well. Finally, we fall back to the generic system serif font.

For headings, we have listed Avenir Next as our first preference, a typeface with many variations that comes preinstalled with modern Mac OS X computers and iOS devices. If this typeface isn't available, the browser looks for Segoe UI, a similar versatile sans-serif font that exists on most versions of Windows computers and Windows Phone devices. Should the browser fail to find that, it will try to use Arial (which is available on a wide variety of platforms), and then finally any generic sans-serif font that is set as the default for the current platform.

Figure 4-3 shows how these fonts look in Safari 9 on Mac OS X compared to Microsoft Edge on Windows 10.

THE MOON

The **Moon** (in Greek: σελήνη *Selene*, in Latin: *Luna*) is Earth's only natural satellite. It is one of the largest natural satellites in the Solar System, and, among planetary satellites, the largest relative to the size of the planet it orbits (its primary). It is the second-densest satellite among those whose densities are known (after Jupiter's satellite Io).

The Moon is thought to have formed approximately 4.5 billion years ago, not long after Earth. There are several hypotheses for its origin; the most widely accepted explanation is that the Moon formed from the debris left over after a giant impact between Earth and a Mars-sized body called Theia.

Orbit

The Moon is in synchronous rotation with Earth, always showing the same face with its near side marked by dark volcanic maria that fill between the bright ancient crustal highlands and the prominent impact craters. It is the second-brightest regularly visible celestial object in Earth's sky after the Sun, as measured by illuminance on Earth's surface.

Although it can appear a very bright white, its surface is actually dark, with a reflectance just slightly higher than that of worn asphalt. Its prominence in the sky and its regular cycle of phases have, since ancient times, made the Moon an important cultural influence on language, calendars, art, and mythology.

THE MOON

The **Moon** (in Greek: σελήνη *Selene*, in Latin: *Luna*) is Earth's only natural satellite. It is one of the largest natural satellites in the Solar System, and, among planetary satellites, the largest relative to the size of the planet it orbits (its primary). It is the second-densest satellite among those whose densities are known (after Jupiter's satellite Io).

The Moon is thought to have formed approximately 4.5 billion years ago, not long after Earth. There are several hypotheses for its origin; the most widely accepted explanation is that the Moon formed from the debris left over after a giant impact between Earth and a Mars-sized body called Theia.

Orbit

The Moon is in synchronous rotation with Earth, always showing the same face with its near side marked by dark volcanic maria that fill between the bright ancient crustal highlands and the prominent impact craters. It is the second-brightest regularly visible celestial object in Earth's sky after the Sun, as measured by illuminance on Earth's surface.

Although it can appear a very bright white, its surface is actually dark, with a reflectance just slightly higher than that of worn asphalt. Its prominence in the sky and its regular cycle of phases have, since ancient times, made the Moon an important cultural influence on language, calendars, art, and mythology.

Figure 4-3. *Our page as it renders with Avenir Next and Georgia on Safari 9 (left) vs. Segoe UI and Georgia on Microsoft Edge (right)*

■ **Note** *Serifs* are the small angled shapes at the end of the strokes of a glyph, found in many classical typefaces. Sans-serif simply refers to fonts without serifs.

This fallback mechanism is a vital feature of the `font-family` property because different operating systems and mobile devices don't all have the same fonts available to them. The choice of font is also more complex than just whether the font exists or not: if the preferred font is missing glyphs used in the text, such as accented characters, the browser will fall back in the font stack for those individual characters as well.

Some research around which default fonts are available on various operating systems can help you choose the right stack for your project. You can find a good starting point at `http://cssfontstacks.com`.

The `sans-serif` and `serif` font families defined at the end of our lists are known as a *generic families*, and act as a catch-all option. We could also have chosen `cursive`, `fantasy`, and `monospace`. The `serif` and `sans-serif` generic families are probably the most common ones to use for text. When selecting typefaces for preformatted text such as code examples, `monospace` tries to pick a font where all the characters have the same width, aligning characters across lines. The `fantasy` and `cursive` generic families are a bit more uncommon, but map to more elaborately ornamented or handwriting-like typefaces, respectively.

■ **Note** You don't strictly need to place in quote marks `font-family` names containing spaces, but it's a good idea to do so. The spec only demands use of quote marks if the `font-family` name is the same as a generic family name, but also recommends it for names containing nonstandard symbols that may trip up the browser. If nothing else, syntax highlighters in code editors often seem to handle names with spaces in them better if they are quoted.

The Relation Between Fonts and Typefaces

The terminology around things like typefaces, font families, and fonts can get very confusing. A *typeface* (also known as a *font family*) is a collection of shapes (known as *glyphs*) for letters, numbers, and other characters that share a style. Typefaces can have several different variations for each glyph, including bold, normal, and light weights, italic styles, different ways of displaying numbers, ligatures that combine several characters into one glyph, and other variations.

Originally, the *font* (or *font face*) was a collection of all the glyphs from a specific variation of a typeface, cast into pieces of metal. This collection was then used in a mechanical printing press. In the digital world, we use the word to mean the file that holds the representation of a typeface. The hypothetical typeface "CSS Mastery" could be just a single font file, or it could be made up from several font files containing "CSS Mastery Regular," "CSS Mastery Italic," "CSS Mastery Light," and so on.

Font Size and Line Height

The default `font-size` value in nearly every browser in existence is 16 pixels, unless the user has changed their preferences. We've kept the default `font-size`, choosing instead to adjust the size of specific elements using the em unit:

```
h3 {
  font-size: 1.314em; /* 21px */
}
```

The em unit when used in font-size is a scaling factor of the elements *inherited* font-size. For our h3 elements, for example, the size is 1.314 * 16 = 21px. We could have set the font-size to 21px as well, but ems are a little more flexible. Most browsers allow users to zoom the entire page, which works fine even with pixels. With ems, the measurements also scales if the user only changes the default font-size in their preferences.

As the em unit scales based on inherited size, we can also scale the font-size for just a part of a page by sizing a parent element. The flipside of this—and the tricky part of using ems—is that we don't want to accidentally scale something just because of its position in the markup. Consider the following hypothetical style rules:

```
p {
  font-size: 1.314em;
}
article {
  font-size: 1.314em;
}
```

The preceding set of rules means that both p and article elements have a font-size of 21px, by default. But it also means that p elements that are *children* of article elements will have a font-size of 1.314em × 1.314em, which calculates as around 1.73em or 28px. This probably wasn't what was intended in the design, so when using relative lengths, you need to keep track of the sizing math.

We could have used percentages in place of ems when it comes to font-size. Setting 133.3% is exactly the same as using 1.333em, and which one you use is a matter of personal preference. As a final flexible measurement, we can use the rem unit. It is a scaling factor, just like the em, but always scales based on the *root element em* size (hence the name rem), meaning the font-size set on the html element. We've used the rem unit to get a consistent margin-top value for all headings:

```
h1, h2, h3, h4, h5, h6 {
  margin-top: 1.5rem; /* 24px */
}
```

When ems are used for box-model dimensions, it relates not to inherited font-size, but the calculated font-size of the element itself. Thus, this measurement would have been different for all heading levels. To get a consistent (but flexible) value, we need to either use the rem, or calculate margins in ems individually for each heading level.

The rem unit is relatively new, and works in all modern browsers. As a fallback for older browsers like Internet Explorer 8 (and earlier), we can use the fault tolerance of CSS to our advantage and declare a pixel measurement for our margin before the rem-based declaration:

```
h1, h2, h3, h4, h5, h6 {
  margin-top: 24px; /* non-scalable fallback for old browsers */
  margin-top: 1.5rem; /* 24px, will be ignored by old browsers */
}
```

▓ **Caution**   There are also *absolute* measurement units based on physical dimensions like mm, cm, in, and pt, which are intended primarily for print style sheets. These should not be used for screen styles. We won't cover print style sheets here, but will cover how to target different media types in Chapter 8.

Font Sizing with Scales

When deciding on which font-size to use, there are no hard rules on which sizes to pick. Mostly it's a matter of making sure the text is large enough to be readable, and then trying to find sizes that make sense in the current context. Some people like to eyeball it, whereas others believe in basing measurements on mathematical relationships.

We've loosely based our three heading sizes on a mathematical scale known as the "perfect fourth." Each increased heading level is one-fourth of its own size larger than the previous level, or (expressed as the inverse relationship) 1.3333333... times the level below it. The sizes have then been rounded to match the nearest pixel size and truncated to three decimal places:

```
h1 {
  font-size: 2.315em; /* 37px */
}
h2 {
  font-size: 1.75em; /* 28px */
}
h3 {
  font-size: 1.314em; /* 21px */
}
```

A scale like this can be a great help when starting work on a design, even if you end up setting the final measurements by feel. You can play around with a bunch of different preset scales in the Modular Scale calculator at http://www.modularscale.com/ (see Figure 4-4).

Figure 4-4. *The Modular Scale calculator allows you to play with combinations of fonts and mathematical sizing scales*

Line Spacing, Alignment, and the Anatomy of Line Boxes

As we set additional measurements for our text, we are going to start to see relationships between various typographic concepts. For this reason, a deeper look at the CSS inline formatting model is necessary, along with some more typographic terminology—at least as it applies to Western writing systems. Figure 4-5 illustrates the various pieces that make up a line of text, using the first two words from the first paragraph of our example.

```
<p>The <strong>Moon</strong>…[etc]</p>
```

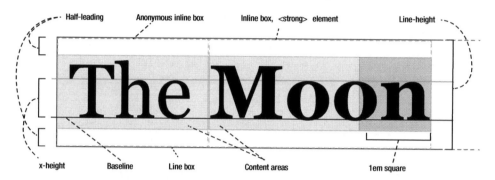

Figure 4-5. *Constituent parts and technical terms of the inline formatting model*

We saw the high-level view of inline formatting in Chapter 3. Each line of text generates a *line box*. This box may be further split in to several *inline boxes*, by representing inline elements (like the `<strong>` element in this case), or the *anonymous inline boxes* in-between them.

Text is drawn in the middle of the inline boxes, on what is known as the *content area*. The height of the content area is the definition of the `font-size` measurement—behind the end of the word "Moon" in Figure 4-5, we see a 1em × 1em square, and how it relates to the size of the glyphs themselves. The traditional typographic term "em" that gave the `em` unit its name has its origins in the size of the uppercase letter "M," but as we can see, this is not a correct definition in web typography.

The upper edge of lowercase letters such as "x" determines what's known as the *x-height*. This height can vary significantly between typefaces, which explains why it's hard to give a general recommendation around exact font sizes—you need to test with the actual font to see what the perceived size is. In Georgia, which we're using here, the x-height is rather tall, making it appear larger than many other fonts at the same `font-size` measurement.

The actual glyphs are then placed as to appear vertically balanced somewhere inside the content area, so that each inline box by default aligns on a common line close to the bottom, called the *baseline*. Glyphs are not necessarily constrained by the content area either: for example, a lowercase "g" could stick out underneath the content area in some fonts.

Finally, the line height defines the total height of the line box. This is more commonly known as *line spacing*, or in typographic terms, *leading* (pronounced as "ledding") due to the blocks of lead typesetters used to separate lines of characters on a printing press. Unlike in mechanical type, the leading in CSS is always applied to both the top and bottom of line boxes.

The `font-size` is subtracted from the total line height, and the resulting measurement is divided in two equal parts (known as *half-leading*). If the `font-size` is 21px and the `line-height` is 30px, each strip of half-leading will be 4.5px tall.

▓ **Note** If a line box contains inline boxes of varying line height, the line height for the line box as a whole will be at least as tall as the tallest inline box.

Setting Line Height

When setting line height, we need to consider what makes sense for the current font. In our article example, we've set a base font-family of Georgia and a line-height of 1.5 for the body element:

```
body {
    font-family: Georgia, Times, 'Times New Roman', serif;
    line-height: 1.5;
}
```

Line height usually ends up somewhere between 1.2 and 1.5. As you tweak the value, you need to find where the lines are neither too cramped nor too spaced apart and disconnected. As a general rule, text with a larger x-height can tolerate more line spacing, as is the case with our text set in Georgia. The length and font-size of the text also matters: shorter runs of smaller text can usually handle a tighter line-height value.

We set line-height with a unitless 1.5, which simply means 1.5 times the current font size. The font-size on the body worked out to be 16px, giving us a default line-height of 24px.

It is possible to set line-height using pixels, percentages, or ems, but remember that all children of the body will inherit this value. A possible "gotcha" is that even for percentages and ems, the inherited line-height is the *computed* pixel value of the line-height, which is not the case for unitless values. By leaving out the unit we ensure that the line-height for a particular element is inherited as a multiplier, always in proportion to its font-size.

Vertical Alignment

In addition to line-height, inline boxes can be affected by the vertical-align property. The default value is baseline, which means that the baseline of the element will align with the baseline of the parent. At the end of our article, we have a reference to the date when we looked it up on Wikipedia, where the ordinal "rd" suffix is marked up with a span:

```
<time datetime="2016-02-23">the 23<span class="ordinal">rd</span> of February 2016.</time>
```

We'll set a superscript alignment for this text (along with a slightly smaller font size) by using vertical-align and the super keyword:

```
.ordinal {
  vertical-align: super;
  font-size: smaller;
}
```

Other possible keywords are sub, top, bottom, text-top, text-bottom, and middle. They all have more or less complicated relationships to the content area and parent line box. Just to give you an example, text-top or text-bottom aligns the top or bottom of the content area with the content area of the parent line box—which only has any effect if the font-size or line-height of the inline box is different from the parent. Like we said: complicated.

Perhaps more intuitive is to shift the vertical alignment of an element's baseline up or down from the parent baseline by a set length—either in px or a length relative to the font size (em or %, for example). It's worth noting that not only line-height values influence the final line spacing of a piece of text. If there is an item in the line box that is shifted using vertical-align, that element will push out the final line box height. Figure 4-6 shows what would happen to a line of text in our article when shifting elements by different vertical-align values.

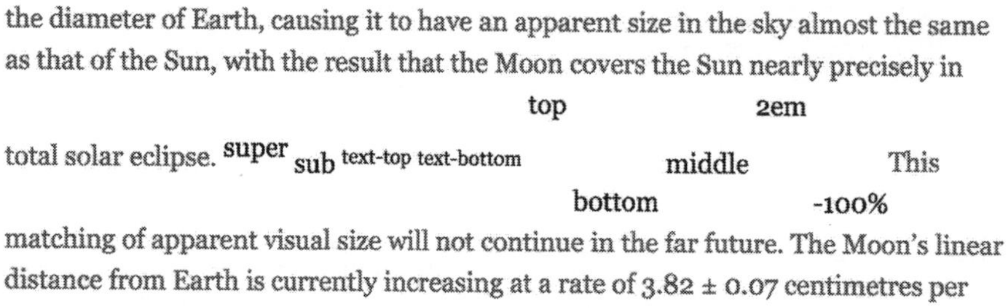

the diameter of Earth, causing it to have an apparent size in the sky almost the same as that of the Sun, with the result that the Moon covers the Sun nearly precisely in

top   2em

total solar eclipse. super sub text-top text-bottom   middle   This

bottom   -100%

matching of apparent visual size will not continue in the far future. The Moon's linear distance from Earth is currently increasing at a rate of 3.82 ± 0.07 centimetres per

Figure 4-6. *The various keywords and values that can be used with* vertical-align. *Note how the top and bottom of the line box are pushed out by the most extreme values, increasing the overall line height for that line*

■ **Note** Inline blocks and images react slightly differently to vertical alignment compared to inline text, as they don't necessarily have a single baseline of their own. We'll use this to our advantage when looking at some layout tricks in Chapter 6.

Font Weights

Next, we set the weight for headings using the font-weight property. Some fonts have numerous variations, like Helvetica Neue Light, Helvetica Neue Bold, Helvetica Neue Black, and more. Rather than declaring the name of a font variation, we use keywords—normal, bold, bolder, and lighter—or numeric values. The numeric values are written as even hundreds, starting at 100, then 200, 300, 400, and so on, up to 900.

The default value of normal is mapped to 400, and bold is 700—these are the most common weights found in most typefaces. The keywords bolder and lighter work a little differently, and are used to make text heavier or lighter than the inherited value.

Values of 100–300 usually map to fonts with "Thin" or "Hairline," "Ultra Light," and "Light" in their names, respectively. Conversely, values of 800 or 900 will map to fonts in the typeface with names including "Ultra Bold," "Heavy," or "Black" in their names. In between those are 500 (Medium) and 600 (Semi-bold or Demi-bold).

As the default for headings, we've set a medium weight of 500, with variations for ultra bold h1 elements and semi-bold h2 elements:

```
h1, h2, h3, h4, h5, h6 {
  font-weight: 500;
}
h1 {
  font-weight: 800;
}
h2 {
  font-weight: 600;
}
```

Both Avenir Next and Segoe UI (our top preferred typefaces) contain lots of weight variations. If a font is missing the desired weight, it may try to emulate bolder weights, but not anything lighter than normal. The results of artificially bolded fonts are sadly often less ideal.

Font Style

Setting the declaration `font-style: italic` picks the italic style from the typeface, if one is present. If not, the browser will try to fake it by slanting the typeface—again, with often less than ideal results. Italic style is often used for either emphasis or to distinguish things usually said with a different tone of voice. In our example, we've wrapped the Latin and Greek names for the Moon with the `<i>` tag. This tag is originally a remnant of presentational markup from early HTML implementations, but has been redefined in HTML5 for the purpose of marking up conventionally italicized runs of text, like names.

```
<p>The <strong>Moon</strong> (in Greek: σελήνη <i lang="el">Selene</i>, in Latin:
<I lang="la">Luna</i>)
```

While the tag doesn't *mean* italic, the browser default style sheet sets the `font-style` to `italic`:

```
i {
  font-style: italic;
}
```

Had we wanted to, we could have redefined this element to display as bold, nonitalicized text:

```
i {
  font-weight: 700;
  font-style: normal;
}
```

Apart from the `italic` and default `normal` values, you can also use the `oblique` keyword (which is another variation of slanted text), but this is rarely used because few fonts come with an oblique style.

Transforming Case and Small-Cap Variants

Sometimes the design calls for text that is shown in a different case than how the HTML source was written. CSS allows you some control over this, via the `text-transform` property. In our example, the h1 is written as capitalized (with uppercase initial letters) in the markup, but forced to display as uppercase via CSS (see Figure 4-7):

```
h1 {
  text-transform: uppercase;
}
```

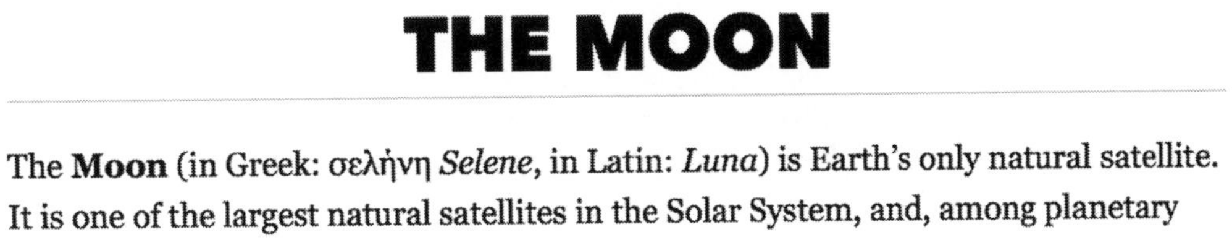

THE MOON

The **Moon** (in Greek: σελήνη *Selene*, in Latin: *Luna*) is Earth's only natural satellite. It is one of the largest natural satellites in the Solar System, and, among planetary

Figure 4-7. *Our h1 is displayed as uppercase*

In addition to the uppercase value, you can also specify lowercase to make all letters lowercase, capitalize to make the first letter of each word uppercase, or none to revert the case to the default as authored in the HTML.

Using Font-Variant

CSS also has a property called font-variant that allows you to pick what's known as small-caps for your font. Small-caps is a variation in the typeface where the lowercase letters are shown as if the shapes of the uppercase (or capital) letters have been "shrunk" to their size. Proper small-caps variations do this with a greater respect for the letter shapes than just plain shrinking them, but these are mostly found in more exclusive font families. Browsers will attempt to fake this for you if no such font is available. We can illustrate this on the abbr tag containing the abbreviation "NASA" in our document (see Figure 4-8):

```
<abbr title="National Aeronautics and Space Administration">NASA</abbr>
```

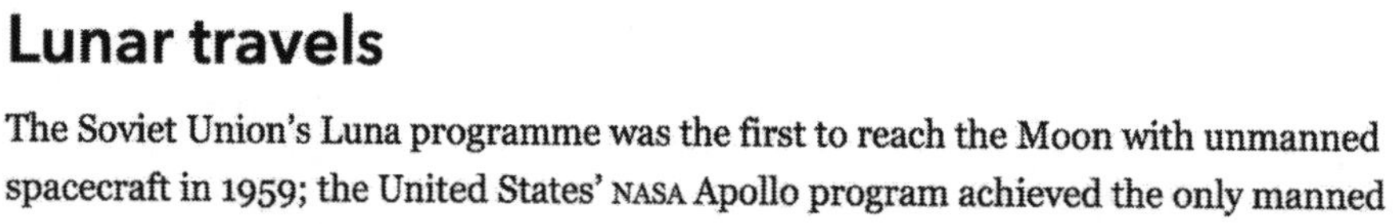

Lunar travels

The Soviet Union's Luna programme was the first to reach the Moon with unmanned spacecraft in 1959; the United States' NASA Apollo program achieved the only manned

Figure 4-8. *Using the font-variant keyword* small-caps *makes the browser shrink the uppercase glyphs down to the x-height*

We'll apply it alongside a text-transform: lowercase rule, as the letters are already uppercase in the HTML source. One final tweak is to set the abbr element with a slightly smaller line-height, as the small-caps variant seems to push the content box down in some browsers, affecting the overall line box height.

```
abbr {
  text-transform: lowercase;
  font-variant: small-caps;
  line-height: 1.25;
}
```

The CSS 2.1 spec defined small-caps as the only valid value for the font-variant property. In the CSS Fonts Module Level 3 spec, this has been expanded to include a large number of values representing ways to select alternate glyphs. Browsers have been slow to adopt these, but luckily there are better-supported ways to achieve this; we'll look at them in the upcoming section on advanced typesetting techniques.

Changing the Space Between Letters and Words

Changing the space between words and individual characters is often best left to the designers of the typeface. CSS does allow you some crude tools to change this though.

The word-spacing property is seldom used, but as you can probably guess it affects the spacing between words. The value you give it specifies how much to add or take away from the *default* spacing, decided by the blank space character width in the current font. The following rule would *add* 0.1em to the default spacing between words in paragraphs:

```
p {
  word-spacing: 0.1em;
}
```

Similarly, you can affect the space between each letter with the `letter-spacing` property. On lowercase text, this is generally a bad idea—most typefaces are designed to let you recognize the shapes of whole words at a time when reading, so messing with the spacing can make text hard to read. Uppercase (or small-cap) glyphs are much better suited to interpret individually, like the case with acronyms. A little extra spacing can actually make them easier to read. Let's try this by adding a little bit of `letter-spacing` to our abbr tags (see Figure 4-9):

```
abbr {
    text-transform: lowercase;
    font-variant: small-caps;
    letter-spacing: 0.1em;
}
```

The Soviet Union's Luna programme was the first to reach the Moon with unmanned spacecraft in 1959; the United States' NASA Apollo program achieved the only manned missions to date, beginning with the first manned lunar orbiting mission by Apollo 8

Figure 4-9. A tiny amount of `letter-spacing` applied to the abbr element

That's the last of our font-related settings and small typographic tweaks. Next up, we'll focus on how the text is laid out, to further ensure a good reading experience.

Measure, rhythm, and rag

Our next area of focus is a crucial factor in making text enjoyable to read: the line length. In typographic terms, this is known as the *measure*. Overly long or short lines disrupt the eye movements across the text and can cause the reader to lose their place or even abandon the text altogether.

There is no exact answer as to what the perfect line length is. It depends on the size of the font, the size of the screen, and the type of text content that is being displayed. What we can do is look to the research and historical advice on general rules for line length, and try to apply them sensibly to our page.

Robert Bringhurst's classic book *The Elements of Typographic Style* notes that body text is usually set between 45 and 75 characters, with the average being around 66 characters. In translating this advice to the Web, typography expert Richard Rutter found that this range works out well there too—at least for larger screens. In the case of very small screens (or large screens viewed far away, like TVs or projections), the size in combination with the distance to the screen may warrant a measure as short as 40 characters.

■ **Note**   We'll come back to typographic challenges specific to responsive web design in Chapter 8.

Applying constraints to line length can be done by setting a width either on elements enclosing the text or on the headings, paragraphs, etc. themselves.

In the case of our body text, the Georgia typeface has relatively wide letter forms, as a consequence of the generous x-height. This means we can probably get away with a measure in the higher range. We've gone for the easy option and set a maximum width of 36em on the `article` element (one character being on average 0.5em), centering it on the page. Should the viewport be narrower than that, the element will shrink down automatically.

```css
article {
  max-width: 36em;
  margin: 0 auto;
}
```

This results in a line length for our paragraph text of about 77 characters on wider viewports, as seen in Figure 4-10. We've chosen to apply the width using ems so that the measure scales nicely even if we—or the user—decide to change the font size.

Figure 4-10. *The* article *element is constrained by a* max-width *of 36em, even if we bump the font size up*

Text Indent and Alignment

By default, our text will be set aligned to the left. Having the left edge of the text straight helps the eye find the next line, keeping the reading pace. For paragraphs following upon paragraphs, it's common to either use a margin in-between of one line space, or indent the text by a small amount to emphasize the shift from one paragraph to the next. We've opted for the latter in setting our article text, using the adjacent sibling combinator and the text-indent property:

```css
p + p {
  text-indent: 1.25em;
}
```

The right edge of the text is very uneven (see previous Figure 4-9), and we'll leave it that way—for now. This uneven shape is known in typographic terms as the "rag" (as in "ragged"). Having the end edge ragged is not a disaster, but you should think very carefully before using for example centered alignment for anything but very short runs of text. Centered text works best for small pieces of user interface copy (like buttons) or short headings, but having both edges ragged destroys readability.

We have, however, centered the h1 of our sample page. We've also given it a bottom border to anchor it visually to the article text below, seen in Figure 4-11.

```
h1 {
  text-align: center;
  border-bottom: 1px solid #c8bc9d;
}
```

THE MOON

The **Moon** (in Greek: σελήνη *Selene*, in Latin: *Luna*) is Earth's only natural satellite.

Figure 4-11. *We've center aligned our h1*

The text-align property can take several keyword values including left, right, center, and justify. The CSS Text Level 3 specification defines a few additional values, including start and end. These two *logical direction* keywords correspond to the writing mode of the text: most Western languages are written from left to right, so if the document language is English, the start value would represent left alignment and end would be right-aligned. In a right-to-left language such as Arabic, this would be inverted. Most browsers will also automatically reverse the default text-direction if you set the dir="rtl" attribute on a parent element, to indicate right-to-left text.

The text-align property can also use the value justify, distributing the space between words so that the text aligns to both the left and right edges, eliminating the ragged right. This is a common technique in printed media, where the copy, hyphenation, and font properties can be trimmed to match the space on a page.

The Web is a different medium, where the exact rendering is up to factors outside our control. Different screen sizes, differing fonts installed, and different browser engines are all things that can affect how the user views our page. If you use justified text, it might end up looking bad and becoming very hard to read, as in Figure 4-12. "Rivers" of whitespace may form running through your text, especially as the measure decreases.

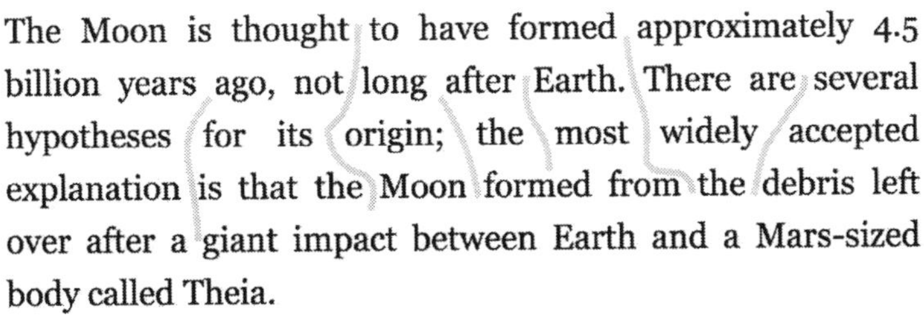

The Moon is thought to have formed approximately 4.5 billion years ago, not long after Earth. There are several hypotheses for its origin; the most widely accepted explanation is that the Moon formed from the debris left over after a giant impact between Earth and a Mars-sized body called Theia.

Figure 4-12. *A paragraph of text where text-align: justify causes "rivers" between words*

The default method browsers use to justify text is a rather clumsy algorithm, with less-refined results than what's found in desktop publishing software. The type of algorithm used can be altered with the text-justify property, but the support for the various values is poor and mostly relates to how to justify the letterforms and words of other types of languages than most Western writing systems.

Interestingly, Internet Explorer supports the nonstandard value newspaper for this property, which seems to use a much more clever algorithm, distributing whitespace both between letters and between words.

Hyphenation

If you're still set on having justified text in your pages, hyphenation may help in eliminating rivers to some degree. You can manually insert what's known as soft hyphens using the ­ HTML entity in your markup. This hyphen will only be visible if the browser needs to break it to fit the line (see Figure 4-13):

```
<p>The <strong>Moon</strong> […] is Earth's only natural satel&shy;lite.[…]
```

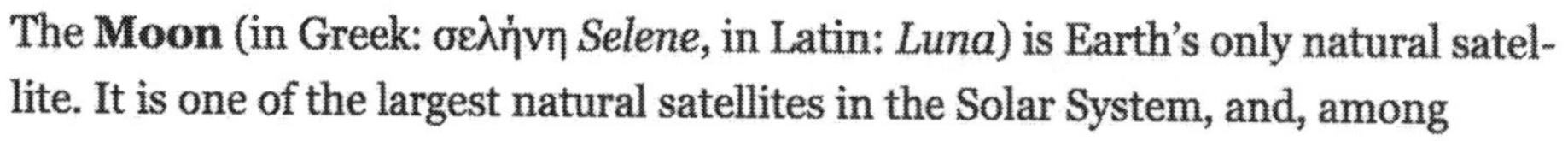

The **Moon** (in Greek: σελήνη *Selene*, in Latin: *Luna*) is Earth's only natural satellite. It is one of the largest natural satellites in the Solar System, and, among

Figure 4-13. Manual hyphenation with soft hyphens

For a longer text like an article, it's unlikely that you'll go through and manually hyphenate every word. With the hyphens property, we can let the browser do the work. It's still a relatively new feature, so most browsers that support it require vendor prefixes. Versions of Internet Explorer before version 10, the stock WebKit browser on Android devices, and, surprisingly, Blink-based browsers like Chrome and Opera (at the time of writing) don't support hyphenation at all.

If you want to activate automatic hyphenation, you need two pieces of code. First, you need to make sure the language code for the document is set, most often on the html element:

```
<html lang="en">
```

Next, set the hyphens property to auto for the relevant elements. Figure 4-14 shows the result as it appears in Firefox.

```
p {
  hyphens: auto;
}
```

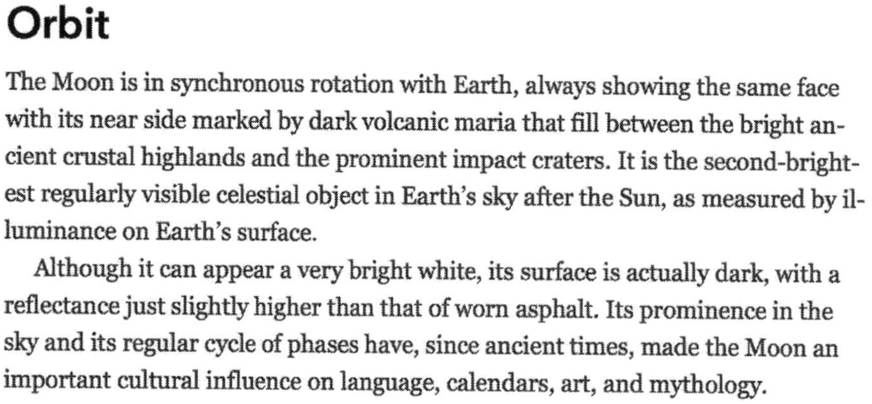

Orbit

The Moon is in synchronous rotation with Earth, always showing the same face
with its near side marked by dark volcanic maria that fill between the bright ancient crustal highlands and the prominent impact craters. It is the second-brightest regularly visible celestial object in Earth's sky after the Sun, as measured by illuminance on Earth's surface.

Although it can appear a very bright white, its surface is actually dark, with a
reflectance just slightly higher than that of worn asphalt. Its prominence in the
sky and its regular cycle of phases have, since ancient times, made the Moon an
important cultural influence on language, calendars, art, and mythology.

Figure 4-14. Activating automatic hyphenation shows a more straight right rag in Firefox

To switch hyphenation off, you can set the hyphens property to a value of manual. The manual mode still respects soft hyphens.

Setting Text in Multiple Columns

While the 36em restriction on the overall article width helps limit the measure, it does waste a lot of space on larger screens. So much unused whitespace! Sometimes, it could make sense to set text in multiple columns, in order to use wider screens more efficiently while keeping a sensible measure. The properties from the CSS Multi-column Layout Module give us tools to do this, dividing the content into equal columns.

The name "Multi-column Layout" can be slightly misleading, as this set of properties does not refer to creating general-purpose layout grids with columns and gutters for separate parts of a *page*, but rather refers to having a part of the page where the content flows in columns like in a newspaper. Trying to use it for other purposes is definitely possible, but perhaps not desirable.

If we were to increase the max-width to something like 70em, we could fit three columns in. We can tell the article to automatically flow the content into columns by setting the columns property to the desired minimum column width (see Figure 4-15). Gaps between columns are controlled with the column-gap property:

```
article {
  max-width: 70em;
  columns: 20em;
  column-gap: 1.5em;
  margin: 0 auto;
}
```

THE MOON

The **Moon** (in Greek: σελήνη *Selene*, in Latin: *Luna*) is Earth's only natural satellite. It is one of the largest natural satellites in the Solar System, and, among planetary satellites, the largest relative to the size of the planet it orbits (its primary). It is the second-densest satellite among those whose densities are known (after Jupiter's satellite Io).

The Moon is thought to have formed approximately 4.5 billion years ago, not long after Earth. There are several hypotheses for its origin; the most widely accepted explanation is that the Moon formed from the debris left over after a giant impact between Earth and a Mars-sized body called Theia.

Orbit

The Moon is in synchronous rotation with Earth, always showing the same face with its near side

marked by dark volcanic maria that fill between the bright ancient crustal highlands and the prominent impact craters. It is the second-brightest regularly visible celestial object in Earth's sky after the Sun, as measured by illuminance on Earth's surface.

Although it can appear a very bright white, its surface is actually dark, with a reflectance just slightly higher than that of worn asphalt. Its prominence in the sky and its regular cycle of phases have, since ancient times, made the Moon an important cultural influence on language, calendars, art, and mythology.

Gravitational pull & distance

The Moon's gravitational influence produces the ocean tides, body tides, and the slight lengthening of the day. The Moon's current orbital distance is about thirty times the diameter of Earth, causing it to have an apparent size in the sky almost the same as that of the Sun, with the result that the Moon covers the Sun nearly precisely in total solar eclipse. This matching of apparent visual size will

not continue in the far future. The Moon's linear distance from Earth is currently increasing at a rate of 3.82 ± 0.07 centimetres per year, but this rate is not constant.

Lunar travels

The Soviet Union's Luna programme was the first to reach the Moon with unmanned spacecraft in 1959; the United States' NASA Apollo program achieved the only manned missions to date, beginning with the first manned lunar orbiting mission by Apollo 8 in 1968, and six manned lunar landings between 1969 and 1972, with the first being Apollo 11. These missions returned over 380 KG of lunar rocks, which have been used to develop a geological understanding of the Moon's origin, the formation of its internal structure, and its subsequent history. After the Apollo 17 mission in 1972, the Moon has been visited only by unmanned spacecraft.

Text fetched from "Moon" article on Wikipedia on the 23rd of February 2016.

Figure 4-15. *The article contents now flow automatically into as many columns as can fit inside the 70em maximum width, as long as they are a minimum of 20em wide*

The columns property is shorthand for setting the column-count and column-width properties. If you set only a column count, the browser will generate a set number of columns, regardless of width. If you set a column width *and* a count, the column width acts as a minimum, while the count acts as a maximum number of columns.

```
columns: 20em; /* automatic number of columns as long as they are at least 20em */

column-width: 20em; /* same as above */

columns: 3; /* creates 3 columns, with automatic width */

column-count: 3; /* same as above */

columns: 3 20em; /* at most 3 columns, at least 20em wide each */

/* the following two combined are the same as the above shorthand: */
column-count: 3;
column-width: 20em;
```

Fallback Width

To avoid excessive line lengths in browsers lacking support for the multi-column properties, we can add rules that set a max-width on the paragraphs themselves. Older browsers will then show a single column but still comfortably readable fallback:

```
article > p {
  max-width: 36em;
}
```

Column Spans

In the preceding example, all elements in the article wrapper flow into the columns. We can choose to opt out some elements from that flow, forcing them to stretch across all columns. In Figure 4-16, the article title and the last paragraph (containing the source link) span across all columns:

```
.h1,
.source {
  column-span: all; /* or column-span: none; to explicitly turn off. */
}
```

THE MOON

The **Moon** (in Greek: σελήνη *Selene*, in Latin: *Luna*) is Earth's only natural satellite. It is one of the largest natural satellites in the Solar System, and, among planetary satellites, the largest relative to the size of the planet it orbits (its primary). It is the second-densest satellite among those whose densities are known (after Jupiter's satellite Io).

The Moon is thought to have formed approximately 4.5 billion years ago, not long after Earth. There are several hypotheses for its origin; the most widely accepted explanation is that the Moon formed from the debris left over after a giant impact between Earth and a Mars-sized body called Theia.

Orbit

The Moon is in synchronous rotation with Earth, always showing the same face with its near side marked by dark volcanic maria that fill between the bright ancient crustal highlands and the prominent impact craters. It is the second-brightest regularly visible celestial object in Earth's sky after the Sun, as measured by illuminance on Earth's surface.

Although it can appear a very bright white, its surface is actually dark, with a reflectance just slightly higher than that of worn asphalt. Its prominence in the sky and its regular cycle of phases have, since ancient times, made the Moon an important cultural influence on language, calendars, art, and mythology.

Gravitational pull & distance

The Moon's gravitational influence produces the ocean tides, body tides, and the slight lengthening of the day. The Moon's current orbital distance is about thirty times the diameter of Earth, causing it to have an apparent size in the sky almost the same as that of the Sun, with the result that the Moon covers the Sun nearly precisely in total solar eclipse. This matching of apparent visual size will not continue in the far future. The Moon's linear distance from Earth is currently increasing at a rate of 3.82 ± 0.07 centimetres per year, but this rate is not constant.

Lunar travels

The Soviet Union's Luna programme was the first to reach the Moon with unmanned spacecraft in 1959; the United States' NASA Apollo program achieved the only manned missions to date, beginning with the first manned lunar orbiting mission by Apollo 8 in 1968, and six manned lunar landings between 1969 and 1972, with the first being Apollo 11. These missions returned over 380 KG of lunar rocks, which have been used to develop a geological understanding of the Moon's origin, the formation of its internal structure, and its subsequent history. After the Apollo 17 mission in 1972, the Moon has been visited only by unmanned spacecraft.

Text fetched from "Moon" article on Wikipedia on the 23ʳᵈ of February 2016.

Figure 4-16. *The first heading and the last paragraph span all columns*

Should we instead choose to let an element in the middle of the flow span all columns, the text will be divided into several vertically stacked column-based flows. In Figure 4-17, the h2 elements are added to the previous rule, showing how the text before and after the heading flows across its own set of columns.

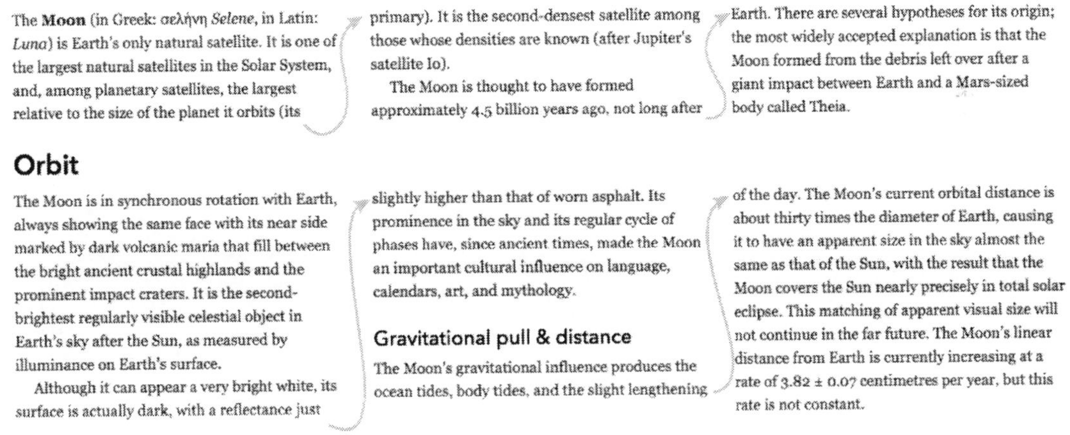

The **Moon** (in Greek: σελήνη *Selene*, in Latin: *Luna*) is Earth's only natural satellite. It is one of the largest natural satellites in the Solar System, and, among planetary satellites, the largest relative to the size of the planet it orbits (its primary). It is the second-densest satellite among those whose densities are known (after Jupiter's satellite Io).

The Moon is thought to have formed approximately 4.5 billion years ago, not long after Earth. There are several hypotheses for its origin; the most widely accepted explanation is that the Moon formed from the debris left over after a giant impact between Earth and a Mars-sized body called Theia.

Orbit

The Moon is in synchronous rotation with Earth, always showing the same face with its near side marked by dark volcanic maria that fill between the bright ancient crustal highlands and the prominent impact craters. It is the second-brightest regularly visible celestial object in Earth's sky after the Sun, as measured by illuminance on Earth's surface.

Although it can appear a very bright white, its surface is actually dark, with a reflectance just slightly higher than that of worn asphalt. Its prominence in the sky and its regular cycle of phases have, since ancient times, made the Moon an important cultural influence on language, calendars, art, and mythology.

Gravitational pull & distance

The Moon's gravitational influence produces the ocean tides, body tides, and the slight lengthening of the day. The Moon's current orbital distance is about thirty times the diameter of Earth, causing it to have an apparent size in the sky almost the same as that of the Sun, with the result that the Moon covers the Sun nearly precisely in total solar eclipse. This matching of apparent visual size will not continue in the far future. The Moon's linear distance from Earth is currently increasing at a rate of 3.82 ± 0.07 centimetres per year, but this rate is not constant.

Figure 4-17. *An element with* `column-span: all` *will divide the column flow into several vertically stacked sets of columns*

The multi-column layout properties are supported in almost every browser, with notable exceptions being IE9 and earlier. Some caveats apply though:

- Almost every browser requires the proper vendor prefix to apply the column properties.

- Firefox does not support the `column-span` rule at all at the time of writing.

- There are quite a few bugs and inconsistencies across browsers. Mostly, things like margin collapse and border rendering happen oddly when elements flow across columns. Zoe Mickley Gillenwater has an article on this and other pitfalls: `http://zomigi.com/blog/deal-breaker-problems-with-css3-multi-columns/`.

Vertical Rhythm and Baseline Grids

We've mentioned how having some mathematical relationships between sizing in typography can help it come together. For example, we used the "perfect fourth" sizing scale as a basis for our heading sizes. We also set a common `margin-top` value for all headings as `1.5rem`, equal to the height of one line of body text, and used the same measurement again for the gaps between columns. Some designers swear by these types of harmonious measurements, letting the base line height act as a metronome for the rest of the design.

In print design, it's common to follow this rhythm closely, so that lines of body text fall on a *baseline grid*, even if headings, quotes, or other pieces break the rhythm now and again. Not only does it help the eye movements when scanning the page, it also helps prevent the printed lines on the other side of the (thin) paper to shine through in double-sided print, as the same baseline grid applies to both.

On the Web, it's much more finicky to get a baseline grid right—especially when dealing with fluid sizes and user-generated content like images. It does make sense to at least try in some circumstances, like with multi-column text. In Figure 4-18, we can see that the baselines of the columns do not quite line up with respect to each other, due to the headings.

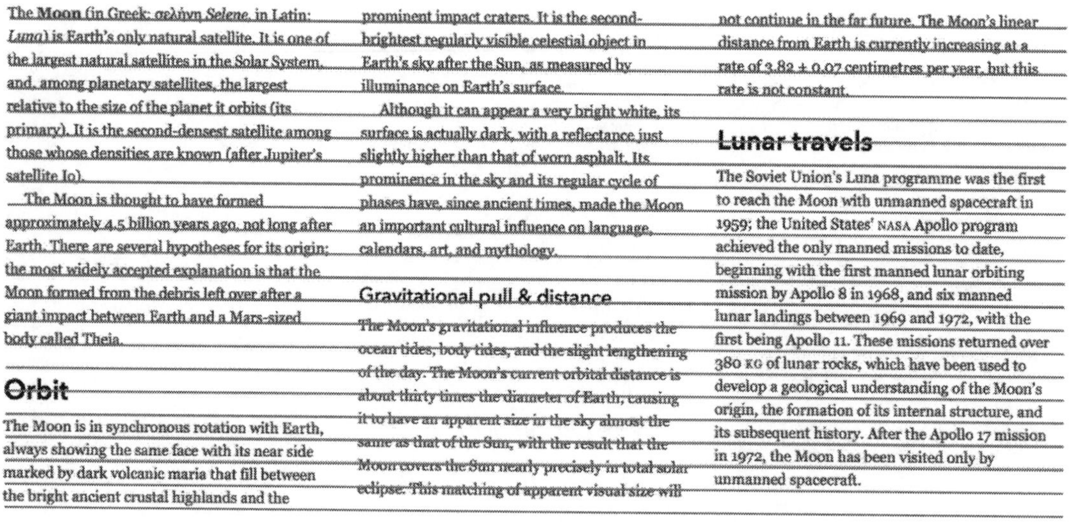

The **Moon** (in Greek: σελήνη *Selene*, in Latin: *Luna*) is Earth's only natural satellite. It is one of the largest natural satellites in the Solar System, and, among planetary satellites, the largest relative to the size of the planet it orbits (its primary). It is the second-densest satellite among those whose densities are known (after Jupiter's satellite Io).

The Moon is thought to have formed approximately 4.5 billion years ago, not long after Earth. There are several hypotheses for its origin; the most widely accepted explanation is that the Moon formed from the debris left over after a giant impact between Earth and a Mars-sized body called Theia.

Orbit

The Moon is in synchronous rotation with Earth, always showing the same face with its near side marked by dark volcanic maria that fill between the bright ancient crustal highlands and the prominent impact craters. It is the second-brightest regularly visible celestial object in Earth's sky after the Sun, as measured by illuminance on Earth's surface.

Although it can appear a very bright white, its surface is actually dark, with a reflectance just slightly higher than that of worn asphalt. Its prominence in the sky and its regular cycle of phases have, since ancient times, made the Moon an important cultural influence on language, calendars, art, and mythology.

Gravitational pull & distance

The Moon's gravitational influence produces the ocean tides, body tides, and the slight lengthening of the day. The Moon's current orbital distance is about thirty times the diameter of Earth, causing it to have an apparent size in the sky almost the same as that of the Sun, with the result that the Moon covers the Sun nearly precisely in total solar eclipse. This matching of apparent visual size will not continue in the far future. The Moon's linear distance from Earth is currently increasing at a rate of 3.82 ± 0.07 centimetres per year, but this rate is not constant.

Lunar travels

The Soviet Union's Luna programme was the first to reach the Moon with unmanned spacecraft in 1959; the United States' NASA Apollo program achieved the only manned missions to date, beginning with the first manned lunar orbiting mission by Apollo 8 in 1968, and six manned lunar landings between 1969 and 1972, with the first being Apollo 11. These missions returned over 380 KG of lunar rocks, which have been used to develop a geological understanding of the Moon's origin, the formation of its internal structure, and its subsequent history. After the Apollo 17 mission in 1972, the Moon has been visited only by unmanned spacecraft.

Figure 4-18. *Our multi-column layout, with a baseline grid superimposed. Some parts fall out of rhythm*

Let's tweak the margins of the headings so that the sum of the top margin, line height, and bottom margin for the two heading levels all add up to a multiple of our base `line-height` value. That way, the baselines should line up across all three columns.

```
h2 {
  font-size: 1.75em; /* 28px */
  line-height: 1.25; /* 28*1.25 = 35px */
  margin-top: 1.036em; /* 29px */
  margin-bottom: .2859em; /* 8px */
}
h3 {
  font-size: 1.314em; /* 21px */
  line-height: 1.29; /* 1.29*21 = 27px */
  margin-top: .619em; /* 13px */
  margin-bottom: .38em;/* 8px */
}
```

Originally, the headings all had a `line-height` value of `1.25`, but we've overridden that where necessary to simplify the math. Overall, the division between `margin-top` and `margin-bottom` is done somewhat by feel. The important thing is that both of these rules sum to a multiple of the base line height: 72px for the h2, and 48px for the h3. The baselines for body text in all three columns should now line up nicely (see Figure 4-19).

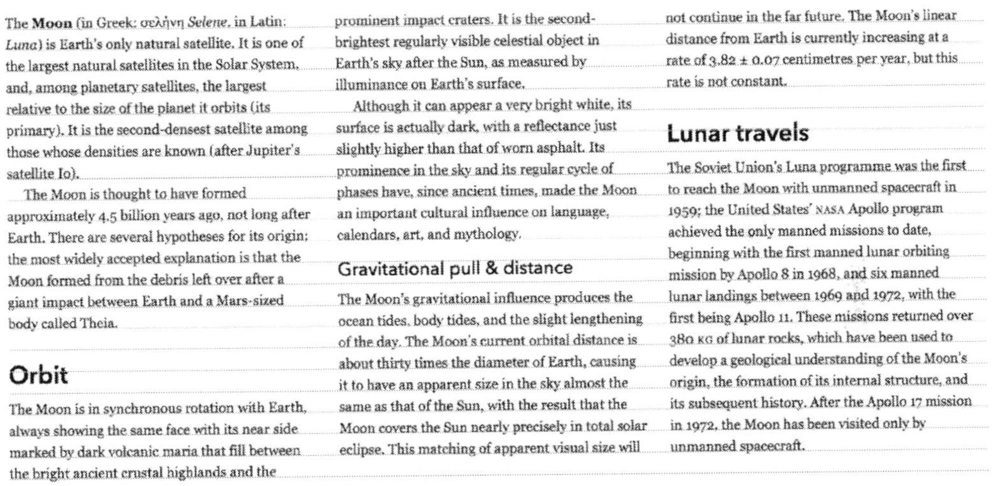

The **Moon** (in Greek: σελήνη *Selene*, in Latin: *Luna*) is Earth's only natural satellite. It is one of the largest natural satellites in the Solar System, and, among planetary satellites, the largest relative to the size of the planet it orbits (its primary). It is the second-densest satellite among those whose densities are known (after Jupiter's satellite Io).

The Moon is thought to have formed approximately 4.5 billion years ago, not long after Earth. There are several hypotheses for its origin; the most widely accepted explanation is that the Moon formed from the debris left over after a giant impact between Earth and a Mars-sized body called Theia.

Orbit

The Moon is in synchronous rotation with Earth, always showing the same face with its near side marked by dark volcanic maria that fill between the bright ancient crustal highlands and the prominent impact craters. It is the second-brightest regularly visible celestial object in Earth's sky after the Sun, as measured by illuminance on Earth's surface.

Although it can appear a very bright white, its surface is actually dark, with a reflectance just slightly higher than that of worn asphalt. Its prominence in the sky and its regular cycle of phases have, since ancient times, made the Moon an important cultural influence on language, calendars, art, and mythology.

Gravitational pull & distance

The Moon's gravitational influence produces the ocean tides, body tides, and the slight lengthening of the day. The Moon's current orbital distance is about thirty times the diameter of Earth, causing it to have an apparent size in the sky almost the same as that of the Sun, with the result that the Moon covers the Sun nearly precisely in total solar eclipse. This matching of apparent visual size will not continue in the far future. The Moon's linear distance from Earth is currently increasing at a rate of 3.82 ± 0.07 centimetres per year, but this rate is not constant.

Lunar travels

The Soviet Union's Luna programme was the first to reach the Moon with unmanned spacecraft in 1959; the United States' NASA Apollo program achieved the only manned missions to date, beginning with the first manned lunar orbiting mission by Apollo 8 in 1968, and six manned lunar landings between 1969 and 1972, with the first being Apollo 11. These missions returned over 380 KG of lunar rocks, which have been used to develop a geological understanding of the Moon's origin, the formation of its internal structure, and its subsequent history. After the Apollo 17 mission in 1972, the Moon has been visited only by unmanned spacecraft.

Figure 4-19. *The multi-column article, now with a vertical rhythm set so that all paragraphs fall on the baseline grid*

Web Fonts

So far in this chapter we've limited ourselves to fonts that are installed locally on a user's computer. Common web fonts like Helvetica, Georgia, and Times New Roman are common precisely *because* they have traditionally been available on popular operating systems like Windows and Mac OS X.

For many years designers wanted the ability to embed remote fonts from the Web, in much the same way as they could embed an image into a web page. The technology to do this has been available since the release of Internet Explorer 4 in 1997, but there hadn't been good cross-browser support until 2009 when Firefox, Safari, and Opera introduced similar technology.

Since then, there has been huge adoption of web fonts. Initially quite experimentally on small blogs and personal sites, this has been followed by large corporations and even government organizations (see Figure 4-20, for example) adopting custom web fonts.

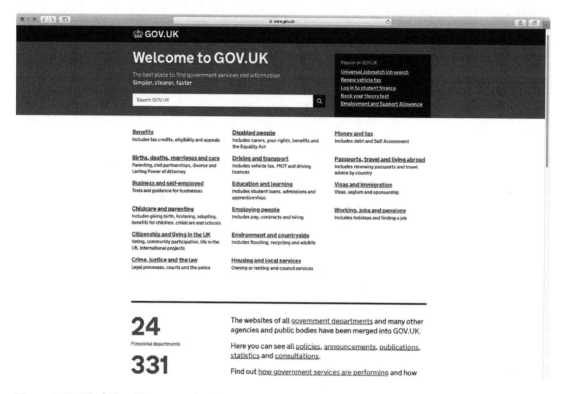

Figure 4-20. *The* http://www.gov.uk *website using a custom font designed by Margaret Calvert and Henrik Kubel*

Licensing

The other complication when dealing with web fonts is licensing. Initially, type foundries were very cautious about allowing their fonts on the Web for individual browsers to download. The fear was this would lead to uncontrollable piracy of their typefaces, and it's taken a few years for this fear to abate.

Most foundries that make their fonts available on the Web require certain security restrictions about how they are served. For example, they might only allow fonts to be downloaded when linked to from a site with a specific domain name, or require that the name of the font on the server changes regularly to avoid hot-linking of fonts.

┌───┐
│   **WEB FONT HOSTING SERVICES**   │
└───┘

The simplest way of experimenting with custom fonts if you haven't yet started doing so is to use a web font service. Commercial services like Adobe Typekit (http://typekit.com), Cloud.typography (http://www.typography.com/cloud), and Fonts.com (http://www.fonts.com) look after all the nitty-gritty of hosting and serving web fonts. There's also Google Fonts (https://www.google.com/fonts), where Google collects and hosts free-to-use fonts from a range of type foundries.

These online services handle the different licensing deals with foundries and the difficult job of converting fonts to the correct file formats, ensuring the correct character sets are included and are well optimized. They then host and serve these fonts from their reliable and high-speed servers.

Choosing a hosted service allows you to license fonts either individually for one-off use or as part of a subscription to a library of fonts. Hosted services take a huge amount of the pain out of dealing with web fonts and allow you to focus on the design and use of them within your web pages.

The @font-face rule

The key to embedded web fonts is the @font-face rule. This rule allows you to specify the location of a font on a web server for a browser to download, and then lets you reference that font elsewhere in your style sheet:

```
@font-face {
  font-family: Vollkorn;
  font-weight: bold;
  src: url("fonts/vollkorn/Vollkorn-Bold.woff") format('woff');
}
h1, h2, h3, h4, h5, h6 {
  font-family: Vollkorn, Georgia, serif;
  font-weight: bold;
}
```

The code in the preceding @font-face block declares that this rule applies when the style sheet uses the font-family value Vollkorn with a bold weight, and then provides a URL for the browser to download the Web Open Font Format (WOFF) file containing the bold font.

Once this new Vollkorn font has been declared, you can use it in a normal CSS font-family property later on in your style sheet. In the previous example, we've chosen to use the bold Vollkorn font for all heading elements on the page.

Font File Formats

Although support for web fonts is now very good across all the main browsers, what's less good is support for consistent font file formats. The history of font formats is long, complicated, and tightly bound to the history of companies like Microsoft, Apple, and Adobe. Luckily, all browser makers are now on board with the standardized WOFF format, with some even supporting the new and more efficient WOFF2. If you need support for IE8 and earlier, ancient versions of Safari, or older Android devices, you may have to complement your code with additional file formats like SVG fonts, EOT, and TTF.

■ **Tip** If you have a font licensed for web font usage, you can create these additional formats using online tools like Font Squirrel (`http://fontsquirrel.com`).

To deal with this inconsistent support, the `@font-face` rule is able to accept multiple values for the `src` descriptor (much like how `font-family` works) along with the `format()` hint, leaving it to the browser to decide which file is most appropriate to download.

Using this feature, we can get almost universal cross-browser support for web fonts, with a `@font-face` rule such as the following:

```
@font-face {
  font-family: Vollkorn;
  src: url('fonts/Vollkorn-Regular.eot#?ie') format('embedded-opentype'),
       url('fonts/Vollkorn-Regular.woff2') format('woff2'),
       url('fonts/Vollkorn-Regular.woff') format('woff'),
       url('fonts/Vollkorn-Regular.ttf') format('truetype'),
       url('fonts/Vollkorn-Regular.svg') format('svg');
}
```

This covers all browsers that support EOT, WOFF (including WOFF2), TTF, and SVG, which means pretty much every browser in use today. It even accounts for quirky behavior in IE6–8, by declaring the first `src` value with a querystring parameter attached. This pattern, known as the "Fontspring @font-face syntax," is documented in detail at `http://www.fontspring.com/blog/further-hardening-of-the-bulletproof-syntax`, along with the formats and edge cases it accounts for.

■ **Note** There are some further gotchas when using web fonts in IE6–8, in particular when using several variations of the same typeface. We won't go into the specifics here, but you can find more background in this article from Typekit: `http://blog.typekit.com/2011/06/27/new-from-typekit-variation-specific-font-family-names-in-ie-6-8/`. We have also documented workarounds in the code samples that come with the book.

In the rest of the examples where we're using web fonts, we'll be using only the WOFF and WOFF2 formats—by using those, we get support for the large majority of browsers while keeping the code simple.

Font Descriptors

The `@font-face` rule accepts a number of declarations, most of them optional. The most commonly used are

- `font-family`: Required, the name of the font family.
- `src`: Required, the URL, or list of URLs, where the font can be obtained.
- `font-weight`: Optional weight of the font. Defaults to `normal`.
- `font-style`: Optional style of the font. Defaults to `normal`.

It's important to understand that these are not the same `font` properties you apply to regular rule sets—they're actually not the normal properties at all, but *font descriptors*. We are not changing anything about the font, but rather explaining which values of these properties, when used in the style sheet, should trigger the use of this particular font file.

If font-weight is set to bold here, it means "use the file inside this block when something set in this font-family has font-weight set to bold." One pitfall is that if this is the *only* instance of Vollkorn available, it will be used for other weights as well, despite not being the correct weight. This is part of the spec for how browsers load and select fonts: the correct font-family is outranking the correct weight.

Many typefaces have different fonts for the various weights, styles, and variants, so you could have several different @font-face blocks referencing the font-family name Vollkorn pointing to different files. In the following example, we're loading two different typefaces, and declaring for which weights and styles each should be used:

```
@font-face {
  font-family: AlegreyaSans;
  src: url('fonts/alegreya/AlegreyaSans-Regular.woff2') format('woff2'),
       url('fonts/alegreya/AlegreyaSans-Regular.woff') format('woff');
  /* font-weight and font-style both default to "normal". */
}
@font-face {
  font-family: Vollkorn;
  src:  url('fonts/vollkorn/Vollkorn-Medium.woff') format('woff'),
        url('fonts/vollkorn/Vollkorn-Medium.woff') format('woff');
  font-weight: 500;
}
@font-face {
  font-family: Vollkorn;
  font-weight: bold;
  src:  url('fonts/vollkorn/Vollkorn-Bold.woff') format('woff'),
        url('fonts/vollkorn/Vollkorn-Bold.woff') format('woff');
}
```

We can then use the correct font file elsewhere in our style sheet by declaring which variation we're after:

```
body {
  font-family: AlegreyaSans, Helvetica, arial, sans-serif;
}
h1, h2, h3, h4, h5, h6 {
  font-family: Vollkorn, Georgia, Times, 'Times New Roman', serif;
  font-weight: bold; /* will use the Vollkorn Bold font. */
}
h3 {
  font-weight: 500; /* will use the Vollkorn Medium font. */
}
```

Applying these styles to the same markup we used in the Moon article example, we get a different look where the Alegreya sans-serif font family used for body text contrasts with the serif Vollkorn used for headings (see Figure 4-21). The h1 and h2 are now using the Vollkorn Bold font file, whereas the h3 uses Vollkorn Medium automatically as the font-weight matches 500.

THE MOON

The **Moon** (in Greek: σελήνη *Selene*, in Latin: *Luna*) is Earth's only natural satellite. It is one of the largest natural satellites in the Solar System, and, among planetary satellites, the largest relative to the size of the planet it orbits (its primary). It is the second-densest satellite among those whose densities are known (after Jupiter's satellite Io).

The Moon is thought to have formed approximately 4.5 billion years ago, not long after Earth. There are several hypotheses for its origin; the most widely accepted explanation is that the Moon formed from the debris left over after a giant impact between Earth and a Mars-sized body called Theia.

Orbit

The Moon is in synchronous rotation with Earth, always showing the same face with its near side marked by dark volcanic maria that fill between the bright ancient crustal highlands and the prominent impact craters. It is the second-brightest regularly visible celestial object in Earth's sky after the Sun, as measured by illuminance on Earth's surface.

Although it can appear a very bright white, its surface is actually dark, with a reflectance just slightly higher than that of worn asphalt. Its prominence in the sky and its regular cycle of phases have, since ancient times, made the Moon an important cultural influence on language, calendars, art, and mythology.

Gravitational pull & distance

The Moon's gravitational influence produces the ocean tides, body tides, and the slight lengthening of the day. The Moon's current orbital distance is about thirty times the diameter

Figure 4-21. *The article example with our new fonts applied*

▓ **Caution**   A common mistake when loading web fonts is to load a bold font inside a `@font-face` block with its `font-weight` descriptor set to `normal`, and then use it for an element that has its `font-weight` property set to `bold`. This causes some browsers to assume that the font doesn't have a proper bold variant and makes them apply a "faux bold" on top of the original bolding.

We can see in the preceding example how the mechanics of font-family work in combination with our new typeface: it turns out that the Alegreya Sans typeface does not contain any Greek letters, which appear in the translated name of the Moon (see Figure 4-22). For these glyphs, the fallback font is used—in this case Helvetica. This is apparent from the differing x-height in the two fonts.

The Moon (in Greek: σελήνη *Selene*, in Latin: *Luna*)

Figure 4-22. *The Greek glyphs use the fallback font from the* font-family *stack. Note how the x-height differs slightly*

The bad news is that we did not load an italic font file for Alegreya, and for missing font styles, the browser instead uses "faux italics" based on the normal style. This becomes even clearer when we look at the source reference paragraph last in the article (see Figure 4-23).

Text fetched from "Moon" article on Wikipedia on the 23rd of February 2016.

Figure 4-23. *Faux italicized text at the bottom of our article*

Luckily, Alegreya contains a wide range of variations, so if we add a new @font-face block pointing to the correct file, this issue should resolve itself for any body text already set as font-style: italic (see Figure 4-24):

```
@font-face {
  font-family: AlegreyaSans;
  src: url('fonts/alegreya/AlegreyaSans-Italic.woff2') format('woff2'),
       url('fonts/alegreya/AlegreyaSans-Italic.woff') format('woff');
  font-style: italic;
}
```

Text fetched from "Moon" article on Wikipedia on the 23rd of February 2016.

Figure 4-24. *Now with true italics*

Web Fonts, Browsers, and Performance

Although web fonts have provided a considerable leap forward for web design, their application comes with certain disclaimers.

It should be obvious that by downloading extra fonts you are subjecting your users to an increased total page weight. Your very first consideration should be limiting how many font files you need to load. It is also very important that if you are hosting your own custom fonts, you must apply appropriate caching headers to minimize network traffic. However, there are other considerations in regard to how browsers actually render the fonts to the screen.

While web fonts are downloading, the browser has two choices for your textual content. First, it can block showing text on the screen until the web font has downloaded and is available for use, known as the *flash of invisible text* (or FOIT). This is the behavior that Safari, Chrome, and Internet Explorer exhibit by default, and it can lead to a scenario where users cannot read the content of your site because the fonts are slow to download. This could be a particular problem for users browsing on slow network connections, as you can see in Figure 4-25.

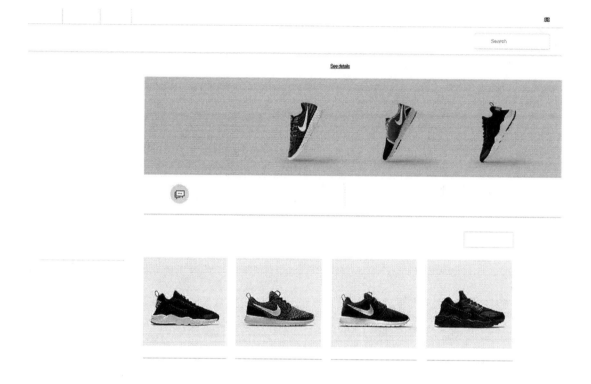

Figure 4-25. A page on http://www.nike.com as it would appear while waiting for fonts to download

The other option for browsers is to show the content in a fallback font while it waits for the browser to download the web font. This gets around the problem of a slow network blocking content, but there's a trade-off in that you get the flash of the fallback font. That flash is sometimes known as the *flash of unstyled text*, or FOUT.

This flash of unstyled text can impact the perceived performance, especially if the metrics of the fallback font are different from the preferred web font you are trying to load. If the page content jumps around too much when the font is downloaded and applied, the user can lose their place in the page.

If you're using web fonts, you can opt to load the fonts via JavaScript to gain some further control over which method is used, and how both web font and fallback are displayed.

Loading Fonts with JavaScript

There is an experimental JavaScript API for loading fonts, defined in the very recent CSS Font Loading specification. Sadly, browser support is not particularly broad yet. Instead, we need to use third-party libraries to ensure a consistent font-loading experience.

Typekit maintain an Open Source JavaScript tool called Web Font Loader (`https://github.com/typekit/webfontloader`). This is a small library that uses the native font-loading API behind the scenes where supported, and emulates the same functionality in other browsers. It comes with support for some of the common web font providers such as Typekit, Google Fonts, and Fonts.com, but also allows for fonts you have self-hosted.

You can download the library or load it from Google's own servers as detailed at `https://developers.google.com/speed/libraries/#web-font-loader`.

Web Font Loader provides a lot of useful functionality, but one of the most useful is the ability to ensure a consistent cross-browser behavior for font loading. In this case we want to ensure that slow-loading fonts never block the user from reading our content. In other words, we want to enable the FOUT behavior across our other supported browsers.

Web Font Loader provides hooks for the following events:

- Loading: When fonts begin loading

- Active: When fonts finishing loading

- Inactive: If font loading fails

In this instance, we'll move all of our `@font-face` blocks into a separate style sheet named `alegreya-vollkorn.css`, placing it inside a subfolder called `css`. We'll then add a small piece of JavaScript to the head of our example page:

```
<script type="text/javascript">
  WebFontConfig = {
    custom: {
        families: ['AlegreyaSans:n4,i4', 'Vollkorn:n6,n5,n7'],
        urls: ['css/alegreya-vollkorn.css']
    }
  };
  (function() {
    var wf = document.createElement('script');
    wf.src = 'https://ajax.googleapis.com/ajax/libs/webfont/1/webfont.js';
    wf.type = 'text/javascript';
    wf.async = 'true';
    var s = document.getElementsByTagName('script')[0];
    s.parentNode.insertBefore(wf, s);
  })();
</script>
```

This code will both download the Web Font Loader script itself and configure which fonts and variations we use (highlighted in bold in the code). The variations we want are described after the `font-family` name: n4 stands for "normal style, weight at 400," and so on. As the fonts found in this style sheet are loading, the script will automatically add generated class names to the `html` element. That way, you can tailor your CSS to the current state of the font loading.

```
body {
  font-family: Helvetica, arial, sans-serif;
}
.wf-alegreya-n4-active body {
  font-family:  Alegreya, Helvetica, arial, sans-serif;
}
```

These two CSS rules mean that before the Alegreya font has loaded, we are showing the fallback font stack in its place. Then, once Alegreya is done loading, the loader script adds the wf-alegreya-n4-active class to the html element, and the browser starts using our newly downloaded font. Not only will we now see a consistent behavior across browsers, but we also have a hook for tweaking the details of our typography for both fallback fonts and web fonts.

Matching Fallback Font Size

With a similar rule applied when the font is loading but not done yet, we can parry differences in font metrics between the web font and the fallbacks. This is important because when the web font replaces the fallback font, you want this change in size to be as discreet and unnoticeable as possible.

In our example, the Alegreya font has a noticeably smaller x-height than Helvetica and Arial (both of which have similar metrics). By tweaking the font-size and line-height slightly, we can match the height pretty closely. Similarly, we can adjust for differences in the character widths by tweaking word-spacing slightly. This way, we end up with a result that much more closely resembles what the text will look like once the web font has loaded.

```
.wf-alegreyasans-n4-loading p {
  font-size: 0.905em;
  word-spacing: -0.11em;
  line-height: 1.72;
  font-size-adjust:
}
```

■ **Tip**   If you're using a vertical rhythm, you might have to adjust these kinds of properties in several places when using this technique, so that the different font sizes still correspond to the base measurement.

The other thing we'll be using the Web Font Loader for is to set the font-size-adjust property once the web font has loaded. This property allows you to specify the aspect ratio between the x-height and the font-size. In cases where a glyph is missing in the preferred font, the fallback font will then be adjusted in size to match that ratio. This usually comes down to about half as tall (a value of 0.5), but it can differ a bit, making the difference between your fallback fonts and your preferred web font quite noticeable. Instead of measuring by hand and setting this value to a number, we can set the keyword auto, and let the browser do the work for us:

```
.wf-alegreyasans-n4-active body {
  font-size-adjust: auto;
}
```

At the time of writing, Firefox is the only browser with shipped support for `font-size-adjust`, with Chrome offering experimental support behind a preference flag. If we view the article example in Firefox, as shown in Figure 4-26, we can see that the Greek glyphs (seen here in Helvetica) now have the same height as the surrounding Alegreya.

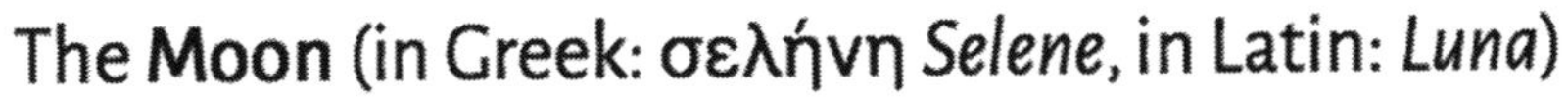

The **Moon** (in Greek: σελήνη *Selene*, in Latin: *Luna*)

Figure 4-26. *Firefox showing the Greek glyphs in Helvetica with adjusted x-height*

Advanced Typesetting Features

OpenType, a font format developed by Microsoft and Adobe in the 1990s, allows for additional characteristics and features of fonts to be included in a font file. If you're using a font file that contains OpenType features (which can be contained in either `.ttf`, `.otf`, or `.woff`/`.woff2` files), you can control a range of CSS features in most modern browsers. These features include kerning, ligatures, and alternative numerals, as well as decorative features like the swashes seen in Figure 4-27.

Figure 4-27. *The names of speakers for the Ampersand conference with swash glyphs from the "Fat Face" typeface*

The CSS Fonts specification has targeted properties for many OpenType features, like `font-kerning`, `font-variant-numeric`, and `font-variant-ligatures`. Support for these targeted properties is not currently available cross-browser, but there are methods for accessing these features through another, more low-level property, `font-feature-settings`, that does have support across many modern browsers. Often, you'll do best to specify both, as some browsers may support the targeted properties but not the low-level settings.

The `font-feature-settings` property accepts values that toggle certain feature sets, by passing it four-letter OpenType codes, optionally with a numeric value. For example, we can enable ligatures—glyphs that combine two or more characters into one—as shown in Figure 4-28.

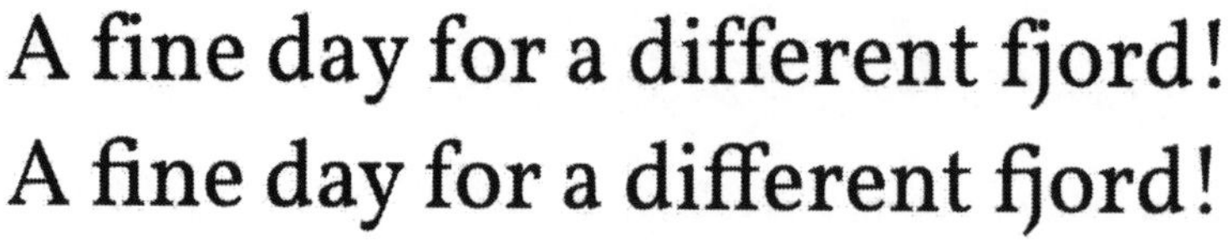

A fine day for a different fjord!
A fine day for a different fjord!

Figure 4-28. *Two pieces of text set in Vollkorn, the first without ligatures and the second with ligatures enabled. Note the difference in the "fi," "ff," and "fj" pairs*

The typeface designer can specify several categories of ligatures, depending on whether they should be used generally or in special cases. To enable the two kinds of ligatures present in the Vollkorn typeface called *standard ligatures* and *discretionary ligatures,* we would use the following rule:

```
p {
  font-variant-ligatures: common-ligatures discretionary-ligatures;
  font-feature-settings: "liga", "dlig";
}
```

Standard ligatures are always enabled by default in browsers supporting OpenType using `font-variant-ligatures`, so they are left out in the first declaration. Certain browsers support the `font-feature-settings` property with a slightly different syntax, and others need a vendor-prefixed version of the property, so a full rule to turn on common and discretionary ligatures would be

```
h1, h2, h3 {
  font-variant-ligatures: discretionary-ligatures;
  -webkit-font-feature-settings: "liga", "dlig";
  -moz-font-feature-settings: "liga", "dlig";
  -moz-font-feature-settings: "liga=1, dlig=1";
  font-feature-settings: "liga", "dlig";
}
```

The syntax differences require a bit of explanation :

- The standard way of affecting an OpenType feature is to use its four-letter code in quotes, optionally followed by a keyword—on or off—or a number. These codes indicate the state for the feature, and if you leave them out (like in the preceding example), they default to on.

- Using 0 for the state also turns the feature off. If the feature only has on and off states, a value of 1 turns it on. Some features have several "states," and these can be selected by using the appropriate numbers for each—what this means depends on the individual font and type of feature you want to activate.

- When several features are affected at once, they need to be separated by commas.

- Most browsers still implement these features as vendor-prefixed, so make sure to include these.

- The older syntax for some Mozilla browsers is a bit different: all of the affected features are named as comma-separated in one quoted string, and the state is affected by using an equals sign and then the number part.

A full list of the OpenType feature codes can be found from Microsoft at `http://www.microsoft.com/typography/otspec/featurelist.htm`. In the rest of the examples, we'll only use the standardized forms of `font-feature-settings` along with the targeted feature properties.

Numerals

Some typefaces include multiple styles of numerals for use in different situations. Many typefaces, such as Georgia or Vollkorn, use old-style numerals by default, where numbers have ascenders and descenders the same way letters do. Vollkorn also includes lining numerals, where numbers sit on the baseline and have the same general height as capital letters. In Figure 4-29, we have toggled explicitly between old-style and lining numerals, using the following code:

```
.lining-nums {
  font-variant-numeric: lining-nums;
  font-feature-settings: "lnum";
}
.old-style {
  font-variant-numeric: oldstyle-nums;
  font-feature-settings: "onum";
}
```

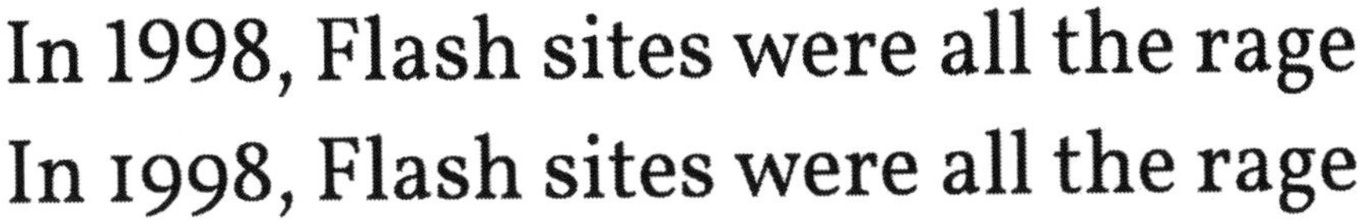

In 1998, Flash sites were all the rage
In 1998, Flash sites were all the rage

Figure 4-29. Lining numerals (top) vs. old-style numerals (bottom) as set in Vollkorn

Most typefaces have numerals with varying width (proportional numerals), just like regular letters. If you're using numbers in a table or list where you need them to line up vertically, you may want to switch to tabular numerals. In Figure 4-30, we have used them combined with lining numerals, configured as follows:

```
table {
  font-variant-numeric: tabular-nums lining-nums;
  font-feature-settings: "tnum", "lnum";
}
```

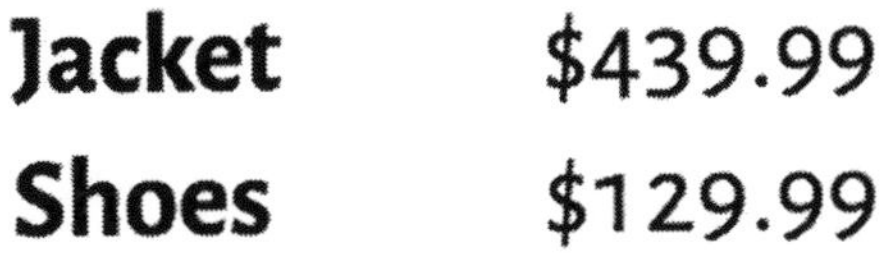

Jacket $439.99
Shoes $129.99

Figure 4-30. Tabular lining numerals as set in Alegreya Sans. Prices on the right line up vertically, despite having different widths

Kerning Options and Text Rendering

High-quality fonts often have data inside them to adjust the space between certain pairs of glyphs. This process of fine-tuning the spacing is known as *kerning*. It means that some letter pairs may need extra space between them to not seem too cramped up with each other, and some even need to overlap slightly so as not seem too far apart. Some examples of common kerning pairs can be seen in Figure 4-31, where we have activated kerning in the Alegreya typeface.

VAT means Value-Added Tax
VAT means Value-Added Tax

Figure 4-31. *A sentence without (top) and with (bottom) detailed kerning activated. Notice how the space shrinks between pairs like "AT," "Ad," and "Ta"*

The text rendering in browsers mostly tries to handle this automatically based on known metrics, but you can also activate the reading of detailed kerning data from individual fonts in many modern browsers. We trigger it by setting the font-kerning property, or activating the kern OpenType feature:

```
.kern {
  font-kerning: normal;
  font-feature-settings: "kern";
}
```

The keyword normal tells the browser to grab the kerning data from the font, if available. A value of auto allows the browser to turn it on when deemed appropriate; for example, it might be ignored for very small text sizes. Finally, you can explicitly turn it off by setting the value to none.

■ **Note**   Activating other OpenType features (like ligatures) may automatically trigger use of kerning data from the font in some browsers, so if you want to turn off kerning but still use ligatures, you need to specify that explicitly. Conversely, using the "kern" feature may also trigger the application of common or standard ligatures.

AVOID THE TEXT-RENDERING PROPERTY

Setting the declaration text-rendering: optimizeLegibility is another trick that activates kerning as well as common ligatures at the same time. It's not part of any CSS standard, but is a property from the SVG specification that tells the browser to pick a method for rendering letter shapes in SVG. It can prioritize performance (optimizeSpeed), more exact shapes (optimizeGeometricPrecision), or more readable shapes (optimizeLegibility).

This property has been around for a while and is fairly well supported, so it's common to see sites using it—it was the only method for activating these features in older WebKit-based browsers before they supported font-feature-settings. However, you should know that there are quite a few serious rendering bugs associated with using this property, so you'd do best to avoid it.

Text Effects

While there is still plenty to explore when it comes to the basics of typography on the Web, there are situations where you want to go nuts with things like headings and logotypes. In this section we'll look at some examples of techniques that let you go above and beyond, for creating eye-catching effects that set your website apart from the rest.

Using and Abusing Text Shadows

The CSS `text-shadow` property lets you draw a shadow behind a piece of text. For longer runs of body text, this is usually not a very good idea, since it often diminishes the readability of your text. For headings or other short pieces of text, it does have some good uses, especially for creating "letterpress" like effects or re-creating the shading of traditional painted signs.

The syntax for `text-shadow` is pretty straightforward. You need to supply lengths for the x- and y-axis offset from the original text (positive or negative), a length for the blur distance (where 0 means a completely sharp shadow), and a color, all separated by spaces (see Figure 4-32):

```
h1 {
    text-shadow: -.2em .4em .2em #ccc;
}
```

Hello from the 90's!

Figure 4-32. *A simple text shadow with some spread applied. Any spread value other than 0 means that the shadow is blurry*

In addition to this, you can create several shadows for one piece of text by using a comma-separated list of shadows. When applying multiple shadows, they are stacked, with the first one defined showing on the top and the others stacking behind it, increasingly further down the stack in the order they're defined.

The ability to add multiple shadows to a single piece of text makes this quite a versatile effect. This is what lets you emulate a "letterpress" effect, where the type seems either impressed into the page or embossed, by adding one darker and one lighter shadow, sticking out above or below the text (see Figure 4-33). The offset of the light vs. dark shadow depends on whether the text is lighter or darker than the background: a darker text with a light shadow above and a darker shadow below usually appears impressed into the page, and vice versa.

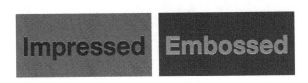

Figure 4-33. *A simple "letterpress" effect*

The following code sample illustrates the two different effects:

```
.impressed {
  background-color: #6990e1;
  color: #31446B;
  text-shadow: 0 -1px 1px #b3d6f9, 0 1px 0 #243350;
}
.embossed {
  background-color: #3c5486;
  color: #92B1EF;
  text-shadow: 0 -1px 0 #243350, 0 1px 0 #def2fe;
}
```

Building further on the technique of multiple shadows, we can create lettering that looks like it's in a pseudo-3D-shaded kind of style, emulating styles from hand-painted signage. Adding a large number of sharp shadows, where the diagonal offset between each shadow is one pixel or less, allows us to achieve this effect:

```
h1 {
  font-family: Nunito, "Arial Rounded MT Bold", "Helvetica Rounded", Arial, sans-serif;
  color: #d0bb78;
  text-transform: uppercase;
  font-weight: 700;
  text-shadow:
    -1px 1px 0 #743132,
    -2px 2px 0 #743132,
    -3px 3px 0 #743132,
    /* …and so on, 1px increments */
    -22px 22px 0 #743132,
    -23px 23px 0 #743132;
}
```

This gives us the funky 70s-inspired look we see in Figure 4-34. The text is set in Nunito, loaded from Google Fonts.

Figure 4-34. *A large number of text shadows with increasing offset creates a diagonal shade from the text*

To further increase the sense of hand-painted signage, we can apply some effects. First, we could create an outline effect with a first batch of white shadows, since sign painters often left some space between the lettering and the shade—this let them work more quickly since the paint in the letters didn't have to dry before they could move on to the shading. We'll need to duplicate the white shadow and use offsets in all directions to make it go all the way around the letters.

Secondly, we can use another trick to make the shade appear to shift in color along with its direction, creating an even more pseudo-3D look, emulating lighting direction. This is achieved by offsetting the individual shadows in a staggered way, where the color alternates between a lighter and a darker color. This way, we're utilizing the stacking of them to make one color stand out more in the horizontal direction, and the other in the vertical. The finished result can be seen in Figure 4-35.

Figure 4-35. *Our finished shaded headline*

Here's how the resulting code for the two tricks described would look:

```
h1 {
  /* some properties left out */
  text-shadow:
      /* first, some white outline shadows in all directions: */
      -2px 2px 0 #fff,
      0px -2px 0 #fff,
      0px 3px 0 #fff,
      3px 0px 0 #fff,
      -3px 0px 0 #fff,
      2px 2px 0 #fff,
      2px -2px 0 #fff,
      -2px -2px 0 #fff,
      /* …then some alternating shades that increasingly stick out in either direction: */
      -3px 3px 0 #743b34,
      -4px 3px 0 #a8564d,
      -4px 5px 0 #743b34,
      -5px 4px 0 #a8564d,
      -5px 6px 0 #743b34,
       /* ..and so on… */
      -22px 21px 0 #a8564d,
      -22px 23px 0 #743b34,
      -23px 22px 0 #a8564d,
      -23px 24px 0 #743b34;
}
```

An in-depth article on this technique for shading and old-style signage for the Web can be found at the Typekit Practice website (`http://practice.typekit.com/lesson/using-shades/`), which also has a wealth of other resources for learning the art of web typography.

Almost all browsers support the text-shadow property, only IE9 and earlier are missing out. As for performance where they are supported, drawing shadows can be quite the expensive operation, so you should only apply shadow effects very sparingly in your designs.

Using JavaScript to Enhance Typography

There are some situations where pure CSS just won't do the trick. For instance, you can target the first letter of a piece of text with the `:first-letter` pseudo-element, but there is no selector for individually targeting the rest of the letters. Your only option if you would want each letter to have a different color, for example, would be to wrap each letter with an element (like a `<span>`, for example) and target those. That approach is not very viable, especially if you don't have manual control over the markup for the elements you want to style.

Luckily, we can treat these kinds of visual effects as an enhancement, and use JavaScript to automatically create the extra hooks. The `lettering.js` jQuery plug-in (http://letteringjs.com) will do just that. One of the people behind this plug-in is designer and developer Trent Walton. Figure 4-36 shows `lettering.js` used in the wild in a heading on his personal website.

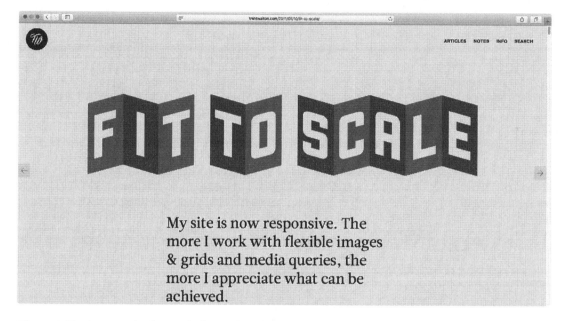

Figure 4-36. *An example of using the `lettering.js` jQuery plug-in, from http://trentwalton.com*

There are a gazillion different other JavaScript-based solutions to help you tweak your text. Here are some examples:

- `fitText.js`: A jQuery plug-in from the same folks behind `lettering.js` (from agency Paravel) to make text resize in relation to the size of the page (http://fittext.js).

- `BigText.js`: A script from Zach Leatherman of Filament Group that tries to make a line of text as big as possible based on its container (https://github.com/zachleat/BigText).

- `Widowtamer`: A script from Nathan Ford of Gridset.com that makes sure to prevent accidental widows by inserting nonbreaking space characters between words of a certain distance from the end of a paragraph (https://github.com/nathanford/widowtamer).

> ■ **Note** SVG enables some really cool text effects, which are generally outside the scope of this book. However, in Chapter 12 we will look at some advanced techniques for visual effects, among them a brief look at scalable text using SVG.

Further Type Inspiration

Typography on the Web is an area that is rich for investigating, experimenting, and pushing the limits of what's possible. There are many hundreds of years of history and tradition to explore, and to investigate what we can apply and how we can apply it sensibly in a web context.

One of the authorities on typography in general is the book *The Elements of Typographic Style* by Robert Bringhurst, which documents and explains much of this tradition. It talks about many of the features we've discussed in this chapter, such as vertical rhythm, and the nuances of hyphenation and word spacing.

The previously mentioned Richard Rutter has spent time thinking about how some of this best practice that Bringhurst has established can be brought over to the Web. *The Elements of Typographic Style applied to the Web* (http://webtypography.net) shows how to apply features of typographic tradition using HTML and CSS, and is well worth a look if you're interested in getting more detailed rules and practices into how you typeset for the Web.

Another great guide to typographic practice, with explanations for how to translate the advice to CSS, is *Butterick's Practical Typography*, available at http://practicaltypography.com/.

Finally, Jake Giltsoff's collection of typography links, "Typography on the Web" (https://typographyontheweb.com), is a great resource of tips on both design and code.

Remember, if you're adding *any* text to a web page, then **you** are typesetting.

Summary

In this chapter, we've gone through the basics of text and font properties in CSS and some tips on how to use them for maximum readability and flexibility. Using the multi-column layout module, we created text set in a newspaper-like format. We saw how systematic distances in line height and other spacing properties can let you set your type to a vertical rhythm.

We looked at how to load custom fonts using the @font-face rule, and the various parameters that affect which font file is loaded. We also had a quick look at how to control the perceived performance of font loading, using the Web Font Loader JavaScript library.

We took a look at some of the more detailed OpenType options available for increased typographic control—ligatures, numerals, and kerning—and how the font-feature-settings property allows us low-level control over how to turn these features on or off.

Finally, we explored some methods of experimenting with more radical typography techniques for headings and poster type, using text shadows and some further help from JavaScript.

In the next chapter, we'll take a look at how to set the stage for your beautifully typeset pages: using images, background colors, borders, and shadows.

CHAPTER 5

■ ■ ■

Beautiful Boxes

In previous chapters you learned that every element of an HTML document is made up of rectangular boxes: from the containers that hold the structural parts of your page, to the lines of text in a paragraph. You then spent the last chapter learning how to style the text content of your pages.

Web design wouldn't be as creative or flexible if we weren't able enhance the look of these boxes, or complement them with colors, shapes, and imagery. This is where the CSS properties for backgrounds, shadows, and borders come in, as well as content images through the img element, and other embedded objects.

In this chapter you will learn about

- Background colors and the different kinds of opacity

- Using background images and the different image formats

- Using the calc() function to do mathematical calculations on lengths

- Adding shadow effects to your boxes

- Using simple and advanced border effects

- Generating gradients with CSS

- Styling and sizing content images and other embedded objects

Background Color

We'll start with a very basic example of adding a color to the background of the entire page. The following code will set our background to a mellow green color:

```
body {
  background-color: #bada55;
}
```

We could also set the background color using the shorter background property:

```
body {
  background: #bada55;
}
```

© Andy Budd and Emil Björklund 2016
A. Budd and E. Björklund, *CSS Mastery*, DOI 10.1007/978-1-4302-5864-3_5

What's the difference between these two properties? The second, background, is a shorthand property that allows you to set a whole host of other background-related properties at the same time. In the preceding example, we only declare a background color in the shorthand, but the other values (for background images) are affected as well—they are reset to their default values. This could unintentionally override something that you've already specifically set, so be careful with that one—we'll examine it in detail further ahead in this chapter.

Color Values and Opacity

In the previous color example, we set the value with the *hexadecimal* notation: a hash character (also known as an *octothorpe, pound sign,* or *number sign*) followed by a six-character string. This string is composed of three sets of two characters each in the range of 0 to F. Hexadecimal means every "number" can have 16 different values, so 0–9 are complemented with A–F representing the 11th to 16th values:

```
0123456789ABCDEF
```

These three pairs represent the red, green, and blue (RGB) values for the color. There are 256 different possible values for each color channel, hence the two characters per color channel ($16 \times 16 = 256$).

Colors where all three pairs have the same values in both places are allowed to be shortened to three characters: #aabbcc becomes #abc, #663399 becomes #639, and so forth.

▓ **Tip**   You can also specify colors using one of the many available color keywords such as red, black, teal, goldenrod, or darkseagreen. There are some pretty weird color keywords—they have their roots in an old graphics system called X11, where the developers in turn chose some of the color keywords from a box of crayons!

It's hard to find any good reason why you'd want to use these keywords—apart from possibly wanting to quickly come up with a color for debugging purposes. We'll move ahead by using the more exact methods.

Setting the RGB values can be done in another way, using the rgb() functional notation. Each value for RGB can be represented as either a number (from 0 to 255) or a percentage (0% to 100%). Here's what the example in the previous section would look like using rgb() notation:

```
body {
  background-color: rgb(186, 218, 85);
}
```

Hexadecimal and rgb() notation have been around since CSS 1. More recently, we have gotten a few new ways to handle color: hsl(), rgba(), and hsla().

First, there is the hsl() functional notation. Both hexadecimal and RGB notations refer to how computers work with colors to display them on a screen—a mix of red, green, and blue. The hsl() notation refers to a different way of describing colors using the hue–saturation–lightness (HSL) model. The hue gets its value from a hypothetical *color wheel* (see Figure 5-1), where the colors gradually shift into each other depending on which degree you choose: red on the top (0 degrees), green one-third of the way around (120 degrees), and blue at two-thirds of the way (240 degrees).

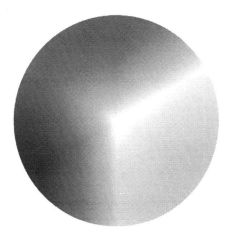

Figure 5-1. *The HSL color wheel*

If you've worked with any type of graphic design software, you've probably seen a color wheel in the color pickers there. To use hsl() syntax, you pass it the degree representing the angle of the circle you'd like to pick, and two percentages. The two percentages represent first the amount of "pigment" (saturation) you would like to use in your color mix, and then the lightness. Here's how the code from earlier would be written in hsl() notation:

```
.box {
  background-color: hsl(74, 64%, 59%);
}
```

It's important to note that there's no qualitative difference in choosing either of these ways to write your color values: they are simply different ways of representing the same thing.

The next new color notation is the turbo-powered version of RGB, called rgba(). The "a" stands for *alpha*, and it is the alpha channel that controls transparency. Here's what we would use if we wanted the same basic background color as the previous example but now want it to be 50% transparent:

```
.box {
  background-color: rgba(186, 218, 85, 0.5);
}
```

The fourth value in the arguments for the rgba() function is the alpha value, and it is written as a value between 1.0 (fully opaque) and 0 (fully transparent).

Finally, there's the hsla() notation. It has the same relationship to hsl() as rgb() has to rgba(): you pass it an extra value for the alpha channel to choose how transparent the color should be.

```
.box {
  background-color: hsla(74, 64%, 59%, 0.5);
}
```

Now that you know how to make colors more or less transparent, it should be noted that there is another way to control transparency in CSS. It can be done via the `opacity` property:

```
.box {
  background-color: #bada55;
  opacity: 0.5;
}
```

This would make our `.box` element the same color and level of transparency as in the previous example. So what is different here? Well, in the previous examples, we made only the background color transparent, but here we're making the whole element transparent, *including any content inside it*. When an element is set to be transparent using `opacity`, it is not possible to make child elements inside it be any less transparent.

In practice, this means that color values with transparency are great for making semitransparent backgrounds or text, while lowered opacity makes the whole element fade out.

■ **Caution**   Be careful with the contrast between the text and the background color! While this book is not about design theory per se, we do want to stress that designing for the Web is about your users being able to take in the information present on the pages you create. Poor choice of color contrast between background and text affects people visiting your site on their phone out in the sun, people with bad screens, people with impaired vision, etc. An excellent resource on color contrast is the site Contrast Rebellion at `http://contrastrebellion.com/`.

Background Image Basics

Adding background color is a great tool for creating more interesting pages. Sometimes we want to go further and use images as backgrounds on our elements, be it subtle patterns, pictograms to explain the user interface, or a bigger background graphic to give the page some extra character (see Figure 5-2). CSS has plenty of tools for doing this.

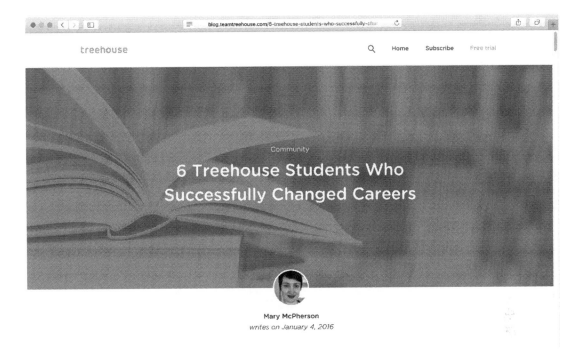

Figure 5-2. The blog on `https://teamtreehouse.com` *uses a faded and colorized background image*

Background Images vs. Content Images

First things first: when is an image a background image? You might be aware that there is an HTML element specifically for adding content images to websites: the `img` element. How do we decide when to use `img` and when to use background images in CSS?

The simple answer is that anything that could be removed from the website and still have it make sense should probably be applied as a background image. Or to put it another way: anything that would still make sense if the website had a completely different look and feel should probably be a content image.

There may be situations where the line is not clear, and you end up bending the rules to achieve a specific visual effect. Just keep in mind that any content images from `img` elements that are purely for decoration on your site may end up in other places where your content would be better left undisturbed: in feed readers and search results, for example.

Simple Example Using Background Images

Imagine we're designing a page to resemble one of those massive headers on a profile page for a social site like Twitter or Facebook (see Figure 5-3).

Figure 5-3. *A profile page on* `https://twitter.com`

Our page will instead be a social network for cats, and throughout this chapter, we'll use various properties to create the beginnings of a header component looking something like Figure 5-4.

Figure 5-4. *Giant header image and profile box with text and profile pic*

We'll start off by adding a default blue-gray background color and a background image along with some dimensions to the big header of the page. Adding a default background color is important, should the image fail to load:

```
.profile-box {
  width: 100%;
  height: 600px;
  background-color: #8Da9cf;
  background-image: url(img/big-cat.jpg);
}
```

The HTML for this component could look something like this:

```
<header class="profile-box">
</header>
```

The result of this can be seen in Figure 5-5: our image is loaded and tiled across the entire profile box.

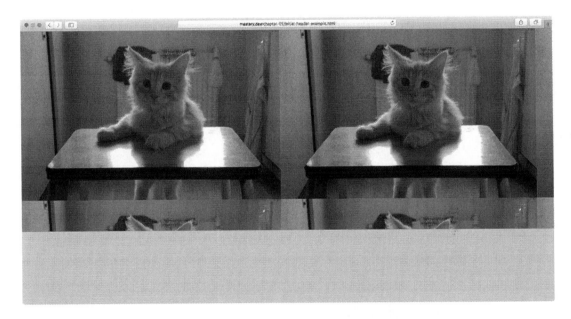

Figure 5-5. *The background image tiled across the profile box in both directions*

Why is it tiled across the whole box like that? Because of the default value of another property related to background images, named background-repeat. The default value, repeat, means that the image repeats across both the x axis and y axis. This is very useful for backgrounds containing patterns, but perhaps not photos. We can constrain this to just either direction by setting the value to repeat-x or repeat-y, but for now we'll remove the tiling effect completely by setting it to no-repeat:

```
.profile-box {
  background-image: url(img/cat.jpg);
  background-repeat: no-repeat;
}
```

The Level 3 Backgrounds and Borders specification redefines this feature with an expanded syntax and new keywords. First, it allows you to specify the repeat value for the two directions with keywords separated with a space, so the following would be equivalent to setting `repeat-x`:

```
.profile-box {
  background-repeat: repeat no-repeat;
}
```

Second, it defines some new keywords. In supporting browsers you can set `space` or `round` as one or both keywords. Using `space` means that if the background image fits inside the element two or more times (without cropping or resizing it), it will be repeated as many times as it fits and spaced apart so that the first and last "copies" of the background image touch the edges of the element. Using `round` means that the image will be resized so that it fits inside the element a whole number of times.

To be honest, these new background repetition features are probably not massively useful. They can be handy if you want to use a symbol or repeating pattern as a background and want to retain some sort of symmetry in the design, but they also make it hard to maintain the aspect ratio of the images. Support is also spotty: older browsers are missing out, but even modern versions of Firefox are missing support.

Loading Images (and other files)

When using the `url()` functional notation as we did in the previous example, we can use a relative URL—`url(img/cat.jpg)`, for example. The browser will try to find the file `cat.jpg` in the `img` subdirectory relative to the file holding the CSS itself. Had the path started with a slash—`/img/cat.jpg`—the browser would look for the image in the top-level `img` directory, relative to the domain the CSS file was loaded from.

We could also use an absolute URL. An example of an absolute URL would be if we went as far as to specify exactly which combination of protocol, domain, and path that leads to the image, like `http://example.com/img/my-background.jpg`.

Apart from absolute and relative URLs, we could opt to load images (and other resources) without pointing to any files at all, but instead embed the data directly inside the style sheet. This is done via something called a *data URI*, where the binary-encoded data inside a file is converted to a long string of text. There are numerous tools to do this for you, including online versions like `http://duri.me/`.

You can then paste that text inside the `url()` function and save the data as part of the style sheet. It looks something like this:

```
.egg {
  background-image:
    url(data:image/png;base64,iVBORwOKGgoAAAANSUhEUgAAAC gAAAAoAQAAAACkhYXAAAAAjElEQVR4AWP…
    /* ...and so on, random (?) data for a long time.. */
...4DwIMtzFJs99p9xkOXfsddZ/hlhiY/AYib1vsSbdn+P9vf/1/hv8//oBIIICRz///
r3sPMqHsPcN9MLvn1s6SfIbbUWFl74HkdTB5rWw/w51nN8vzIbrgJDuI/PMTRP7+ByK//68HkeUg8v3//WjkWwj5GOR+
+w5WyV8P1gsxB2EmwhYAgeerNiRVNyEAAAAASUVORK5CYII=);
}
```

The starting bit with `data:image/png;base64` tells the browser what kind of data to expect, and the rest is the actual pixel data of the image converted to a string of characters.

There are good and bad effects of using embedded data URIs—the main reason for using them is to reduce the number of HTTP requests, but at the same time they increase the size of your style sheets quite a bit, so use them very sparingly.

Image Formats

You can use image files of several different formats on the Web, all of them either as content images or background images. Here's a brief run-down:

- **JPEG:** A bitmap format that can be highly compressed but with some quality loss in details, suitable for photos. No support for transparency.

- **PNG:** A bitmap format that has a lossless compression, which makes it unsuitable for photos (it would create very large files) but can achieve quite small file sizes for "flatter" graphics like icons or illustrations. Can have alpha-transparency.

- **GIF:** An older bitmap format, similar to PNG, that is mostly used for animated pictures of cats. To be serious, it has largely been replaced by PNG for everything except animated images: PNG does have support for that too, but the browser support is a bit behind. GIF supports transparency, but not with alpha levels, so edges often look jagged.

- **SVG:** A vector graphics format that is also its own markup language. SVG can be either embedded directly into web pages or referenced as the source for background images or content images.

- **WebP:** A new format, developed by Google, that has very efficient compression and combines the features of JPEG (heavily compressable) with those of PNG (alpha transparency). So far, browser support is very spotty (only Blink-based browsers like Chrome and Opera), but that may change fast.

All of these except SVG are bitmap formats, meaning that they contain data pixel by pixel, and have intrinsic dimensions (meaning a "built-in" width and height). For graphic elements with high levels of details, like photos or detailed illustrations, that makes sense. But for many uses, the really interesting format is SVG, which instead contains instructions around how to draw specific shapes on the screen. This allows SVG images to be resized freely or shown on a screen with any pixel density: they will never lose any sharpness or level of detail.

SVG is a topic big enough for several books on its own (and indeed, many such books exist), but we still hope to give you some glimpses of the flexibility of SVG throughout this book (especially in Chapter 11, when we look at some of the more cutting-edge visual effects in CSS). SVG is an old format (it has been around since 1999), but in recent years browser support has become wide enough to make SVG a viable alternative. The only holdouts are the somewhat ancient versions of Internet Explorer (version 8 and earlier) and earlier versions of WebKit browers on Android (version 2 and earlier).

Background Image Syntax

Back in Figure 5-5, we started to create the profile page example with a background image in JPEG format, since it's a photo. So far, we've placed it in the background of our element, but it doesn't look very good yet. We'll go through the properties that let you adjust a background image.

Background Position

We could try positioning our image in the center of the element. The position of a background image is controlled with the `background-position` property.

We have also used a bigger version of the image file to make sure it covers the element even on larger screens (see Figure 5-6). Sides will get clipped at smaller screens, but at least the image is centered.

```
.profile-box {
  width: 100%;
  height: 600px;
  background-color: #8Da9cf;
  background-image: url(img/big-cat.jpg);
  background-repeat: no-repeat;
  background-position: 50% 50%;
}
```

Figure 5-6. *Our page with a bigger, centered background image to cover the whole element*

You can set the `background-position` property value using either keywords or units like pixels, ems, or percentages. In its simplest form, the value consists of two subvalues: one for the offset from the left, one for the offset from the top.

■ **Note**   Some browsers support the `background-position-x` and `background-position-y` properties, which position the image individually on each axis. These started out as nonstandard properties in IE, but are being standardized. They are still not supported in Mozilla-based browsers at the time of writing.

If you set these values using pixels or ems, the top-left corner of the image is positioned from the top-left corner of the element by the specified number of pixels. So if you were to specify a vertical and horizontal position of 20 pixels, the top-left corner of the image would appear 20 pixels from the left edge and 20 pixels from the top edge of the element. Background positioning using percentages works slightly differently. Rather than positioning the top-left corner of the background image, percentage positioning uses a corresponding point on the image. If you set a vertical and horizontal position of 20 percent, you are actually positioning a point 20 percent from the top and left edges of the image, 20 percent from the top and left edges of the parent element (see Figure 5-7).

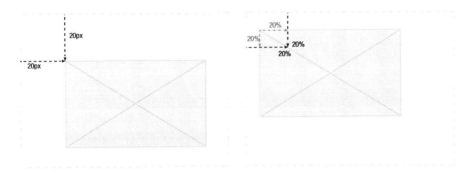

Figure 5-7. *When positioning background images using pixels, the top-left corner of the image is used. When positioning using percentages, the corresponding position on the image is used*

Keyword alignment works by replacing one or both of the x- and y-axis measurements with left, center, or right for the x axis or top, center, or bottom for the y axis. You should get into the habit of always declaring these in the order of x first, then y. This is for both consistency and readability, but also to avoid mistakes: the spec allows you to change the order if you use two keywords (like top left), but disallows this when one is a keyword and one is a length. The following would be broken:

```
.box {
  background-position: 50% left; /* don't do this */
}
```

The constraints of background positioning have been bugging designers for a long time. Consider the design in Figure 5-8: we have some text of an unknown length that has an icon image at the rightmost edge, with some whitespace around it. Using pixels or ems to position the image would be rather useless, because we don't know how far from the *left* edge the image is supposed to sit.

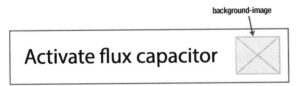

Figure 5-8. *A piece of text with an icon as a background image at the right edge*

Previously, the only solution, apart from giving the icon its own wrapper element and positioning that instead, would be to use a background image and position it 100% from the left edge and have the whitespace on the right baked into the image file itself as transparent pixels. This isn't very elegant, because it doesn't give us control over this whitespace by means of CSS. Luckily, the Level 3 Backgrounds and Borders spec has our backs!

The new syntax for `background-position` allows us to do exactly what we hoped for as just described: we can prefix each distance with the corresponding edge keyword we want to use as reference. It looks like this:

```
<p>
  <a href="/activate" class="link-with-icon">Activate flux capacitor</a>
</p>

.link-with-icon {
  padding-right: 2em;
  background-image: url(img/icon.png);
  background-repeat: no-repeat;
  background-position: right 1em top 50%;
}
```

The previous example means that we position the image 1 em from the right edge and 50% from the top. Problem solved! Sadly, this version of the syntax doesn't work in IE8 or Safari before version 7. Depending on your use case, it could work as an enhancement, but it's kind of hard to have it gracefully degrade in unsupported browsers.

Introducing Calc

We could actually achieve the same results with the example in the previous section by introducing another CSS construct with perhaps slightly wider support: the `calc()` functional notation. Using `calc` gives you a way to leave it to the browser to calculate any sort of number for you (angles, pixels, percentages, etc.). It even works with mixed units that are not known until the page is rendered! This means you could say "100% + x number of pixels," for example—very useful for any situation where something sized or positioned in percentages collides with other distances set in ems or pixels.

In the case of the "background image positioned from the right" problem we previously discussed, we could use the `calc()` notation to express the same position on the x axis:

```
.link-with-icon {
  /* other properties omitted for brevity. */
  background-position: calc(100% - 1em) 50%;
}
```

▨ **Note**   Internet Explorer 9 does support the `calc()` notation, but sadly has a serious bug when using it specifically with `background-position`, causing the browser to crash. Hence, the previous example will be mostly theoretical. The `calc()` function is useful for a lot of other situations though—element sizing, font sizing, and others.

The calc() functional notation works with the four operators for addition (+), subtraction (-), multiplication (*), and division (/). You can have several values in a calc() expression; the declaration in the following rule set would be fully valid as well:

```
.thing {
  width: calc(50% + 20px*4 - 1em);
}
```

> ▓ **Note**   When using calc(), you need spaces on both sides of an operator when using addition and subtraction. This apparently is required to more clearly distinguish the operator from any *sign* on the number, such as the length -10 px.

The calc() notation is defined in the Level 3 Values and Units specification, and it has pretty decent support. As with the "four-value" background position you saw earlier, IE8 and earlier, along with older WebKit browsers, are missing out on the fun. Some slightly older versions of WebKit-based browsers do support it but may require a prefix in the form of -webkit-calc().

Background Clip and Origin

By default, the images you use for backgrounds will be painted across the border box of the element, meaning that they will potentially cover the element all the way to the visible edge. Note that since they are painted underneath any border, a semitransparent border will potentially show on top of the image.

The background-clip property can change this behavior. The default corresponds to background-clip: border-box. Setting the value padding-box switches to clipping the image inside of the border, covering the padding box, and the value content-box clips the image inside any padding, to the content box. Figure 5-9 shows the difference.

```
.profile-box {
  border: 10px solid rgba(220, 220, 160, 0.5);
  padding: 10px;
  background-image: url(img/cat.jpg);
  background-clip: padding-box;
}
```

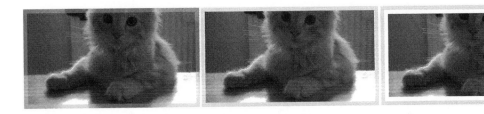

Figure 5-9. *The difference between background clipped to border-box (left), padding-box (middle), and content-box (right)*

Even if the `background-clip` value is changed, the default origin (i.e., the reference point where the image starts off being positioned) for the background position is still the top-left corner of the padding box, meaning that the positioning values start from just inside of any border on the element.

Fortunately, you can affect the origin position too, via the `background-origin` property. It accepts the same box-model-related values as `background-clip`: `border-box`, `padding-box`, or `content-box`.

Both `background-clip` and `background-origin` are part of the Level 3 Backgrounds and Borders spec mentioned earlier. They have been around for a while but still lack support in really old browsers: again, IE8 is the primary laggard, but this time even older Android browsers have implemented the properties, albeit with `-webkit-` prefixes.

Background Attachment

Backgrounds are attached to the element they are shown behind. If you scroll the page, the background scrolls with it. It is possible to change this behavior via the `background-attachment` property. If we want the background of our header image to "stick" to the page as the user scrolls down, we can use the following code:

```
.profile-box {
  background-attachment: fixed;
}
```

Figure 5-10 tries to capture the behavior of the background as the user scrolls the page: it gives the appearance of the header getting hidden behind the rest of the page, which can be a cool effect.

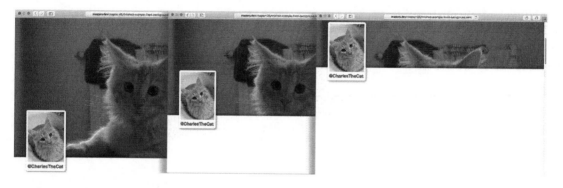

Figure 5-10. *Our profile header with a fixed background attachment*

Apart from `fixed` and the default value, `scroll`, you can set the `background-attachment` to `local`. It's hard to illustrate on paper, but the `local` value affects the attachment inside the scroll position of the element: it causes it to scroll with the element content when it has scrollbars, via setting the `overflow` property to either `auto` or `scroll` and having content tall enough to stick out of the element. If we do that on the header, the background image will scroll with the element as the page is scrolled, but also scroll along with the content as the internal scroll position changes.

The `local` value is relatively well supported across desktop browsers, but more shaky across their mobile counterparts: it's reasonable to assume that some mobile browser makers ignore this property (as well as the `fixed` value) since element scrolling is unusual and can have usability impacts on small screens with touch scrolling. Indeed, the spec also allows implementers to ignore `background-attachment` if it is deemed inappropriate on the device. Mobile browser expert Peter-Paul Koch has an article on the subject (as well as a treasure trove of other mobile browser tests) at his site QuirksMode.org (`http://www.quirksmode.org/blog/archives/2013/03/new_css_tests_c_2.html`).

Background Size

In the example in the previous section, we used a larger image to cover the profile box. This means it gets clipped when it's viewed in a smaller browser window. It might also have gaps to the side when the window gets really big. Assuming we want to prevent this and have the contents retain their aspect ratio while scaling with the page, we need to make use of the background-size property.

By setting background-size to explicit length measurements, you can either resize the background image to a new, fixed measurement or have it scale with the element.

If we still had the big file and wanted to display it smaller for some reason, we could give it new pixel measurements:

```
.profile-box {
  background-size: 400px 240px;
}
```

Getting the image to scale along with the box means we need to switch to using percentages. You could potentially set percentages for both width and height, but these percentages will not be related to the intrinsic size of the image, but the size of the container: if the height of the container changes with the content, that might distort the aspect ratio of our image.

A much more sensible way of using percentages is to use percent for one value and the keyword auto for the other. For example, if we want the image to be 100% wide (the x axis, the first value) and keep its aspect ratio (see Figure 5-11), we can use the following:

```
.profile-box {
  background-size: 100% auto;
}
```

Figure 5-11. *Setting the background size with percentages and the auto keyword allows the background to cover the width of the element, regardless of the viewport size*

Using percentages gives us some flexibility, but not for all situations. Sometimes, we may wish to make sure the background never gets cropped, and in the profile header example, we may wish to make sure the background always covers the entire area of the element. Luckily, there are some magical keywords that take care of this for us.

First off, we can use the keyword `contain` as our background size. This means that the browser will try to make the image as large as possible without distorting its aspect ratio or clipping it: it's almost like the previous example, but it automatically determines which value should be `auto` and which one should be 100% (see Figure 5-12).

```
.profile-box {
  background-size: contain;
}
```

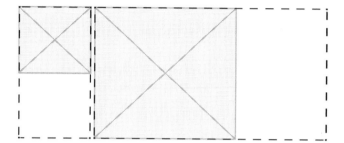

Figure 5-12. *Using the* `contain` *keyword as the background size prevents cropping*

In a tall and narrow element, a square background would be at most 100% wide but could leave vertical gaps; in a wide element, it would be at most 100% tall but leave horizontal gaps.

The second keyword value we can use is `cover`: this means that the image is sized to completely cover every pixel of the element without distorting the image. This is what we want in our profile page example. Figure 5-13 shows how a square background on a narrow but tall element would fill the height but clip the sides, and a wide element would clip the top and bottom while filling the element width, configured as follows:

```
.profile-box {
  background-size: cover;
}
```

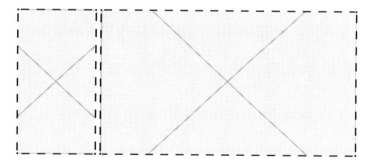

Figure 5-13. *Using the* `cover` *keyword to completely cover the surface of the element while cropping the background*

As with the properties for clip and origin, `background-size` is a relatively new background property, and support levels are similar.

Background Shorthand

As we saw in the beginning of the chapter, there is a `background` shorthand syntax for setting many of the background-related properties at the same time. In general, you can specify the different values in any order you please—the browser will figure out from the various keywords and syntaxes what you mean. There are a couple of gotchas though.

The first is that since length pairs can be used for both `background-position` and `background-size`, you need to write them together, with `background-position` first, then `background-size`, and separate them with a slash (`/`) character.

The second is the `*-box` keywords for `background-origin` and `background-clip`. The following rules apply:

- If only one `*-box` keyword is present (`border-box`, `padding-box`, or `content-box`), both values are set to the declared value.

- If two `*-box` keywords are present, the first one sets `background-origin`, and the second sets `background-clip`.

Here's an example of combining a whole bunch of the various background properties:

```
.profile-box {
 background: url(img/cat.jpg) 50% 50% / cover no-repeat padding-box content-box #bada55;
}
```

And as we said at the start of the chapter, be careful with the background shorthand: it automatically sets all the values you don't mention back to their default values. If you do use it, put the shorthand declaration first, then override specific properties as necessary. It may be tempting to use shorthands as often as possible to save a few keystrokes, but as a general rule for writing code, explicit code is often less error-prone and easier to follow than implicit code.

Multiple Backgrounds

So far, we've treated the background image as though you would always use a single image for the background. This used to be the case, but the background properties defined in the Level 3 Backgrounds and Borders spec now allow you to specify *multiple* backgrounds for a single element, with corresponding multiple values syntax for each of the properties. Multiple values are separated by commas. Here's an example, shown in Figure 5-14:

```
.multi-bg {
  background-image: url(img/spades.png), url(img/hearts.png),
                    url(img/diamonds.png), url(clubs.png);
  background-position: left top, right top, left bottom, right bottom;
  background-repeat: no-repeat, no-repeat, no-repeat, no-repeat;
  background-color: pink;
 }
```

Figure 5-14. *Multiple overlapping backgrounds on one element*

The background layers are stacked top to bottom as they are declared, the first one on top and the last one on the bottom. The color layer ends up behind all of them (see Figure 5-15).

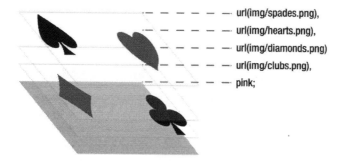

url(img/spades.png),
url(img/hearts.png),
url(img/diamonds.png)
url(img/clubs.png),
pink;

Figure 5-15. *Multiple background layers stack top to bottom, in the order declared. The color layer is always at the bottom*

You can also declare multiple background shorthand values:

```
.multi-bg-shorthand {
  background: url(img/spades.png) left top no-repeat,
              url(img/hearts.png) right top no-repeat,
              url(img/diamonds.png) left bottom no-repeat,
              url(img/clubs.png) right bottom no-repeat,
              pink;
}
```

With this syntax, you are only allowed to declare a color on the last background layer, which makes sense considering the order seen in Figure 5-15.

If any of the background properties have a list of values that is shorter than the number of background images, lists of values are cycled. This means that if the value is the same for all of them, you only need to declare it once: if it alternates between two values, you only need to declare two, etc. So the recurring no-repeat in the previous example could have been written as follows:

```
.multi-bg-shorthand {
  background: url(img/spades.png) left top,
              url(img/hearts.png) right top,
              url(img/diamonds.png) left bottom,
              url(img/clubs.png) right bottom,
```

```
            pink;
    background-repeat: no-repeat; /* goes for all four */
}
```

Since the multiple-background stuff is from the Level 3 spec, once again it's not available in some older browsers. A lot of the time, you can achieve a perfectly acceptable fallback for older browsers by using a combination of the single-value background syntax:

```
.multi-fallback {
    background-image: url(simple.jpg);
    background-image: url(modern.png), url(snazzy.png), url(wow.png);
}
```

Just like in other examples in the book, older browsers will get the simpler first image and discard the second declaration, while newer browsers will ignore the first since the second one overrides it.

Borders and Rounded Corners

We mentioned the humble border as part of the box-model properties in Chapter 3. In modern browsers, we have some further control over borders, allowing us to spice them up with images and rounded corners—so we finally get to create something other than sharp rectangles!

First a quick recap of the border properties of old:

- You can set the properties for each side of a border separately, or all of them at the same time.

- You set the width of the whole border with `border-width` or set a specific side with, e.g., `border-top-width`. Remember that the width of the border contributes to the overall size of the box, unless specifically told otherwise by the `box-sizing` property.

- Likewise, you set the color of the whole border with `border-color` or set a specific side with, e.g., `border-left-color`.

- The style of the border, `border-style` (or `border-right-style`, etc.) is set by keyword: `solid`, `dashed`, or `dotted` are pretty common ones to use. There are also some more exotic ones, like `double` (draws two parallel lines on the surface specified by `border-width`), `groove`, and `inset`, for example. To be honest, these are seldom useful: both because they look funky, and because you leave the control of how they look to the browser—it's not really specified in the standards. You can also remove the border completely by setting `border-style: none`.

- Finally, you can set all of the border properties with the `border` shorthand. The shorthand sets width, style, and color of all sides to the same value, like this: `border: 2px solid #000;`.

Border Radius: Rounded Corners

For a long time, rounded corners were at the top of the wish list for developers. We'd spend countless hours coming up with new hacks using images that were scalable and worked cross-browser. In fact, previous editions of this book described them in detail. Today, we are fortunately well past that. Just about the only browsers around that don't support the `border-radius` property are old IE versions (8 and down) and Opera Mini. The thing about rounded corners is that they are most often a nice-to-have feature and not crucial to the usability of the page, so we think it makes sense to use the standardized property instead of burdening some of the weakest browsers (in terms of performance) with even more code, to emulate something that exists in all others.

Border Radius Shorthand

This time, we'll start with the shorthand property—since it's the most common use case—making all of the corners on a box rounded.

The border-radius property allows you to set all of the corner at once by simply declaring a length value. Let's add a profile photo box to our example and make the corners rounded. First, some markup:

```
<header class="profile-box" role="banner">
  <div class="profile-photo">
    <img src="img/profile.jpg" alt="Charles the Cat">
    <h1 class="username">@CharlesTheCat</h1>
  </div>
</header>
```

Here is the added CSS to size and position our profile photo box to poke out of the bottom of the header area, as well as give it a border to stand out from the background (see the result in Figure 5-16):

```
.profile-box {
  position: relative;
  /* other properties omitted for brevity */
}

.profile-photo {
  width: 160px;
  min-height: 200px;
  position: absolute;
  bottom: -60px;
  left: 5%;
  background-color: #fff;
  border: 1px solid #777;
  border-radius: 0.5em;
}
```

Figure 5-16. Rounded corners on the profile photo component

More Complex Border-Radius Syntax

You can also use the shorthand property to set each value individually. This is done by starting with the top-left corner, then going around clockwise:

```
.box {
  border-radius: 0.5em 2em 0.5em 2em;
}
```

Each length value in this declaration is already a shorthand, since it represents the same radius on both the horizontal and vertical axes of each corner. If you want different values for these—i.e., an asymmetric corner shape—you can specify each axis as a list of values (first horizontal, then vertical) and separate the two with a slash:

```
.box {
  border-radius: 2em .5em 1em .5em / .5em 2em .5em 1em;
}
```

If values are reflected diagonally across corners, you can leave out the bottom-right and bottom-left corners; if only two or three values are present, the rest will be filled in:

```
.box {
  border-radius: 2em 3em; /* repeated for bottom right and bottom left. */
}
```

In the previous example, the first value sets the top-left and bottom-right corners, and the second sets the top-right and bottom-left corners. Had we included a third value for the bottom-right corner, the bottom-left corner would get the same value as the top-right corner.

Setting a Border Radius on a Single Corner

You can, of course, set the value for a single corner, using `border-top-left-radius`, `border-top-right-radius`, etc.

You supply these single-corner properties with the same length(s) for the radius as in the previous shorthand examples: either one length value, that creates a symmetric corner, or two length values separated by a slash, where the first sets the horizontal radius and the second sets the vertical radius.

Here's the code for a single symmetrical rounded corner as applied to our profile photo box, as seen in Figure 5-17:

```
.profile-photo {
  border-top-left-radius: 1em;
}
```

Figure 5-17. *A version of our profile photo box with only the top-left corner rounded*

Creating Circles and Pill Shapes with Border Radius

So far, we've been talking about setting the radius using a length value, but you can also use percentages. When you set the border-radius in percentages, the x radius relates to the width and the y radius relates to the height of the element. This means we can easily create circular shapes by taking a square element, and then setting its border radius to at least 50%.

Why "at least"? Well, there's really no reason you should set a value higher than 50% for all corners, but it might be useful to know that when two corner curves start overlapping, both axes are decreased until they don't anymore. For symmetric corners on a square, any value higher than 50% will always yield a circle (see Figure 5-18). Note that a *rectangular* element with the same border radius would become an oval, as the radius is decreased proportional to the size in that direction:

```
<div class="round"></div>
<div class="round oval"></div>

.round {
  width: 300px;
  height: 300px;
  border-radius: 50%;
  background-color: #59f;
}
.oval {
  width: 600px;
}
```

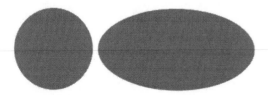

Figure 5-18. *A circle and an oval from using border-radius: 50%*

Circles are often desired, but ovals not so much. Sometimes, we want a "pill shape"—a rectangular oblong element with semicircle. The technical term for this shape (shown in Figure 5-19) is an *obrund*. Percentages or exact length measurements won't help us create such a shape, unless we know the exact measurements of the element, which is rarely the case in web design.

Figure 5-19. *Using a large* border-radius *to create pill shapes*

We can, however, use a quirk of border-radius calculation to create this shape. We saw that the radius is decreased when it no longer fits. But when it's set set to a length (*not* a percentage), the radii don't relate to the size of the element, and they end up being symmetric instead. So to create the semicircle edges of an obrund, we can cheat and use a length that we know is *longer* than the radius needed to create a half-circle edge, and the shape will create itself:

```
.obrund {
  border-radius: 999em; /* arbitrarily very large length */
}
```

As a final note on border radii, you should be aware of how they affect the shape of the element on the page. We've finally found a way to create something other than rectangles, but alas: they will still behave as if they were a rectangle covering the original surface of the box, in terms of layout. One thing that *has* changed in terms of how the shape of the element is interpreted is that the clickable (or "touchable") surface of an element follows the corner shape. Keep this in mind when creating rounded corner buttons, links, etc., so that the clickable surface doesn't become too small.

Border Images

The Level 3 Backgrounds and Borders spec also allows you to define a single image to act as the border of an element. What good is a single image, you may ask? The beauty of the border-image property is that it allows you to slice up that image into nine separate sectors, based on rules for where to "cut," and the browser will automatically use the correct sector for the corresponding part of the border. Known as nine-slice scaling, this technique helps avoid the distortion you'd normally get when resizing images to cover boxes. It's a little difficult to visualize, so an example is in order.

The canonical example of using a border image is perhaps to create something like a picture frame for an element. The source for the picture frame is a square image with a 120-pixel side length. If you draw lines 40 pixels from the top, right, bottom, and left edges of the box, you will have divided the box up into nine sectors (see Figure 5-20).

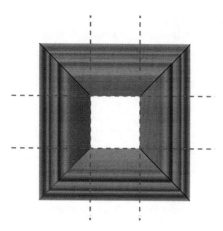

Figure 5-20. *The source file for our border image, with the division points drawn on top for illustration purposes*

The border-image property will automatically use the images in each sector as a background for the corresponding border part. The image slice in the top-left corner will be used as the image for that corner, the slice in the top-middle bit will be used for the top border, the slice in the top-right corner for that respective corner, and so on. The slice in the center is by default discarded, but you can change this behavior as well.

You can also tell the browser how to treat the top, right, bottom, and left bits when it comes to covering the border. They can be stretched, repeated, or spaced, rounding the number of whole repetitions that are shown: it works much like the newer background-repeat keywords. By default, the middle slices on each side are stretched, which works well for our purposes.

In order to show the border images, the border width also needs to be set—the measurements will stretch each slice according to the border width for that particular segment.

Applying this graphic as a border image, we can create something like the "motto" we see in Figure 5-21.

Figure 5-21. *Border images stretched to fit the element*

Here's how the CSS for this component looks:

```
.motto {
  border-width: 40px solid #f9b256;
  border-image: url(picture-frame.png) 40;
  /* ...same as border-image: url(picture-frame.png) 40 40 40 40 stretch; */
}
```

The preceding code will load the image picture-frame.png, slice it 40 pixels from each of the four edges, and stretch the middle slices on the top, right, bottom, and left sides. Note that the "20 pixels" measurement for the slicing guides is given without the px unit; this is a quirk having to do with differences between vector images (SVG) and bitmap images.

Another thing worth mentioning about the preceding example is that you need to put the `border` shorthand (if used) before the `border-image` property. The spec demands that the shorthand resets *all* border properties, not just the ones it sets by itself.

As you'd expect, there are specific border image properties to set each value separately. In fact, there's a whole heap of values that allows you to control how border images work. The thing is that we could probably count the number of times we've used `border-image` during our careers on one hand, so we won't go into more detail here.

Border image support *was* high on the wish list for many web designers a few years back, mostly because it would make it easy to create rounded corners without hacks. Now that we have `border-radius`, that need is a lot less acute. Of course, depending on the design of your project, border images might be a good fit—it's easy to see how a grungier aesthetic might benefit from bitmap images as borders, for example.

If you want to dive deeper into the intricacies of border image properties, check out Nora Brown's article on CSS Tricks: `http://css-tricks.com/understanding-border-image/`. Support for the `border-image` property is fairly broad—mostly, it's Internet Explorer 10 and earlier that is missing support. Sadly, there are quite a few bugs and quirks present even in supporting browsers.

Box-Shadow

Leaving background images and borders aside for now, we'll explore another way to add visual effects to your page: shadows. It used to be that designers had to jump through hoops to add shadows to their designs, using extra elements and images. Not any more!

CSS lets you add shadows using the `box-shadow` property. It's very well supported. In fact, pretty much only really old versions of IE (version 8 and earlier) and Opera Mini are missing out. To support older Android WebKit browsers (and some other ancient WebKit versions), you need the `-webkit-` prefix. Firefox (and other Mozilla-based browsers) has had unprefixed support for long enough to safely skip the `-moz-` prefix.

You've already seen the syntax for `text-shadow` in the previous chapter: `box-shadow` has a very similar syntax, but adds some extra goodies.

Let's add a shadow to the profile photo box to illustrate, using the following markup and CSS (Figure 5-22 shows the result):

```
.profile-photo {
  box-shadow: .25em .25em .5em rgba(0, 0, 0, 0.3);
}
```

Figure 5-22. A profile image box with a subtle shadow added

The syntax in this example is exactly the same as the text-shadow version: two values for x and y offsets, then a blur radius value (how much the edge of the shadow blurs), and finally a color, using rgba(). Note how the shadow also follows the corner shape of the rounded box!

Spread Radius: Adjusting the Size of the Shadow

The box-shadow property is a bit more flexible than text-shadow. For example, you can add a value after the blur radius that specifies a *spread radius*: how large the shadow should be. The default value is 0, meaning the same size as the element it's applied to. Increasing this value makes the shadow bigger, and negative values make the shadow smaller (see Figure 5-23).

```
.larger-shadow {
  box-shadow: 1em 1em .5em .5em rgba(0, 0, 0, 0.3);
}
.smaller-shadow {
  box-shadow: 1em 1em .5em -.5em rgba(0, 0, 0, 0.3);
}
```

Figure 5-23. *A box shown with different values of spread radius*

Inset Shadows

Another extra box-shadow feature that makes it more flexible than text-shadow is the inset keyword. Applying an inset shadow means that the element is assumed to be the surface that the shadow is cast on, creating the effect of it being "knocked out" of the background. For example, we could use the inset shadow effect to make it look like the background of our profile header is a little bit sunken into the page, behind the profile photo and the rest of the content. We'll add the following to the profile box ruleset (see Figure 5-24):

```
.profile-box {
  box-shadow: inset 0 -.5em .5em rgba(0, 0, 0, 0.3);
}
```

Figure 5-24. *Detail of the profile header component, showing an inset box shadow on the bottom edge of the large background*

Multiple Shadows

Just like with `text-shadow`, you can apply multiple shadows to a single element, separating the different values with commas. We'll look at an example of how this would work combining it with a "flat" shadow technique and removing the blur radius completely.

If you leave out the blur radius or set it to 0, you'll end up with a shadow that has a completely sharp edge. This can be beneficial as it allows you to step away from the mental model of pseudo-realistic shadows and start considering them more as generated "extra boxes" behind the element they're applied to that don't affect the layout—very handy for all sorts of effects.

One useful example is to create multiple "fake borders" on an element. The `border` property only allows you to draw one border (except the weird `double` keyword, but that doesn't count). Using shadows with a 0 blur radius and a different spread radius, you can create several border-like fields (see Figure 5-25). Since they don't affect layout, they act more like the `outline` property.

```
.profile-photo {
  box-shadow: 0 0 0 10px #1C318D,
              0 0 0 20px #3955C7,
              0 0 0 30px #546DC7,
              0 0 0 40px #7284D8;
}
```

Figure 5-25. *Using multiple shadows and the spread radius to draw fake outlines*

Using CSS Gradients

A common use case in designs is to have color gradients as backgrounds for elements, adding a subtle sense of depth to the page. Loading image files containing the gradients works fine, but CSS also has a mechanism to draw gradient images for you. This is done with the various flavors of gradient functional notation, in combination with any property that accepts images, including background-image. Let's say we have a profile page where the user hasn't uploaded a background image yet (see Figure 5-26), and we want to show a gradient background as a default:

```
.profile-box {
  background-image: linear-gradient(to bottom, #cfdeee 0%, #8da9cf 100%);
}
```

Figure 5-26. A linear gradient applied to the profile box background

As gradient images created with CSS have no specific size, this gradient will initially cover the entire element unless you specifically give it measurements using `background-size`.

Browser Support and Browser Prefixes

Gradients are supported in most modern browsers. Internet Explorer 9 (and earlier) and Opera Mini are the most notable exceptions. Some slightly older WebKit-based browsers only have support for the linear gradient versions. In the coming sections, we'll see that there's more than one type of gradient.

■ **Note**   The syntax for CSS gradients has changed several times over the years since they were first introduced as a nonstandard property in Safari. There are three different syntaxes, and depending on the level of browser support you need, you might need to use several versions at once, with various vendor prefixes. In the interest of keeping this section manageable and not too confusing, we'll go through them with the latest unprefixed syntax. You can read up on the various syntaxes in this article: `http://www.sitepoint.com/using-unprefixed-css3-gradients-in-modern-browsers/`.

Linear Gradients

The previous example uses the `linear-gradient()` function to draw a gradient along a hypothetical line going from the top to the bottom of the element. The angle of this line, in this case a keyword pair (`to bottom`), is the first argument of the function, followed by a comma-separated list of color stops. The color stops define points along the gradient line where the color changes, and in this case we start with a lighter blue-gray at 0% and end with a darker shade of blue at 100%, meaning the bottom of the element.

We can specify the direction by using the to keyword, followed by a side (top, right, bottom, left) or a corner (top left, bottom right, etc.), the latter making the gradient diagonal. It starts from the opposite corner or side, and the gradient line always goes through the center of the image area. We could also use an angle, written in the deg unit, where 0 degrees means up/north and then increasing clockwise up until 360 degrees, just like the HSL color wheel. In that case, the degree means which direction the gradient is drawn in, so it still starts opposite of the direction we're pointing at. Here's a gradient running at 45 degrees:

```
.profile-box {
  background-image: linear-gradient(45deg, #cfdfee, #4164aa);
}
```

Here the gradient line does not start at the edge of the background image area. Instead, it is automatically scaled so that any colors at 0% and 100% coincide with the corners of the image. Figure 5-27 explains how this works.

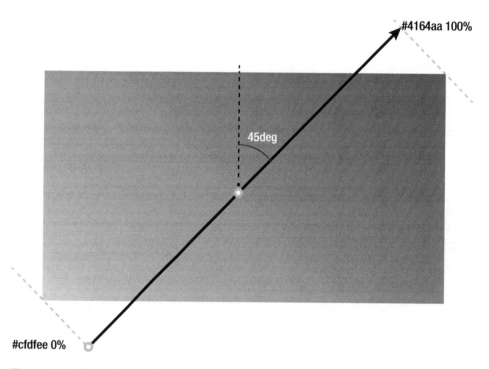

Figure 5-27. *The position and scale of the gradient line in a diagonal gradient*

Defaults and Color Stop Positions

Since going from top to bottom (180deg) is the default, and 0% and 100% are implicit for the first and last color stops, respectively, we could actually shorten our first example (refer to Figure 5-26) like this:

```
.profile-box {
  background-image: linear-gradient(#cfdfee, #8da9cf);
}
```

Any additional color stops without specified positions would end up proportionately spaced in between 0% and 100%—if there were five colors, they would be at 0%, 25%, 50%, 75%, and 100%:

```
.profile-box {
  background-image: linear-gradient(red, green, blue, yellow, purple);
}
```

We can use other measurements than percentages for the color stops, giving us further control over how the gradient is drawn:

```
.profile-box {
  background-image: linear-gradient(#cfdfee, #8da9cf 100px);
}
```

This would draw a gradient that starts light blue at the top, then shifts to the darker blue over 100 pixels, and then stays that color until the bottom edge of the background image area.

Radial Gradients

You can also use radial gradients to create color shifts that happen along a hypothetical *gradient ray*, extending outward in all directions from a central point, in the shape of a circle or an ellipse.

The syntax for radial gradients is a little more involved. You can specify the following properties:

- Which type of shape: circle or ellipse.

- The radius of the gradient ray, determining the size of the gradient area. Circles only accept one size measurement (for the radius), while ellipses accept two for the radius on the x axis and y axis, respectively. Ellipses can use any length or a percentage, where the percentage is relative to the background image size in that axis. Circles only accept lengths, not percentages. There are also keywords representing where the edge of the gradient area ends, so that either the gradient can extend to fit *within* the farthest or closest side from the center (closest-side and farthest-side) or the edge of the gradient shape touches the closest or farthest corner of the image area (closest-corner or farthest-corner).

- The position of the center of the shape using positional values much like the background-position property. These values are preceded by the at keyword, to differentiate them from the size.

- Color stops (as many as you like) along the way as the shape expands, comma-separated.

An example could look like this:

```
.profile-box {
  background-image: radial-gradient(circle closest-corner at 20% 30%, #cfdfee, #2c56a1);
}
```

This would give us a circular radial gradient with its center located at 20% on the x axis and 30% on the y axis, extending so that the circumference of the circle touches the closest corner. Outside of the circle, the final color-stop color continues to cover the whole background image area (see Figure 5-28).

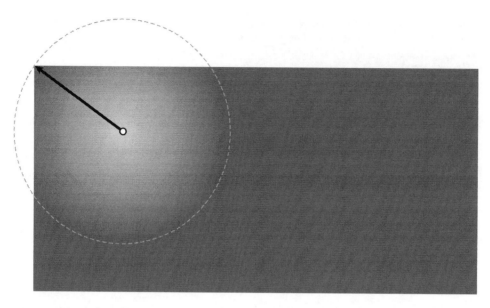

Figure 5-28. *Our profile page header with a circular radial gradient, positioned at 20% 30% and sized to expand to the closest corner*

Considering our profile box example shape, we might want a centered radial gradient, with an elliptical shape. Let's try something a bit more psychedelic (see Figure 5-29):

```
.profile-box {
  background-image: radial-gradient(#cfdfee, #2c56a1, #cfdfee, #2c56a1, #cfdfee, #2c56a1);
}
```

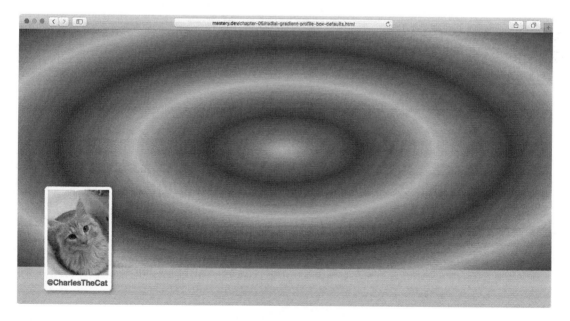

Figure 5-29. *Several repeated color stops in a radial gradient*

We've actually left off the part declaring it an ellipse that is centered and covers the whole element (by extending to the farthest corner); all those properties are covered by the default values in this case. But it seems a bit tedious to repeat those color stops like that, doesn't it? That's where repeating gradients come in.

Repeating Gradients

At some point along the line (or ray) in which they expand and shift colors, normal gradients stop at a final color. There are also repeating gradient functions, both linear and radial (see Figure 5-30), that repeat the sequence of color stops for as long as their size allows (via either the `background-size` property or the element size). For example, here's a repeating linear gradient:

```
.linear-repeat {
  background-image: repeating-linear-gradient(#cfdfee, #2c56a1 20px);
}
```

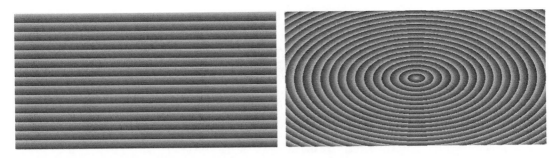

Figure 5-30. *Repeating gradient functions repeat the list of color stops across the entire background image area*

And here's a repeating radial gradient:

```
.radial-repeat {
  background-image: repeating-radial-gradient(#cfdfee, #2c56a1 20px);
}
```

Gradients as Patterns

Gradients don't necessarily need to be smooth transitions over several pixels. They could just as well change from one pixel to the next, allowing us to create more crisp lines and circles. Combining this with the ability to layer multiple background images on top of each other gives us a tool to declaratively create simple background image patterns, without needing to ever open image editing software!

The trick to creating crisp patterns is to position the color stops the right way. For example, to draw a simple vertical line, we'll need to put the adjacent color stops right up next to each other, so there is no space where the color shifts gradually (see Figure 5-31):

```
body {
    background-color: #fff;
    background-image: linear-gradient(
        transparent,
```

```
        transparent 50%,
        rgba(55, 110, 176, 0.3) 50%
      );
    background-size: 40px 40px;
  }
```

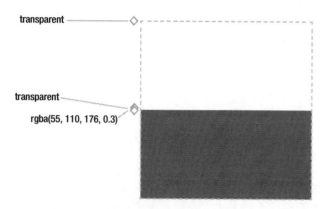

transparent

transparent

rgba(55, 110, 176, 0.3)

Figure 5-31. *The second and third color stops are both positioned at 50%, creating a sharp shift between colors*

Depending on the browser, you might see that it doesn't manage to get the line perfectly crisp, but actually fades over 1 px to either side. This will likely be improved as browsers get better at rendering gradients, but it should be good enough for more subtle patterns.

Rather than using a repeating linear gradient across the whole element, we have used a single gradient, and then sized and repeated the resulting image with the background properties. This lets us control the scale of the line without affecting the color stops. By adding another gradient image, this time running horizontally, we can build a "table-cloth" pattern (see Figure 5-32):

```
body {
    margin: 0;
    background-color: #fff;
    background-image: linear-gradient(
        transparent,
        transparent 50%,
        rgba(55, 110, 176, 0.3) 50%
      ),
    linear-gradient(
        to right,
        transparent,
        transparent 50%,
        rgba(55, 110, 176, 0.3) 50%
      );
    background-size: 40px 40px;
  }
```

Figure 5-32. Drawing a background pattern with two linear gradient lines

It's not a huge step to imagine the wealth of shapes you could conjure up using (overlapping) multiples of the basic shapes of lines, triangles (half-filled diagonal linear gradients), circles, and ellipses.

A great source of inspiration is Lea Verou's CSS3 Patterns Gallery at `http://lea.verou.me/css3patterns/` (see Figure 5-33).

Figure 5-33. Lea Verou's CSS3 Patterns Gallery

135

Drawing with CSS

Combining gradient patterns with box shadows and pseudo-elements gives you plenty of opportunities for creative effects *without loading a single image*. Another inspiring resource is "A Single Div" (http://a.singlediv.com), a project from artist and designer Lynn Fisher. It is a collection of illustrations done in CSS, where each piece only requires a single element in the markup, and no images (see Figure 5-34).

Figure 5-34. *Illustrations from "A Single Div"*

Just remember that at some point, the code for these CSS drawings may become less understandable and maintainable than just creating an SVG (or PNG) image file and using that instead. It's also worth keeping in mind that even though gradients avoid loading an external image resource, they can have quite the performance impact themselves—particularly on resource-constrained devices like phones. Radial gradients especially are worth keeping to a minimum.

Styling Embedded Images and other Objects

When styling images in the flow of a document, you are dealing with content that is different from the other boxes that make up your page. This is becasue images can have an inherent width and height in pixels, a set aspect ratio that needs to be respected, or both. In a flexible design, where the content depends on the width of the browser window, you need to use CSS to tame images and other embedded objects.

▓ **Note**   Loading a different image for the current rendered size—known as *responsive images*—is a hugely important topic for performance, but one we're leaving aside for now. We'll come back to it Chapter 8, on responsive techniques.

The Flexible Image Pattern

Making images flexible without either displaying them larger than their inherent dimensions or distorting the aspect ratio can be achieved using a technique originally made famous by Richard Rutter (http://clagnut.com/blog/268/). At its core, you only need the following rule:

```
img {
  max-width: 100%;
}
```

The max-width property as applied to images means that the image will shrink to respect the boundaries of the container it is placed in, but it will not grow *outside of its intrinsic size* if the container is wider (see Figure 5-35).

Figure 5-35. *A bitmap image that is 320 pixels wide with* max-width: *100% shown at a container width of 100 pixels vs. a container width of 500 pixels*

We can augment this rule to cover a few more bases by extending it to the following:

```
img {
  width: auto;
  max-width: 100%;
  height: auto;
}
```

Why the extra rules? Well, sometimes markup authors or content management systems put width and height attributes with the image dimensions in the HTML source.

Setting width and height to auto is there partly to override these attributes, but also to counter a bug in IE8 where images without a declared width attribute will sometimes not scale correctly.

New Object-Sizing Methods

Sometimes, you end up wanting to apply sizes to img elements and other embedded objects (like video or object elements) that have a different aspect ratio to the media that is being displayed inside them. For example, you may have a rectangular image file as a user avatar placeholder (see Figure 5-36), but you want to use CSS to display it as a square.

Figure 5-36. *A rectangular user avatar image*

Some new magic properties and keywords that have recently been standardized and are making their way into browsers allow you to size and position the *content* of these types of elements in a more flexible way. Using the property object-fit, we can size the contents of the image much like with the newer background-size keywords, preserving the aspect ratio:

```
img {
  width: 200px;
  height: 200px;
}
img.contain {
  object-fit: contain;
}
img.cover {
  object-fit: cover;
}
img.none {
  object-fit: none;
}
img.scaledown {
  object-fit: scale-down;
}
```

Figure 5-37 illustrates the difference between these keywords, when displaying an image at a set size that isn't matched by the intrinsic dimensions.

Figure 5-37. *Examples of a fixed-size image with contents sized using different keywords of the object-fit property*

The default behavior for object-fit is fill, meaning that the contents of the image will stretch with the element dimensions, which may cause the aspect ratio to distort.

The cover and contain keywords work the same as their counterparts in the background-size property. When using none, the exact dimensions of the original image are used, regardless of the size of the element. Finally, there's scale-down, which chooses automatically between none and contain, picking the smallest resulting dimensions. The resulting image is centered, but can be positioned using object-position, in a similar way that you would position a background image.

So far, support is limited to recent versions of Chrome, Opera, Safari, and Firefox, although Safari does not support object-position at the time of writing. No versions of IE or Edge support this behavior, although Edge is likely to follow the rest and support these properties soon.

Aspect-Ratio Aware Flexible Containers

For bitmap images, as we saw in previous sections, the aspect ratio is built-in: they have a set width and height, and as long as you set the height to auto and only change the width (or vice versa), things will still look right.

But what happens if the element you're styling doesn't have an intrinsic aspect ratio, and you want to give it one, while still keeping it flexible and resizable?

This is the case with iframe and object elements and, to a certain extent, SVG content. One common example is the markup you get when embedding videos from sites like YouTube or Vimeo into a page:

```
<iframe width="420" height="315" src="https://www.youtube.com/embed/dQw4w9WgXcQ"
frameborder="0" allowfullscreen></iframe>
```

If we set a flexible width like this:

```
iframe {
  width: 100%; /* or any other percentage, really…*/
}
```

…that would result in an iframe that is 100% wide, but still 315 pixels high because of the height attribute. Since the video has a set aspect ratio, we want the height to adjust automatically.

Setting an auto height or removing the attribute wouldn't work since the iframe doesn't have an intrinsic height—it would most likely become 150 pixels tall instead. Why 150 pixels? Well, the CSS specs dictate that replaced content (such as iframes, images, object elements, etc.) that doesn't have a specified nor intrinsic size fall back to a measurement of 300 pixels wide and/or 150 pixels tall. Weird but true.

To get around this, we need to apply some clever CSS trickery. First, we put the iframe in a wrapper element:

```
<div class="object-wrapper">
    <iframe width="420" height="315" src="https:////www.youtube.com/embed/dQw4w9WgXcQ"
frameborder="0" allowfullscreen></iframe>
</div>
```

Then, we make the wrapper box have a size that is the same aspect ratio as the object we want to embed. To figure this out, we take the original height (315 pixels) and divide it by the original width (which is 420 pixels) to get a resulting ratio: 315/420 = 0.75. So the height is 75% of the width.

Next, we set the height of the wrapper to 0, but set the padding-bottom to the number we arrived at—75%:

```
.object-wrapper {
  width: 100%;
  height: 0;
  padding-bottom: 75%;
}
```

You might remember from Chapter 3 that when vertical padding and margins are set in percentages, they actually refer to the *width of the containing block*—in this case, the width is 100% (same as the containing block), so the padding is 75%. We have now created a block with a set aspect ratio.

Finally, we position the embedded object inside the wrapper. Even if the wrapper has a height of 0, we can use absolute positioning to place elements inside the "aspect ratio–aware" padding box:

```
.object-wrapper {
  width: 100%;
  height: 0;
  position: relative;
  padding-bottom: 75%;
}
.object-wrapper iframe {
  position: absolute;
  top: 0;
  right: 0;
  bottom: 0;
  left: 0;
}
```

That's it! Now we have a way to embed flexible objects into our pages, as well as create other aspect ratio–preserving elements. Figure 5-38 shows the process.

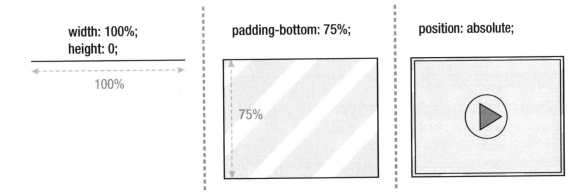

Figure 5-38. *Creating an aspect ratio–aware container*

One caveat exists: if we wanted the wrapper to be anything other than 100% wide, we would have to recalculate the padding-bottom measurement. Therefore, it might be a good idea to use yet another wrapper to achieve further flexibility; we can then size the outer wrapper as wide as we like, set the inner wrapper to be 100% wide, and be done with it.

This technique was spearheaded by developer Thierry Koblentz, and you can read an in-depth explanation of it at http://alistapart.com/article/creating-intrinsic-ratios-for-video.

Reducing Image File Sizes

When you use images as part of your design, you need to make sure you don't send unnecessarily large images to your users. Sure, you can use CSS to scale and crop them, but every unnecessary pixel incurs a performance penalty. Downloads taking too long, batteries draining, and processors wasting time resizing images are all enemies of a good user experience.

The first step to reducing unnecessary file sizes is to optimize your images. Image files often include loads of metadata that browsers don't really need to display the images properly, and there are programs and services that can help you strip that stuff away from the file. Addy Osmani has a nice roundup at https://addyosmani.com/blog/image-optimization-tools/. Many of the tools he mentions are part of automated task-runners—we will return to look at these kinds of workflows in Chapter 12.

If you're working with PNG images for simpler graphics, you might also get huge reductions in file sizes by reducing the number of colors in the image. If you're using alpha transparency in your images, most image editing software will only let you export it in the PNG24 format. The fact is that even the simpler (and much smaller) PNG8 format can contain alpha transparency, so you can get even more gains by converting your graphics to that. There are web-based services like https://tinypng.com that help you convert PNG files online, as well as several stand-alone apps for all operating systems. Some professional image editing programs like Photoshop have this functionality built-in in more recent versions.

If you're using SVG graphics, you should know that most image editors that handle SVG export files that have lots of unnecessary data in them. One very useful tool for optimizing SVG is Jake Archibald's OMGSVG (https://jakearchibald.github.io/svgomg/)—an online tool that lets you tweak a range of parameters to make your files more lean, and it even works offline!

We'll dive further into the techniques for analyzing and debugging performance in Chapter 12.

Summary

In this chapter, we've looked at a whole lot of techniques for styling the boxes that make up a page. We explored how to use the various color syntaxes, and how to use transparency. We've looked at how to master background images and how to position, size, repeat, and crop them in relation to the element box.

We've also shown you how to use borders, and how to break out of the boxy defaults by using border-radius to create rounded corners, and even circles.

We had a go at using shadows, both as a means to create depth in a page (as inset or outset shadows on a box) and as a means to draw "extra rectangles" to create other visual effects. Furthermore, we looked at how to use linear and radial gradients, both as subtle effects and as a way to make the browser draw image patterns for you.

We went through the differences between content images and background images, and how to style your content images flexibly—as well as other embedded content, including aspect ratio–aware containers.

We will come back to some more advanced (but less broadly supported) visual effects in Chapter 11. Meanwhile, in the next chapter, we'll finally combine our knowledge of sizing, styling, and positioning boxes and text into doing proper layout for the Web, using both old and new techniques and properties.

CHAPTER 6

■ ■ ■

Content Layout

A web page, at the most basic level, is made up of different blocks of content: headings, paragraphs, links, lists, images, videos, etc. These elements can be grouped together thematically; a headline, some text, and an image making up a news story. By controlling the position, size, order, and spacing of the items inside each component, we can better convey their function and meaning.

This content is often further grouped into the layout of the page as a whole. We are going to look at how we can systematically lay out whole pages in the next chapter. In this chapter, we're going to stay zoomed in on the individual content blocks and how to lay them out.

We have already briefly touched on using positioning and floats for layout, and they both have strengths and weaknesses. You can also coax other properties like table display modes and inline blocks to play their part in layout, with their own pros and cons. The new *Flexible Box Layout Module*—or *flexbox* for short—provides a whole host of properties to control ordering, orientation, alignment, and sizing. Flexbox is a powerful tool, and we'll cover it in detail.

In this chapter, we'll look at the following:

- Common use cases for absolute vs. relative positioning, and z-index

- Using floats, inline blocks, and table display for layout purposes

- Mastering vertical alignment and vertical centering

- Orientation, alignment, ordering, and sizing with flexbox

Using Positioning

In Chapter 3, we suggested that positioning is not the best tool for high-level layout, as it takes elements out of the flow of the page. On the flipside, this is what makes positioning an important part of CSS. In this section, we'll briefly examine some scenarios where positioning can be a useful tool.

As a quick recap from Chapter 3:

- Elements are initially positioned as *static*, meaning that block-level elements stack up vertically.

- We can give elements *relative* positioning, allowing us to nudge them around relative to their original position without altering the flow of elements around them. Doing so also creates a new positioning context for descendant elements. That last fact is what makes relative positioning really useful. Historically, the ability to nudge elements around was an important ingredient in many old-school layout hacks, but these days we can often get by without them.

© Andy Budd and Emil Björklund 2016
A. Budd and E. Björklund, *CSS Mastery*, DOI 10.1007/978-1-4302-5864-3_6

- *Absolute* positioning allows us to give an element an exact position with regard to the nearest positioning context, which is either an ancestor with a positioning other than static, or the html element. In this model, elements are lifted out of the page flow, and put back relative to their positioning context. By default, they end up where they originally should have ended up were they static, but without affecting the surrounding elements. We can then choose to change their position, relative to the positioning context.

- *Fixed* positioning is basically the same as absolute, but the positioning context is automatically set to the browser viewport.

Absolute Positioning Use Cases

The very nature of absolute positioning makes it an ideal candidate for creating things like overlays, tooltips, and dialog boxes that sit on top of other content. Their position can be given with the top, right, bottom, and left properties. There are a couple of things that are good to know about absolute positioning that can help you write more efficient code.

Using the Initial Position

For this example, we're using an article about spaceships, where we want to introduce some sort of inline comments. We want to display them as small comment bubbles in the margins, as shown in Figure 6-1.

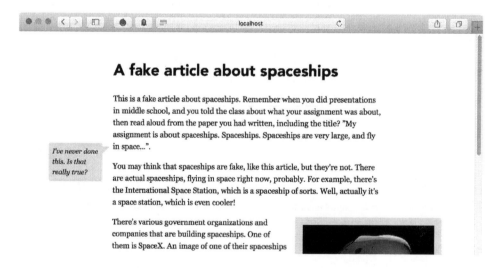

Figure 6-1. *Showing in-page comments next to the article*

Each comment is an aside element sitting after the paragraph the comment refers to:

```
<p>This is a fake article[...]</p>
<aside class="comment"> I've never done this. Is that really true?</aside>
<p>You may think[...]</p>
```

To get the comment to display right at the end of the paragraph it is referring to, we need to position it absolutely. The trick is that we *don't* have to give it an exact offset from the top of the article container to position it correctly in the vertical direction.

Absolutely positioned elements will retain the position they would have as static elements when offsets from the positioning context are left undefined, so the first step is to just leave the comment where it is (see Figure 6-2):

```
.comment {
 position: absolute;
}
```

then read aloud from the paper you had written, including the title? "My assignment is about spaceships. Spaceships. Spaceships are very large, and fly in space...".

I've never done this. Is that really true? ke, like this article, but they're not. There are actual spaceships, flying in space right now, probably. For example, there's the International Space Station, which is a spaceship of sorts. Well, actually it's

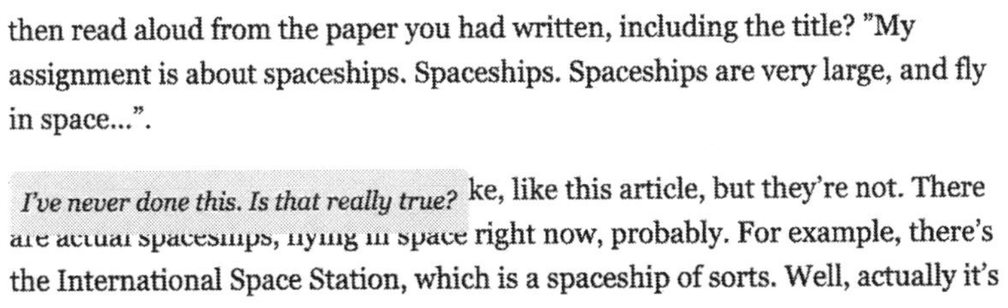

Figure 6-2. *Applying absolute positioning to the comment lifts it out of the flow, but by default leaves it in the place where it would originally have ended up with a static position*

Now we need to shift the comment up and to the left, so that it sits in the space next to the end of the preceding paragraph. This nudging sounds like a job for relative positioning, but we can't have an element be absolutely positioned and relatively positioned at the same time. If we would use directional offsets (top, right, left, and bottom) to position it, we would be dependent on both the parent positioning context and the exact size of surrounding elements. Luckily, we don't have to! Instead, we can use negative margins to nudge the element:

```
.comment {
  position: absolute;
  width: 7em;
  margin-left: -9.5em;
  margin-top: -2.5em;
}
```

Negative margins are completely valid in CSS, and have some interesting behaviors:

- A negative margin to the left or top will pull the element in that direction, overlapping any elements next to it.

- A negative right or bottom margin will pull in any adjacent elements so that they overlap the element with the negative margin.

- On a floated element, a negative margin opposite the float direction will decrease the float area, causing adjacent elements to overlap the floated element. A negative margin in the direction of the float will pull the floated element in that direction.

- Finally, the behavior of negative margins to the sides is slightly moderated when used on a nonfloating element without a defined width. In that case, negative margins to the left and right sides both pull the element in that direction. This *expands* the element, potentially overlapping any adjacent elements.

In the case of our comment bubble, we use negative margins to the left and top to pull the element into place, much like if we were using relative positioning.

Bonus: Creating Triangles in CSS

In the comment bubble shown in Figure 6-1, the little triangle shape pointing to the previous paragraph is in turn absolutely positioned relative to the comment bubble. It is created as a pseudo-element, and given a triangular shape using an old clever trick with borders. (It goes back at least as far as 2001—see this page from Tantek Çelik: http://tantek.com/CSS/Examples/polygons.html.) Figure 6-3 shows how it works.

```
.comment:after {
  position: absolute;
  content: '';
  display: block;
  width: 0;
  height: 0;
  border: .5em solid #dcf0ff;
  border-bottom-color: transparent;
  border-right-color: transparent;
  position: absolute;
  right: -1em;
  top: .5em;
}
```

0 × 0 px element

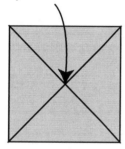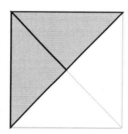

Figure 6-3. *Creating an arrowhead with a zero-size element and borders. As the right and bottom edges are made transparent, a triangle shape is left*

Here we are creating a 0 × 0–pixel block that has a .5 em border—but only the top and right border edges have any color, so we end up with a triangle, since the border edges of the corners are rendered with a slant. A handy way to generate triangles without images! We then position the triangle so it sticks out of the top right of the comment box (see Figure 6-4).

assignment is about s]

in space...".

I've never done this. Is that really true?

You may think that sp are actual spaceships,

Figure 6-4. *Positioning the triangle in relation to the contents of the comment*

Automatic Sizing Using Offsets

At the other end of the scale, it helps to know how elements react when they are absolutely positioned with many or all of the offsets declared. Without any declared *size*, the absolutely positioned element will fall back to the size needed to contain the contents within it. When we declare offsets from opposing sides of the positioning context, the element will stretch to accommodate the size it needs to fulfill these rules.

For example, we could have a situation where we want to size something at a set distance from the edges of another element, but without using a specific size on either element. For example, we might have a box with text in it on top of an image, as shown in Figure 6-5.

```
<header class="photo-header">
  <img src="images/big_spaceship.jpg" alt="An artist's mockup of the "Dragon" spaceship">
  <div class="photo-header-plate">
    <h1>SpaceX unveil the Crew Dragon</h1>
    <p>Photo from SpaceX on <a href="https://www.flickr.com/photos/spacexphotos/16787988882/">
    Flickr</a></p>
  </div>
</header>
```

Figure 6-5. *The semitransparent box on top of the image is absolutely positioned relative to the right, bottom, and left sides. The distance to the top is decided by the content*

Assuming we don't want the semitransparent "plate" holding the heading to take up a specific width, we can instead position it from the right, bottom, and left sides and let it figure out its measurements as well as the top edge position by itself:

```
.photo-header {
  position: relative;
}
.photo-header-plate {
  position: absolute;
  right: 4em;
  bottom: 4em;
  left: 4em;
  background-color: #fff;
  background-color: rgba(255,255,255,0.7);
  padding: 2em;
}
```

Regardless of the dimensions of the image, the plate will now sit at the bottom of the image at 4 ems from the bottom and sides. This gives us something that works nicely at different screen sizes—the top edge of the plate will adjust to the content height if there are line breaks (see Figure 6-6).

Figure 6-6. *At a smaller screen size, the text will wrap as the box grows upward*

Positioning and z-index: Stacking Context Pitfalls

One final component of using positioning in a smart way is to have a good grip on z-index: the stacking order of elements. We mentioned the basics in Chapter 3: elements with a position other than static are arranged into stacks based on their depth in the source tree, like playing cards being dealt on top of one another. Changing the z-index changes their order in the stack.

Any element that has an explicit z-index declaration set to a positive value is higher in the stack than an element without one. Elements with negative values are shown behind elements without a z-index.

But the z-index is not the only thing controlling how elements are stacked. We also have the concept of a *stacking context*. Stretching the deck-of-cards analogy a bit, each card can also be its own deck, and cards can only be sorted in relation to the current deck level. There's always a *root stacking context* to begin with, and positioned elements with a z-index other than auto are sorted inside that. As other contexts are formed, they create a hierarchy of stacks.

Specific properties and values create these new stacking contexts. For example, an element with position: absolute and a z-index declaration set to anything but auto will form a stacking context for descendant elements inside it.

From inside a stacking context, it doesn't matter how large or small the z-index value is: you can't reorder something in relation to *another* stacking context (see Figure 6-7).

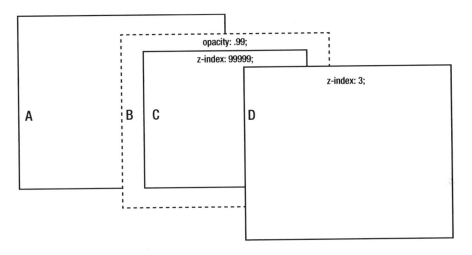

Figure 6-7. *Containers A, B, C, and D are all absolutely positioned, where C is a child element of B. Containers C and D have z-index applied, but since container B has an opacity lower than 1, it creates a new stacking context, separate from the others. The z-index will not place C in front of D, no matter how high the number*

One of these triggering rules is setting opacity to values lower than 1. An element with lowered opacity needs to be rendered separately (together with its descendant elements) before being placed onto the page, so these rules are there to make sure no outside elements can be interleaved between the semitransparent elements as this takes place. There is a code example in the files accompanying the book that lets you play with this very situation.

Further ahead in the book, we'll encounter other examples, like the transform and filter properties, which can also trigger the creation of new stacking contexts. At the end of this chapter, we'll get to some peculiarities with using z-index and flexbox.

Horizontal Layout

Generally speaking, a web page grows in the vertical direction as content is added. Any block container you add (a div, an article, an h1-h6, etc.) is going to stack up vertically, since they display as blocks with an automatic width. Because of this, one of the most basic layout challenges occurs when you want to give blocks of content a width and space them out *horizontally* next to each other.

We have already seen an example of designing a small "media component" in Chapter 3 using floats. This pattern, with an image (or other kind of media) on one side and a piece of text on the other, is an excellent example of an atomic pattern of layout: "this thing sits next to this other thing, and they belong together." If you look at any website, you are sure to see this pattern repeated again and again (see Figure 6-8).

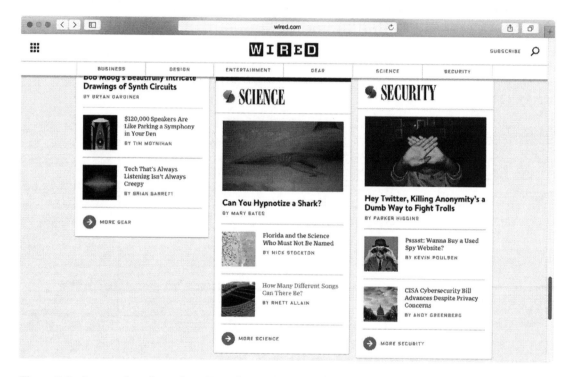

Figure 6-8. *A screenshot of a section of Wired.com. How many "media objects" can you spot?*

There are a number of other common patterns that appear on a broad range of websites out there. Many of them have to do with horizontal layout. Newer standards like flexbox have been created to cater for horizontal layout (and more), but until there's universal support for flexbox, chances are that you will need to co-opt floats, inline-block display, or table display modes to create horizontal layout patterns.

Using Floats

In the spaceship article, we have an example of the most basic use of floats. The figure floats to the right, allowing the line boxes of the text to flow around and below it (see Figure 6-9). We have also used a negative margin-right to pull the image out some distance from the text.

```
<p>You may think[...]</p>
  <figure>
    <img src="images/spaceship.jpg" alt="The Dragon spaceship in orbit around Earth.">
    <figcaption>The "Dragon" spaceship, created by SpaceX. Image from <a href="https://www.
    flickr.com/photos/spacexphotos/16787988882/">Flickr.com</a></figcaption>
  </figure>
<p>There's various [...]</p>
figure {
  background-color: #eee;
  margin: 0;
  padding: 1em;
  float: right;
  max-width: 17em;
  margin-right: -8em; /* pull to the right */
  margin-left: 1em;
}
```

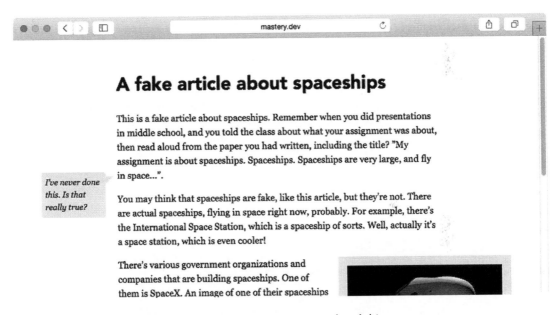

Figure 6-9. Using a floated figure, pulled out using negative margin-right

In Figure 6-10, we have removed the negative margin, and constrained the figure to take up 50% of the width. We've also added a second figure immediately following the first. Both figures will now sit horizontally next to each other.

```
figure {
  float: right;
  width: 50%;
}
```

a space station, which is even cooler!

Artist mockup of Mars landing. Image
from *Flickr.com*

The ”Dragon” spaceship, created by
SpaceX. Image from *Flickr.com*

There's various government organizations and companies that are building

Figure 6-10. *Two floated figures at 50% width, sitting next to each other*

This effect—floated items acting as "columns" in a "row"—has formed the basis of countless techniques for CSS layout. As discussed in Chapter 3, there are some quirks of floats that can trip you up. Remember, floats are not actually in the flow of the page, so you may need to have an element that contains the floats. Usually, that's accomplished either by applying clear to a (pseudo-)element inside the container, or a rule to make the container a new block formatting context. Floats will also wrap into multiple rows if necessary, but can get stuck on preceding floats sticking out from the row above.

Floats can also offer some limited reordering of horizontal content, independent of the source order. For example, we can switch places of the figures by floating them left instead of right (see Figure 6-11).

a space station, which is even cooler!

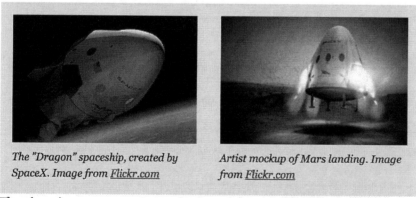

The ”Dragon” spaceship, created by
SpaceX. Image from *Flickr.com*

Artist mockup of Mars landing. Image
from *Flickr.com*

There's various government organizations and companies that are building

Figure 6-11. *Switching places of the figures by floating in the other direction*

Because of the ubiquitous browser support and relative versatility of floats, they have become the go-to solution for many variations on horizontal layout. We'll come back to using them in Chapter 7, when we build a small grid system for high-level page layout. But there are other CSS properties that allow us to create horizontal layout patterns, with different pros and cons of their own, as we'll see in the upcoming sections.

Inline Block as a Layout Tool

Lines of text are a form of horizontal layout in themselves—at least in languages written left-to-right or right-to-left. When we use inline elements (such as span, time, or a), they line up horizontally in the same direction as the text. We can also place *inline blocks* into that flow, creating elements that line up horizontally but act as blocks in terms of visual formatting and can have other blocks inside them.

For example, let's add some metadata to the bottom of our spaceship article, consisting of an author name with a photo and an e-mail address. We've also added a couple of extra spans as styling hooks:

```
<p class="author-meta">
  <!-- image from Jeremy Keith on Flickr: https://flic.kr/p/dwFRgH -->
  <img class="author-image" src="images/author.jpg" alt="Arthur C. Lark">
  <span class="author-info">
    <span class="author-name">Written by Arthur C. Lark</span>
    <a class="author-email" href="mailto:arthur.c.lark@example.com">arthur.c.lark@example.
com</a>
  </span>
</p>
```

The contents of the `.author-meta` paragraph will now line up, with the bottom edge of the image sitting on the baseline of the text. Any whitespace character, including for example the line break between the image and the line where the author info starts, will be rendered as a blank space. The width of that space depends on the font family and the font size (see Figure 6-12).

 Written by Arthur C. Lark arthur.c.lark@example.com

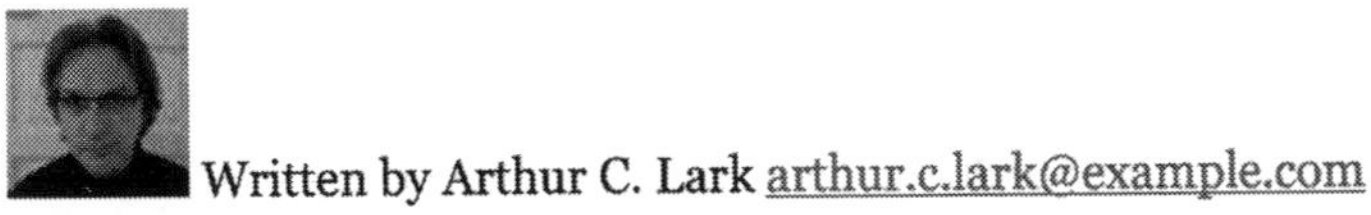

Figure 6-12. *Our author metadata. Note the whitespace between image and text.*

Next, we'll turn the image and the author info into inline blocks:

```
.author-image,
.author-info {
  display: inline-block;
}
```

In terms of rendering, the component looks the same at this stage. The difference is that we can start treating the image and the info as blocks. For example, we can put the name and e-mail address inside the author info on separate lines next to the image, by changing them to display as blocks:

```
.author-name,
.author-email {
  display: block;
}
```

153

We are now fairly close to the visual result of, for example, a floated image next to a block of text (as in the "media block" example from Chapter 3). One difference is that the last baseline of the author info block is aligned with the bottom of the image. We see the result in Figure 6-13, where we've also added a dotted outline around both image and author info to visualize how the two elements relate.

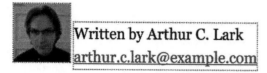

Figure 6-13. *The baseline of the author info is now aligned with the bottom of the image*

We can now shift the author info relative to the image by changing the `vertical-align` property. When the alignment is set to `top`, the top of the author info block will align with the top of the image (see Figure 6-14).

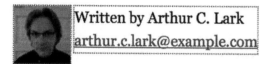

Figure 6-14. *Aligning the author info to the top of the image with* `vertical-align: top`

Vertical Centering with Inline Block

Now, let's say that the design we want is for the author info block to be vertically centered in relation to the image. It may be tempting to try something like this:

```
.author-info {
  vertical-align: middle;
}
```

...but that probably won't have the effect you expected! Figure 6-15 shows the results.

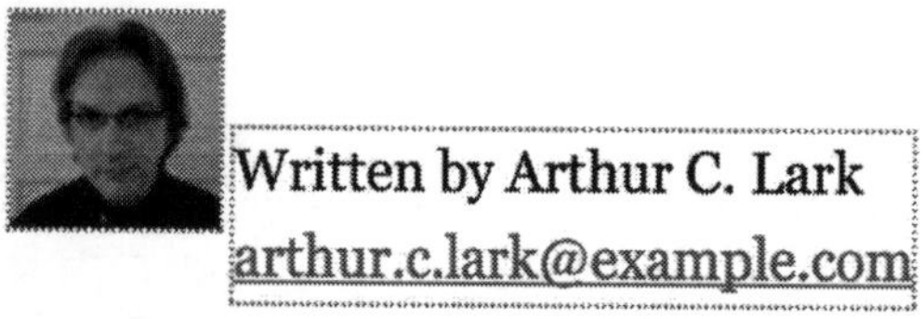

Figure 6-15. *The position of the author info when using* `vertical-align: middle`

This is where it gets somewhat tricky. The keyword `middle` when applied to inline blocks means "align the vertical center of this inline block with the middle of the x-height of the line of text." In this instance, there *is* no inline text. Therefore, the image (being the tallest element on the line) is what determines the height of the line box and where the baseline ends up. The center of the x-height thus ends up just above the bottom of the image. In order to center the author info on the vertical center of the image, we need to make both elements refer to the same "middle":

```
.author-image,
.author-info {
  vertical-align: middle;
}
```

With the image being an inline block, it too becomes vertically centered on the same vertical point as the author info, resulting in the layout we wanted, shown in Figure 6-16.

Figure 6-16. *Applying* `vertical-align: middle` *to both image and author info vertically centers them on the same point*

The rules for how the baseline of line boxes is decided, and how it affects inline and inline-block elements, are rather complicated. If you want to dive deep, we recommend Christopher Aue's article "Vertical-Align: All You Need To Know" (`http://christopheraue.net/2014/03/05/vertical-align/`). For the purpose of using inline block display as a layout tool, there are two important takeaways in terms of vertical alignment:

- To make inline blocks align to the top (much like floats do), set `vertical-align: top`.

- To vertically center contents with regard to each other, make sure they are all inline blocks, and then use `vertical-align: middle`.

Vertical Centering Inside a Container Element

That last bullet point in the previous list enables us to vertically center content inside a container of *any* height, with a bit of trickery. The only prerequisite is that the `height` of the container is set to a definite length.

For example, let's assume we want to make the author info block 10em tall, and center the author image and info inside it, vertically and horizontally. First of all, we apply a height to the `.author-meta` block. We'll also add a border to make the changes a little easier to spot (see Figure 6-17).

```
.author-meta {
  height: 10em;
  border: 1px solid #ccc;
}
```

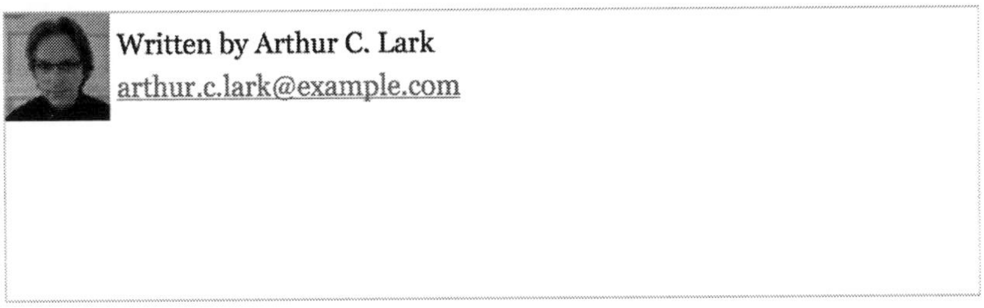

Written by Arthur C. Lark
arthur.c.lark@example.com

Figure 6-17. *The* `.author-meta` *block with* `height` *and border added*

The vertical alignment of photo and author info does not yet happen in relation to the container block, but to the hypothetical line of text they are sitting on. In order to align them vertically we need to add *another* inline block element, which takes up 100% of the height. This element will force the alignment point for the `middle` keyword to end up in the middle of the container. For this, we'll use a pseudo-element. Figure 6-18 shows how the hypothetical baseline gets calculated when this "ghost element" is added.

```
.author-meta:before {
  content: '';
  display: inline-block;
  vertical-align: middle;
  height: 100%;
}
```

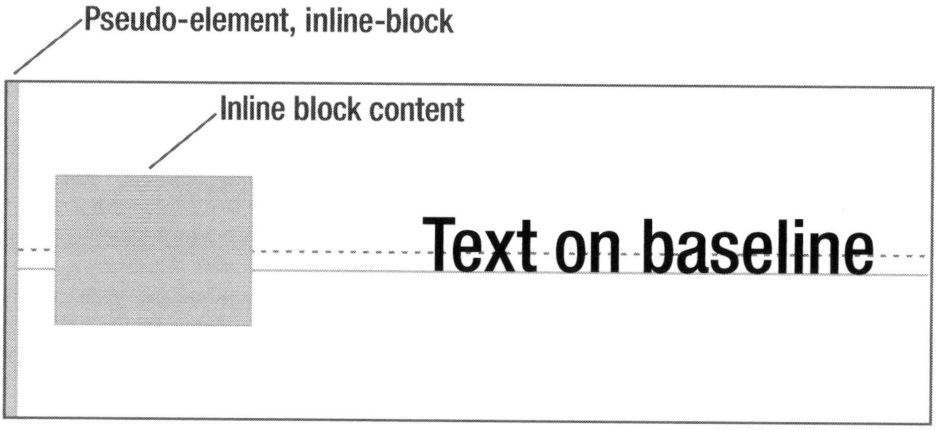

Figure 6-18. *Using a 100% tall pseudo-element to force the* `middle` *keyword to end up representing the vertical center of the container*

At this point, the whole `.author-meta` container will in effect have a single line box taking up the whole height. As the pseudo-element is an inline block with vertical alignment set to `middle`, the other inline blocks will be vertically aligned to the center of the container. All we need to do now is to center the content horizontally. As inline blocks respond to text alignment, we need to use `text-align`:

```
.author-meta {
  height: 10em;
  text-align: center;
  border: 1px solid #ccc;
}
.author-info {
  text-align: left;
}
```

This results in the contents of `.author-meta` being centered horizontally as well as vertically, as shown in Figure 6-19.

Written by Arthur C. Lark
arthur.c.lark@example.com

Figure 6-19. *The contents are now horizontally and vertically centered*

In actual fact, the horizontal centering is not exactly right. Remember that any whitespace character in the line box will be rendered as a single blank space? The pseudo-element will create one such space, pushing the content to the right by a few pixels. We can negate the width of the blank space by applying a negative margin to the pseudo-element:

```
.author-info:before {
  margin-right: -.25em;
}
```

Why -.25em? In this instance, it happens to be the width of a whitespace character in the current font. This is a bit of a "magic number," and will vary with the font used. As such, it is not very robust, and not something that we recommend for any systematic layout work. In our next horizontal layout example, we'll focus on a more detailed application of inline-block as a layout tool.

Getting the Details Right: Battling Whitespace

When dealing with horizontal layouts where each block takes up an exact width, the whitespace issue becomes much more noticeable. We'll work through building another common component to highlight how to fix this issue when using inline blocks, with fewer magic numbers.

This time we're creating a navigation bar, consisting of four link items, where each item takes up exactly one-fourth of the width. We start with the markup:

```
<nav class="navbar">
  <ul>
    <li><a href="/home">Home</a></li>
    <li><a href="/spaceships">Spaceships</a></li>
    <li><a href="/planets">Planets</a></li>
    <li><a href="/stars">Stars</a></li>
  </ul>
</nav>
```

The CSS gives us some basic styling in terms of colors and fonts, and outlines to highlight the edges between items. Each item is set to 25% width, so that four items should fit in the navigation bar as a whole:

```
.navbar ul {
  font-family: Avenir Next, Avenir, Century Gothic, sans-serif;
  list-style: none;
  padding: 0;
  background-color: #486a8e;
}
```

```
.navbar li {
  text-transform: uppercase;
  display: inline-block;
  text-align: center;
  box-sizing: border-box;
  width: 25%;
  background-color: #12459e;
  outline: 1px solid #fff;
}
.navbar li a {
  display: block;
  text-decoration: none;
  line-height: 1.75em;
  padding: 1em;
  color: #fff;
}
```

We use box-sizing: border-box to make sure that any borders or padding of individual items are included in the 25% width of each item. The navigation bar itself is given a blue-gray background, while the items have a slightly darker blue background, with white link text.

Now to the result, which can be seen in Figure 6-20.

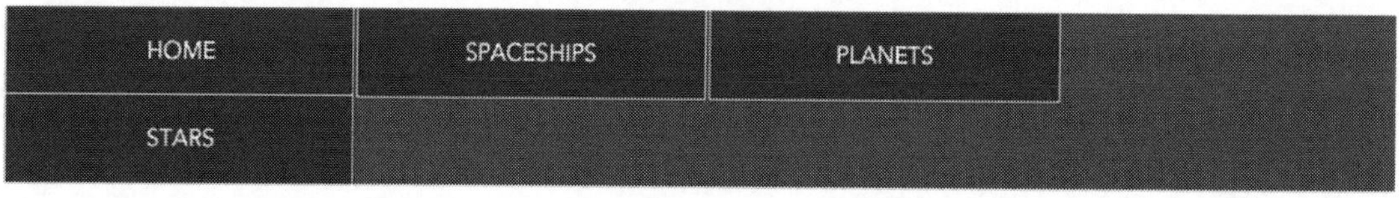

Figure 6-20. *The list sadly doesn't fit on one line, and the items are spaced apart*

The linebreaks in the HTML source are rendered as blank space characters, adding to the 25% width of each item and causing the line to wrap. We could eliminate these whitespace characters, for example, by putting all of the <li> tags on one line, but such demands on markup formatting are brittle.

Our preferred method of fixing this is a little brutal. It works by setting a font-size of 0 on the container itself (thus causing a blank space character to have zero width), and then resetting the size on the items:

```
.navbar ul {
  font-size: 0;
}
.navbar li {
  font-size: 16px;
  font-size: 1rem;
}
```

This gets rid of the whitespace in a predictable manner, making the items fit nicely into the container, as shown in Figure 6-21.

| HOME | SPACESHIPS | PLANETS | STARS |

Figure 6-21. *A navbar with four equal-width items*

There are a couple of downsides of this technique. The first has to do with inherited font sizes. Assuming we use a 16-pixel font size on the navbar, we can no longer use em units or percentages to inherit a flexible font size for the list items—it would only become a multiple of 0. Instead, we can retain flexible sizing by basing the size on the root font size using the rem unit. For browsers that don't support the rem unit (mostly Internet Explorer 8 and older), the pixel-based measurement acts as a fallback.

The second downside has to do with slightly older WebKit-based browsers, where a font-size of 0 is not always respected—the stock WebKit-based browser on early versions of Android 4, for example. As we'll see further ahead in the chapter, we often use inline block display only as a fallback for older browsers, and then layer on more modern techniques like flexbox. As even these older Android browsers support flexbox—albeit an older flavor—whitespace problems are likely to become a nonissue.

■ **Tip** Should you for some reason need to use the inline block technique with a perfect fallback in these older Android browsers, there's a final trick involving fonts. It works by using a tiny custom font, only containing a blank space character with a zero width, on the parent element. The original font-family is then reset on the child elements. See this demo by developer Matthew Lein for the details: https://matthewlein.com/articles/inline-block-no-space-font/.

Using Table Display Properties for Layout

The rows in a table have the exact qualities we're looking for in the navbar example: a number of "cells" dividing the space between them, never slipping down on multiple rows. This is one of the reasons why actual HTML tables were co-opted for layout in the early days of the web. These days, we can borrow the display modes from tables via CSS, without resorting to table-based markup.

If we change the navigation bar example to use the display mode of a table for the ul element, and set each of the items to display as a table cell, we get the same look as when we used inline blocks:

```
.navbar ul {
  /* some properties omitted for brevity. */
  width: 100%;
  display: table;
  table-layout: fixed;
}
.navbar li {
  width: 25%;
  display: table-cell;
}
```

This gives us the exact same appearance as in the previous inline block example (shown in Figure 6-21).

Note that we have set the ul element to be 100% wide. This is to make sure the navbar expands to fill its parent. Unlike regular blocks, tables without a set width have a "shrink to fit" width unless the contents of the cells push them out to fill their parent container.

There are two algorithms for how the width of each column in a table row is calculated. By default, the browser will use the "auto" algorithm. It is somewhat undefined, standards-wise, but it basically allows the table to adapt the width of the columns based on the cell contents of the table as a whole.

The other algorithm is the "fixed" table layout. Using `table-layout: fixed`, column widths are determined based on the first row of the table. Any declared widths on the first row encountered "win," and if subsequent rows have wider content, that content will wrap into multiple lines inside the cells, or overflow.

While setting the `table-layout` to `fixed` is not technically necessary in this example, it's common to use it when using table display modes as a layout tool, to avoid any surprises from the automatic mode.

When using the table display modes for layout purposes, you should be aware that other quirks of table rendering apply as well. For example, it's not possible to apply margins to an element rendered as a table cell, and the behavior of positioning as applied to table cells is shaky at best. We will come back to HTML tables and CSS table display modes in Chapter 9.

Vertical Alignment in Table Cells

Another useful aspect of table display modes is that vertical alignment works slightly differently in that context. Setting `vertical-align: middle` on an element displaying as a `table-cell` will align the contents of the cell to the vertical middle, without any extra trickery. Figure 6-22 shows what happens if we add a set height to the list displaying as a table, and vertically align the list items to `middle`.

```
.navbar ul {
  display: table;
  height: 100px;
}
.navbar li {
  display: table-cell;
  vertical-align: middle;
}
```

Figure 6-22. *Adding a height and vertical centering to list items displaying as table cells*

Pros and Cons of the Different Techniques

When considering floats, inline blocks, and table display modes as tools for horizontal layout as well as vertical alignment, how do we determine which one to use? There are pros and cons for each method:

- **Floats** are able to wrap onto multiple lines, as are inline blocks. Floats also "shrink-wrap" down to a size based on their contents, which can be a useful behavior. On the negative side, floats may give you grief when it comes to containing or clearing them, and when floated items get stuck on taller preceding floats. On the other hand, floats are somewhat source order independent, as you can float some elements on a row right and the others left.

- **Inline blocks** have whitespace issues, but those are solvable, albeit with some hacky solutions. On the positive side, inline blocks can also wrap onto multiple lines, they give you some control over vertical alignment, and they have the same "shrink-wrap" sizing behavior as floats.

- Using **table display modes** for horizontal layout also works great, but only for nonwrapping rows of content. They have the same quirks as tables, meaning, for example, that they are unaffected by margins, and the items inside cannot be reordered. They also allow simple vertical centering of their contents.

Flexbox

The Flexible Box Layout module, known as flexbox, is one of the newer sets of CSS properties we can use to create layouts. It consists of a number of properties relating to both a container element (the *flex container*) and its direct children (*flex items*), as well as how those child elements behave. Flexbox can control several aspects of the flex items:

- Size, based on both content and available space

- Direction of the flow: horizontal or vertical, forward or reverse

- Alignment and distribution on both axes

- Ordering, regardless of source order

If using inline blocks, floats, and table properties for layout felt hacky to you, flexbox is likely the solution you want. It was developed as a direct response to the various common scenarios we have looked at so far in this chapter, and more.

Browser Support and Syntax

Flexbox is supported in the latest versions of all major browsers. With some adjustment of syntax and vendor prefixes, you can get it to work for a wide range of slightly older browsers as well.

To achieve support in IE10 and older WebKit browsers, you'll need to complement the standard syntax we use in this chapter with vendor-prefixed and somewhat different properties, as the syntax for flexbox has changed a lot over various iterations of the spec. There are numerous tools and articles describing how to do this, such as the "Flexy Boxes" code generator (`http://the-echoplex.net/flexyboxes/`).

Note that Internet Explorer 9 and earlier do not support flexbox at all. We will discuss some fallback strategies for these browsers later in the chapter.

Understanding Flex Direction: Main and Cross Axis

Flexbox allows you to define an area of the page where a bunch of elements can be controlled in terms of order, size, distribution, and alignment. The boxes inside that space line up in one of two directions: by default horizontally (as a row) or vertically (as a column). That direction is known as the *main axis*.

The boxes inside can also be shifted and resized in the direction running perpendicular to the main axis: this is known as the *cross axis* (see Figure 6-23). Usually, the most important measurement for creating layouts with flexbox is the size along the main axis: width for horizontal layouts and height for vertical layouts. We refer to that size as the *main size* of the item.

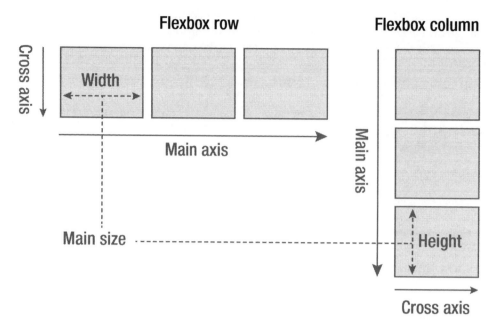

Figure 6-23. *Defining the main axis and the cross axis in row vs. column mode, and their respective main size properties*

Going back to the navigation bar example we first saw in Figure 6-20 (a wrapper with an unordered list containing links), we can easily convert it to a horizontal flex container. Assuming the rest of the styling (colors, typography, link styles, borders) is the same, we need a minimal amount of CSS. We don't need any specific properties on the list items themselves just yet, and there is no width declared on the items (see Figure 6-24):

```
.navbar ul {
  display: flex;
  /* this also implies flex-direction: row; unless told otherwise */
}
```

Figure 6-24. *The navbar created with flexbox*

As you can see in Figure 6-24, the items line up horizontally, and shrink to their minimum size based on the content inside them. One way of looking at it is as if we've taken the block flow and rotated it 90 degrees.

The items also bunch up on the left side, which is the default behavior when the language direction is left to right. If we change the flex-direction property to row-reverse, the items will start from the right edge and flow right to left (see Figure 6-25). Note that the order is also reversed!

```
.navbar ul {
  display: flex;
  flex-direction: row-reverse;
}
```

Figure 6-25. *Flowing items in the row-reverse direction*

Items inside a flex container shrink down to this size if no other sizing is in place. This means that items in rows automatically get a minimum width, and items in columns get a minimum height, both based on the minimum size of the contents inside each item.

Alignment and Spacing

We can use flexbox to distribute the items along the row in various ways. Flexbox calls distribution along the main axis *justification*, while distribution on the cross axis is called *alignment*. (As a memory aid, remember that the horizontal direction is the default, and text justification, in horizontal writing systems, happens in the horizontal direction as well. The trick is to remember which one is which when the direction changes.)

Now we can distribute the items on the main axis with various keywords and the `justify-content` property. The default value that causes the items to align in the current text direction (in this case left to right) is called `flex-start`. Using `flex-end` causes them to move over to the other side (see Figure 6-26), but this time keeping the same order. Figures 6-27, 6-28, and 6-29, respectively, show the other keywords: `center`, `space-between`, and `space-around`.

Figure 6-26. *Using* `justify-content: flex-end` *to move items over to the right*

Figure 6-27. *Centering flex items with* `justify-content: center`. *Extra space is placed on the outer sides of the edge items*

Figure 6-28. *Using* `justify-content: space-between`. *Extra space is placed in between the items*

Figure 6-29. *Using* `justify-content: space-around`. *Space is divided equally and placed on both sides of each item. Note that space between items does not collapse*

Flexbox does not allow you to justify individual items with these keywords. However, setting `margin` values with the keyword `auto` has a slightly different meaning when applied to flexbox items, and we can put that to use here. If an element has `margin` set to `auto` on one side and there is space left in the container, that margin expands to fill the available space. This can be used for patterns where all items except one need to be arranged to one side. For example, we could place all items to the right, but put the "Home" item to the left (see Figure 6-30):

```
.navbar li:first-child {
  margin-right: auto;
}
```

Figure 6-30. *Using* `margin-right: auto` *on the first item eats up all the space that's left, pushing the rest of the items to the right*

Note that using an `auto` margin like this will negate the effects of any justification on the other items, since there is no space left to distribute. You can still put individual margins on the other elements though.

Cross-Axis Alignment

So far we have only approached the basic problem of horizontal layout, which is a breeze with flexbox. Flexbox also allows us to control how the other axis works. If we increase the height of either the flex container itself or one of the items, we find that the default properties have an interesting effect (see Figure 6-31):

```
.navbar ul {
  min-height: 100px;
}
```

Figure 6-31. *The items will stretch to fill the flex container in the cross-axis dimension by default*

It seems we automatically have equal-height items! The default value for the `align-items` property, which controls cross-axis alignment, is `stretch`. This means that all flex items will fill the available space. We can also set a value of `flex-start`, `center`, or `flex-end` (see Figures 6-32 to 6-34, respectively) to make the items shrink back to their original size and align with the top, middle, or bottom of the navigation bar.

Figure 6-32. *Using* `align-items: flex-start`

164

Figure 6-33. *Using* `align-items: center`

Figure 6-34. *Using* `align-items: flex-end`

Finally, you can use the `baseline` keyword to align the baseline of the text inside items to the baseline of the container, similar to how inline blocks work by default. This can be useful if you have boxes of varying sizes, where you want them placed differently on the cross-axis but aligned among themselves.

In Figure 6-35, we have added a class name representing the currently active item:

```
<ul>
    <li><a href="/home">Home</a></li>
    <li class="navbar-active"><a href="/spaceships">Spaceships</a></li>
    <li><a href="/planets">Planets</a></li>
    <li><a href="/stars">Stars</a></li>
</ul>
```

Figure 6-35. *Using a class of* `navbar-active` *to show the selected state*

The active item has been given a larger `font-size` and a `z-index` of 1:

```
.navbar .navbar-active {
    font-size: 1.25em;
}
```

The larger active item now determines the baseline, and the other items align themselves accordingly.

Aligning Individual Items

As well as aligning all the items as a group, you can set an individual alignment on the cross-axis for each item. We could, for example, have the "Home" item align to the top left, and the rest to the bottom right (see Figure 6-36):

```
.navbar ul {
    min-height: 100px;
    align-items: flex-end;
}
.navbar li:first-child {
    align-self: flex-start;
    margin-right: auto;
}
```

Figure 6-36. *Individual alignment using* `align-self`

Vertical Alignment with Flexbox

Finally, flexbox alignment solves the vertical alignment problem with very little code. When there is a single item in the container, we only need to set the parent as a flex container and then set the `margin` declaration on the item we want to center to `auto` in all directions. Remember, margins set to `auto` on flex items will expand to "fill" in all directions.

```
<div class="flex-container">
    <div class="flex-item">
      <h2>Not so lost in space</h2>
      <p>This item sits right in the middle of its container...<p>
    </div>
  </div>
```

We can now center the `.flex-item` horizontally *and* vertically with the following CSS, regardless of the size of container or item. In this instance, we make the container be as tall as the viewport (using `height: 100%` on both the `html`, `body` and `.flex-container` elements), just to visualize the result, seen in Figure 6-37.

```
html, body {
  height: 100%;
}
.flex-container {
  height: 100%;
  display: flex;
}
.flex-item {
  margin: auto;
}
```

Figure 6-37. *Vertical and horizontal centering with flexbox and auto margin*

When there are several items inside the flex container—like in our author metadata example—we can cluster them to the horizontal and vertical center using the alignment properties (see Figure 6-38). To achieve this, we set both justification and alignment to center. (By the way, this works for single items too, but the margin: auto method requires a bit less code.)

```
.author-meta {
  display: flex;
  flex-direction: column;
  justify-content: center;
  align-items: center;
}
```

Written by Arthur C. Lark
arthur.c.lark@example.com

Figure 6-38. *Easy vertical centering of multiple elements with flexbox*

Flexible Sizes

Flexbox gives us a lot of control over sizing. It's part of what makes flexbox so great for detailed content layout, but it is also, by far, the most complex part of flexbox. Don't worry if this section feels overwhelming at first—flexible sizing is one of those things you need to work with before it "clicks."

The Flexible Sizing Properties

This is where the "flex" in flexbox comes in, as defined in the three properties flex-basis, flex-grow, and flex-shrink. These properties are set on each flex item, not on the container.

- **flex-basis** regulates what the "preferred" size of the item is on the main axis (width or height), before it's corrected based on the available space. It can be set to either a length (like 18em, for example), a percentage (which is based on the main axis size of the container), or the keyword auto, which is the default value.

  The auto keyword sounds like it sets width or height to auto, but that's actually not the case. Instead, it means that the item will get its main size from the corresponding property (width or height) if that's set. If the main size is not set, the element will be sized according to its contents, a bit like a float or an inline block,

  You can also set the value to content, which also sets the size based on the contents of the item, but *disregarding* any main axis size set with width or height (unlike auto). Note that the content keyword is a newer addition to flexbox, and support is spotty at the time of writing.

- **flex-grow** regulates what will happen if there is space left when each element has been given its preferred size via flex-basis: you supply it with a number, known as a *flex factor*, that works out as a fraction of the extra space. We'll explain how the fractions work in a second. The default value for flex-grow is 0, which means that items will not grow beyond the size they get from flex-basis.

- **flex-shrink** works similarly to flex-grow but in reverse: how will the elements shrink if there isn't enough room? When flex-shrink comes into play, the calculation is a little more involved—we'll revisit it further ahead. The default value is 1, meaning that all items will shrink proportionately compared to their preferred size if there is not enough space.

Understanding how flex-basis plays with flex-grow and flex-shrink is the tricky part. Flexbox uses a rather complex algorithm to calculate sizing, but it gets easier to handle if we simplify it down to two steps:

1. Determine a hypothetical main size by looking at flex-basis.

2. Determine the actual main size. If there is any space left in the container after putting the items inside the container with their hypothetical main size, they can grow. This growth is based on the flex-grow factor. By the same token, if there is too little space to fit them, the items can shrink down based on the flex-shrink factor.

We can piece these properties together by working through an example. In this example, we imagine a container that is 1000 pixels wide. There are two child items inside the container in the markup. One of them contains a short word, causing this particular element to take up 200 pixels in width. The other contains a long word, and takes up 400 pixels in width (see Figure 6-39). The items are not yet placed inside the container.

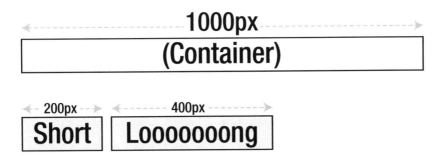

Figure 6-39. *A flex container at 1000 pixels wide, and two flex items, not yet placed in the container*

If these items have flex-basis set to auto and no explicit width value declared, as follows, they retain this content-based size when placed into the container (see Figure 6-40), taking up a total of 600 pixels of the available width. This is the default behavior for flex-basis, and the same as we have seen in the navigation bar example so far.

```
.navbar li {
  flex-basis: auto; /* default value. */
}
```

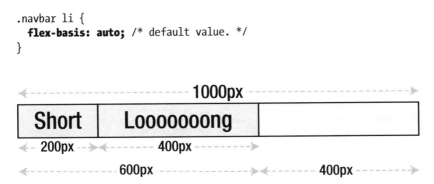

Figure 6-40. *The items take up a total of 600 pixels of the available 1000 pixels, leaving 400 pixels of unused space*

As there is space left to distribute, flex-grow comes into play. By default flex-grow is set to 0, which does nothing to change the sizes of the items. But what happens when we set flex-grow for both items to 1?

```
.navbar li {
  flex-basis: auto;
  flex-grow: 1;
}
```

What do the 1's and 0's represent? Well, it's a bit like in a cocktail recipe: 1 part this, 2 parts this, 3 parts soda water. It doesn't represent a specific measurement, only parts of a whole.

In this case, there are two items. Both will now grow equally, by *1 part* of the available space, meaning they each will grow by half the remaining space, or 200 pixels. This means that the first item will be resized to a final size of 400 pixels, and the second will be 600 pixels, adding up to fill the container exactly, as shown in Figure 6-41.

169

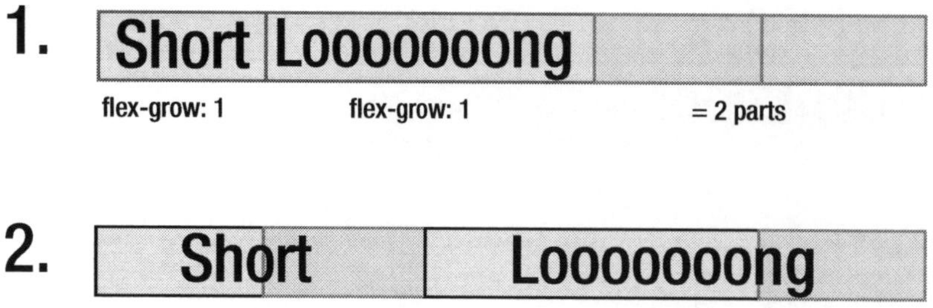

Figure 6-41. *Both items grow by 1 part of the remaining 400 pixels, or 200 pixels each*

We could also have set individual `flex-grow` factors for the items:

```
.navbar li:first-child {
  flex-grow: 3;
}
.navbar li:last-child {
  flex-grow: 1;
}
```

This would result in the first item receiving three-fourths of the available space and the second item receiving one-fourth. As a result, both items end up being 500 pixels wide! Figure 6-42 shows how the layout algorithm works the sizing in this instance.

Figure 6-42. *The first item will grow by three-fourths of the available space, while the second only grows by one-fourth*

The items in this example happened to end up equally wide. If we want items to divide the whole space proportionally between them regardless of content, there are better flexbox techniques, as we'll find out next.

Sizing Purely with Flex Factors

In the first step of the simplified flexbox layout algorithm we used in the previous section, the items were sized based on the width of their contents, using a `flex-basis` of `auto` and no explicit `width` declaration. If we were to assume that the `flex-basis` was `0`, the consequence would be that no space would be allocated in the first step. *All of the space* inside the container would remain in step 2, to be divided according to flex factors and setting the final size of the items.

In Figure 6-43, the items have a flex-basis of 0, and flex-grow set to 1. This means there are two parts making up the total space to be divided, so each item will take up exactly half of the allocated space. This effect is close to calculating and using percentages for layout, with the added bonus that flexbox doesn't care how many items there are—they will automatically be resized to fit the total width.

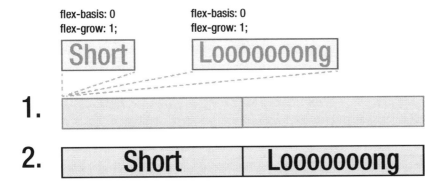

Figure 6-43. *Two items with a* flex-basis *set to* 0 *will take up zero space in the first step of the algorithm. They will then be sized entirely based on their* flex-grow *factors*

This time, we'll use the flex shorthand for setting flex-grow, flex-shrink, and flex-basis at the same time, declared in that order and separated by spaces:

```
.navbar li {
  flex: 1 0 0%;
}
```

Note the percentage sign after the flex-basis last in the value: the flex-basis in the shorthand can't be unitless, so you must use either 0% or another unit like 0px in this instance.

If we wanted the first item to take up twice as much space as any other item, we could give it a flex-grow factor of 2:

```
.navbar li {
  flex: 1 0 0%;
}
.navbar li:first-child {
  flex-grow: 2;
}
```

Applying this to the navbar markup with four items from earlier, we get a navbar where the first item takes up two-fifths of the width (or 40%), followed by three items taking up one-fifth (or 20%) each (see Figure 6-44).

HOME	SPACESHIPS	PLANETS	STARS

Figure 6-44. *Example of* navbar *where the first item is set to grow by 2 units, and the rest by 1 unit*

Shrinking Flex Items

When the items to be placed inside a flex container add up to more than the available space, we can allow them to shrink based on the flex-shrink property. The mechanics are a little more involved than flex-grow. The idea behind more complex rules for shrinking items is to prevent small items from shrinking down to nothing just because a larger item causes the total width to overshoot. Allowing an item *more* space is fairly straightforward (as we saw with flex-grow), and happens in proportion to the available space. When shrinking happens, it does so slightly differently.

Going back to our hypothetical 1000-pixels-wide navigation bar, let's imagine there are two child items, each with a preferred size set via flex-basis. Together, they overshoot the width of the container by 300 pixels, as shown in Figure 6-45.

```
.navbar li:first-child {
    flex: 1 1 800px;
}
.navbar li:last-child {
  flex: 1 1 500px;
}
```

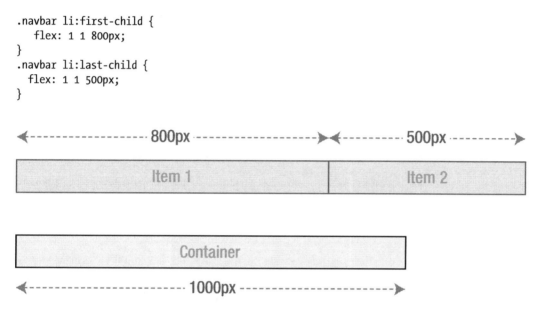

Figure 6-45. *Two flex items, whose combined flex-basis overshoots the container width*

The combined preferred width (800 + 500 = 1300) overshoots the size of the container by 300 pixels, and both items have a flex-shrink value of 1. You'd be forgiven for thinking both items shrink by 150 pixels each to make room—but this is not what will happen. Instead, each item will shrink in proportion to both its flex-shrink factor and the flex-basis. Technically, each item's flex-shrink factor is multiplied by the flex-basis. Next, that value is divided by the sum of multiplying the flex-shrink factor of every item with its flex-basis. Finally, the result of that division is multiplied by the negative space, giving us the amount of space to shrink the item by.

This is a lot to keep in your head, but the gist of it is this: items with a larger preferred size will shrink more (in relation to the flex-shrink factor) than those with a smaller preferred size. Even if both our items have a flex-shrink factor of 1, they will shrink by different amounts. If we work through the calculations for the first item, the result is this:

```
((800 × 1) / ((800 × 1) + (500 × 1))) * 300 = 184.6
```

The first item will shrink by 184.6 pixels. Going through the same math for the second item should then give us the remainder:

```
((500 × 1) / ((800 × 1) + (500 × 1))) * 300 = 115.4
```

...which means the second item will shrink by 115.4 pixels, adding up neatly to the 300 pixels of decreased width needed to fit both inside the flex container (see Figure 6-46).

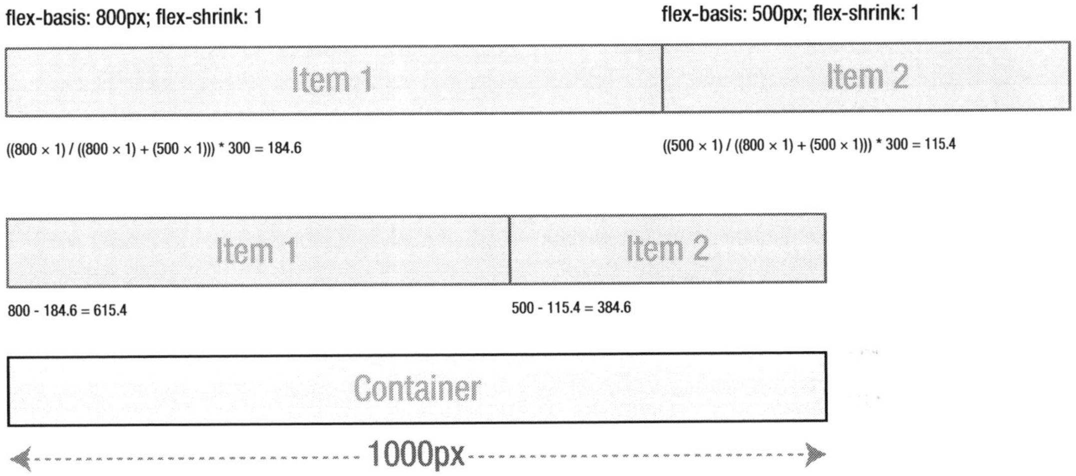

flex-basis: 800px; flex-shrink: 1   flex-basis: 500px; flex-shrink: 1

| Item 1 | Item 2 |

((800 × 1) / ((800 × 1) + (500 × 1))) * 300 = 184.6   ((500 × 1) / ((800 × 1) + (500 × 1))) * 300 = 115.4

| Item 1 | Item 2 |

800 - 184.6 = 615.4   500 - 115.4 = 384.6

| Container |

◄------------------------------ 1000px ------------------------------►

Figure 6-46. *The rather more complex* flex-shrink *calculation*

Will you need to know this by heart when using flexbox? Most likely the answer is "no." But if you're struggling to make a layout work, realizing that flex-shrink works differently compared to flex-grow may prevent you from tearing your hair out.

Wrapping Flexbox Layouts

In the navigation bar and author metadata examples, we worked with only one row of content. Just like inline blocks or floats, flexbox allows us to flow the content into several rows (or columns), but with increased control.

■ **Caution**   The properties for wrapping into multiple rows or columns are from a newer version of the spec. Browsers supporting the old flexbox spec, such as older versions of Safari, the stock Android browser before version 4.4, and Firefox before version 28, do not support wrapping.

This time, we'll be working with a list of tags, representing categories of planets. It's an unordered list of items with links, much like the navigation bar, but where the number of items can be much larger, making it unfeasible to fit them all on one row. We're giving each item a background color, and the shaped appearance of a physical luggage tag using the same kind of pseudo-element trick we used for the comment bubbles (see Figure 6-47).

Figure 6-47. *Our list of tags*

The markup is simple enough:

```
<ul class="tags">
  <li><a href="/Binary_planet">Binary planet</a></li>
  <li><a href="/Carbon_planet">Carbon planet</a></li>
  <!-- …and so on… -->
</ul>
```

The styling for the tags is a little more involved, but nothing we haven't seen before:

```
.tags {
  border: 1px solid #C9E1F4;
  margin: 0;
  padding: 1em;
  list-style: none;
}
.tags li {
  display: inline-block;
  margin: .5em;
}
.tags a {
  position: relative;
  display: block;
  padding: .25em .5em .25em .25em;
  background-color: #C9E1F4;
  color: #28448F;
  border-radius: 0 .25em .25em 0;
  line-height: 1.5;
  text-decoration: none;
  text-align: center;
}
.tags a:before {
  position: absolute;
  content: '';
  width: 0;
  height: 0;
  border: 1em solid transparent;
  border-right-width: .5em;
  border-right-color: #C9E1F4;
  left: -1.5em;
  top: 0;
}
```

174

With the preceding styling, the tags are declared as inline blocks, and will wrap nicely. Now it's time to layer on the flexbox enhancements. First we turn the list into a flex container, and tell it to allow rows to wrap using the flex-wrap property set to wrap:

```
.tags {
  display: flex;
  flex-wrap: wrap;
  margin: 0;
  padding: 0;
  list-style: none;
}
```

At this point, the list looks pretty much exactly like it did initially. But now we have all the power of flexbox to control the direction, size, and alignment of rows.

Wrapping and Direction

To start with, we can reverse the direction of the rows, just like we did initially with the navigation bar. When the flex-direction changes to row-reverse, items will start at the top right and flow right to left, wrapping into right-aligned rows, as shown in Figure 6-48.

Figure 6-48. *Reversing the flow with* flex-direction: row-reverse

We can also reverse the vertical flow, so that the rows start at the bottom and wrap upward! In Figure 6-49, flex-direction is set to row-reverse, and flex-wrap is set to wrap-reverse.

Figure 6-49. *Using the* wrap-reverse *keyword to flow content from bottom to top*

▓ **Note** Flexbox directions are *logical directions*, which means they depend on text direction for what counts as start and end edges. If you're building, for example, an Arabic language site with right-to-left text, the horizontal directions will be reversed (providing you set the correct dir attribute in the markup), while the vertical directions stay the same.

Flexible Sizing in Wrapping Layouts

Another benefit of flexbox layout in multiple rows is that the flexible sizing allows us to fill rows evenly (see Figure 6-50). The flex-grow calculation happens on a per-row basis, so items will grow only as much as needed to fill the current row.

```
.tags li {
  flex: 1 0 auto;
}
```

Figure 6-50. *Applying a* flex-grow *factor to create perfectly filled-out rows*

When viewed at a slightly different size, the last item wraps onto the last row, becoming uncomfortably wide (see Figure 6-51). Unfortunately, there's no mechanism to address specific rows in a wrapping flexbox layout. We can't tell items to become inflexible if they're on the last row, for example.

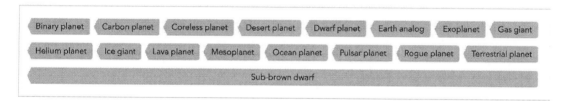

Figure 6-51. *The last tag becomes very wide when wrapping onto the last row by itself and growing to fill the space*

We'll solve the immediate problem by setting a max-width property on the tags, so that they stay flexible within a certain limit (see Figure 6-52):

```
.tags li {
  display: inline-block;
  margin: .5em;
  flex: 1 0 auto;
  max-width: 14em;
}
```

Figure 6-52. *By setting a reasonable* max-width *on the tag items, we can prevent items from growing to uncomfortable lengths*

Generally, the ability to fill available space is a core strength of flexbox. Combining flex-grow with min- and max-width, we can build very smart wrapping flexbox layouts, where items stay within reasonable measurements no matter the screen size or how many items there are. We'll dive further into techniques for this in Chapter 8, where we discuss responsive web design, and how to adapt layouts to their context.

Aligning all Rows

In our earlier review of the cross-axis alignment properties (align-items and align-self), we saw how flexbox allows us to align *items* with respect to the flex-start, center, baseline, and flex-end points of a single row. In a wrapping layout, we can align the rows or columns themselves, with regard to the container.

If we set a min-height of 300px on the taglist container, the effect of the align-content property becomes clear. By default, it is set to stretch, meaning each row will stretch to fill its share of the container height. If we inspect items, we can see that each li element will stretch to fill a third of the height, as shown in Figure 6-53.

```
.tags {
  display: flex;
  flex-wrap: wrap;
  min-height: 300px;
  /* align-content: stretch; is implied here */
}
```

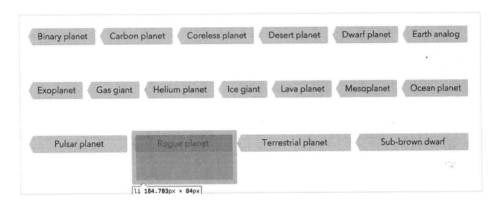

Figure 6-53. *Each row is stretched so that the combination of all rows fills the container*

The effect of align-content is pretty much exactly as how you'd distribute content on the main axis using justify-content. We can now distribute the content to flex-start (the top of the container), flex-end (the bottom), center (clustered to the middle), or separated using space-between or space-around.

Column Layout and Individual Ordering

With the flexbox order property, you are completely free from source order. You can simply tell the browser which order you want the boxes in. By default, all items are given the order value of 0, and items with the same order value are sorted in the order they appear in the source.

Flexbox gives us complete control of this ordering. In our next flexbox example, we'll leave the horizontal layout techniques, and create a small "article teaser" component, where an excerpt from our spaceship article is shown, along with the heading, an image, and a link to continue reading the whole thing. We'll show this as single column.

177

Starting with the markup, we'll put each of the component parts in order of importance:

1. The heading with the article title

2. The teaser text

3. An image illustrating the article topic

4. A link to the article

```
<div class="article-teaser">
  <h2>The Dragon and other spaceships</h2>
  <div class="article-teaser-text">
    <p>There are actual spaceships…</p>
  </div>
  <img src="images/medium_spaceship.jpg" alt="The Dragon spaceship in orbit around Earth.">
  <p class="article-teaser-more">
    <a href="/spaceships">Read the whole Spaceship article</a>
  </p>
</div>
```

The article teaser can be seen in Figure 6-54. We've added some basic styling for this component, mostly dealing with margins, colors, and typography. This particular styling is not important for the example, so we'll leave it out for now.

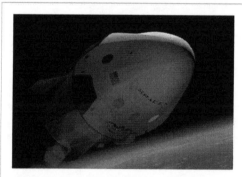

Figure 6-54. The first iteration of our article teaser component

Visually, the design could perhaps benefit from putting the image first, to catch the eye of a potential reader. But in terms of the markup, it doesn't quite make sense to put the image first. For example, we may want users of screen readers to have the article title read as the first element within the teaser.

To acheive this reordering, we need to turn the `.article-teaser` container into a flexbox column:

```
.article-teaser {
  display: flex;
  flex-direction: column;
}
```

Next, we give the image an `order` value lower than the default 0, so that it appears first (see Figure 6-55):

```
.article-teaser img {
  order: -1;
}
```

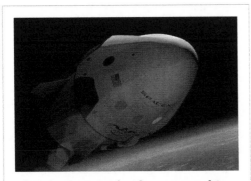

The Dragon and other spaceships

There are actual spaceships, flying in space right now, probably. For example, there's the International Space Station, which is a spaceship of sorts. Well, actually it's a space station, which is even cooler!

Read the whole Spaceship article

Figure 6-55. *Our reordered article teaser*

If we had wanted the heading first, for example, we could have set order values on the heading and image:

```
.article-teaser h2 {
  order: -2;
}
.article-teaser img {
  order: -1;
}
```

…and the rest of the items would remain as they were, as they retain their order value of 0. The order values you set don't have to be sequential (we could have used -99 and -6 for header and image respectively), and they can be either positive or negative. As long as they are numbers that can be compared, the items will reorder themselves accordingly. Just remember that 0 is the default.

▦ **Caution**   It is worth emphasizing that reordering items using flexbox is simply a visual shift. Things like tab order and the order in which a screen reader speaks the content will not be changed by the order property. For this reason, it is important to make sure that HTML source is still logical, and not use flexbox as an excuse for sloppy markup practices.

Nested Flexbox Layouts

As our final example, we'll show that flexbox layout can be nested, with some really useful results.

We'll reuse the article teaser example, but this time there's two teasers that we want to show next to each other. For this purpose, we'll add a wrapper element, set to display as a flexbox row:

```
<div class="article-teaser-group">
  <div class="article-teaser">
    <!-- first article teaser contents… -->
  </div>
  <div class="article-teaser">
    <!-- second article teaser contents… -->
  </div>
</div>
```

The wrapper element is set to display as a flexbox row:

```
.article-teaser-group {
  display: flex;
}
```

In Figure 6-56 we can see the now familiar effect that flex items will by default stretch in the cross-axis direction, creating two equal-height article teasers.

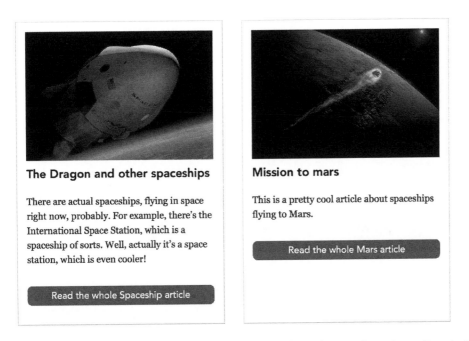

Figure 6-56. *Our two article teasers are now nested flexbox columns, also acting as items inside the flexbox row*

We've seen equal-height items with flexbox before. But when the items are also flexbox containers like this, we can pull one final trick. We can see that the content in the second teaser is much shorter than in the first, creating an off-balance impression between the high-contrast "read more" link components in the two teasers. Flexbox can help us in this situation as well.

Remember that margins set to auto on flex items eat up any remaining space, in each direction? Setting margin-top: auto on the "read more" element will push it to the bottom of the column, making it line up with the component next to it (see Figure 6-57):

```
.article-teaser-more {
  margin-top: auto;
}
```

The Dragon and other spaceships

There are actual spaceships, flying in space right now, probably. For example, there's the International Space Station, which is a spaceship of sorts. Well, actually it's a space station, which is even cooler!

Read the whole Spaceship article

Mission to mars

This is a pretty cool article about spaceships flying to Mars.

Read the whole Mars article

Figure 6-57. Using `margin-top: auto` *on the link pushes it to the bottom of the column, creating a neater impression*

This is a type of layout for dynamic content that would have been a hassle to get right using older techniques like floats, inline blocks, and positioning. And when flexbox is not supported, it falls back to a simpler but perfectly workable design—which leads us nicely to our next topic.

Flexbox Fallbacks

While flexbox is widely supported in theory, there will still be situations where you will want to fall back on techniques like floats or inline blocks. You may have to support older versions of Internet Explorer (prior to IE10). There may be browser bugs preventing you from realizing a flexbox layout even across browsers that claim support. Or maybe you want a wrapping behavior that works consistently with old Android phones. You get the picture.

Luckily, there are some nuggets of wisdom in how flexbox was designed that allow you to implement these fallbacks.

First, since flexbox is a display mode on the containers, browsers that don't understand the `flex` keyword will ignore it. This means that you can let nonsupporting browsers display the container itself as a normal block.

Second, you can add `float` declarations to flex items, or set them to display as `inline-block` without affecting the flexbox layout. The `float` and `clear` properties have no effect on flex items, and setting a different `display` value will not affect the layout of the box. This gives you a great opportunity to start using flexbox for horizontal layouts today. First, you'd create a simple layout that works everywhere, and then enhance that with flexbox—for example, making use of the automatic margins, vertical alignment, or other nice-to-have embellishments.

In some cases, you might want to differentiate solely between browsers that do understand flexbox and those that don't. In those cases, we recommend that you use a JavaScript library like Modernizr (http://modernizr.com) for detecting the capabilities of the browser, giving you class name hooks on which to base your styles. We'll take a closer look at the Modernizr technique in Chapter 7.

If you only care about the most modern implementations of the spec in the latest browsers, you can also use the @supports notation, specifically designed to differentiate styling based on browser support:

```
@supports (flex-wrap: wrap) {
  /* flexbox rules here */
}
```

In this instance, we've limited the @supports block to browsers that understand both the conditional rule syntax and the flex-wrap: wrap declaration, which is only present in browsers implementing the latest syntax. There are plenty of browsers that understand variations of flexbox but not @supports, and vice versa. This construct can be handy when you only want to apply some very new aspect of flexbox, or work around bugs in older implementations.

The important aspect of this technique is to have the simpler fallback solution as your baseline, and then layer the flexbox enhancements on top of that.

Flexbox Bugs and Gotchas

Since flexbox is both fairly new and has gone through several iterations of different syntaxes, there are quite a few of bugs and inconsistencies to consider.

To keep track of flexbox bugs in slightly older browsers, check out Philip Walton's community-curated "Flexbugs" repository (https://github.com/philipwalton/flexbugs), where both bugs and workarounds are listed.

Apart from pure bugs, there are a couple other things that may trip you up:

- The sizing of images, videos, and other objects with an intrinsic aspect ratio is tricky when they become flex items. The spec has changed with regard to this over time, so your best bet is probably to add a wrapper element around such objects, letting the wrapper act as the flex item.

- Flex items also have what's known as an *implied minimum width*. In practical terms, this means that a flex item may refuse to shrink below its content-based size, despite being told to do so via flexible sizing. Overriding the min-width property or setting an explicit main size overrides this behavior.

- The painting order of flex items is determined by the order property if present. This can affect overlapping of items, just like with z-index.

- Furthermore, flex items can be given a z-index without having to give them a position other than static—unlike normal blocks. If given a z-index, that index will override the stacking order. A flex item with z-index set also creates a new stacking context.

- Some elements have rendering models that are a little bit outside the normal. For example, button and fieldset elements have default rendering that doesn't quite follow the normal rules for CSS styling. Trying to make those elements act as flex containers can fail horribly.

Summary

In this chapter, we've looked at several common content layout patterns and various use cases for them. We've seen how you can use inline blocks, table display modes, and floats for layout purposes, and their respective trade-offs.

We also looked at some useful patterns for using absolute or relative positioning, in combination with margins, to achieve some effective patterns.

Finally, we took a deep dive into the flexbox standard, finding more efficient ways to distribute, size, align, and order items horizontally and vertically.

In the next two chapters, we are going to scale up our efforts in layout-land. First we'll look at how to apply layout techniques to layout systems for whole pages, and get to grips with the new Grid module, specifically created for that scenario. Then we're going to see how to adapt our designs to varying screen sizes, using the techniques of responsive web design.

■ ■ ■

CHAPTER 7

Page Layout and Grids

This chapter is all about a systematic approach to creating page layouts. In the previous chapter, we focused on layout from the perspective of individual page components. The priority of and relationships between the individual components is a good place to start when designing the overall layout of a page. But at some point, you'll start to find recurring patterns for the overall structure. This chapter is all about codifying these structures into reusable solutions: containers, into which you can "pour" your content.

As you create these containers, you will most likely work with a grid system of predetermined sizes and ratios. This chapter will explore different ways of creating such a system in CSS. At first we will look at more traditional techniques, then later enhance them with flexbox. In the second half we will look at the upcoming CSS Grid Layout specification.

In this chapter you'll learn about

- A systematic approach to page layouts

- The terminology around page grids

- Building robust page layouts with floats and inline blocks, enhanced by flexbox

- Using the Grid Layout module

Planning your Layout

When it's time to start turning design into fully functional templates, it can be tempting to jump straight in and start marking up your page and writing the CSS. The risk is that you can paint yourself into a corner very quickly. A small amount of planning can save a lot of hassle further down the line. Or, as the saying goes, "Measure twice; cut once."

The important thing at this stage is to find the repeating patterns and the essence of the design system you are trying to translate into code.

Grids

When talking about the overall layout system for a site, the *grid* is a word that comes up often. It refers to the basic set of rules that the designer has used to divide the layout into a number of rows and columns (see Figure 7-1 for an example). Spaces between rows and columns are known as *gutters*. By talking about an element that spans three columns with gutters on the left and right sides, both designers and developers have a more clear picture of what is being built. This systematic approach to layout gives a certain predictability and stability. It still allows you to step away from the grid and have asymmetric parts of your layout—but that is usually the exception rather than the rule.

© Andy Budd and Emil Björklund 2016
A. Budd and E. Björklund, *CSS Mastery*, DOI 10.1007/978-1-4302-5864-3_7

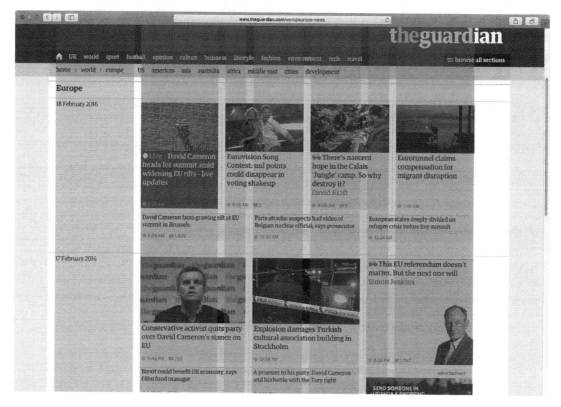

Figure 7-1. *Illustrated overlay view of column and gutter sizes used on* http://www.theguardian.com. *This view uses mainly a mix of five columns total, and three nested columns in the rightmost four*

Traditional Grid Terminology

Grids are far from being an invention of web designers; they have been around in various forms for centuries in graphic design. In web design, we often simplify the terminology down to just rows, columns, and gutters, but there is a richer vocabulary for grids used in traditional print design.

In the more traditional sense, rows and columns are names for whole strips of a grid, spanning the whole width or height. An individual cell of the grid, spanning one column and one row, is known as a *unit* or *module*. Units are then combined to form larger areas with certain ratios—one area could be three columns wide and two rows tall, for example. These combinations of units, vertically and horizontally, are traditionally called *fields* or *regions*.

The number of units in total across a grid is often based on a number that can be divided in several ways to create different ratios. For example, a 24-column grid can be further divided into 4 columns, each 6 units wide, or 3 columns of 8 units each, and so on.

The traditional meanings of these terms are perhaps not required knowledge to build grids for the Web. On the other hand, it won't hurt to have a bit of a grasp on them when communicating with colleagues, or creating naming conventions for your code. Having a common naming scheme helps greatly in creating a structured codebase right from the get-go—often you will use them to create helper classes for your design.

Layout Helper Classes

Class names are an obvious candidate as hooks to hang your layout styles on. For a very simple site, you may end up with just a couple of class names dictating the base of your layout. The class names you use for controlling a two-column blog layout may look as simple as the following:

```
.main-content {}
.secondary-content {}
```

As you work on more complex sites, you may find repeated patterns that are not clearly identifiable as belonging to a specific content hierarchy. This makes it slightly harder to name your classes in a reusable way. To create reusable styles, a lot of people use more visually descriptive class names, like the following:

```
.column { /* general column styles */ }
.column-half { /* taking up 50% of the row width */ }
.row { /* general row styles */ }
```

These class names are in a strict sense presentational, which means that you are putting information about presentation in your HTML. On the other hand, they are highly readable, reusable, and allow you to solve problems of layout *once*.

The alternative at the other end of the spectrum would be to collect all the selectors that have a certain style in common in a list:

```
.thing,
.other-thing,
.third-thing,
.fourth-thing {
  /* styles in common here */
}
```

The benefit of this organization is that you won't need to hook these styles up with any single name in HTML, but instead can add and remove from the list of selectors. The risk is that the number of selectors can get out of hand and tough to scan. It also presents a problem in terms of code organization. When the styles are split up based on similar styles rather than on the basis of reusable components, you risk having to jump around in your CSS to an uncomfortable degree when doing edits to a specific part of your site.

Naming schemes are a hugely challenging part of creating high-quality code, and tying presentation and markup together is a tricky trade-off. In this chapter, we'll try to walk the middle road of using a small number of layout helper classes while keeping the ties to presentation as light as possible. It is a highly compact way of creating layout systems, allowing for rapid prototyping and consistent styling. We will get back to the challenges of creating modular and reusable CSS systems in Chapter 12.

Regardless of whether you have created the visual design yourself or if you're coding up someone else's design, you will thank yourself down the line for creating something that is robust and well thought out. Having names for the component parts of the layout system also helps greatly when you need to collaborate with other designers and developers on a team. If your design is very complex, you might even benefit from incorporating solutions from ready-made CSS layout frameworks.

Using Ready-Made Design Grids and Frameworks

Since CSS layout can be tricky, and the patterns you find when planning them are often found repeatedly across many site designs, there are a number of ready-made CSS frameworks or libraries that include some sort of grid system.

Many of them work quite well, and allow you to quickly assemble designs that are supported across browsers. That is a very good thing, and it can potentially save you tons of effort. Especially for layouts with complex relationships between sizes, tools like Gridset (`https://gridsetapp.com`) that help you generate your CSS can be really helpful (see Figure 7-2).

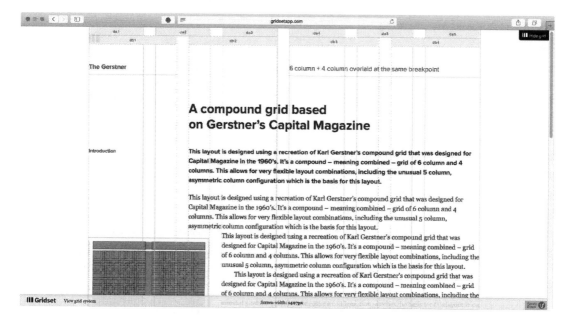

***Figure 7-2.** Gridset is a tool that helps you generate grid rules for your layouts*

The downside is that many of the larger CSS frameworks come with a complete set of layout rules for situations that your design might not need. This means including code in your project that is never used but still takes up bandwidth both over the wire and in your head—having CSS in your project that you yourself don't understand can be a bad thing.

Whether you should choose third-party code over something that you've built yourself always depends on the situation. If you're building a quick prototype to test something out, it's probably fine to use a prebuilt library. For moderately complex sites, you may find yourself having to modify an existing library so much that it would actually make more sense to build it yourself.

Fixed, Fluid, or Elastic

You might have come across the terms *fixed layout*, *fluid layout*, and *elastic layout* before. These refer to how we constrain the sizes of the elements in a specific layout.

- **Fixed layouts:** Layouts where we impose a specific measurement on the layout of our page. For instance, we could say "Our page is 960 pixels wide and that's that." This was the trend for a long time, as it gave designers and developers a great deal of control over the design. For years, designers debated which dimensions to base their layouts on: "Do most users have screens that are 1024 pixels wide, or is it safe to assume everyone has a 1280-pixel-wide monitor these days?"

- **Elastic layouts:** Layouts where the flexibility comes with sizing the components of the layout in ems. That way, proportions of the layout are preserved even if the user resizes the text. This can then be combined with minimum and maximum widths, so that the page respects the screen size a little better. Even if elastic layouts are somewhat dated today, borrowing the idea of using a maximum width set in ems is a good way to constrain fluid layouts.

- **Fluid layouts:** Also known as *liquid layouts*, layouts where the elements are sized with percentages, and ratios between the sizes (and sometimes also the distances between them) remain constant. The actual size in pixels varies with the size of the browser window. This is in a way the default mode of the Web, where block-level elements have no defined width but instead fluidly adjust to the available space.

People are still building fixed layouts, because of the sense of control they give from the designer's point of view. But this control is something being imposed on the person visiting the site, and fixed-width sites work poorly with the diversity of devices and screen sizes that exist today.

As you might have guessed, it's best to avoid fixed-width designs, letting your layout become fluid and adapt to the device it's being viewed on. This method of letting the design respond to its environment is one of the cornerstones of what is known as *responsive web design.*

▦ **Note** Creating responsive layouts requires a few more ingredients. We'll examine those in Chapter 8, but in this chapter, we'll assume that we are dealing with layout for bigger screens, to keep the examples simple.

Creating a Flexible Page Layout

In this section, we're going to go through some practical tips on how to create a system of styles that helps you create solid, flexible, and reusable page layouts.

A lot of the techniques and CSS properties in this section are variations of the same techniques you saw in Chapter 6, but with a slightly more high-level perspective.

We are going to re-create a layout similar to what we find in some sections on http://www.theguardian.com (see Figure 7-3), which have a few different variations on columns and horizontal sections.

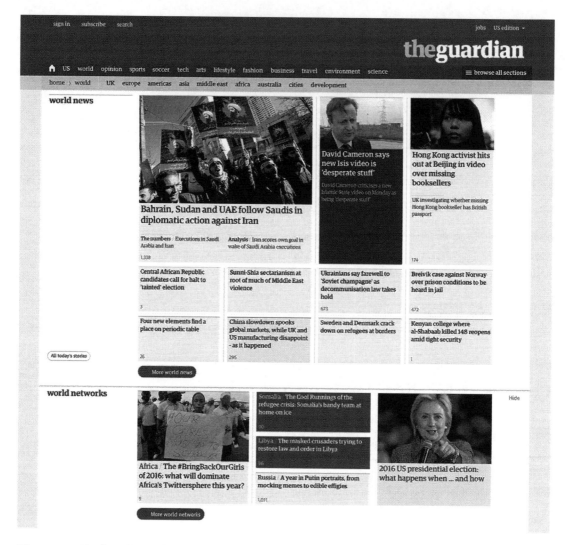

Figure 7-3. *The "World news" subsection on* `http://www.theguardian.com`*. We can see some variations of different numbers of columns and different sizes*

If we were to break this design down into a simplified sketch of just the major layout patterns, we would end up with something like what we see in Figure 7-4. For the rest of this section, we'll try to re-create this layout.

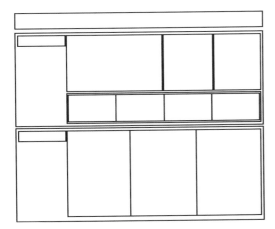

Figure 7-4. *A sketch of the different size columns in the layout*

What's not showing in the sketch is that the layout as a whole is centered in the page, and is capped by a maximum width. We'll start by creating the rules for that kind of wrapper element.

Defining a Content Wrapper

It's very common to use some sort of wrapper element that holds the contents of the page, like this:

```
<body>
    <div class="wrapper">
        <h1>My page content</h1>
    </div>
</body>
```

You *could* use the body element for this—after all, it's already there (or should be!)—but a lot of the time you end up wanting more than a single wrapper. There could be a site-wide navigation bar with a different width outside of the wrapper, or just stacked sections covering the whole screen width that have centered wrappers inside them.

Next, we need to set some rules for how this wrapper behaves. We'll give it a width combined with a maximum width and center it using automatic margins. For fluid layouts, it's very common to use a width set in percentages, slightly less than the full width of the window. The maximum width is then set in relation to the font size, using ems:

```
.wrapper {
  width: 95%;
  max-width: 76em;
  margin: 0 auto;
}
```

The body element comes with its own default margin as well, so we'll need to remove that or it will interfere with our styles. In Chapter 2 we mentioned "reset" styles like Eric Meyer's CSS Reset and Nicolas Gallagher's Normalize.css: they take care of things like this for you to create a consistent baseline, but sometimes it's a good idea to start slowly and build up your own styles. We'll keep it simple for this example:

```
body {
  margin: 0;
}
```

The result in Figure 7-5 gives us a good foundation. We've taken a number of decisions in these few lines of code:

- The main wrapper should normally take up 95% of the viewport width.

- With the shorthand `margin: 0 auto`, we've told it to have no margin at the top or bottom, and automatically divide the empty space to its left and right (leaving 2.5% on either side), which centers it on the page.

- At a maximum, the wrapper should be 76 ems wide. This equates to 1216 pixels based on the default font size of 16 pixels, but will automatically change if the user bumps up the font size setting in their browser. This `76em` number is not any kind of hard rule: it's just what looked right when trying out the layout.

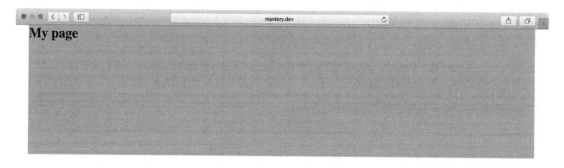

Figure 7-5. *Our content wrapper—we've temporarily given it a background color and some height to see the effects of the style*

We are parrying a number of factors that are subject to change. We don't know how large the screen is, so we don't want to tie ourselves down to any specific pixel size for the overall width. We also don't know what the user's font settings are.

What we do know is that we want a centered wrapper with at least some space on the sides, no matter the screen size. We also want to cap the layout width at some point, to prevent things like line length getting out of hand. If the user has a different font size setting than the normal 16px default, the maximum width will follow.

The specific measurements you choose will change to accommodate the design you're working on, but the principle is the same: find the basic constraints you want to set for the overall content wrapper, but don't define them too strictly. Instead, make sure you optimize for a changing environment.

"Optimize for change" is incidentally a mantra you will hear in all fields of software design. We have established principles for what our layout wrapper should do, without being overly specific about pixel measurements. Elements using the wrapper class can now be edited in one go.

We can make use of the consistency of the `wrapper` class straight away, using it in three different places. We'll add a masthead section for our fictional newspaper, and a navigation bar. These will both be full-width elements, but with an inner wrapper constraining the content centered within them. The main element holding the page-specific content comes after those two blocks.

```html
<header class="masthead">
  <div class="wrapper">
    <h1>Important News</h1>
  </div>
</header>
<nav role="navigation" class="navbar">
  <div class="wrapper">
    <ul class="navlist">
        <li><a href="/">Home</a></li>
        <!-- ...and so on -->
    </ul>
  </div>
</nav>
<main class="wrapper">
  <!-- the main content goes here -->
</main>
```

We won't go into the styling of the masthead and navbar (see Figure 7-6) here, but the CSS is available in the code examples for the book, and we have covered how to create a navbar component in Chapter 6.

Figure 7-6. *Using the wrapper class to center elements within two stacked page sections*

Row Containers

Next, we focus on the behavior of horizontal groups of content. The only thing we want them to do at this stage is to contain any floated elements within. In Chapter 3, we saw how we can use the `overflow` property to achieve float containment, by creating a new block-formatting context. While the overflow method is often the easiest way for smaller components, in this case we'll use a clearing pseudo-element instead. These larger sections of a page are more likely to have positioned content sticking out of the row container, so messing with overflow may come back to bite us.

```css
.row:after {
  content: '';
  display: block;
  clear: both;
  height: 0;
}
```

Creating Columns

We have our row container, and we want to divide it into columns. First things first: pick a method of horizontal layout. As we saw in the previous chapter, there are a number of ways of doing this. Using floats is probably the most commonly used technique and has pretty much universal browser support, so let's start there. Floating items to the left by default seems a good choice for left-to-right languages.

In case we want to add borders or padding directly on the column container without changing the width, we should also set the box-sizing method to border-box:

```
.col {
  float: left;
  box-sizing: border-box;
}
```

Next, we need to decide on a method of sizing the columns. A lot of CSS libraries use explicit presentational size classes to size individual columns:

```
.col-1of4 {
  width: 25%;
}
.col-1of2 {
  width: 50%;
}
/* ...etc */
```

That kind of approach is very helpful for quick prototyping, when you're likely to work at a desktop or laptop computer. Based on the preceding rules, a three-column layout where the leftmost column occupies half the width becomes very easy to declare in your markup:

```
<div class="row">
  <div class="col col-1of2"></div>
  <div class="col col-1of4"></div>
  <div class="col col-1of4"></div>
</div>
```

The downside of this kind of technique is the heavy emphasis on one particular layout. When we later want to adjust how the layout responds to various screen sizes, the naming scheme will not make as much sense.

If we want to retain the strategy of reusable class names for sizing, we will be left with *some* ties between markup and presentation. We can choose to make these ties looser by using other class names, without mentioning the specific width or ratio. Using a metaphor from the musical world, we can, for example, create a rule for row containers that normally have four equal parts—a *quartet*:

```
.row-quartet > * {
  width: 25%;
}
```

We're targeting direct children of the row container with the universal selector here. This is to keep the specificity of this general rule low. Since the universal selector has a specificity value of 0, we can override this width with a single class name later on. The following markup would now create a row with four equal-width columns:

```
<div class="row row-quartet">
  <div class="col"></div>
  <div class="col"></div>
  <div class="col"></div>
  <div class="col"></div>
</div>
```

Any deviation from this "tempo" inside .row-quartet would now get its own overriding class name, but without a layout-specific class. The example of the three-column layout from before would now look slightly different:

```
<div class="row row-quartet">
  <div class="col my-special-column"></div>
  <div class="col"></div>
  <div class="col"></div>
</div>
.my-special-column {
  width: 50%;
}
```

We can now complement the row rules with more "tempo" classes as needed:

```
.row-quartet > * {
  width: 25%;
}
.row-trio > * {
  width: 33.3333%;
}
```

In the sketch of the layout we're building, both subcategory sections have a header area that takes up the leftmost one-fifth of the page, and a content area that takes up the remaining four-fifths. In the first subsection, there's also a bigger article column, taking up 50% of the content area.

```
.subcategory-content {
  width: 80%;
}
.subcategory-header {
  width: 20%;
}
.subcategory-featured {
  width: 50%;
}
```

The HTML:

```html
<section class="subcategory">
  <div class="row">
    <header class="col subcategory-header">
      <h2>Sub-section 1</h2>
    </header>
    <div class="col subcategory-content">
      <div class="row row-quartet">
        <div class="col subcategory-featured"></div>
        <div class="col"></div>
        <div class="col"></div>
      </div>
      <div class="row row-quartet">
        <div class="col"></div>
        <div class="col"></div>
        <div class="col"></div>
        <div class="col"></div>
      </div>
    </div>
  </div>
</section>
<section class="subcategory">
  <div class="row">
    <header class="col subcategory-header"></header>
    <div class="col subcategory-content">
      <div class="row row-trio">
        <div class="col"></div>
        <div class="col"></div>
        <div class="col"></div>
      </div>
    </div>
  </div>
</section>
```

USING EXTRA WRAPPER ELEMENTS

In this example, we've used extra nested elements with a class of row for the "inner" column groups. You could also add the row class to the col items themselves. While being sparse with your markup is a nice feeling and generally a good practice in many circumstances, it can also backfire if conceptually different rules start to clash. Adding an extra element to separate them in some places minimizes the risk of this happening, despite being somewhat redundant.

Putting this together with the wrapper and a simple header gets us a long way toward our "page skeleton." As listed next and shown in Figure 7-7, we have also added a few placeholder content headings and some minimum heights to the columns, as well as an outline. (Outlines are a handy trick for visualizing and debugging layouts, since they don't affect the sizing of elements.)

```css
.col {
  min-height: 100px;
  outline: 1px solid #666;
}
```

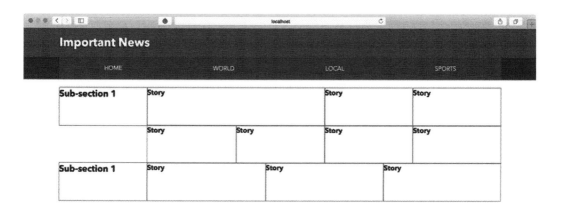

Figure 7-7. *Our page layout is now beginning to take shape*

Now that we have our grid classes working for us, we can easily combine or extend them with more measurements to create even more complex layout patterns. Next, we'll add some dummy content inside each container and add in the details.

Here's how an article with an image looks in markup:

```html
<div class="col">
  <article class="story">
    <img src="http://placehold.it/600x300" alt="Dummy image">
    <h3>Cras suscipit nec leo id.</h3>
    <p>Autem repudiandae...</p>
  </article>
</div>
```

Figure 7-8 shows how it looks when we incorporate this dummy content.

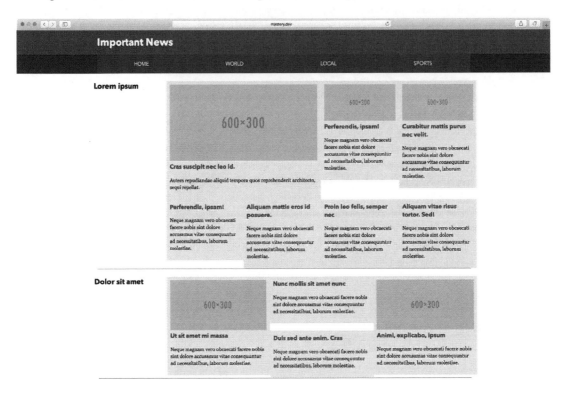

Figure 7-8. *Now we have added some content inside the grid cells to see how our layout holds up, along with some light typographic styling*

We have used an `article` element with a class name of `story` inside the column containers. The extra element separates layout from content and gives us a portable solution instead of overloading the wrappers themselves.

The dummy content styling simply consists of a background color, a little bit of padding, and a rule to make any images inside the stories become fluid to fill up the width of the element:

```
.story {
  padding: .6875em;
  background-color: #eee;
}
.story img {
  width: 100%;
}
```

Fluid Gutters

It is now glaringly obvious that we need to add some spacing between our columns, to allow the layout some breathing room. This is where gutters come in.

In a fluid layout, you can either go for fluid gutters set in percentages, or gutters that are set in a fixed length, commonly set relative to the font size. Either way you choose, one of the most common techniques is to set equal amounts of spacing on both sides of the column element, each side being half as wide as the intended total gutter size (see Figure 7-9).

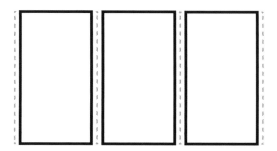

Figure 7-9. *Adding equal amounts of space on both sides of the columns, each one-half of the total gutter width*

If you need to set background colors or images directly on the columns and still want them spaced apart, it may make sense to use margins as gutters. It also makes sense if you need to cater for *really* old browsers like IE7 that don't even support box-sizing. Considering this is a fluid layout, you will want to use margins set with percentages, since mixing percentages and other lengths becomes tricky to handle without using calc(), which is also not supported in older browsers.

In any case, it's useful to know how to calculate margins in percentages, to make them play nicely with other widths. In the previous example, we have used a font size of 16 pixels and a line height of 1.375, which equals 22 pixels. Let's say we want the gutters to equal the line height of the text on reasonably wide screens, connecting the typographic measurement to our grid. We start with the widest point of our layout, 76 ems or 1216 pixels.

Since margins are relative to the containing block, we calculate the ratio of gutter to the total width in the same way we calculate a relative font size: divide the desired measurement by the whole width. Dividing 22 by 1216 gives us 0.018092105, so around 1.8% for one whole gutter. Finally, we divide that in half, to give us the amount of margin to put on either side of each column, and end up with 0.9%:

```
.col {
  float: left;
  box-sizing: border-box;
  margin: 0 0.9% 1.375em;
}
```

We have also added a bottom margin to space the rows of content apart by the height of one line of text. Note that the vertical spacing is set in ems rather than percentages, since the line height is not relative to the screen size, so we want to keep that relationship intact.

Taking a look at the example in progress will show us a broken layout (see Figure 7-10) since the margins add to the measurements of columns. Not even box-sizing: border-box can get us out of that one, so we'll need to revise the column widths.

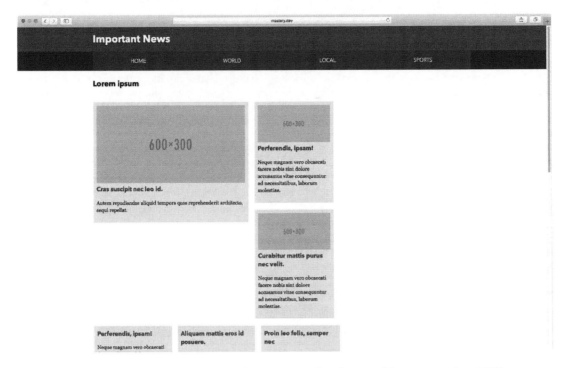

Figure 7-10. *Our layout is now broken, since the margins make columns add up to more than 100%*

To fix the column width calculations when using margins for fluid gutters, we need to subtract 1.8% from each column width:

```
.row-trio > * {
  width: 31.53333%;
}
.row-quartet > * {
  width: 23.2%;
}

.subcategory-featured {
  width: 48.2%;
}
.subcategory-header {
  width: 18.2%;
}
.subcategory-content {
  width: 78.2%;
}
```

This gives us the working version we see in Figure 7-11. In the screenshot, we have narrowed the browser window slightly, and you can see the gutters narrowing along with it.

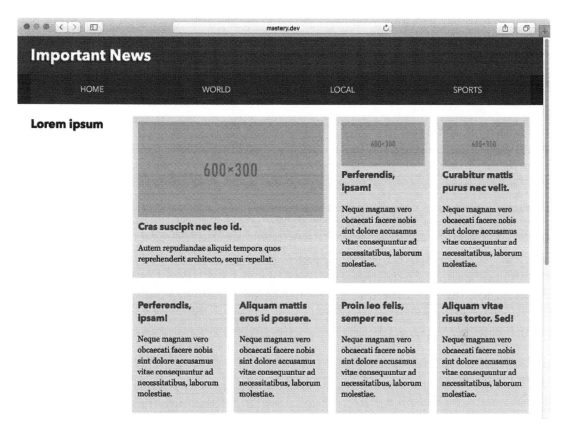

Figure 7-11. *Our page now has fluid gutters, growing and shrinking with the page width*

Negating the Outer Gutters

At this point, we have a working system representing rows, fluid columns, and fluid gutters. The remaining work has to do with getting the details right and minimizing the risk of visual discrepancies.

First off, the margins that we use to create gutters cause an extra indent on the right and left sides of the outer container, which may not be desirable. Nesting columns inside further row containers compounds this problem (see Figure 7-12). We could negate the left margin on the first item and the right margin on the last item to counter this situation. But that would further complicate the math involved in calculating column and gutter widths.

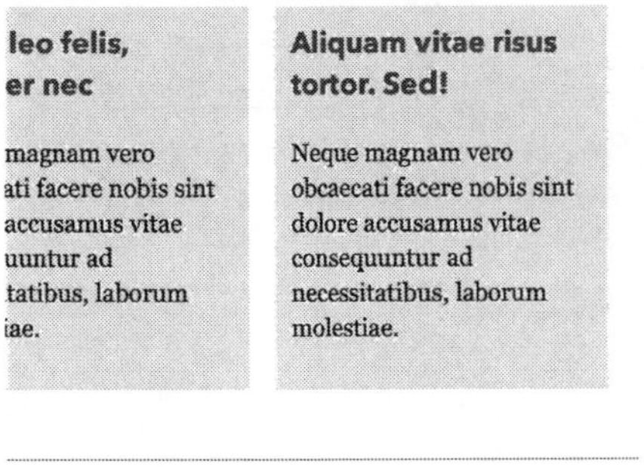

**leo felis,
er nec**

magnam vero
ati facere nobis sint
accusamus vitae
uuntur ad
tatibus, laborum
iae.

**Aliquam vitae risus
tortor. Sed!**

Neque magnam vero
obcaecati facere nobis sint
dolore accusamus vitae
consequuntur ad
necessitatibus, laborum
molestiae.

Figure 7-12. *The article containers end up being some distance from the right edge of the section border, because of the outer margins that we apply to each column to create gutters*

Instead, we'll use a trick with negative margins to alleviate this problem. We mentioned in Chapter 6 that nonfloating block elements without a specified width expand their width when given negative margins to the left *and* right.

Since we opted to use a separate element to act as our row containers (rather than letting column elements double as rows for any nested columns), we are in a fine position to use this fact to our advantage. We amend the grid rules by saying that each row container has a negative margin on each side equal to one-half the gutter (see Figure 7-13):

```
.row {
  margin: 0 -.9%;
}
```

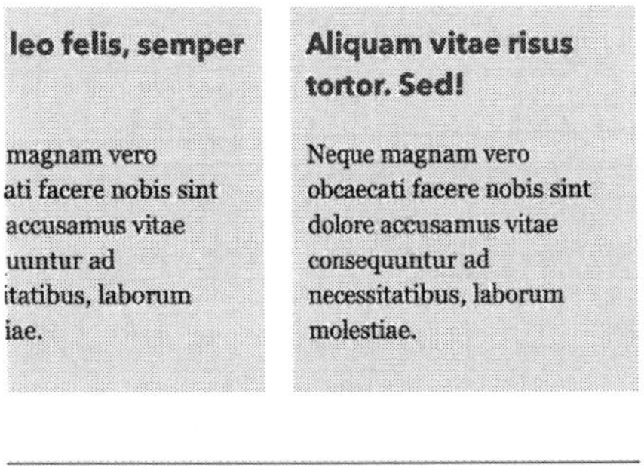

leo felis, semper

magnam vero
ati facere nobis sint
accusamus vitae
uuntur ad
itatibus, laborum
iae.

**Aliquam vitae risus
tortor. Sed!**

Neque magnam vero
obcaecati facere nobis sint
dolore accusamus vitae
consequuntur ad
necessitatibus, laborum
molestiae.

Figure 7-13. *Using negative margins on row container elements, we counter the extra indent and compounding margins of nested rows*

Alternate Gutter Strategies

In order to further simplify the column width calculations, we can make use of the box-sizing property and set the gutters using padding instead.

If we continue using fluid gutters, we only need to shift the gutter measurement to become padding instead. We can now go back to expressing the measurements of the columns as proper fractions of the whole again, without factoring in the width of the gutter:

```css
.col {
  float: left;
  box-sizing: border-box;
  padding: 0 .9% 1.375em;
}
.row-trio > * {
  width: 33.33333%;
}
.subcategory-featured {
  width: 50%;
}
/* ...etc */
```

This also leaves the road open to using gutters set with a typographic measurement instead: we can use ems to set the gutter to be relative to the font size rather than the width of the grid. In the following example (see Figure 7-14), the gutter size is the same as the line height, creating equal vertical and horizontal spacing between columns regardless of the width of the grid.

```css
.col {
  float: left;
  box-sizing: border-box;
  /* one half of the line-height as padding on left and right: */
  padding: 0 .6875em 1.375em;
}
```

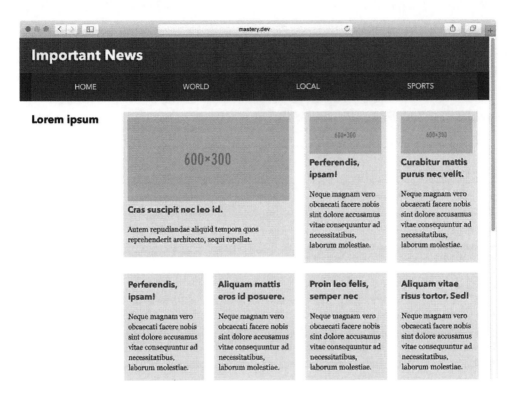

Figure 7-14. *With "elastic" gutters set in relation to the font size, gutters stay the same no matter the width of the content*

Enhanced Columns: Wrapping and Equal Heights

So far we've used floats as our method of choice for creating the layout. As we saw in the previous chapter, we have a range of other tools at our disposal. We'll briefly look at some examples of employing these in the same generic way as our floated columns. This will help us create even more flexible layouts.

Wrapping Column Rows with Inline Blocks

If you look closely at the screenshot from The Guardian (see Figure 7-15), you'll note that the bottom of the topmost subsection actually has two rows of headline links. In our version of the layout, we so far only have one row of slightly bigger story previews.

Figure 7-15. *The bottom part of the top subsection contains two rows of stories*

Using floats for wrapping lines of containers is a tricky affair: if one of the items is taller, the floats might get stuck, creating an ugly stepped effect.

To counter this, we can create a generic class name that we employ where content is expected to wrap into several rows. For containers with this class name, we'll employ `inline-block` display using the font-sizing technique we used in Chapter 6. As we do so, we need to set the negative margin of the row container in `rem` units, since the `font-size` of the element itself is now 0. For full backward compatibility, we use a fallback to pixel measurements for IE 8.

```
.row-wrapping {
  font-size: 0;
  margin: 0 -11px;
  margin: 0 -.6875rem;
}
.row-wrapping > * {
  float: none;
  vertical-align: top;
  display: inline-block;
  font-size: 16px;
  font-size: 1rem;
}
```

At this point, we can add as many story previews as we like, and they will wrap neatly after filling up four items in a row. But before we view the results, we'll polish the details a little further using flexbox.

Using Flexbox for Equal-Height Columns

Just as we saw in Chapter 6, flexbox can help with creating equal-height columns. When creating a systematic layout, we want to have some specific rule sets that apply only when flexbox is supported.

To be able to detect flexbox support, we'll add a small script at the top of the page. We will use Modernizr for this, which adds class names to the `html` element for each feature that is supported. On `https://modernizr.com` you can create your own detection script file with only the detection code you need. For this example, we'll add detection only for the various flexbox features to keep the file small.

After creating your detection script, you put it inside a JavaScript file that you load in the `head` element of your page, *before* loading any CSS files. The order is important, since the detection needs to happen on load, before styles are applied.

```
<script src="modernizr.js"></script>
```

We can now start coding our solution using prefixed classes, and be confident that only browsers with support will see it. The `flexbox` class indicates modern flexbox support, and the `flexwrap` class indicates support for wrapping flexbox items into multiple rows or columns.

In the full code examples, you'll find that we have combined these with the `flexboxtweener` class, which indicates support for the version of flexbox shipped in IE10.

First, we'll turn the standard rows into flexbox rows:

```
.flexbox .row {
  display: flex;
}
```

Already at this point, we have created equal-height columns, a direct effect of the default stretching of flex items to fill the parent.

Since we use a wrapper element around the contents of each column, we need to sprinkle on some more flexbox magic to get the content to fill the columns evenly. Each column is made a columnar flexbox container in itself, where the direct children are set to fill up the space evenly as any extra space is distributed:

```
.flexbox .col {
  display: flex;
  flex-direction: column;
}
.flexbox .col > * {
  flex: 1;
}
```

The shorthand flex: 1 is a special case of the flex shorthand that sets flex-grow to 1, flex-shrink to 1, and flex-basis to 0.

Finally, we augment the class used for wrapping rows so that they too utilize the equal-height mechanisms of flexbox:

```
.flexwrap .row-wrapping {
  display: flex;
  flex-wrap: wrap;
}
```

Looking at the example layout, displayed in Figure 7-16, shows us neat rows and columns, filling up the space perfectly.

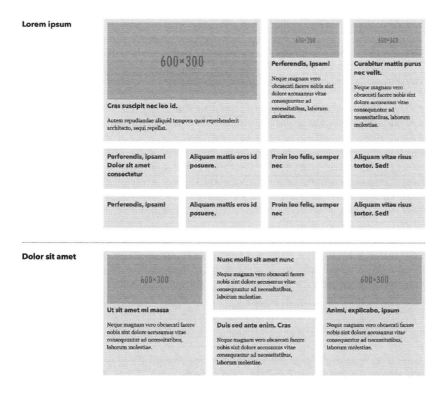

Figure 7-16. *The rows and columns of our grid now fill up their containers perfectly, adjusting to the tallest content within each row*

At this point, we have created a small flexible system of rules for creating page layouts. We can achieve consistency in our rows, columns, and gutters by recombining simple sets of class names. This is essentially what ready-made grid rules in CSS frameworks like Bootstrap and Foundation do for you, but often with a heavier reliance on presentational class names.

Starting out simple like we did in this chapter allows you to create the grid rules specifically needed for your project, keeping the code small and manageable (the final example file has about 80 lines of generously spaced code for the whole grid system, including all browser prefixes).

Flexbox as a General Tool for Page Layout

In the previous chapter, we looked at flexbox as a power tool for detailed and flexible content layout. In this chapter, we have sprinkled it on top of a more backward-compatible float-based layout system. This strategy is very robust, and it is in fact the exact same strategy that The Guardian has employed for their page layout—if you dig into their page source, you'll find lots of similarities!

We saw in Chapter 6 why this "sprinkling flexbox on top" strategy works so well—flexbox was designed to ignore floats and display properties on flex items. This makes it easy to use flexbox to polish float-based layouts. The flex items adopt the width, margins, padding, and so forth from the properties already set. But is flexbox the right tool for the job of creating full-page layout and grid-like structures?

There is nothing (aside from lacking support in older browsers) stopping you from using flexbox as the core method for page layout, despite it not being conceived explicitly for that purpose. After all, neither were floats! Still, there are both upsides and downsides to using flexbox as a high-level layout tool.

Pros and Cons

On the positive side, flexbox is fast—at least in browsers implementing the most modern specification. Modern flexbox is generally more performant than, for example, floats. The implementations of the oldest flexbox specification generally performed quite poorly though, so you should apply it carefully for older browsers.

Flexbox also makes it very easy to take a part of a page and, with very few lines of code, divide it up into flexible pieces, using grow and shrink factors. This ability to accommodate content regardless of the number of items is a clear benefit for creating grid-like layouts.

On the negative side, since this flexibility requires recalculation as content loads inside the items, it can lead to a jumpy experience when first loading a page. For example, an image loading in one flexible item can "push" the other items as the item grows to accommodate the new content.

The example we worked on earlier relies on the default flex values for rows (where elements do not automatically grow) combined with explicit widths to minimize the jumpy effect.

Layout in One or Two Dimensions

All of the methods we have looked at for layout so far, including flexbox, are variations of lining things up to create rows and columns. Even if some of them allow wrapping of content into several rows (and thus stacking into the vertical dimension), they are basically one-dimensional—content flows left-to-right, right-to-left, or top-to-bottom (see Figure 7-17), but items cannot span rows and columns at the same time. This means we need to subdivide layouts using wrapper elements.

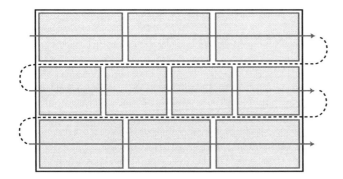

Figure 7-17. *All the layout methods we have looked at so far (even the ones with wrapping rows) are one-dimensional in the sense that the content flows in one direction*

In the early days of web layout, one of the few tools to create layout was using actual HTML table elements. One of the reasons that practice stuck around long after CSS was a viable alternative was that it actually enabled us to create two-dimensional layouts—items inside the table could have colspan and rowspan attributes allowing them to take part in complex layout scenarios, like in Figure 7-18.

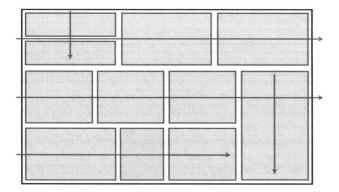

Figure 7-18. *Layout in two dimensions—see if you can spot how many container elements you would need to achieve this layout with floats or flexbox*

With CSS layouts to date, we have come to accept that any subsection in the layout may need its own container element, and that layout is something we apply to the individual elements. But the upcoming CSS Grid Layout module aims to change all that.

The CSS Grid Layout Module: 2D Layout

When it comes to the macro level of page layout, none of the techniques we've looked at so far has been a complete solution for controlling order, placement, and sizing in a two-dimensional grid. The CSS Grid Layout module defines the first set of CSS properties to specifically do this.

Using the Grid Layout module allows us to remove a lot of the extra elements we've added to control layout, dramatically simplifying our markup. It also shifts the burden of setting column or row dimensions from the elements themselves up to a single containing element representing a grid on the page.

WARNING: EXPERIMENTAL PROPERTIES AHEAD!

It should be noted that the Grid Layout spec is the least supported layout technology in this chapter, and is still in the experimental stage at the time of writing.

Google Chrome Canary, Firefox Developer Edition, Safari Technology Preview and the WebKit Nightly prerelease browser versions all have reasonably comprehensive implementations of Grid Layout. The Chrome Canary implementation tends to be the most updated—we recommend that you try the examples out in that version. It does require you to turn on the preference flag "Enable Experimental Web Platform Features."

Internet Explorer was, surprisingly, the first browser to support Grid Layout. It shipped with Internet Explorer 10, but at that time the spec looked a bit different, and did not support all of the functionality. To get the basics working there, you need to change the syntax up a bit, and use the `-ms-` prefix for the grid properties. Microsoft Edge also supports this older syntax.

In this chapter, we'll only look at the standard syntax as it is defined today. If you want to adapt the syntax for IE10-11 and Microsoft Edge, have a look at the Microsoft Developer Network pages for Grid Layout (`http://msdn.microsoft.com/en-us/library/ie/hh673533(v=vs.85).aspx`).

Understanding the Grid Terminology

Figure 7-19 shows you a fully fledged grid, as it's defined in CSS.

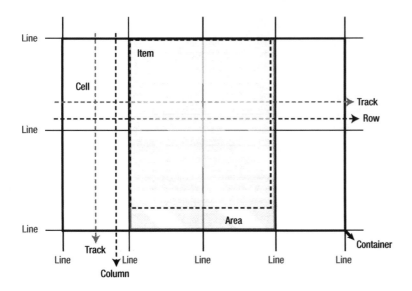

Figure 7-19. *A grid container and its component parts*

Here's what's going on:

- An element set to display as a grid is called a *grid container*—that's the thicker outer part in the figure.

- The container is then divided up into parts—known as *grid cells*—by *grid lines*, slicing through the grid container.

- These lines create strips running horizontally and vertically, called *grid tracks*. Horizontal tracks are *grid rows* and vertical tracks are *grid columns*.

- The combined rectangular surface covered by a set of adjacent cells is known as a *grid area*.

- Direct children of a grid container are called *grid items*. These can be placed in grid areas.

You may note that these terms have little in common with the more traditional grid terminology we outlined at the start of the chapter. Designers like Mark Boulton have criticized this difference in terminology (http://markboulton.co.uk/journal/open-letter-to-w3c-css-working-group-re-css-grids), but the people writing the specification decided that it was better to use names from the concept of tables and spreadsheets to get the ideas of a grid across to developers. For better or worse, these names are what we are stuck with.

Defining Rows and Columns

To create the grid, we need to tell the browser the number and behavior of its rows and columns. To achieve the 4×2 grid in Figure 7-19 using our trusty old wrapper div as a container, we need to set the display mode to grid. We also supply measurements for rows and columns, called the grid template:

```
.wrapper {
    display: grid;
    grid-template-rows: 300px 300px;
    grid-template-columns: 1fr 1fr 1fr 1fr;
}
```

The preceding code has given us a grid with two rows that are 300 pixels tall each, and four equal-width columns across them. It also generates the grid lines at the edges of each column and row—we'll need to use those later.

The unit we use for the column widths is new: the fr unit stands for *fraction* (of available space). It's pretty much the same flexible unit as we've seen in the flexbox flex-grow-factors, but here it's gotten its very own unit notation, presumably to keep from confusing it with other unitless numbers. The available space is the space that is left after any grid tracks are sized with either an explicit length or according to their own content.

Each fr unit here thus represents a fourth of the available space in the grid; had we added a fifth column of 1fr, each unit would represent one-fifth of the available space.

We could also have mixed and matched units in the rows and columns: you can pretty much choose any type of length measurement. For example, the columns could be declared as 200px 20% 1fr 200px, giving us two fixed-width 200-pixel columns at the edges, with the second column from the left being 20% of the overall space, and the third one taking up any space that is left after that—the fr unit deals with remaining space after other lengths have been calculated, just like in flexbox.

Making Grids for Our Page Subsections

Looking at the example page section we have been working with so far, we can now slice each subsection into a grid. The simplest possible grid for the first section would be three rows and five columns. The columns need to be one-fifth of the total width, and the rows can have an automatic height, depending fully on the content (see Figure 7-20).

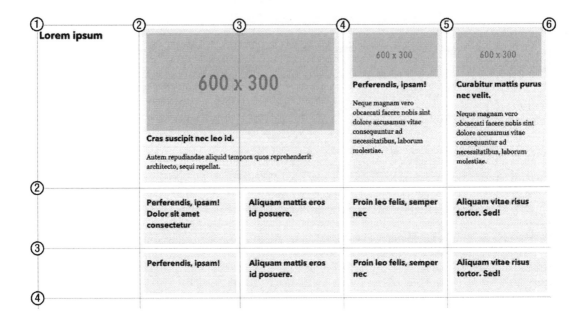

Figure 7-20. *Creating a grid container from the first page subsection requires us to slice it into five columns and three rows. Numbers indicate the resulting grid lines*

The markup needed for the content can now be radically simplified. We are still going to use a wrapper element for the grid container to separate it from any subsection styling, but inside that all the stories are just direct child elements:

```
<section class="subcategory">
  <div class="grid-a">
    <header class="subcategory-header">
      <h2>Lorem ipsum</h2>
    </header>
    <article class="story story-featured">
      <!-- The slightly bigger article goes here -->
    </article>
    <article class="story">[...]</article>
    <article class="story">[...]</article>
    <!-- ...and so on, for all our articles. -->
  </div>
</section>
```

Next, we'll define this particular grid setup in CSS. As we saw from "slicing" the grid in Figure 7-20, we'll need three rows of automatic height and five columns each taking up an equal fraction of the space:

```
.grid-a {
  display: grid;
  grid-template-rows: auto auto auto;
  grid-template-columns: repeat(5, 1fr);
  margin: 0 -.6875em;
}
```

212

You can also see a new functional notation that comes with grids: the ability to repeat a track declaration for columns or rows a specified number of times instead of typing out every track individually.

Since grid tracks are not represented by any specific element in the Document Object Model (DOM), we can't size them with min-width, max-width, etc. To achieve the same functionality in grid track declarations, the minmax() functional notation has been introduced. For example, we could set the last two rows to be at least 4em tall, but other than that take up an equal amount of the available space:

```
.grid-a {
  display: grid;
  grid-template-rows: auto minmax(4em, 1fr) minmax(4em, 1fr);
  grid-template-columns: repeat(5, 1fr);
  margin: 0 -.6875em;
}
```

If you want to compress the grid track definition into a single shorthand, you can use the grid-template property, where you can supply row definitions and column definitions, separated by a slash:

```
.grid-a {
  display: grid;
  grid-template: auto minmax(4em, 1fr) minmax(4em, 1fr) / repeat(5, 1fr);
  margin: 0 -.6875em;
}
```

Placing Items on the Grid

To place items on the grid, we need to reference the grid lines where they start and end. For example, the subsection header takes up the entire leftmost column. The most verbose way of putting it there is setting properties for the starting and ending lines in both dimensions (see Figure 7-21):

```
.subsection-header {
  grid-row-start: 1;
  grid-column-start: 1;
  grid-row-end: 4;
  grid-column-end: 2;
}
```

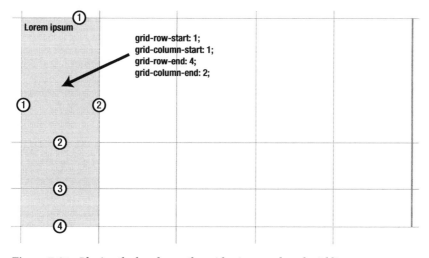

Figure 7-21. *Placing the header on the grid using numbered grid lines*

213

We can simplify that somewhat by setting the starting and ending lines in a single declaration, using the grid-row and grid-column properties respectively. Starting and ending lines in each property are separated with a slash character.

```
.subsection-header {
  grid-row: 1/4;
  grid-column: 1/2;
}
```

If we were unsure how many rows there would be in the grid but still wanted the header to span all of them, we would want to specify that it ends on the last row. Grid Layout allows you to count the lines backward using a negative index, so the ending line of the last declared track is always -1. The default span is always one cell, so we could also omit the last part of the grid-column value:

```
.subsection-header {
  grid-row: 1/-1;
  grid-column: 1; /* equivalent to grid-column: 1/2 */
}
```

Finally, we can compact the values even further into the grid-area property: it takes up to four values separated by slashes. They specify, in order, grid-row-start, grid-column-start, grid-row-end, and grid-column-end.

```
.subsection-header {
  grid-area: 1/1/-1;
}
```

In the preceding code snippet, we have left out the fourth argument, indicating the end placement in the column direction. You can do this with both of the end-direction arguments, as the grid positioning will then default to the item spanning one grid track in either direction.

Grid Item Alignment

When you place items on the grid, they automatically become as wide and as tall as the grid area you place them in. The automatically expanding height is very similar to how flex row items work in flexbox. This is no coincidence.

Both flexbox and Grid Layout specify the behavior of child items in terms of the CSS Box Alignment specification—a standard that takes care of alignment and justification in several CSS contexts.

Just like in flexbox rows, vertical alignment can be controlled with align-items and align-self. The alignment defaults to stretch, which causes the items to expand vertically to fill the area. The same values as in flexbox (but without the flex- prefix) are used here, for example start, end, or center—Figure 7-22 explains the differences.

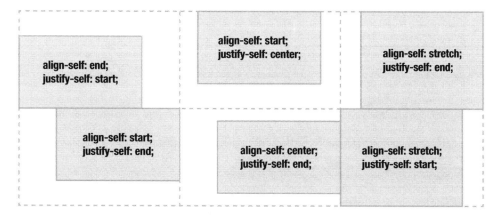

Figure 7-22. *Some possible values for alignment of grid items*

Grid items behave like block-level elements, and automatically fill the width of the grid area they are placed in, unless you give them another measurement. Percentages for width are based on the grid area the item sits in, not the grid container.

If your grid items don't fill the whole width of the area where they're placed, you can also justify them left, right, or center inside that area with the `justify-items` and `justify-self` properties.

Just like in flexbox, you use `align-self` on individual items, but in the Grid Layout context, you can also set `justify-self`. On the grid container, `align-items` or `justify-items` sets a default alignment for the items.

Aligning the Grid Tracks

In the same way you can align items inside grid areas when they don't take up the whole area, you can align the grid tracks themselves inside the container. As long as the track sizes don't add up to cover the whole size of the grid container, you can use `align-content` (vertically) and `justify-content` (horizontally) to shift the tracks.

For example, the columns in the following grid declaration don't add up to the whole size of the container:

```
.grid {
  width: 1000px;
  grid-template-columns: repeat(8, 100px); /* 800px in total */
}
```

You can now choose where the remaining space inside the container ends up. By default, `justify-content` computes to `start`. Figure 7-23 shows the possible values and their effects.

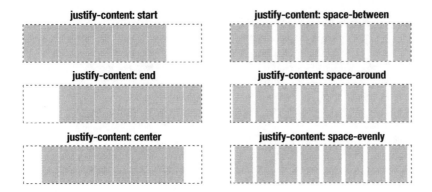

Figure 7-23. *Shifting grid tracks with* justify-content

In a similar way, you can align tracks vertically (if the container has a fixed height) using the same keywords with the align-content property.

Gutters in Grid Layout

There are several ways to create gutters inside your grids. You can avoid declaring them with the grid properties altogether by using margins on the items themselves. You can also use grid track alignment (see for example the space-between example earlier), or create empty grid tracks that act like gutters.

If you need a fixed-size gutter that stays the same between all tracks, the simplest way is to use the grid-column-gap and grid-row-gap properties, as follows. This creates fixed-size gutters that act as if the grid lines themselves had a width—comparable to column-gap in multicolumn layout or border-spacing in tables.

```
.grid {
  display: grid;
  grid-template-columns: repeat(5, 1fr);
  grid-column-gap: 1.5em;
  grid-row-gap: 1.5em;
}
```

Automatic Grid Placement

In the news site subsection we're working with, the leftmost column is reserved for the header, but the rest of the space is simply packed with the .story elements. It wouldn't be too hard to position them using, for example, :nth-of-type() selectors and explicit grid positions, but that would be rather tedious:

```
.story-featured {
  grid-area: 1/2/2/4;
}
.story:nth-of-type(2) {
  grid-area: 1/4/2/5;
}
/* ...and so on */
```

216

Luckily for us, the Grid Layout spec has something called *automatic placement*. It is part of the property defaults for Grid Layout, and without changing anything items are laid out, by source order, in the first available cell in the first row where there is an empty column. As rows fill up, the grid continues on the next row and any empty cells there.

This means we only need to specify the following in order for the Grid Layout algorithm to do its job:

- The grid definition

- The header area

- That the featured article spans two columns

Everything else is just packed in order. The full code for replicating the float-based grid we created earlier (but with the much cleaner markup) looks like this:

```
.grid-a {
  display: grid;
  grid-template-rows: auto auto auto;
  grid-template-columns: repeat(5, 1fr);
}
.subcategory-header {
  grid-row: 1/-1;
}
.story-featured {
  grid-column: span 2;
}
```

That's *five declarations* in total for controlling the actual layout! Admittedly, the full code example has more rules for padding and gutters created with margins, but that's just the same as previous float-based examples. Figure 7-24 shows how the `.story` items fill up the grid.

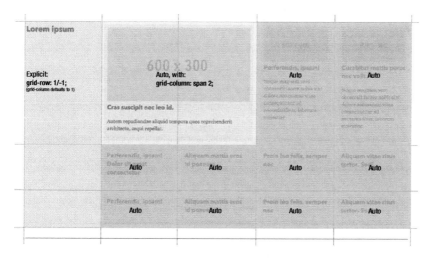

***Figure 7-24.** Only the subsection header has any explicit placement—and even that makes use of the default placement of column 1. The rest of the items are placed column by column, row by row*

Order of Automatic Placement

The automatic placement defaults suit us well in this example. There are several things that allow us to control the placement further, without being explicit about where the items end up.

In the example we have played with so far, the source order lines up neatly with the order that the grid places the items in. We can also make use of the order property, as with flexbox, to control the order in which items are processed. Items default to an order value of 0, and any integer value, including a negative one, is permitted.

```
.story:nth-of-type(2),
.story:nth-of-type(3) {
  order: -2;
}
.story-featured {
  order: -1;
}
```

This changes the layout so that the featured story becomes the third item to be placed on the grid: the second and third stories come first (represented by the second and third article elements with the class of .story inside the grid wrapper). After that, all of the other stories that default to order: 0 are placed, as shown in Figure 7-25.

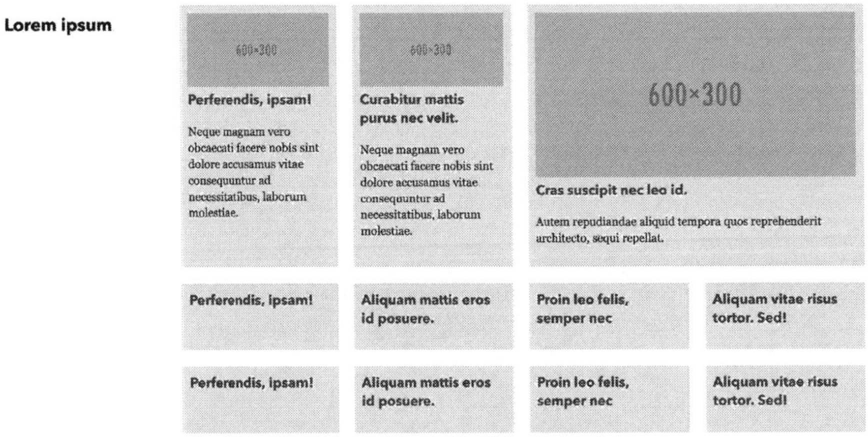

Figure 7-25. *Changing the* order *property determines the order in which the automatic layout happens*

■ **Note**   There's nothing stopping you from placing several items overlapping the same grid area. The order property also affects the order in which they are painted in that case. You can further control the stacking of grid items using z-index, without setting any specific positioning properties, just like with flexbox. Each grid item also forms its own stacking context.

Switching the Automatic Placement Algorithm

By default, automatic placement happens row by row. You can set it to place column by column instead, and this is controlled by the `grid-auto-flow` property:

```
.my-row-grid {
  grid-auto-flow: row; /* default value */
}
.my-columnar-grid {
  grid-auto-flow: column;
}
```

The placement algorithm is very simple by default: it makes one pass and tries to find the next sequence of grid cells where the item to be placed fits. When items span several cells, this can lead to holes in the grid (see Figure 7-26).

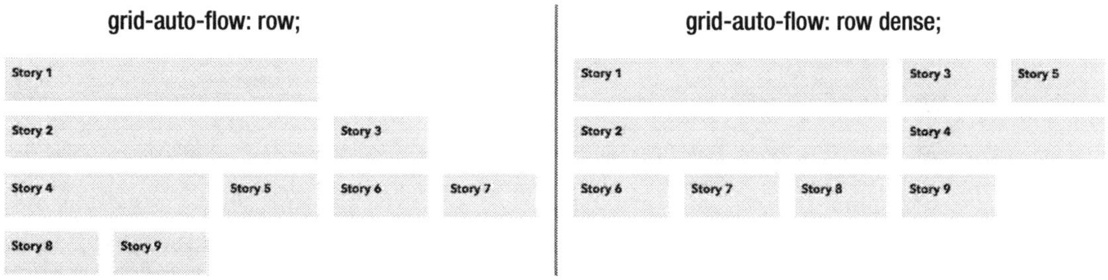

Figure 7-26. *When items span several cells, the default sparse algorithm can cause gaps. When using the dense algorithm, the items are more efficiently packed*

If we change the algorithm to use something called the dense mode (sparse is the default), the automatic placement algorithm goes back to the start for each pass, trying to find the first empty slot. This leads to a more densely packed grid.

```
.grid {
  grid-auto-flow: row dense;
}
```

Grid Template Areas

The "named template areas" syntax in CSS Grid Layout is perhaps one of the weirdest parts of CSS. It allows you to specify in a very visual way how things are going to be laid out. As it is perhaps more suitable for simple grids, let's look at the second subsection from the example we have been working with (see Figure 7-27). We'll say that we want to fit two stories and a couple of ads into this layout.

Figure 7-27. *The second subsection, with a header to the left, two story blocks, and a couple of ads in between them*

In the markup for this section, we want to list the contents in order of priority—the header comes first, then the articles, and finally the ads:

```
<section class="subcategory">
  <div class="grid-b">
    <header class="subcategory-header"></header>
    <article class="story"></article>
    <article class="story"></article>
    <div class="ad ad1"></div>
    <div class="ad ad2"></div>
  </div>
</section>
```

We can then declare the grid layout using the grid-template-areas property:

```
.grid-b {
  display: grid;
  grid-template-columns: 20% 1fr 1fr 1fr;
  grid-template-areas: "hd st1 . st2"
                       "hd st1 . st2";
}
```

The grid-template-areas property takes a space-separated list of quoted strings that themselves are made up of space-separated *custom identifiers* for each row of the grid. You are free to choose names for these identifiers as long as they don't clash with existing CSS keywords.

Cells with the same name that are next to each other across columns or rows make up *named grid areas*. These areas have to be rectangular. The areas marked with dots are anonymous cells, with no name.

We have arranged the rows visually so they line up top-to-bottom, which is optional but helps—notice how they form a visual representation of our layout? It's like ASCII art describing the grid (Figure 7-28 shows the resulting grid areas).

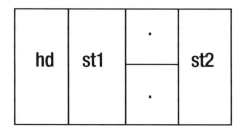

Figure 7-28. *The resulting named grid areas based on our template*

The template for the columns gives the first column 20%, and the rest each take up one-third of the remaining 80% using fr units.

In order to place items on this grid, we can now use the grid-area property again, but this time with the custom area names that we have defined:

```
.grid-b .subcategory-header {
  grid-area: hd;
}
.grid-b .story:nth-child(2) {
  grid-area: st1;
}
.grid-b .story:nth-child(3) {
  grid-area: st2;
}
```

The reason we don't have any named areas or specific placement of the ads is that we don't have to, in this example. They simply default to the automatic placement algorithm and end up the two remaining empty cells. All done!

Now when the boss inevitably comes and asks you to slot in five more ads before and underneath the stories, you only have to add them last in the markup and tweak the grid-template-areas (see Figure 7-29):

```
.grid-b {
  display: grid;
  grid-auto-columns: 1fr;
  grid-template-areas: "hd ... ... ..."
                       "hd st1 ... st2"
                       "hd ... ... ...";
}
```

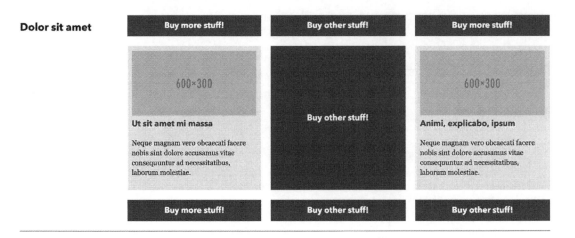

Figure 7-29. *Further ads slotted into the grid layout*

This example also shows a variation on the dot pattern for denoting unnamed cells. The spec allows for multiple adjoining dots to represent a single anonymous cell in order to allow you to line up your template strings more neatly.

Closing Words on Grid Layout

We have looked at the most important features of Grid Layout, but there is more to learn. The Grid Layout specification is large and complex, as it allows you to choose a number of ways to express your grid structure.

It may be a while before Grid Layout is the default way to do layout—browsers that don't understand it are bound to be around for a few more years, at least. Since it affects a very significant part of our pages, it is hard to layer on progressively, without falling back to just a simple column of page elements. There is at least one JavaScript-based polyfill to be found, created by Francois Remy (`https://github.com/FremyCompany/css-grid-polyfill`).

As with any new technique, it remains to be seen how we designers and developers come up with creative ways of working Grid Layout into the sites we build. But as it will be present in most browsers very soon (if not already as you read this book!), it will be a good idea to start using Grid Layout as soon as possible.

Summary

This chapter has been all about a systematic approach to designing layout systems for web pages, thinking in terms of rows, columns, and gutters. We started out building a backward- and forward-compatible grid system using floats, with inline blocks and flexbox properties jumping in to take the design even further.

For the entire history of CSS, we have needed to have nested element structures in place in order to create structures to hold our layouts. This applies even for flexbox layouts, which are otherwise a very powerful layout tool. We devoted the second half of this chapter to the CSS Grid Layout specification, where a lot of these concerns are addressed. Layout using grid properties shifts the grid creation from individual elements to the grid container, and we only need to place and align the items into the correct position.

Armed with this understanding, we are now ready to master yet another layer of thinking in web design: adapting your page to the multitude of different devices and form factors out there. So buckle up and get ready for the next chapter: Responsive Web Design & CSS.

CHAPTER 8

■ ■ ■

Responsive Web Design & CSS

When the iPhone made its debut in 2007, it marked a significant jump in the experience of browsing on a mobile device. People scrambled to make separate sites optimized for mobile and touchscreens, leading to the artificial notion of the "mobile web" and the "desktop web."

Today, you can find browsers in phones ranging from the tiny to the almost comically oversized; small tablets, large tablets, small and large computers, TVs, watches, and all kinds of game consoles.

Creating a separate site for each of these form factors and input types is impossible, and the lines will only get more blurred. The notion of building one site that adapts to the device it is viewed on—a *responsive* site—has become the norm.

Responsive web design is simple in principle, but gets complex when you delve into the details. In this chapter, we'll look at the techniques in CSS, and to some extent HTML, that give you a solid understanding of responsive web design from first principles.

We'll cover

- The history and reasoning behind responsive web design

- How viewports, media types, and media queries work

- Basic "mobile first" strategy when creating responsive sites

- When and where to create breakpoints

- Responsive examples using modern techniques like flexbox, grid layout, and multi-column layout

- Responsive typography and responsive media content

A Responsive Example

The most tangible part of responsive web design, from the point of view of CSS, is the use of fluid layouts that adapt based on the size of the viewport. We'll start this chapter by rewriting the first part of the news site example from Chapter 7 as a responsive layout.

Starting Simple

For narrower viewports, like those on mobile devices, a simpler layout will usually suffice. A single column of items, ordered by priority of the content (as they should be in the HTML source), is a common approach, as shown in Figure 8-1.

© Andy Budd and Emil Björklund 2016
A. Budd and E. Björklund, *CSS Mastery*, DOI 10.1007/978-1-4302-5864-3_8

Figure 8-1. *A single-column layout for narrower screens*

In terms of the layout code, this means removing styles from the example we used in Chapter 7 rather than adding them. We can remove almost all mentions of specific widths. The only thing we set as basic styling is the padding and margin of rows and columns. We will also set the columns to be floated and 100% wide, keeping the rules that make sure rows contain any floated children.

```
.row {
  padding: 0;
  margin: 0 -.6875em;
}
.row:after {
  content: '';
  display: block;
  clear: both;
}
.col {
  box-sizing: border-box;
  padding: 0 .6875em 1.375em;
  float: left;
  width: 100%;
}
```

Introducing Our First Media Query

If we view the design at a slightly wider size, we could potentially fit more onto the screen at the same time. We could, for example, let the second and third stories take up half the container width, as shown in Figure 8-2.

Figure 8-2. *Two stories fit side by side under the featured story on slightly wider screens*

By resizing the window and trying to find where it would make sense to show two stories side by side, we end up with a minimum width of about 560 pixels, or 35 ems. This is where we need to add something called a *media query*, which triggers the rules inside it only if the minimum width requirement is fulfilled:

```
@media only screen and (min-width: 35em) {
  .row-quartet > * {
    width: 50%;
  }
  .subcategory-featured {
    width: 100%;
  }
}
```

If you've ever done any programming in JavaScript, PHP, Python, Java, etc., you've probably seen the if statement—"if this condition is true, do this." Media queries using the @media rule, much like its cousin the @supports rule, are like if statements for CSS, specifically geared toward capabilities of the environment in which the page is shown. In this particular case, the browser viewport needs to be at least 35 ems wide. The width at which we introduce a media query is commonly called a *breakpoint*.

Note that the measurement where we place the breakpoint has nothing to do with the measurement of any particular class of device—mobile or otherwise. It is simply a point where we could use the space in a better, more efficient way. We should avoid setting breakpoints based on specific device widths, as new devices are created all the time. In the end, we will not be able to tear down the artificial divide of "mobile web" and "desktop web" by creating further division.

We will take another look into structuring media queries and breakpoints later in this chapter. For now, the important thing to remember is that CSS inside a media query is only applied when a certain condition is met.

Finding Further Breakpoints

Continuing to increase the size of the browser window, we find more places where it would make sense to use the space more efficiently. At about 800 pixels (50 ems), we could place four stories side by side, and let the featured story take up half the width (see Figure 8-3). This is starting to resemble the initial "unresponsive" example, but the subcategory header still stays on top of the stories.

```
@media only screen and (min-width: 50em) {
  .row-quartet > * {
    width: 25%;
  }
  .subcategory-featured {
    width: 50%;
  }
}
```

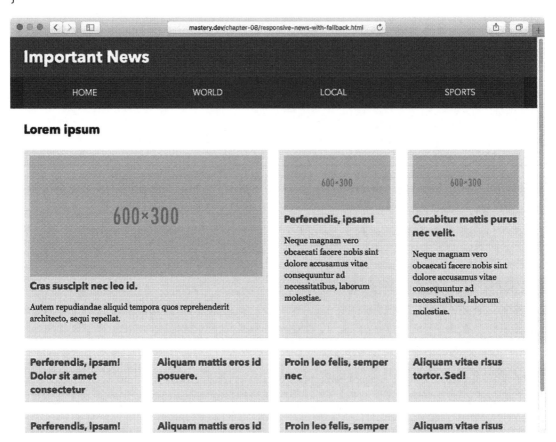

Figure 8-3. *The content area now houses four columns, while the featured article takes up twice that size. The header stays on top though.*

226

Finally, we find that we can fit the header in to the side of the stories at around 70 ems, or 1120 pixels (see Figure 8-4).

```
@media only screen and (min-width: 70em) {
  .subcategory-header {
    width: 20%;
  }
  .subcategory-content {
    width: 80%;
  }
}
```

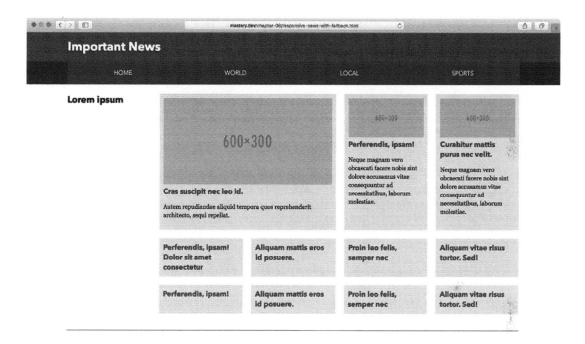

Figure 8-4. *As the window gets wider, we can add another media query to adjust the header to work as a sidebar*

At this point, we have re-created a responsive version of this example, covering four different layouts. We've also made some further tiny stylistic tweaks that aren't covered here. The full example code (which you can find with the files accompanying the book) includes these tweaks, as well as the viewport declaration that makes responsive layouts work on mobile devices. (We'll dive into the details of the viewport later in the chapter.)

The relatively short snippets of code in the previous example encapsulate a number of useful techniques and principles. We started with a bare-bones single-column layout, and used media queries to create scopes where the design changes—this is the basis for a robust approach to responsive web design. Before we go any further in exploring responsive coding techniques, we'll take a look at where responsive web design came from.

The Roots of Responsiveness

Designer and developer Ethan Marcotte coined the term "responsive web design" in an article of the same name, published on A List Apart (`http://alistapart.com/article/responsive-web-design`) in 2010 (see Figure 8-5). In that article, he used the term to describe designs where the combination of fluid grids, flexible embedded objects (like images or video), and media queries adapt the design to work regardless of screen size. The article later turned into a book of the same name, and the ball was rolling.

Illustration by Kevin Cornell

Responsive Web Design

by **Ethan Marcotte** · May 25, 2010

Figure 8-5. *The article that started it all. Fun fact: the illustration itself is responsive—go find the article and resize the browser window!*

While responsive web design as a phenomenon is still relatively new, the roots of adapting a single design to work on multiple types of devices are older than the name.

On the technical level, the components of responsive web design already existed before the term was coined. Media queries (and their predecessor, media types) would not have been standardized if there weren't some people anticipating the need for layouts that adapted to the browser. In fact, one of the major inspirations for Ethan's article was a piece by John Allsopp from 2000 called "A Dao of Web Design" (`http://alistapart.com/article/dao`). In that article, John argues that good web design is more about adapting to the user and less about enforcing pixel-perfect control. It took us a while to get there, but things are changing.

By 2010, media queries were gaining wider support. It was also a point in time when browsing on mobile devices was becoming a common thing. By bringing the techniques together and coining the term responsive web design, Ethan put a name to a direction that the Web had wanted to move in for quite a while.

Responsive web design is fast becoming the de facto way of designing web pages, and may soon just be seen as "good web design." Until then, responsive web design is a useful term to describe the specific methods of making a design work on multiple devices and multiple screen sizes.

Responsive beyond CSS

Today, responsive techniques are used on sites big and small. Ethan's three main pillars of responsiveness still form the basis of responsive web design, but they are complemented with even more tools for adaptation. One of the most common is to use JavaScript to add interactivity or change the presentation of our pages on different devices.

For example, you have probably seen the now ubiquitous "hamburger menu." A common pattern is to have a global navigation menu expanded at larger screen sizes, but hidden underneath a button on smaller viewports (see Figure 8-6). Usually, there is some amount of JavaScript involved to change the menu depending on the viewport size. It's important to point out that the initial content and markup are still the same, independent of what device is used to view the site. This "core experience" can then be transformed in any way you like using scripting.

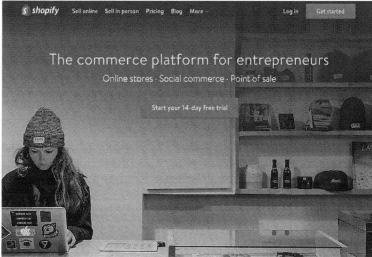

Figure 8-6. *Shopify is one of many sites using a "hamburger menu" on smaller viewports*

This pattern should be a familiar one: loading a core set of resources first and only loading further resources as the capabilities of the device are determined. Responsive web design is indeed another example of progressive enhancement.

We will try to focus on the parts of responsive web design that we can affect with CSS in this chapter, with a brief excursion into responsive images. If you want to start looking at more advanced patterns for responsive sites, Brad Frost has a large collection of patterns and code examples called "This Is Responsive" (https://bradfrost.github.io/this-is-responsive/).

The first step to mastering responsive CSS is to understand the canvas we have to work with—the viewport.

How Browser Viewports Work

The viewport is the rectangle in which a web page is shown. It is the area that affects our layout: how much space we have in terms of CSS. To get the viewport to play nicely with our responsive designs, we need to understand how it works and how to manipulate it. On desktop browsers, the concept of a viewport is mostly straightforward. We have a number of CSS pixels to play with and we use the space inside the viewport as best we can.

There is an important distinction to be made here, which is that CSS pixels are not the same things as physical pixels. The pixels we talk about when measuring things in CSS has a very fluid relationship to the physical pixels of the screen, decided by factors like the hardware, the operating system, the browser, and whether the user has zoomed the page in or out.

As a thought experiment, we can imagine two `div` elements placed directly in the `body` element of a page. If we set the first `div` to have `width: 100%`, and the second to have a width set in `px`, at which `px` measurement are they the same width? That measurement is the width of the current viewport in CSS pixels, regardless of how many physical pixels are used to display it.

As a concrete example, the iPhone 5 has a physical screen width of 640 pixels, but as far as CSS is concerned, the viewport width is 320 pixels. There is a scaling factor in play here—each CSS pixel on this particular device is shown using 2×2 physical pixels (see Figure 8-7).

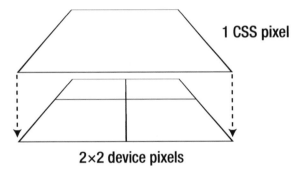

Figure 8-7. *The difference between CSS pixels and device pixels on a high-resolution device*

This ratio between "virtual" CSS pixels and the actual hardware pixels currently ranges from 1 (where each CSS pixel = 1 physical pixel) up to around 4 (where each CSS pixel = 4×4 hardware pixels), depending on the device.

The good news is that since we only need to keep track of the CSS pixels for the sake of responsive layouts, the pixel ratio is largely irrelevant. The bad news is that we need to dig a little deeper into the real-world mechanics of viewports to understand how to bend them to our will.

Nuances of the Viewport Definition

Touchscreen smartphones and other mobile devices stirred things up a bit. They made much heavier use of zooming to be able to handle web pages not suited for viewing on such a small screen. This caused device makers to invent new concepts affecting the viewport. Mobile platform strategist Peter-Paul Koch (`http://quirksmode.org`) has published extensive research into how these different levels of viewports work, and has also tried to give them helpful names.

Default and Ideal Viewports

As smartphone browsers appeared, there weren't many sites optimized for screens of that size. As a consequence, browsers on most mobiles (as well as tablets) are hard-wired to show a desktop-sized viewport by default, allowing non-optimized sites to fit. Usually, they emulate a viewport width of somewhere around 1000 CSS pixels, effectively zooming out the page. We call this the *default viewport*. This is why we have to jump through some hoops when we want responsive designs to display correctly.

As the default viewport is an emulated viewport size, it follows logically that there is a viewport definition closer to the dimensions of the device itself. This is what we call the *ideal viewport*. The ideal viewport varies depending on device, operating system, and browser, but usually ends up being around 300 to 500 CSS pixels in width for phones, and 800 to 1400 CSS pixels for tablets. In the iPhone 5 example from earlier, this is where the 320-pixel width comes from.

In responsive design, this is the viewport we design for. Figure 8-8 shows a comparison between loading the mobile-optimized `http://mobile.nytimes.com`, which uses the ideal viewport, and loading the "desktop version" of the same site, showing the zoomed-out desktop layout using the default viewport.

Figure 8-8. *The mobile site for the New York Times website uses the ideal viewport for layout (left). If you switch to the "Desktop" site, you get the zoomed-out default viewport look (right), emulating a 980-pixel width.*

Visual and Layout Viewports

Having set the scene by differentiating between the default viewport and the ideal viewport on phones and tablets, we get to a common, more intuitive definition for both with regard to how viewports actually work. We call the basic rectangle inside of which a web page is shown the *visual viewport*. This means the browser window, minus any buttons, toolbars, scrollbars, etc. (known as "browser chrome") that surround the actual web content.

As we zoom in on a page, some parts of the layout end up outside of the visual viewport, as shown in Figure 8-9. The rectangle we are looking at now is still the visual viewport, but we now refer to the hypothetical rectangle constraining the layout of the *whole page* as the *layout viewport*. This split between visual viewport and layout viewport works conceptually in the same way on desktop browsers as on phones and tablets.

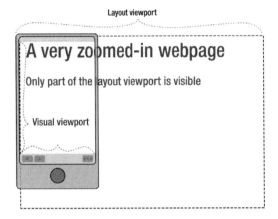

Figure 8-9. *The visual viewport and the layout viewport on a zoomed-in site viewed on a phone*

As you can see, there is more than meets the eye when it comes to the viewport. The bottom line is that in responsive web design, we aim to design our pages to adapt to the *ideal viewport* of each device. Desktop browsers don't need any special treatment since the ideal viewport is equal to the default viewport there. But on phones and tablets, we need to opt out of the fake measurement of the default viewport and make it equal to the ideal viewport. This is done with a small piece of HTML known as the *meta viewport* tag.

Configuring the Viewport

We can make devices that have a different default viewport use the ideal viewport by adding a small tag inside the head element of our pages. It looks like this:

```
<meta name="viewport" content="width=device-width, initial-scale=1">
```

This tells the browser that we would like to use the ideal measurements of the device (the device-width) as the basis for the viewport width. There's also another preference set here: the initial-scale=1 bit. That part sets the zoom level to match the ideal viewport, which also helps to prevent some odd scaling behavior in iOS. Most devices will assume device-width when a zoom level is set, but both are needed for full compatibility across devices and operating systems.

Setting initial-scale to a value higher than 1 means you are zooming the layout further, and by doing so you're decreasing the size of the layout viewport, since fewer pixels fit. Conversely, setting the value lower zooms out and sets the layout viewport to be larger in terms of CSS pixels.

Other Values and Combining with Initial-Scale

You can also set width inside the viewport to a pixel measurement instead of the device-width keyword, effectively locking down the layout viewport to a value of your choice. If you combine it with an initial-scale value, mobile browsers across the board will pick the *larger* of the two.

DON'T DISABLE ZOOMING!

You can lock zooming to certain levels by setting maximum-scale and minimum-scale properties (to a numeric value) inside the meta viewport tag. You can also disable zoom completely by setting user-scalable=no. It's not uncommon to see meta viewport tags like this one:

```
<meta name="viewport" content="initial-scale=1.0, maximum-scale=1.0, minimum-scale=1.0, user-scalable=no">
```

This keeps your users from zooming pages on mobile devices, which means that your pages are less accessible.

Even if you take care in designing pages where text is legible and actionable parts of the page (like links and buttons) are sufficiently sized, that may not be the opinion of users with lowered vision or motor difficulties.

Locking down the zoom factor has been preferred by some developers to make web applications behave more like their native app counterparts. Doing so also resolved some bugs and quirky behavior related to zooming and positioning on older platforms, but those bugs are getting fixed as the mobile platforms mature.

We think that locking the zoom factor sounds like throwing out the baby with the bathwater—universal access is, after all, one of the big benefits of building for the Web.

Device Adaptation and CSS @viewport

Declaring the viewport properties in a <meta> tag is the best approach for now, but it is also a nonstandard mechanism, as you could probably tell from the previous section. Apple introduced it as a proprietary switch in the Safari browser that came with the first iPhone, and others followed suit.

Since this is part of how pages are rendered, it makes sense that the viewport properties should be part of CSS. There is a proposed standard for this, called CSS Device Adaptation. It recommends that instead of the meta viewport tag, we should have something like this in the head of our pages:

```
<style>
@viewport {
  width: auto;
}
</style>
```

Placing the viewport declaration inside of a style element in the HTML instead of in the actual CSS file is a small but important detail. The browser should not have to wait for the CSS file to be downloaded before knowing about the viewport size. Keeping that information as part of the HTML file prevents the browser from doing extra work once any external CSS files arrive.

So far the @viewport declaration has not been widely implemented. At the time of writing, it is only partially supported in Internet Explorer 10+ on Windows and Windows Phone 8. Blink-based browsers like Chrome and Opera implement it behind a hidden setting on some platforms. It is perhaps the most likely candidate for controlling the viewport in the future, but not hugely important as this book is written.

There are a couple of small caveats to this technique, as expected with an experimental technology: developer Tim Kadlec has a good article on the pitfalls (http://timkadlec.com/2013/01/windows-phone-8-and-device-width/).

Media Types and Media Queries

Now that we have a thorough understanding of viewports as the spaces in which we constrain our layouts, it is time to move into the "how" of responsive design: adapting your designs with media queries. We started the chapter with a quick example, but this time we're diving deeper, starting with the predecessors of media queries: media types.

Media Types

The ability to separate styles based on the capabilities of the device started with media types. These were defined in HTML 4.01 and CSS 2.1, and were created to let you target certain types of environments: screen styles, styles for print, styles for TVs, etc.

You could target a media type by adding a media attribute to a link element, like so:

```
<link rel="stylesheet" href="main.css" media="screen, print">
```

The preceding snippet means that this style sheet is meant for both screens (any type of screen) and when the page is printed. If you didn't care about what type of media it was used for, you could put all as the value, or just omit the media attribute. Comma-separated lists of valid types means that any one of them can match, and if none matches, the stylesheet is not applied.

You could also put the media type selection as part of the CSS file. The most common way is to use it with the @media syntax, like this:

```
@media print {
  /* selectors and rule sets for print media go in here */
  .smallprint {
    font-size: 11pt;
  }
}
```

There are several more media types to choose from: among them are handheld and tv. Those sound like they should be useful for responsive design, but sadly they're not. For various reasons, browser makers have shied away from explicitly transmitting what type of device they belong to, so the only useful types are pretty much screen, print, and all.

Media Queries

Since we want to target not only the type of device but also the capabilities of that device, the CSS 3 Media Queries specification was created. It defined extensions to the base of media types. Media queries are written as a combination of the media type and a *media condition* consisting of a *media feature* inside parentheses. There are also a few other new keywords in the media selection syntax, offering some additional logic.

A media query could look like this on a link element:

```
<link rel="stylesheet" href="main.css" media="screen and (min-width: 600px)">
```

This declares that the main.css file should be used for any screen media matching the media condition where the viewport is at least 600 CSS pixels wide.

■ **Note** A lot of browsers still download the CSS file, even if the media query does not currently match. This means that you should be careful not to overdo the use of link elements with media queries—you might be unnecessarily creating extra requests for your users, which is a serious performance issue.

The same statement would look like this combined with the @media rule inside of your CSS file:

```
@media screen and (min-width: 600px) {
  /* rules go here */
}
```

The and keyword acts like glue between the media types and any conditions we are testing for, so our query can have several media conditions:

```
@media screen and (min-width: 600px) and (max-width: 1000px) {}
```

Multiple media queries can be chained together with a comma character, which acts as an "or." The rules inside the block will be applied if any of the media queries is true. If all of the media queries are false, it will be skipped.

You can omit the media type completely and still use the media condition part of the statement:

```
@media (min-width: 30em) {/*...*/}
/* ...is the same as... */
@media all and (min-width: 30em) {/*...*/}
```

You can also negate media queries with the not keyword. The following means the rules inside are valid for any medium but screens:

```
@media not screen {
  /* non-screen styles go here. */
}
```

We also have the only keyword, which was introduced as a way to keep older browsers from misunderstanding media queries.

When a browser that doesn't support media queries sees screen and (min-width: ..., it's supposed to discard the whole thing as one badly declared media type and move on. However, some old browsers seem to stop after seeing the first string of screen, recognize it as a valid media type, and apply the styles for all screens.

Thus, the only keyword was introduced in the Media Queries specification. When old browsers see it at the beginning, they discard the whole @media rule since there is no such thing as an only media type. All browsers that *do* support media queries are required to ignore the only part as if it wasn't there.

To be really safe against older browsers applying the wrong styles, you should declare any media query that you need to scope to a specific media type like this:

```
@media only screen and (min-width: 30em) {/*...*/}
```

If you don't care about the specific media type, you could shorten it to this:

```
@media (min-width: 30em) {/*...*/}
```

Dimensional Queries

Out of `width` and `height`, the `width` dimension (with its `min-` and `max-` prefixes) is the true workhorse of responsive web design. When Peter-Paul Koch of QuirksMode.org ran a survey among web developers and designers about media queries (`http://www.quirksmode.org/blog/archives/2013/11/media_queryrwdv.html`), he found that the width-related media queries were the most popular to use, by a landslide.

The reason width is so important is that the default way we create web pages is to utilize the horizontal layout only up until we fill the viewport. In the vertical direction, we can let things grow as much as we like, and let the user scroll. It makes sense that we want to know when we run out of (or gain more) horizontal space for our layouts.

STAY AWAY FROM DEVICE MEASUREMENTS

We can also ask the browser about `device-width` and `device-height`. This does not always mean the same thing as the viewport measurements, but rather the dimensions of the screen in its entirety.

The sad thing is that many developers have used `device-width` interchangeably with normal `width` queries, leading to mobile browser makers following suit to make sure sites work on their browsers. The device-measurement queries have also been deprecated in the upcoming version of the Media Queries specification. All in all, `device-width` and `device-height` are quite confusing, so stay away unless you are forced to use them for some reason.

Further Dimensions: Resolution, Aspect Ratio, and Orientation

While the queries for viewport dimensions are likely to make up the vast majority of media query usage, it should be noted that we could query other aspects of the device. For example, we could change the layout only when the device width is less than the device height, meaning it is in portrait orientation:

```
@media (orientation: portrait) {
  /* portrait orientation styles here. */
}
```

Similarly, we can apply rules only when, for example, the viewport matches a certain minimum aspect ratio:

```
@media (min-aspect-ratio: 16/9) {
  /* only applied when the viewport aspect ratio is at least the widescreen 16:9 ratio. */
}
```

We mentioned earlier that the pixel ratio of the device is largely irrelevant. That is true when it comes to *layout*. Further ahead in the chapter, we'll use `min-resolution` media queries to adapt which image to load, where the pixel ratio is very important.

Media queries are likely to be extended in the future, to be able to detect other aspects of the user's device and environment. While there are plenty of exciting advancements on the horizon (and even some experimental support already in browsers), we'll focus on the most useful queries in this book, preparing you for what works today.

Browser Support for Media Queries

The basic media queries are supported *almost* everywhere. Sadly, as with many other "CSS 3" features, browsers like IE8 and older are a bit behind the times.

There are various tactics you can use to counter this, and either serve a fixed-width layout to these older browsers or use a polyfill—a script that fakes support for missing features.

One such script is `Respond.js` from Scott Jehl (`https://github.com/scottjehl/Respond`). In browsers that don't support media queries, it looks through all the linked CSS files and searches for the media query syntax. It then applies or removes those sections based on the screen dimensions, emulating how the native media queries would work.

There are some downsides to using `Respond.js`. For example, the script doesn't work with media queries directly inside `style` elements in the page. There are other edge-case constraints to consider, so be sure to consult the instructions on the website before using `Respond.js`.

If using JavaScript for this doesn't work for you, you could lock the design down to a specific "desktop" width in old versions of IE by using a separate style sheet, and include that using conditional comments.

Conditional comments are a weird feature that existed in IE up until (but not including) IE10. They make it possible to wrap pieces of HTML in something that all other browsers regard as a normal comment, but IE can reach in and get at the HTML hidden inside. A special syntax lets you target individual or grouped versions of IE.

The conditional comment for serving these wide-screen styles to desktop IE would need to consider old versions of IE, while still not targeting IE in old versions of Windows Phone. It looks something like this:

```
<!--[if (lt IE 9) & (!IEMobile)]>
<link rel="stylesheet" href="oldIE.css" media="all">
<![endif]-->
```

This strategy depends on your putting the rest of your rules in a style sheet where the small-screen styles are the "default" and the wider-screen styles are scoped by media queries. That is a good idea anyway, which we'll see in the next section.

Structuring CSS for Responsive Design

In the initial example at the start of the chapter, we stripped out the widths and layout rules from the code, and added them back scoped to `min-width` media queries. This approach is not just an efficient pattern in terms of how little code you need to write; it is also part of an important strategy.

Mobile First CSS

You may have heard the term "mobile first." It is a strategy around how to focus your design and development efforts. Mobile devices have small screens, are harder to type on, and usually have weaker processors and less memory than their desktop counterparts. They are also the devices that are closest at hand to a great deal of people.

By focusing on these devices first in the design and development process, we start with a set of constraints that emphasize what is at the core of a digital product. As we scale a website or app to work on other devices, we can make use of the expanded capacity.

Had we done it the other way around, we would need to cram existing features into a more constrained platform—a much harder feat.

The same mindset can be applied to CSS, even if you are rewriting a project initially conceived as a "desktop" site.

The first rules in your CSS files form the basic experience both for the smallest screens and for browsers that don't understand media queries:

- **Typographic basics:** Sizes, colors, line heights, headings, paragraphs, lists, links, etc.

- **Basics of "boxes":** Any specific border styles, padded items, flexible images, background colors, and some limited background images

- **Basic components for getting around and consuming content:** Navigation, forms, buttons

As you test these styles on mobile devices and browsers of various kinds and sizes, you will find that they start breaking at some point. Line lengths will become too long, items will become too far apart, and so forth. When this happens you should consider adding a media query at that point—that's why it's called a *breakpoint*. To reiterate, this can be any measurement: it's more important that the code adapts to the *contents* of the site than to the pixel measurements of any specific device.

```css
/* start off with the baseline and small-screen styles. */
.myThing {
  font-size: 1em;
}
/* ...then adjust inside min-width media queries: */
@media only screen and (min-width: 23.75em) {
  .myThing {
    width: 50%;
    float: left;
  }
}
/* ...and further adjustments... */
@media only screen and (min-width: 38.75em) {
  .myThing {
    width: 33.333%;
  }
}
```

You'll recognize the method from how we rewrote the news site example at the start of the chapter. This is the "mobile first" mindset translated into code. It also reflects how mobile first, responsive web design, and progressive enhancement go hand in hand. Writing as little code as possible while still catering for as many devices as possible is a sure sign you are doing something right!

> ## MEDIA QUERIES AND EMS
>
> Writing media queries with ems, as we have done here, is a way of further strengthening your design against changing environments. Most browsers will scale pixel-based queries as you zoom in desktop browsers, but users can also choose to change the base font size rather than zooming.
>
> Using ems as a measurement makes sure your layout scales with that case as well, since it relates to the base font size of the document.
>
> Note that media queries set in ems always relate to the base font size in the browser preferences, *not* the font size of the `html` element (`1rem`) that you can adjust in CSS.

Max-Width Queries for Efficient Small-Screen Styles

With the `min-width` query as our primary tool, we can layer on adjustments for increasingly wider viewports. But the `max-width` query is not to be underestimated. Sometimes, we might have some styles that make sense on a smaller screen but not on bigger ones. This means that we have to first declare the style and then negate it, if using `min-width`. Using `max-width` queries can cut down on the effort.

As a condensed example (no pun intended!), you might want to use a narrow typeface for some headings on smaller viewports, in order to prevent excessive line wrapping (see Figure 8-10).

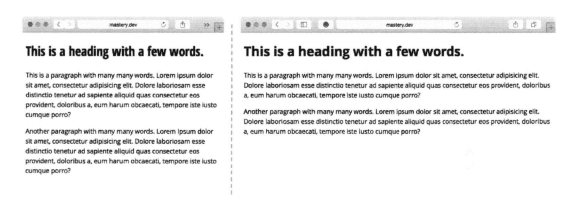

Figure 8-10. *One example of responsive typography could be to use a narrower typeface on smaller viewports to avoid excessive line wrapping*

Using the `min-width` query and the "mobile first" CSS strategy, this scenario could look like this:

```
body {
  font-family: 'Open Sans', 'Helvetica Neue', Arial, sans-serif;
}
h1,h2,h3 {
  font-family: 'Open Sans Condensed', 'Arial Narrow', Arial, sans-serif;
}
```

239

```
@media only screen and (min-width: 37.5em) {
  h1,h2,h3 {
    font-family: 'Open Sans', 'Helvetica Neue', Arial, sans-serif;
  }
}
```

The highlighted parts indicate how the base `font-family` declaration needs to be repeated in order to negate the small-screen styles of condensed headings. If we were to use a `max-width` query instead, we get a slightly shorter example with no repetition, and thus less code to maintain:

```
body {
  font-family: 'Open Sans', 'Helvetica Neue', Arial, sans-serif;
}
@media only screen and (max-width: 37.5em) {
  h1,h2,h3 {
    font-family: 'Open Sans Condensed', 'Arial Narrow', Arial, sans-serif;
  }
}
```

Of course, there are other types of media queries that you could use to change your site. As with so many things, the specific details of each project make it all come down to a bit of "it depends." But using the `min-width` query as your workhorse chimes well with the idea of using media queries as a form of progressive enhancement.

Where to Place Your Media Queries

The example with basic, "unscoped" styles first, followed by `min-width` queries, works well as an example of the basic structure of a style sheet containing media queries.

Media queries can serve slightly different purposes though: either to tweak a small detail or to rearrange the whole layout. Often these two categories of media queries also appear at slightly different measurements, so it makes sense to treat them differently.

There is no hard rule on how to pick your own structure, but we find that it makes sense to group the different kinds of media queries slightly differently:

- Media queries that affect the overall layout of your pages are usually related to a handful of class names that describe the major components of your site, and across a handful of screen sizes. It often makes sense to place them close to these layout rules.

- If you have specific media queries that only tweak one specific component of the site, put the media query code next to the rules describing that component.

- Finally, if you find that a lot of changes to layout as well as several smaller tweaks to individual components end up at the same breakpoints, it may be better to put them all at the end of the style sheet. In doing so, you are keeping with the pattern of starting with the "unscoped" rules, and then getting more specific with overriding styles.

The important takeaway is that there is no definite place in your CSS where all your media queries need to be placed. That also means that it's up to you as a developer to create the structure and conventions required to suit you or your team.

▓ **Caution**   Media queries do not add to the specificity of the selectors within them, so you need to make sure that the structure and order of where you put them doesn't mean that they are overridden elsewhere in the source code. Putting them last does not guarantee that they will override anything: they still follow the normal rules of the cascade.

More Responsive Patterns

The "mobile first" way of writing CSS is an example of a fundamental pattern for responsive design. There are plenty of other patterns for making your design more flexible and more responsive though, and as new technologies emerge, we will create and refine even more of them. This section contains a few good ones.

Responsive Text Columns

The CSS 3 Multi-column Layout specification we encountered in Chapter 4 was one of the first parts of CSS to have responsive patterns built in from the start, long before the term was coined. By using a column width rather than a set number of columns, the content will flow into as many columns as fit in the container (see Figure 8-11).

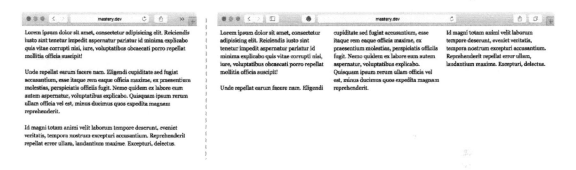

Figure 8-11. *On narrower viewports, the paragraphs flow into a single column, and on wider viewports multiple columns appear automatically*

```
<div class="multicol">
  <p>Lorem ipsum [...]<p>
  <!-- ...etc -->
</div>
```

The CSS is a single line for the column declaration—no media queries necessary!

```
.multicol {
  column-width: 16em;
}
```

It bears repeating that text in multiple columns should be used sparingly on the Web. There is definitely a use case for it though. As long as the text is not overly long such that it forces the user to scroll up and down even on wider screens, it is a way to reclaim horizontal space without using a measure that is uncomfortably wide.

Responsive Flexbox without Media Queries

Flexbox is another part of CSS that has a degree of responsiveness built in. Without using any media queries, we can create components that adapt their layout to the available space.

Let's say we want to build a widget where you order spare parts for your time machine, by clicking buttons to increase or decrease the number of parts in your shopping basket (see Figure 8-12).

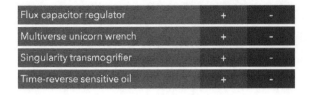

Figure 8-12. *Our widget for ordering parts*

The list of parts is an unordered list, where each item has the following structure:

```
<ul class="ordering-widget">
  <li class="item">
    <span class="item-name">Flux capacitor regulator</span>
    <span class="item-controls">
      <button class="item-control item-increase" aria-label="Increase">+</button>
      <button class="item-control item-decrease" aria-label="Decrease">-</button>
    </span>
  </li>
  <!-- ...and so on. -->
</ul>
```

By styling the item name and the button controls with flexible sizes, we can create a component that changes layout when there's not enough space to house them both on the same row.

First, some reset styles for the list, and basic typographic rules:

```
.ordering-widget {
  list-style: none;
  margin: 0;
  padding: 0;
  font-family: 'Avenir Next', Avenir, SegoeUI, sans-serif;
}
```

Then we turn each item into a wrapping flex row:

```
.item {
  color: #fff;
  background-color: #129490;
  display: flex;
  flex-wrap: wrap;
  font-size: 1.5em;
  padding: 0;
  margin-bottom: .25em;
}
```

The name of each item needs to be at least 13 ems wide to fit the longest names, but should otherwise expand to fill the available space:

```
.item-name {
  padding: .25em;
  flex: 1 0 13em;
}
```

Next up, the span element wrapping the two buttons should also fill the available space, and be at least 4em wide. It also acts as a flex container for the buttons.

```
.item-controls {
  flex: 1 0 4em;
  display: flex;
}
```

Each button is in turn a flex item taking up an equal amount of space. The rest of the styles are mostly to neutralize default styling of the button element (we'll get back to styling form controls in Chapter 9):

```
.item-control {
  flex: 1;
  text-align: center;
  padding: .25em;
  cursor: pointer;
  width: 100%;
  margin: 0;
  border: 0;
  color: #fff;
  font-size: inherit;
}
```

All that's left is the background colors for the buttons themselves:

```
.item-increase {
  background-color: #1E6F6D;
}
.item-decrease {
  background-color: #1C5453;
}
```

That's all the styles for the responsive widget! Here comes the interesting bit: when the button controls (the .item-controls element) run out of space to fit comfortably on the same line as the fixed-width .item-name element, they will naturally wrap to a second row. Since the .item-controls element has a flex-grow factor of 1, it will expand to take up the whole second row (see Figure 8-13). Each button will in turn grow to take up half of the row in itself.

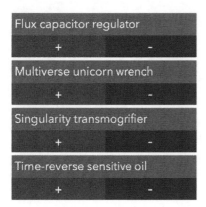

Figure 8-13. *When space is tight, the buttons end up underneath the item name*

Flexible, Container-Relative Components

In the preceding example, we have created another responsive component without resorting to media queries, keeping the complexity of the CSS down. This wrapping behavior, while simple, would not be possible with floats or inline block display.

It's also important to note that this type of flexible component does not respond to the size of the viewport, but rather the actual available space inside the component where it is rendered. This is often what we actually want to achieve.

While media queries are great for adapting layouts based on the viewport, they do not take into account that one particular component can appear in multiple places, rendered at different widths. Put another way, if a component appears in a narrow sidebar, we want it to display using styles that make sense in a narrow context, regardless of the viewport size. Until we have some form of "container queries" (which are being worked on—see `https://github.com/ResponsiveImagesCG/cq-usecases`), techniques like flexbox help us get partway there.

Responsive Grids with Grid Template Areas

The Grid Layout properties allow you to shift a lot of the layout work from the individual elements up to the grid container. This next pattern drastically simplifies the process of making a page layout responsive when using the named template areas syntax we saw in Chapter 7.

■ **Note**   As a reminder, Grid Layout still has very spotty browser support as this is written. However, it is likely to be an important ingredient in responsive layouts in years to come.

If we look at the second subsection of the news site example from Chapter 7, we can adapt it into a fully responsive layout with relatively few changes. But first, a recap of the markup structure:

```
<section class="subcategory">
  <div class="grid-b">
    <header class="subcategory-header"></header>
    <article class="story"></article>
```

```
      <article class="story"></article>
      <div class="ad"></div>
      <div class="ad"></div>
    </div>
</section>
```

The markup contains the section header, two articles, and two ads. Without applying any layout styles (grid layout or otherwise), they line up as full-width blocks on the page. This works quite well on small viewports (see Figure 8-14).

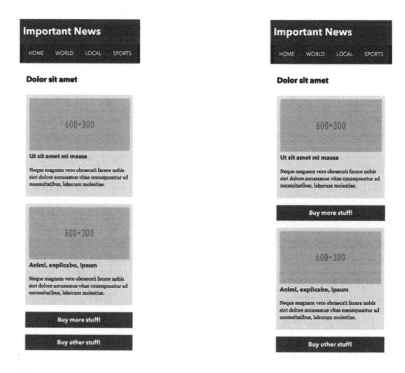

Figure 8-14. *To the left, the unstyled single-column layout. To the right, an ad injected in between stories by using a grid template.*

The source order features what's important in the page content with the stories appearing first in the markup, followed by the ads. But what if the ad sales team needs us to inject ads in between stories on the mobile view, so the ads don't get lost at the bottom of the page?

We can use a grid declaration to take care of that. First we need to define the grid area names for the header and stories:

```
.grid-b .subcategory-header {
  grid-area: hd;
}
.grid-b .story:nth-of-type(1) {
  grid-area: st1;
}
.grid-b .story:nth-of-type(2) {
  grid-area: st2;
}
```

Without using a media query, we can now define the basics of the grid container, and the row order of the single column inside. The grid template now takes control of the ordering of items within a single column of content. The ads now automatically flow into the unnamed areas (represented by dots) in between stories.

```
.grid-b {
  display: grid;
  grid-template-columns: 1fr;
  grid-template-areas: "hd" "st1" "." "st2" ".";
}
```

When there is a little more space, we can change the story part into a 2×2 grid by adding a new template inside a media query (see Figure 8-15).

```
@media only screen and (min-width: 37.5em) {
  .grid-b {
    grid-template-columns: 1fr 1fr;
    grid-template-areas: "hd   hd "
                         "st1 ..."
                         "... st2";
  }
}
```

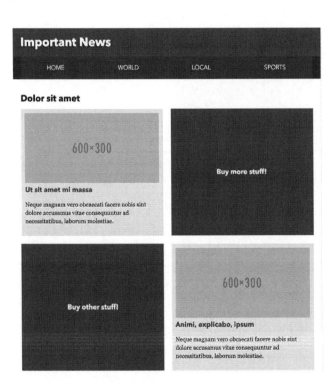

Figure 8-15. *For slightly bigger viewports, the stories and ads are now in a checkered formation*

Remember, we can use an arbitrary number of consecutive dots to denote an anonymous grid area, to line up our template strings more neatly.

In viewports that are slightly larger still, the header remains on top of the content, but the stories and ads form the same three-column layout that we saw in the example from Chapter 7 (see Figure 8-16):

```
@media only screen and (min-width: 55em) {
  .grid-b {
    grid-template-columns: 1fr 1fr 1fr;
    grid-template-areas: "hd  hd hd "
                         "st1 .. st2"
                         "st1 .. st2";
  }
}
```

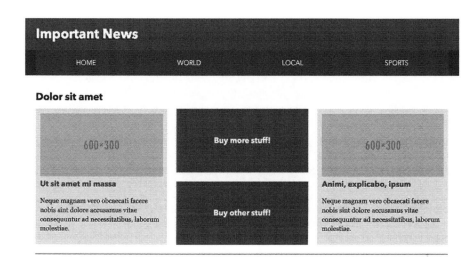

Figure 8-16. *The header goes across the top, and the stories and ads form a three-column/two-row layout*

Finally, we switch to the layout using the sidebar header plus the three-column layout (see Figure 8-17).

```
@media only screen and (min-width: 70em) {
  .grid-b {
    grid-template-columns: 20% 1fr 1fr 1fr;
    grid-template-areas: "hd st1 . st2"
                         "hd st1 . st2";
  }
}
```

Figure 8-17. *The sidebar header now fits comfortably next to the three columns*

As you can see, the Grid Layout properties allow us to redefine the whole grid at certain breakpoints without ever touching the respective components. You can of course use the other methods of grid positioning for responsive layouts, but the grid template areas feature is particularly well suited for responsive work. Just remember that nonsupporting browsers will fall back to a single-column layout, so it may be a while before this is your weapon of choice for responsive grids.

Going beyond Layout

So far, we have gotten acquainted with the details of how viewports and media queries work, along with a sampling of responsive layout techniques. But responsive websites need to deal with more than just layout. In this section, we'll look at some techniques to make sure other aspects of our sites adapt as well. We'll start with media, first as background images and then as embedded page content.

Responsive Background Images

Making background images adapt to the size of the screen in CSS is fairly straightforward, since we have access to media queries.

For our example, we'll revisit the page header example from Chapter 5 (the social network for cats, remember?). The markup consists of a single element, acting as the header for the page—we'll leave out the rest of the contents of the header for now, focusing on just applying the background.

```
<header class="profile-box" role="banner"></header>
```

We'll use two different image files as backgrounds. The smaller version is 600 pixels wide and cropped to a square, while the larger version is 1200 pixels wide, with a looser crop (see Figure 8-18).

small-cat.jpg

big-cat.jpg

Figure 8-18. *Our two cat images*

For the smallest viewports, we will use the tightly cropped smaller version:

```
.profile-box {
  height: 300px;
  background-size: cover;
  background-image: url(img/small-cat.jpg);
}
```

Now when the viewport gets larger than the background image, it is scaled up (by the background-size: cover declaration), and starts to look blurry. At this point, we can swap it for the larger image:

```
@media only screen and (min-width: 600px) {
  .profile-box {
    height: 600px;
    background-image: url(img/big-cat.jpg);
  }
}
```

This simple example illustrates two things. First, that we can use media queries to deliver the most appropriately sized image for the viewport. Second, we can use responsive backgrounds not only for loading image sources of different resolutions, but also to art-direct responsive designs by cropping background images differently based on the viewport.

Using Resolution Queries to Switch Images

In the previous example, we changed the image based on the dimensions of the viewport. But we may also want to load images of different resolutions for the same viewport size, based on the pixel ratio of the device. With images, the actual pixel dimensions of the image and CSS pixels need to work together. An image with the intrinsic size of 400 by 400 pixels will be displayed as 400 by 400 *CSS pixels* even on high-resolution screens. This means the image will be scaled up, losing sharpness in the process. If we want to load a larger, sharper image only on high-resolution devices, we need to use resolution queries.

Let's say we want to serve a `medium-cat.jpg` file even to the smallest viewport, but only if it has a pixel ratio of at least 1.5. This `medium-cat.jpg` file is the same square crop, but 800×800 pixels in size. The number 1.5 is somewhat arbitrary, but it makes sure that the larger image is used on most high-resolution phones and tablets, where 1.5 is in the lowest range. You can always add further media queries (and more detailed image sizes) for higher resolutions—just keep an eye on the file size for the images!

In order to switch out the image based on pixel ratio, the standardized media feature to test for is called `resolution`, so we check for `min-resolution` using the `dppx` unit ("device-pixels per pixel"). Not all devices support this standardized query though, so we complement it with a check for the `-webkit-min-device-pixel-ratio`, predominantly used by Safari. The measurement for the latter is a unitless number.

```
@media (-webkit-min-device-pixel-ratio: 1.5),
       (min-resolution: 1.5dppx) {
  .profile-box {
    background-image: url(medium-cat.jpg);
  }
}
```

Combining queries for dimensions with queries for resolution, you can make sure the most optimal image gets loaded for each device class.

OLDER RESOLUTION QUERY SYNTAXES

You may encounter various other recommendations for resolution queries. There are nonstandard queries like the extremely odd `min--moz-device-pixel-ratio`, used in very old Firefox browsers, as well as `min-resolution` queries set in the `dpi` unit.

The `dpi` unit is the only supported unit for the standardized `min-resolution` query in some older implementations, most notably Internet Explorer 9–11. Sadly, the IE implementation gets the `dpi` number for the device wrong, which causes the high-resolution image to be loaded by mistake in some circumstances.

Using only the `-webkit-min-device-pixel-ratio` query in combination with the `min-resolution` query (and the `dppx` unit) is likely to cover a wide majority of users running high-resolution devices, and keeps the code complexity to a minimum, which is why we recommend it, despite the lack of IE support. For further reading, see this blog post from W3C's Elika Etemad: `https://www.w3.org/blog/CSS/2012/06/14/unprefix-webkit-device-pixel-ratio/`

Responsive Embedded Media

One of the trickier aspects of responsive web design is getting the flexibility of content images, video, and other embedded objects right. With background images in CSS, we can let media queries do a lot of the work. With things embedded into the page, the logic of CSS is not always there to help the browser make the right decisions.

Some of this is technically beyond the scope of CSS, but it's important to grasp these issues since they affect the performance of the sites you build in such a massive way.

Responsive Media Basics

In Chapter 5, we already encountered one of the most basic techniques to make images, video, and other objects behave in a fluid way. Setting a `max-width` of 100% makes the element fluid, while still not growing outside of its intrinsic dimensions:

```
img, object, video, embed {
  width: auto;
  max-width: 100%;
  height: auto;
}
```

While the preceding rule is somewhat naïve, it represents a good baseline to prevent fixed-width elements sneaking into your fluid and responsive designs. Each usage situation may require different sizing methods though.

The "aspect-ratio aware container" trick from Chapter 5 is especially useful for creating flexible containers for videos. It also helps with a number of sizing issues for SVG content; Sara Soueidan has written a good article on how to size SVG responsively (`http://tympanus.net/codrops/2014/08/19/making-svgs-responsive-with-css/`).

Responsive Images and the srcset Attribute

While sizing images is relatively straightforward, it doesn't solve the bigger issue with loading the *right* image. Image file size is the number one factor in overall page weight, and the Web is getting heavier at an alarming rate. Today, the average web page is well over 2MB, with images accounting for more than 60% of that weight (see Figure 8-19).

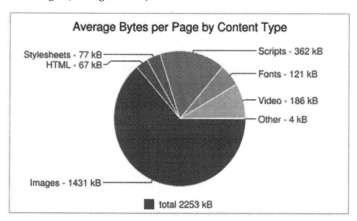

Figure 8-19. *Screenshot from `http://httparchive.org`: the distribution of size in bytes between different content on an average web page, February 2016*

251

When responsive web design was introduced, many developers exacerbated the file size problem by serving the same image to every device, regardless of screen size or capability. This meant serving the largest image, and scaling it down for smaller viewports, to keep it looking sharp. This was bad not only because of overall page weight; scaling images requires processor time and lots of memory space, neither of which is abundant on devices like phones.

Browsers do something called *pre-parsing* of HTML, where assets like images start to download even before the browser has finished constructing the full page in memory, or executed any JavaScript. This makes it impossible to solve responsive images in a sane way using scripting alone. This is why there has been a big effort in the last few years to standardize responsive images. One of the resulting improvements is the srcset attribute.

The srcset attribute, along with its companion attribute sizes, is in its simplest form an extension to the img element. It allows you to specify a couple of different things about the image:

- Which are the alternate source files for this image, and how wide are they in pixels?

- How wide, in terms of CSS, is the image supposed to be at various breakpoints?

By supplying this information in markup rather than CSS, the pre-parser can decide as quickly as possible which image to load.

An early version of the srcset syntax was originally introduced a couple of years back in WebKit-based browsers. It only deals with the target resolution and allows you to specify a list of alternate image sources, along with a minimum ratio of physical pixels to CSS pixels known as an "x-descriptor." For the featured article in the news section example, we could use the 600×300 image for default resolutions or nonsupporting browsers, but switch to a twice-as-large image when the ratio is higher (see Figure 8-20):

```
<img src="img/600x300.png" srcset="img/1200x600.png 1.5x" alt="Dummy image">
```

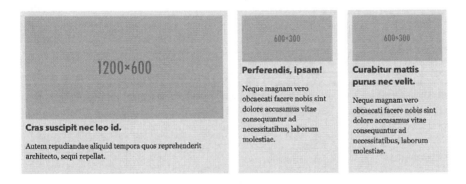

Figure 8-20. *Viewing the news example page on a high-resolution screen, with the x-descriptor syntax used to load a higher resolution "featured article" image (leftmost article)*

Resolution switching does not regard at which size the image will be shown. To do that, you need to add the sizes attribute, and describe how wide the image is rather than the intended pixel ratio.

This is where `srcset` syntax gets a little bit tricky. If we have a number of source images containing the same graphic at varying sizes (ranging from 300×150 to 1200×600), we combine them with a list of pairs of media conditions and width measurements, describing how the image will be used. We can express the intended sizes as precisely as we wish, using, for example, viewport-relative units and the `calc()` functional notation, borrowed from CSS:

```
<img src="img/xsmall.png"
    srcset="img/xsmall.png 300w,
            img/small.png 400w,
            img/medium.png 600w,
            img/large.png 800w,
            img/xlarge.png 1200w"
    sizes="(min-width: 70em) 12.6875em,
           (min-width: 50em) calc(25vw * 0.95 - 2.75em),
           (min-width: 35em) calc(95vw / 2 - 4.125em),
           calc(95vw - 1.375em)"
    alt="Dummy image" />
```

We'll break this down piece by piece. Apart from the normal `src` and `alt` attributes, we have `srcset`. It describes a list of image URLs, and a clue for the browser on how wide they are in actual pixels—not CSS pixels. This syntax, with a `w` character after the width, is called a *width descriptor*.

```
srcset="img/xsmall.png 300w,
        img/small.png 400w,
        ..."
```

Next, we'll need to explain to the browser how we intend to use the image. We do this by supplying a list of widths, each one optionally starting with a media condition, just like in a media query. It's important to note that these expressions are not CSS, so they don't follow the rules of the Cascade where the last declared matching rule wins. Instead, the first matching rule short-circuits the evaluation and wins, so we start with the widest media condition. The last size doesn't need a condition, as it acts as a fallback measurement and matches the smallest screens.

```
sizes="(min-width: 70em) 12.6875em,
       (min-width: 50em) calc(25vw * 0.95 - 2.75em),
       (min-width: 35em) calc(95vw / 2 - 4.125em),
       calc(95vw - 1.375em)"
```

The measurements after the media condition are calculations on approximately how wide the image will be shown at the various breakpoints, based on the current responsive layout. This is a trade-off with responsive images: we effectively need to put some information about our CSS into the markup. We can't use percentages here, since those are relative to the CSS style calculations, but we can use viewport units like `vw`, and ems. The em-unit size here corresponds to the default font size of the browser, just like with media queries.

■ **Note**   The `vw` unit is related to the viewport width, where 1 unit is 1% of the viewport. We'll come back to viewport-relative units a little later in the chapter.

Finally, the browser decides on the best candidate for the current viewport dimensions, and downloads that image.

It make take you a while to fully grasp how the srcset and sizes attributes fit together. The end result is that by supplying the browser with a list of image files and the intended width of the img element, the browser will figure it out for you.

This may result in the loading of a larger file based on images already existing in the cache, or a smaller file based on bandwidth constraints, low battery, etc. Similarly, it will figure out if you are on a device with a high-density screen and load the larger image, without having to specify this in the markup.

The Picture Element: Art Direction, File Type Support, and More

Apart from switching between source images of various resolutions, there are a few more important use cases for responsive images:

- We may want to crop the image differently on smaller versus larger screens, because of the difference in both rendered size and viewing distance—just like in the background image example. When we're using only srcset/sizes, the browser may assume that the source files all have the same aspect ratio and only differ in their resolution.

- We may want to load images in a different file format based on what the browser supports. We have already mentioned the WebP format in Chapter 5, but there are other formats as well, such as the JPEG2000 format (supported by Safari) and the JPEG-XR format (supported by IE and Edge), and more. A lot of these formats have significant file-size savings compared to the formats supported cross-browser.

The standardized solution to these issues is the picture element. It acts as a wrapper around an <img> tag and adds further capabilities on top of the srcset and sizes attributes.

We could complement the srcset markup from the responsive news site example with loading images in the WebP format where supported. The markup now looks like this:

```
<picture>
  <source type="image/webp"
          srcset="img/xsmall.webp 300w,
                  img/small.webp 400w,
                  img/medium.webp 600w,
                  img/large.webp 800w,
                  img/xlarge.webp 1200w"
          sizes="(min-width: 70em) 28em,
                 (min-width: 50em) calc(50vw * 0.95 - 2.75em),
                 calc(95vw - 1.375em)" />
  <img src="img/xsmall.png"
       srcset="img/xsmall.png 300w,
               img/small.png 400w,
               img/medium.png 600w,
               img/large.png 800w,
               img/xlarge.png 1200w"
       sizes="(min-width: 70em) 28em,
              (min-width: 50em) calc(50vw * 0.95 - 2.75em),
              calc(95vw - 1.375em)"
       alt="Dummy image" />
</picture>
```

While this is very verbose, the logic is only a little more complex. The <img> tag and all its contents are the same. What's new is the <picture> wrapper, and the <source> tag inside it, repeating much of the patterns from the <img>.

First of all, the img still needs to be there inside the picture element—the function of the picture and source elements is to choose which image file becomes the final source for the img. Besides, it acts as a fallback for browsers lacking in support for picture.

We still have the srcset and sizes attributes on the img, but let's leave them for a minute. When the browser encounters a picture element with an img inside it, it will start going through any source elements to try and find a match for what the img element could display. In our example, there's only one source element, but there could be several:

```
<source type="image/webp" ...>
```

Our source element has a type attribute set to image/webp, so it will only continue to be evaluated as a potential match if the browser knows about that file type.

Next, the source element has the same kind of srcset and sizes attributes as the img element has, but the source files listed in the srcset attribute are all WebP files:

```
<source type="image/webp"
        srcset="img/xsmall.webp 300w,
                img/small.webp 400w, ..."
        sizes="(min-width: 70em) 28em,
               (min-width: 50em) calc(50vw * 0.95 - 2.75em)...">
```

If the browser manages to match one of these, that file will be loaded as the source for the img element. If no source element has a match, it finally goes to the img element itself, and checks any attributes there. As a last resort if nothing matches (or the picture syntax is unsupported), the src attribute is used.

At this point, the example negotiates both resolution *and* image file-type support for us. If we compare the example when viewed in Firefox on a high-resolution screen and Chrome on a standard-resolution screen, each browser will choose the most appropriate image for us. In Figure 8-21, we see that Chrome loads a smaller WebP file, and Firefox picks the high-resolution PNG file.

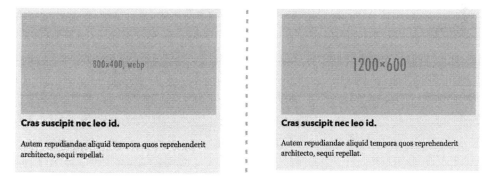

Figure 8-21. *Chrome (left) on a standard-resolution screen loads a smaller WebP file. Firefox (right) on a high-resolution screen loads the high-resolution PNG file.*

In the preceding example, we check the media conditions in the `sizes` attribute to match a display width with a breakpoint. If we wanted to have even more control over which source is used when, we could also use a `media` attribute on the `source` element itself, with full media queries inside it:

```
<picture>
  <source media="(min-width: 70em) and (min-resolution: 3dppx)" srcset="..." />
  <img src="..." alt="..." />
</picture>
```

Combined like this, you get a great deal of control over which files load when. The difference from `srcset` is that the browser will *not* make a judgment call for you in terms of selecting which `source` element to use. The selection inside the `srcset` attribute is still up to the browser, but it must use the first `source` element that matches either on the `media` or the `type` attribute.

This means increased control for you as developer. For example, it makes sense when you want art-directed images, with different crops for different viewports. But it also brings a greater responsibility to be careful. After all, the goal is to reduce unnecessarily large downloads.

For most cases, `srcset` and `sizes` will be enough, but with `picture`, you're bringing out the big toolbox.

Browser Support and Picturefill

At the time of writing, the latest versions of almost all browsers have full support for the `srcset` and `sizes` syntax. Some browsers (most notably slightly older versions of Safari) offer partial support, using the syntax with x-descriptors. Internet Explorer 11 (and earlier) is completely left out.

Support for the `picture` element is slightly weaker, but catching up. Chrome, Opera, Firefox, and Microsoft Edge have already shipped support. As this is being written, Safari is just about to ship support on both OS X and iOS, starting with Safari 9.1 on desktop and iOS 9.3.

The nice thing is that `srcset` and `picture` solutions were designed to have a fallback, in that both rely on the existing `img` element if support isn't there. This means that you can still go ahead and implement a solution using these technologies right now, with a sensible fallback image size. As responsive images can have a drastic impact on performance, you might get even further if you use a polyfill.

There is an official JavaScript-based polyfill for these standards, called Picturefill (`http://scottjehl.github.io/picturefill/`). You may remember from the start of this section that JavaScript will not be enough for a proper solution of the responsive images solution. That's still true, and the polyfill comes with a few caveats:

- You will need to have a "fake" `src` attribute on the `img` element to avoid double downloads in nonsupporting browsers. This means that browsers where the JavaScript polyfill doesn't load and `picture` is not supported will not see any images at all.

- IE before version 10 will ignore `source` elements in HTML unless they are children of a `video` element (the `source` element plays a similar role for loading videos), so if you need to use `picture` with `source` file types targeting IE, you'll need to fiddle with conditional comments to add a "fake" `video` element to your markup. Details are in the documentation for Picturefill.

■ **Note** For the picture element example accompanying the book, you'll see that we haven't used the hack for IE—this is because IE does not understand the WebP format anyway, so polyfilling that particular feature is not necessary.

Responsive Typography

It's easy to understand why layout is important for responsive design. Typography is probably equally important when designing for all different types of devices. Not only are the sizes of screens different, but we also interact with different types of devices in different ways. In this section, we'll go through the most important considerations for adapting your typography across various form factors.

Different Devices, Different Measures

When we read on a larger screen, we are often comfortable with a measure of around 45 to 70 characters per line. For smaller screens such as phones, a measure of upward of 70 characters would mean that the type would be uncomfortably small. This means that we need to adjust the size on smaller screens so that the average line length is closer to 35 to 45 characters.

When the number of characters per line gets smaller, we can often decrease the line-height a little bit. If you set a line-height of around 1.5 for desktop-sized type, you can probably get away with 1.3 for the smallest screens.

When deciding on a size, you are influencing the measure—these two are always linked. So how do you decide on a comfortable size for the body text of your site?

One easy way is to sit in front of your screen at a comfortable distance, and then hold up a physical book or magazine at your normal reading distance. Compare the size of the text in the book with the size of the text on your screen (see Figure 8-22). Is the text on the screen smaller or larger? Usually, you will end up with a text size of around 20 pixels to match that of the book.

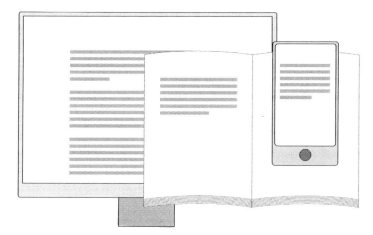

Figure 8-22. *Holding a book at comfortable reading distance as a guide, you can find the right size and measure for other devices*

It is very common for text on the Web to be set a lot smaller than that. This is probably more out of habit among designers and developers than the actual readability of the text. The conventions are changing though, and sites where the reading experience is front and center are leading the way. As an example, https://medium.com uses a font size of 22 pixels for body text viewed on a desktop browser.

Repeating the same experiment on a phone, you are likely to find that you hold the phone a little bit closer than you would hold a book. Experimenting with the measure is likely to land you at a font size of 16–18 pixels.

To judge if the measure is in the accepted range for a particular combination of screen size and font, you can use a trick from designer Trent Walton. He simply added a special character at the character position where the accepted range starts and stops, and tested that as the paragraph text on the device (http://trentwalton.com/2012/06/19/fluid-type/):

```
<p>Lorem ipsum dolor sit amet, consectetur adip *isicing elit, sed do eius mod* tempor incidid.</p>
```

The asterisks in that paragraph are positioned at character numbers 45 and 70. This means that the measure is too long whenever they are both on the first line. When testing on a mobile device, the first line break of the paragraph should be close to (or before) the first asterisk.

When you have found a good font size and measure for the smallest and the biggest screens, you have a good foundation for the rest of the responsive typography of your site. The next step is to implement it, and as with so many other things, there are many ways to do it. Some of those ways are more flexible than others.

Using Flexible Font Sizes

We often talk about pixel sizes when discussing typography, but as we saw in Chapter 4 on typography, there are other ways of describing sizes and distances.

Font sizing with relative lengths like em, rem, and the viewport units (vw, vh, vmin, and vmax) is a very efficient way to size our text across different screen sizes. These units give us a way to make small adjustments for various form factors by updating the font size at a higher level and then letting that cascade down for all elements. These are Cascading Style Sheets, after all.

Setting the Base Font Size

Pretty much every browser has a base font size set to 16 pixels in its user agent style sheet. We are free to change that by changing the font size on the html element. Media queries based on em units are always based on the base size set by the *browser*, so for reasons of consistency in the CSS for a responsive site, you might want to set your new base on the body element instead.

Using a base font size that works well for the smallest screens makes sense, as it allows us to apply the "mobile first" strategy to our typography as well. Our next task is to set the font sizes of things that may differ from the base size: headings, lists, menus, and other bits of content. We mentioned the importance of using flexible font sizes in responsive design, and now it's time to dive into that technique. We will need to scale our whole typography up as we target bigger and bigger screens.

If your font size was set in pixels, you could end up with a style sheet that looks like this:

```
p { font-size: 16px; }
h1 { font-size: 36px; }
h2 { font-size: 30px; }
h3 { font-size: 26px; }
/* ...etc */
@media only screen and (min-width: 32.5em) {
  p { font-size: 18px; }
  h1 { font-size: 40px; }
  /* ...and on and on... */
}
@media only screen and (min-width: 52em) {
  p { font-size: 20px; }
  h1 { font-size: 44px; }
  /* oh no, there's more... */
}
```

You can see where this is going: pixel-based font sizes make it terribly tedious to rescale a layout. Using relative sizes makes rescaling much easier:

```
p { font-size: 1em; }
h1 { font-size: 2.25em; }
h2 { font-size: 1.875em; }
h3 { font-size: 1.625em; }
/* ...etc */
@media only screen and (min-width: 32.5em) {
  body { font-size: 1.125em; /* done! */ }
}
@media only screen and (min-width: 52em) {
  body { font-size: 1.25em; } /* done! */
}
```

This technique is highly efficient, but hardly enough. Making a typographic system scale is not as simple as just changing the base font size at a few breakpoints. For example, you might want to have huge headlines relative to the body text for very large screens, but a somewhat more moderate difference in size for mobiles. If you want a good foundation, Jason Pamenthal's comprehensive article "A More Modern Scale for Web Typography" (http://typecast.com/blog/a-more-modern-scale-for-web-typography) offers both advice and boilerplate code to get you started (see Figure 8-23).

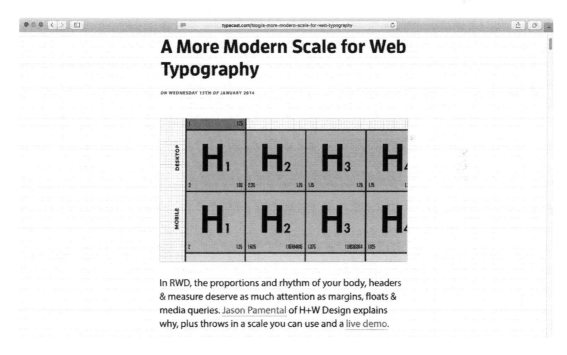

Figure 8-23. Jason Pamenthal's article on responsive typography is a handy resource

Using flexible measurements allows you to scale your font sizes (and other relative measurements like `margin`, `line-height`, and `padding`) up and down inside media queries, and then spend time tweaking the things that don't scale uniformly. That's much more efficient than redeclaring everything for each breakpoint.

Viewport-Relative Units for Typography

The em and `rem` units are flexible, since they don't represent any specific pixel measurement. The next step in flexible sizing is tying the size of your fonts to the size of the viewport, using viewport-relative units. With these units, the value 1 is equal to 1% of either the viewport width or the viewport height:

- `vw` represents the viewport width.

- `vh` represents the viewport height.

- `vmin` represents the smallest of either width or height.

- `vmax` represents the biggest of either width or height.

Getting your head around how viewport units work can be tricky at first. Let's try out an example.

```
p {
  font-size: 5vw;
}
```

What does `5vw` mean? Well, assuming you view a paragraph set with that size on a viewport that is 400 pixels wide (like in some mobile browsers), it would be five times as big as 1% of the viewport width, and 1% is 4 pixels. The math becomes $5 \times 4 = 20$ pixels.

In a way, this gives us the ultimate in responsive typography, as the type will change without any media queries. This is also the risk with viewport-relative units: you risk missing something that shouldn't scale too far, that becomes too big or too small at the extremes. In the example from the previous paragraph, we're doing OK for typical mobile screen sizes, but how large would the type be for desktop-sized browsers? Well, assuming a viewport width of 1400 pixels (for example), the size would be $14 \times 5 = 70$ pixels. That's a little on the massive side!

This means that we still need to cap the ranges somehow. One very creative method, documented by developer Mike Riethmuller in his article "Precise control over responsive typography" (`http://madebymike.com.au/writing/precise-control-responsive-typography`), is to get very creative with the CSS `calc()` function. As `calc()` has its own quirks and bugs, we often have to resort to setting breakpoints where we redefine the `font-size`, even when set in viewport-relative units. Regardless of method, the benefit is that anything set with viewport relative sizes scales nicely even *between* the breakpoints.

Viewport units are relatively well supported across browsers. They are supported in IE since version 9, and in all the latest versions of Chrome, Firefox, and Safari. Support is missing in the stock Android browser before version 4.4 and in Opera Mini. There are a few quirks though:

- IE9 implements the `vmin` unit as `vm`.

- IE9, IE10, and Safari 6–7 are missing the `vmax` unit.

- Safari 6–7 on iOS also has a some severe bugs where viewport units are completely messed up (see `https://github.com/scottjehl/Device-Bugs/issues/36`).

Tweak and Test

Responsive typography is a fairly new way of looking at type. As with responsive layout, we are tasked with trying to find ways of thinking about it as a system, and we need that system to translate to any form factor and device. At the same time, the bottom line is very much the same. There are basic rules of style, sizing, and measure to follow, but for each situation, you need to test, tweak, and test again. Choosing a method for building your CSS is important, but the final goal should be a great experience for the person using what you build, regardless of device.

Summary

In this chapter, we have looked at how to structure responsive CSS—for layout, for images, and for typography. We took a deep dive into the technical foundations of how responsive design works, deciphering various viewports and how to make them behave the way you want when using CSS.

We also looked at a range of examples on how to use new specifications like flexbox and Grid Layout to adjust responsive layouts, with or without media queries. We have seen how to implement responsive images using new additions to CSS as well as the new standards for responsive content images. Finally, we examined some considerations for typography on different form factors.

In the next chapter, we'll focus on another important area for styling: forms and tables. We will see that there are responsive challenges there as well.

■ ■ ■

CHAPTER 9

Styling Forms and Data Tables

Forms are an incredibly important part of modern web applications. They allow users to interact with systems, enabling them to do everything from leaving comments to booking complicated travel itineraries. Forms can be as simple as an e-mail address and a message field, or they can be hugely complex, spanning multiple pages.

As well as needing to capture user data, web applications increasingly need to display this data in an easy-to-understand format. A table can be the best way to show complex data, but it needs to be carefully designed to avoid being overwhelming. The collection of elements that make up tables is one of the more complex bits of HTML, and easy to get wrong.

Form and data table design have been relatively neglected in favor of higher-profile areas of design. However, good information and interaction design can make or break a modern web application.

In this chapter, you will learn about

- Creating attractive and accessible data tables

- Making tables work for responsive layouts

- Creating simple and complicated form layouts

- Styling various form elements, including custom styling of checkboxes and select menus

- Providing accessible form feedback

Styling Data Tables

Tabular data is information that can be arranged in columns and rows. A calendar view of a month is a good example of something that could be marked up as a table.

Even relatively simple data tables can be hard to read if they contain more than a few rows and columns. Without separation between data cells, information blurs together, resulting in a jumbled and confusing layout (see Figure 9-1).

© Andy Budd and Emil Björklund 2016

A. Budd and E. Björklund, *CSS Mastery*, DOI 10.1007/978-1-4302-5864-3_9

January 2015						
Mon	**Tue**	**Wed**	**Thu**	**Fri**	**Sat**	**Sun**
29	30	31	1	2	3	4
5	6	7	8	9	10	11
12	13	14	15	16	17	18
19	20	21	22	23	24	25
26	27	28	29	30	31	1

Figure 9-1. *Compact data tables can be very confusing at first glance*

Conversely, tables with a lot of whitespace can also be very difficult to read, as columns and cells start to lose their visual association with each other. This is particularly problematic when you're trying to follow rows of information on tables with very large column spacing, such as the one in Figure 9-2. If you are not careful, it is easy to accidentally stray into the wrong row when moving between columns. This is most noticeable in the middle of the table where the hard edge of the top and bottom of the table provide less of a visual anchor.

	January 2015					
Mon	**Tue**	**Wed**	**Thu**	**Fri**	**Sat**	**Sun**
29	30	31	1	2	3	4
5	6	7	8	9	10	11
12	13	14	15	16	17	18
19	20	21	22	23	24	25
26	27	28	29	30	31	1

Figure 9-2. *Widely spaced tables can also be difficult to immediately comprehend*

Thankfully, the readability of your data tables can be greatly improved by applying some basic design techniques. The dates in Figure 9-3 have been given breathing room with a little line height and a default width. The table head is clearly distinguished with different text styles and a border, and the various states involving the current date and which days are on the weekend are clearly marked. The result is an easy-to-use calendar widget.

January 2015

Mon	Tue	Wed	Thu	Fri	Sat	Sun
29	30	31	1	2	3	4
5	6	7	8	9	10	11
12	13	**14**	15	16	17	18
19	20	21	22	23	24	25
26	27	28	29	30	31	1

Figure 9-3. *Styled data table*

Table-Specific Elements

If tables can be difficult for sighted users, imagine how complicated and frustrating they must be for people using assistive technologies such as screen readers. At the most basic level, tables are created from the table element, and consist of tr elements (table rows) and td elements (table cells). Fortunately, the HTML specification includes further elements and attributes intended to increase the accessibility of data tables.

Table Captions

A table caption element acts as a heading for the table. Although not a required element, it is always a good idea to use a caption wherever possible. In this example, we're using the caption to show users which month they are looking at:

```
<table class="cal">
  <caption><strong>January</strong> 2015</caption>
</table>
```

thead, tbody, and tfoot

Using thead, tfoot, and tbody allows you to break tables into logical sections. For instance, you can place all of your column headings inside the thead element, providing you with a means of separately styling that particular area. If you choose to use a thead or tfoot element, you must use at least one tbody element. You can only use one thead and tfoot element in a table, but you can use multiple tbody elements to help break complicated tables into more manageable chunks.

Row and column headings should be marked up as th rather than td. Table headings can be given a scope attribute value of row or col to define whether they are row or column headings. The scope attribute can also be given a value of rowgroup or colgroup if they relate to more than one row or column. The days of the week label the columns, so they should have the scope attribute set to col.

```
<thead>
  <tr>
    <th scope="col">Mon</th>
    <!-- ...and so on -->
    <th scope="col">Sun</th>
  </tr>
</thead>
```

col and colgroups

The tr element offers a target to style whole rows. But what about columns? We could use :nth-child to select table cells, which could get messy. The col and colgroup elements are there for this very purpose. A colgroup is used to define a group of one or more columns, represented by the col element. The col elements themselves don't have any content, but rather stand in for the table cells in one particular column of the actual table.

```
<colgroup>
    <col class="cal-mon">
    <col class="cal-tue">
    <col class="cal-wed">
    <col class="cal-thu">
    <col class="cal-fri">
    <col class="cal-sat cal-weekend">
    <col class="cal-sun cal-weekend">
</colgroup>
```

The colgroup needs to be placed inside the table element, after any caption but before any thead, tfoot, or tbody elements.

You then apply styling to the col (or colgroup) elements instead of all the table cells in a specific column, like (for example) all Saturdays and Sundays in a calendar. The properties you can style for columns are severely limited. You can style background properties, border properties, and width and visibility, but that's it.

To top that off, visibility for columns can only have the value visible or collapse, and even that is not very well supported in browsers. The value collapse is supposed to not just hide but collapse the dimensions of portions of a table, which would be handy in some situations, but it's just one of those things that some browser-makers seem to have skipped.

Finished Table Markup

Putting all of these HTML elements and attributes together, you can create the basic outline for the calendar table shown in Figure 9-1.

```
<table class="cal">
  <caption><strong>January</strong> 2015</caption>
  <colgroup>
    <col class="cal-mon">
    <!-- ...and so on -->
    <col class="cal-sat cal-weekend">
    <col class="cal-sun cal-weekend">
  </colgroup>
```

```
<thead>
  <tr>
    <th scope="col">Mon</th>
    <!-- ...and so on one per day.-->
    <th scope="col">Sun</th>
  </tr>
</thead>
<tbody>
  <tr>
    <td class="cal-inactive">29</td>
    <td class="cal-inactive">30</td>
    <td class="cal-inactive">31</td>
    <td><a href="#">1</a></td>
    <td><a href="#">2</a></td>
    <td><a href="#">3</a></td>
    <td><a href="#">4</a></td>
  </tr>
  <!-- ...and so on, one row per week... -->
  <tr>
    <td><a href="#">26</a></td>
    <td class="cal-current"><a href="#">27</a></td>
    <!-- ...and so on -->
    <td><a href="#">31</a></td>
    <td class="cal-inactive">1</td>
  </tr>
</tbody>
</table>
```

We've wrapped all the days with a placeholder anchor element (assuming the calendar component takes you somewhere or does something when you click a date). We have also added a couple of class names to represent the current day (`.cal-current`) and days that fall outside of the current month (`.cal-inactive`).

Styling the Table Element

The CSS specification has two table border models: separate and collapsed. In the separate model, borders are placed around individual cells, whereas in the collapsed model, cells share borders. We want cells to share a single 1-pixel border, so we set the `border-collapse` property of our table to `collapse`.

Tables also have a sizing algorithm for their cells, which we can control via the `table-layout` property. By default, a value of `auto` is used, which basically leaves it up to the browser to determine widths of cells based on their content. By changing it to `fixed`, any cell widths are determined based on the width of cells in the first row of the table or any `col` or `colgroup` elements. This gives us more control via CSS.

Next, we set the font stack and center all the text in the table. Finally, we will add a width and a maximum width to create a fluid component that takes up as much space as it can without being unreadably wide.

```
.cal {
  border-collapse: collapse;
  table-layout: fixed;
  width: 100%;
  max-width: 25em;
  font-family: "Lucida Grande", Verdana, Arial, sans-serif;
  text-align: center;
}
```

Styling the Table Contents

The groundwork has been set, so it is now time to start adding the visual style. To make the table caption look a little more like a regular heading, we'll increase the font size and line height. We will also align it to the left and give it a border to separate it from the table head.

```
.cal caption {
  text-align: left;
  border-bottom: 1px solid #ddd;
  line-height: 2;
  font-size: 1.5em;
}
```

Next, we'll use the col elements to set a pink background for the weekend days. Remember, background properties are among the few things you can change for whole columns. We will use a highly transparent color so it blends in with any background, but supply a fallback declaration to a solid color before that, to accommodate older browsers.

```
.cal-weekend {
  background-color: #fef0f0;
  background-color: rgba(255, 0, 0, 0.05);
}
```

Next, we'll style the individual cells. All cells need a bit more line height, and we'll supply them with a width. By default, tables have a layout algorithm that assigns space according to the content of the cells. This causes the columns to be just slightly different because of the difference in size of the weekday table headings. We can assign a width equal to one-seventh of the table width (14.285%) to correct this. In fact, the width only needs to be *at least* one-seventh of the table width—if the cells add up to more than 100% (when using the fixed table layout model), they will each be proportionally reduced in size until they fit. If we wanted to make the cells equally wide regardless of how many there are, we could set their width to 100%. While this is a handy trick, in this case we've left the width as one-seventh of the total, for clarity's sake. You can read more about table layout quirks in this CSS-Tricks article by Chris Coyier: https://css-tricks. com/fixing-tables-long-strings/.

Table cells also have a default padding in some browsers, which we'll want to remove. We'll also add a faint border for the table cells, but not heading cells.

```
.cal th,
.cal td {
  line-height: 3;
  padding: 0;
  width: 14.285%;
}
.cal td {
  border: 1px solid #eee;
}
```

To separate the table head from the table data (the actual dates), we will add a thicker border. This should be as easy as setting a border on the thead element.

```
.cal thead {
  border-bottom: 3px solid #666;
}
```

This will work fine in most browsers (Chrome, Firefox, Safari, Opera, etc.) but sadly not in Internet Explorer or Edge. Borders in a table, no matter if they are on a table cell, a row, or a group of rows (thead or tbody for example), all get mashed together in the collapsing table model we have chosen. Fortunately, most browsers will override vertical borders when a border is set across a whole row. IE and Edge will try to join each of the right and left borders with the border on the thead element, creating ugly gaps (see Figure 9-4).

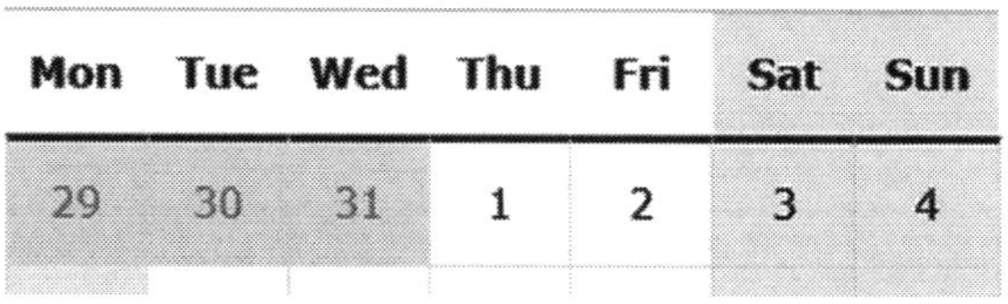

Mon	Tue	Wed	Thu	Fri	Sat	Sun
29	30	31	1	2	3	4

Figure 9-4. *IE and Edge both let the vertical borders crash into the horizontal border on the table head, creating gaps*

There *are* ways around this. We could opt out of the collapsed border model and add more rules for the individual table cell borders, but in this instance, we will leave it as is. Should you come across this problem and need it to look exactly the same in IE as in other browsers, you might have to resort to either the separate border model or using something like a background image instead.

Next up, we'll deal with the anchor links representing the clickable days inside the calendar widget. We will remove the underline, give them a dark purple color, and set them to display as blocks. This causes them to expand to fill the whole table cell, creating a much larger clickable area. Finally, we'll add rules for the hovered and focused states, where we show a translucent background-color (using the same fallback technique to a solid color as before).

```
.cal a {
    display: block;
    text-decoration: none;
    color: #2f273c;
}

.cal a:hover,
.cal a:focus {
  background-color: #cde7ca;
  background-color: rgba(167, 240, 210, 0.3);
}
```

As the finishing touch, we'll add styles for the other states of the calendar dates. We have dates falling outside of the current month, so we will give them a faded color and make it very clear that they cannot be selected by using a different pointer.

For the current date, we'll change the background color to another slightly translucent tone. The translucent colors of the various states blend together, so we will automatically have different resulting colors depending on if we have a current date, current date being hovered, current date being hovered inside of the "weekend," etc., all without any extra rules (see Figure 9-5).

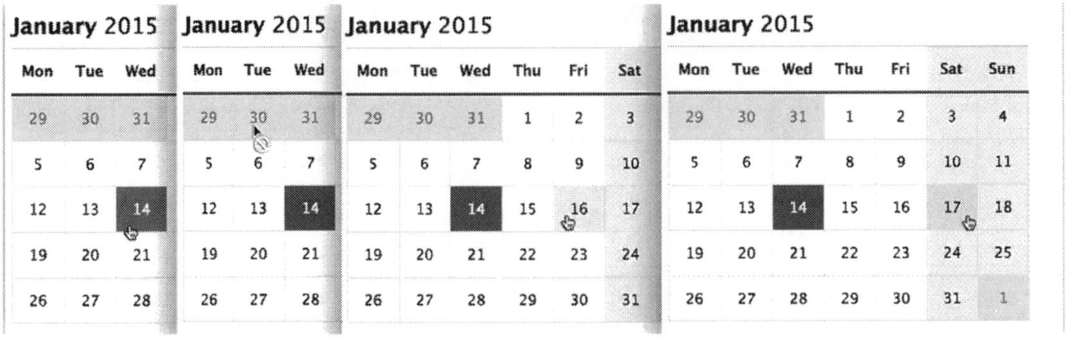

Figure 9-5. *We have added various subtle states for the hovered, current, and inactive dates*

```
.cal-inactive {
  background-color: #efefef;
  color: #aaa;
  cursor: not-allowed;
}
.cal-current {
  background-color: #7d5977;
  background-color: rgba(71, 14, 62, 0.6);
  color: #fff;
}
.cal-current a {
  color: #fff;
}
```

And there you have it, a beautifully styled calendar as seen in Figure 9-3.

Responsive Tables

Tables demand space by their very nature. They have the concept of two axes built in, and require more width as the number of columns increases. The consequence is that complex tables tend to require quite a bit of space, which clashes with the responsive goal of being able to display things comfortably on all screens, big and small.

We have previously mentioned that tables (and each component of a table) have their own display mode in CSS. We can use this to make things that are not tables borrow the "grid nature" of tables, for layout purposes. But we can also use the reverse strategy, and make tables not display as tables! We'll adopt this as a method of making tabular data fit on a smaller screen.

Linearizing a Table

When we have a table with a large number of columns, we can flip it so that each row is represented as a block consisting of both the table header texts and the values for that row. Let's create an example table to visualize this, with a bunch of data for car models. The end result will look something like Figure 9-6 on larger screens.

Tesla car models

Model	Top speed	Range	Length	Width	Weight	Starting price
Model S	201 km/h	426 km	4 976 mm	1 963 mm	2 108 kg	$69 900
Roadster	201 km/h	393 km	3 946 mm	1 873 mm	1 235 kg	$109 000

Figure 9-6. *A table of data for car models, with some simple styling*

For smaller screens, each row gets its own block. The table heading row is hidden, and the column labels are instead printed out before each piece of data. It will look something like Figure 9-7.

```
<table class="cars">
  <caption>Tesla car models</caption>
  <thead>
    <tr>
      <th scope="col">Model</th>
      <th scope="col">Top speed</th>
      <th scope="col">Range</th>
      <th scope="col">Length</th>
      <th scope="col">Width</th>
      <th scope="col">Weight</th>
      <th scope="col">Starting price</th>
    </tr>
  </thead>
  <tbody>
    <tr>
      <td>Model S</td>
      <td>201 km/h</td>
      <td>426 km</td>
      <td>4 976 mm</td>
      <td>1 963 mm</td>
      <td>2 108 kg</td>
      <td>$69 900</td>
    </tr>
    <tr>
      <td>Roadster</td>
      <td>201 km/h</td>
      <td>393 km</td>
      <td>3 946 mm</td>
      <td>1 873 mm</td>
      <td>1 235 kg</td>
      <td>$109000</td>
    </tr>
  </tbody>
</table>
```

Tesla car models

Model S	
Top speed:	201 km/h
Range:	426 km
Length:	4 976 mm
Width:	1 963 mm
Weight:	2 108 kg
Starting price:	$69 900

Roadster	
Top speed:	201 km/h
Range:	393 km
Length:	3 946 mm
Width:	1 873 mm
Weight:	1 235 kg
Starting price:	$109 000

Figure 9-7. *The table as linearized for small screens*

The styling for this table consists of some simple rules for borders, fonts, and a "zebra-striping" technique, where each even row of the table has a different background color:

```
.cars {
  font-family: "Lucida Sans", Verdana, Arial, sans-serif;
  width: 100%;
  border-collapse: collapse;
}

.cars caption {
  text-align: left;
  font-style: italic;
  border-bottom: 1px solid #ccc;
}

.cars tr:nth-child(even) {
  background-color: #eee;
}
.cars caption,
.cars th,
.cars td {
  text-align: left;
  padding: 0 .5em;
  line-height: 2;
}
.cars thead {
  border-bottom: 2px solid;
}
```

If we resize the screen, we find that at around 760 pixels wide, this table starts getting really cramped and hard to read (see Figure 9-8). That is where we need to place a breakpoint and start changing things.

Tesla car models

Model	Top speed	Range	Length	Width	Weight	Starting price
Model S	201 km/h	426 km	4 976 mm	1 963 mm	2 108 kg	$69 900
Roadster	201 km/h	393 km	3 946 mm	1 873 mm	1 235 kg	$109 000

Figure 9-8. *Our table starts getting cramped at around 760 pixels wide*

Tables have a lot of default styles and display modes. If we were to go the "mobile first" route and change the default styling to then use a min-width condition to reset the defaults for larger screens, we could be in for a lot of work. That's why we'll use a max-width condition instead, to specifically target this special case at smaller screens:

```
@media only screen and (max-width: 760px) {
  .cars {
    display: block;
  }
  .cars thead {
    display: none;
  }
  .cars tr {
    border-bottom: 1px solid;
  }
  .cars td, .cars th {
    display: block;
    float: left;
    width: 100%;
    box-sizing: border-box;
  }
  .cars th {
    font-weight: 600;
    border-bottom: 2px solid;
    padding-top: 10px;
  }
  .cars td:before {
    width: 40%;
    display: inline-block;
    font-style: italic;
    content: attr(data-label);
  }
}
```

The table cells are now set to display as blocks and take up 100% of the width, stacking them on top of each other inside the rows. The table header is completely hidden. To retain the association between the column labels and the individual values inside the td elements, we have inserted the label for each column as a data-label attribute on each table cell in the markup:

```
<th scope="row">Model S</th>
<td data-label="Top speed">201 km/h</td>
<td data-label="Range">426 km</td>
<td data-label="Length">4 976 mm</td>
<!-- ...and so on -->
```

We can now use the :before pseudo-element to inject these labels before each row of cell content. We can get at contents of element attributes by using the attr() functional notation with the content property—a handy trick for revealing extra bits of data hidden in HTML. The repetition of the labels in the markup is a small but necessary price to pay to avoid hard-coding the value of the labels inside the CSS.

Apart from some further style changes to keep the table readable, there are some other important parts of the code in the previous example.

First, we have set the table itself to display: block. This isn't necessary for presentation, but it helps with accessibility. Switching the display mode of a table shouldn't change how screen readers interpret it, but it does. This means that some screen readers get confused when there is a table in the markup but with table cells set to display as regular blocks (via CSS) inside it. Setting the table itself to display as a block seems to trigger these screen readers to read the table as a flow of text instead, which keeps the content accessible, despite losing the tabular nature. Jason Kiss of AccessibleCulture.org has a helpful article explaining the differences in various screen readers, at http://accessibleculture.org/articles/2011/08/responsive-data-tables-and-screen-reader-accessibility/.

The second thing we have done to make this solution work is to add a float declaration to the table cells. This is only necessary to counter a bug in IE9, which does support media queries, but does not seem to accept changing the display mode of table cells to block inside of an @media rule. It does apply floats, however, which effectively turns the cells into blocks as a side effect. Setting the width of the cells to 100% counters the shrink-wrapping effect of the float and guarantees they line up vertically just like blocks are supposed to.

Advanced Responsive Tables

Linearizing tables for small viewports is just one of the solutions to creating responsive tables. There are several ways to solve the same problem, and to be quite honest, it is still a fairly new problem as this book is being written. There is no "one size fits all" solution, but there are a few strategies to choose from. Most rely on JavaScript to manipulate the markup when needed, combined with CSS. The various strategies are all variations of some basic mechanisms:

- Introduce some sort of scrolling mechanism for the columns of the table when the screen is too small. For example, the first column could be fixed in place and act as an anchor that helps you know which row you are looking at, and the rest of the columns can scroll.

- Hide columns as the screen gets smaller, so that only the most important things are shown.

- Link to a larger version of the table in a separate window, where the user must rely on zoom instead.

- Make it possible to show and hide columns with a toggle mechanism.

If you need to support complex responsive table scenarios, you might find the tool Tablesaw a good fit (http://www.filamentgroup.com/lab/tablesaw.html), if nothing else as an inspiration for design patterns. It is a collection of jQuery plug-ins that helps you achieve some of the strategies mentioned in the previous list.

Styling Forms

Forms are where visitors of a web page actually do something else than consume content. It can be to fill out a contact form, write a contribution to be published, enter payment information, or finally click the "Buy now" button. It's quite obvious that these are very valuable activities, but despite being very important, forms are often poorly designed and coded.

Perhaps one of the reasons for this is that forms have always been a bit of a pain to code. They have a lot of moving parts and have traditionally been hard to style. This is because many form controls are implemented as *replaced content*, meaning that controls like the arrow in the drop-down menu in a `select` element isn't actually represented by any HTML element. It's more of a black box that the browser throws in there whenever you declare a `<select>` tag in the markup. This is largely to ensure consistency with the default UI controls of the operating system the user is currently on.

We can, however, style at least some parts of the appearance of form controls. For the parts we can't style, we can sort of fake the appearance of a custom control with some creative coding.

Forms are also about more than the form controls themselves, so this section covers both how to mark up and style components that make for an attractive HTML form. It should be noted that it is by no means a comprehensive guide to the various aspects of HTML forms – there are just too many elements and attributes for us to cover them all here.

A simple Form Example

Short and relatively simple forms are easiest to fill in when the form labels appear vertically above their associated form elements. Users can simply move down the form step by step, reading each label and completing the following form element. This method works well for short forms collecting relatively simple and predictable information such as contact details (see Figure 9-9), but it is also a very good baseline for viewing forms on smaller viewports such as mobile browsers.

Figure 9-9. *Simple form layout*

Fieldsets and Legends

HTML provides a number of useful elements that can help add structure and meaning to a form. The first one of these is the fieldset element. A fieldset is used for grouping related blocks of information. In Figure 9-9, three fieldsets are used: one for the contact details, one for the comments, and one for the "Remember me" preference.

To identify the purpose of each fieldset, you can use a legend element. Legends act a little like a fieldset's heading, usually appearing vertically centered over the top border of the fieldset and indented a little to the right. By default fieldsets are often rendered as having a double border. This slightly unusual appearance is implemented by different browsers in different ways. It seems to be a special case in the browser's rendering engine, and throwing normal CSS properties at it to undo the odd positioning rarely has the effect you expect. We'll get back to countering that as we style our form.

Labels

The label element is an extremely important one, as it can help add structure and increase the usability and accessibility of your forms. As the name suggests, this element is used to add a meaningful and descriptive label to each form element. In many browsers, clicking the label element will cause the associated form element to gain focus.

The real benefit of using labels is to increase form usability for people using assistive devices. If a form uses labels, screen readers will correctly associate a form element with its label. Screen reader users can also bring up a list of all the labels in a form, allowing them to audibly scan through the form in much the same way as a sighted user would visually scan through them.

Associating a label element with a form control can be done in one of two ways: either implicitly by nesting the form control inside the label element:

```
<label>Email <input name="comment-email" type="email"/><label>
```

or explicitly by setting the for attribute of the label equal to the id attribute value of the associated form element:

```
<label for="comment-email">Email<label>
<input name="comment-email" id="comment-email" type="email"/>
```

You will notice that this input, and most of the form controls in this chapter, contain both a name attribute and an id attribute, since we will most often not nest the input inside the label. The id attribute is required to create the association between the form input and the label, while the name attribute is required so that the form data can be sent back to the server. The id and name don't have to be the same, but it can be a handy convention to keep them identical when possible, for the sake of consistency.

Labels associated with form controls using the for attribute don't need to be near those controls in the source code; they could be in a completely different part of the document. From a structural point of view, separating form controls from their labels is rarely wise and should be avoided wherever possible.

Input Fields and Text Areas

In our simple example, we have two types of form control elements: input and textarea. Text areas are for typing in multiple lines of text, as in the comment field. The cols and rows attributes can be used to set a default size of the text area, mostly to indicate the approximate length of the expected content. We will be free to further style the textarea with CSS later.

```
<textarea name="comment-text" id="comment-text" cols="20" rows="10"></textarea>
```

The input element is a more versatile form control. By default, it renders as a single-line text input, but the type attribute can change this to a variety of different form controls. Setting type="password" creates an input where the value is obscured, and type="checkbox" creates a checkbox. There are a lot of different values for the type attribute, many of them added in HTML5. Some are mostly variations of the text input but with special behavior behind the scenes—for example, email, url, and search. Some types create very different interface controls where supported, like checkbox, radio, color, range, and file. Apart from type, there is also a whole host of attributes to use on the inputs, to declare the expected format.

The different types of form inputs and their attributes are useful for automatic validation of forms. We will briefly look at that later in the chapter, but for now, we'll settle on another big benefit. On devices with an onscreen keyboard, changing the type triggers the software keyboard to change its layout. If we add an e-mail field and a URL field with the correct types, the keyboard on smartphones and tablets will automatically adjust to make it easier to type in the correct value when we focus each field (see Figure 9-10).

Figure 9-10. *When the input has the type="email" attribute, the software keyboard shows a layout more suitable for typing an e-mail address*

Since the default value of the type attribute is text, older browsers without support for HTML5 will ignore these newer types and fall back to just a normal input. This makes choosing the newer input types a very helpful enhancement for us to make.

Putting the Fieldset Together

Using the structural elements we have looked at so far, we can start laying out our form by marking up the contents of the first fieldset. The unstyled fieldset is shown in Figure 9-11.

Figure 9-11. *The unstyled fieldset*

Inside of the form, we have wrapped the fieldset elements with a div, for reasons that will become clear in a minute. Each combination of label and input is also wrapped with a p element. It used to be that input elements were not allowed as direct children of a form element. That is no longer the case in HTML5, but the standard does still recommend that you wrap labels and form controls with a block element like p, since they semantically represent distinct "phrases" of content inside the form.

We have also added a class name of field to each of these paragraphs, in order to have a specific styling hook if we want to separate them from other kinds of paragraphs inside the form later. Furthermore, we've separated out the fields that contain a text-entry component by giving them the class name field-text.

```
<form id="comments_form" action="/comments/" method="post">
  <div class="fieldset-wrapper">
    <fieldset>
      <legend>Your Contact Details</legend>
      <p class="field field-text">
        <label for="comment-author">Name:</label>
        <input name="comment-author" id="comment-author" type="text" />
      </p>
      <p class="field field-text">
        <label for="comment-email">Email Address:</label>
        <input name="comment-email" id="comment-email" type="email" />
      </p>
      <p class="field field-text">
        <label for="comment-url">Web Address:</label>
        <input name="comment-url" id="comment-url" type="url" />
      </p>
    </fieldset>
  </div>
</form>
```

If you want to change fieldset and legend elements from their default appearance, your best bet is to not style the actual fieldset element itself, but rather just remove as much default styling as possible and then add a wrapper element around the fieldset. Your styles will then be added to the wrapper element instead.

To unstyle the `fieldset`, we'll give it the following rules:

```
fieldset {
  border: 0;
  padding: 0.01px 0 0 0;
  margin: 0;
  min-width: 0;
  display: table-cell;
}
```

We removed the default `border` and `margin`. We've also set the `padding` to 0—with the exception of the top padding, which is set to a tiny amount (`0.01px`). This is to counter weird behavior in some WebKit-based browsers, where any margin on the element after the `legend` gets transferred to the top of the `fieldset` element. Giving the `fieldset` a tiny bit of `padding-top` stops this bug.

On to the next oddity: some browsers (WebKit- and Blink-based) have a default minimum width for `fieldset` elements, which we override—if not, the `fieldset` will sometimes stick out of the viewport in the smallest sizes, creating horizontal scrollbars. Firefox also has a minimum width for `fieldset` elements, but it's hard-coded and overriding `min-width` there doesn't help. The solution is to change the display mode to `table-cell`. That messes with IE, so we need to use a Mozilla-specific nonstandard rule block to only target Mozilla-based browsers:

```
@-moz-document url-prefix() {
  fieldset {
    display: table-cell;
  }
}
```

The `@-moz-document` rule allows users of Mozilla-based browsers to override the styles of specific sites in their user style sheets, but it works in author styles as well. Normally, you'd put a specific URL in the `url-prefix()` function, but leaving it empty means it works regardless of the URL. Admittedly, this is an ugly hack, but it represents the last piece in the puzzle for removing the default styles of our `fieldset`. Now we can focus on styling the wrapper.

We'll give the wrapper a background, some margin and padding, and a subtle shadow. Older browsers that don't support the `box-shadow` property get a border instead, which is then removed using the `:root` pseudo-class as a prefix to the selector. This simply refers to the HTML element (being the root element of the document), but IE8 and other older browsers do not understand this selector, so they will get the border.

```
.fieldset-wrapper {
  padding: 1em;
  margin-bottom: 1em;
  border: 1px solid #eee;
  background-color: #fff;
  box-shadow: 0 0 4px rgba(0, 0, 0, 0.25);
}
:root .fieldset-wrapper {
  border: 0;
}
```

As for the legend, we'll just remove the default padding and add a little extra to the bottom, to increase the space between it and the form fields. Margins, sadly, have inconsistent effects on legend elements, so we'll avoid those. Lastly, we'll change its display mode to table. This hack allows it to wrap into multiple lines in IE if necessary, which is otherwise impossible.

```
legend {
    padding: 0 0 .5em 0;
    font-weight: bold;
    color: #777;
    display: table;
}
```

At this point, the fieldset itself is looking good, as shown in Figure 9-12, and we can turn our attention to the fields.

Figure 9-12. *The fieldset has now lost the double border and weird positioning of the legend, and has gained a background and a shadow*

Styling Text Input Fields

Next, we will add a rule to make the form controls inherit the font properties from the rest of the document. This is to override the browser defaults: the font size inside input fields, for example, is otherwise set to a smaller size than the normal text in the document.

```
input,
textarea {
    font: inherit;
}
```

Positioning the labels so they appear vertically above the form elements is very simple. A label is an inline element by default. Setting its display property to block will cause it to generate its own block box, forcing the input elements onto the line below.

The default width of text input boxes varies from browser to browser, but we can control that with CSS. To create a flexible input field, we'll set the width in percent by default, but with a maximum width of the field wrapper set in ems, so that it does not become uncomfortably wide. This will work well on most screen sizes. We will also need to change the box-sizing property to take borders and padding into account when calculating what 100% means.

```
.field-text {
    max-width: 20em;
}
```

```
.field-text label {
  cursor: pointer;
}
.field-text label,
.field-text input {
  width: 100%;
  box-sizing: border-box;
}
```

The cursor property for the labels is set to pointer, making it clearer for mouse-based users that this is a clickable element. The labels are also included in the rule above that sets the width, so they have the same width as the inputs.

Finally, we will tweak the styles of the text inputs slightly. We will give them subtle rounded corners, set a border color, and add some padding:

```
.field-text input {
  padding: .375em .3125em .3125em;
  border: 1px solid #ccc;
  border-radius: .25em;
  -webkit-appearance: none;
}
```

Setting the border property often removes any OS-specific border appearance and inset shadows that may show when rendering text inputs. Some WebKit-based browsers (like Safari on iOS) still show an inset shadow, so to get rid of that we set the proprietary -webkit-appearance property to none.

▓ **Note**   There isn't a standardized appearance property, but both -webkit-appearance (WebKit- and Blink-based browsers) and -moz-appearance (Firefox) let you override some rendering details for OS-specific controls. Normally, you'd do best to steer clear of these, but they can be useful for *removing* browser-specific styling of input elements.

Handling the Focused State

After changing the border of the input element, we need to pay attention to the focused state of the element as well. Most browsers show some form of outline or glow around the input element when it is focused. This marker helps users distinguish which field is focused, and can be removed by overriding either the outline property or the border property, depending on the browser. As soon as we're affecting *either* of these properties, we need to make sure that we haven't unintentionally made the form inaccessible for keyboard users.

This means that for cross-browser compatibility it's necessary to take care of the focused state ourselves. We'll add a different border color on :focus, as well as a subtle blue glow by using box-shadow (see Figure 9-13). Having done that, we can also set the outline property to 0 when focused in order to avoid a double marker of the focused state in some browsers.

```
.field-text input:focus {
  box-shadow: 0 0 .5em rgba(93, 162, 248, 0.5);
  border-color: #5da2f8;
  outline: 0;
}
```

281

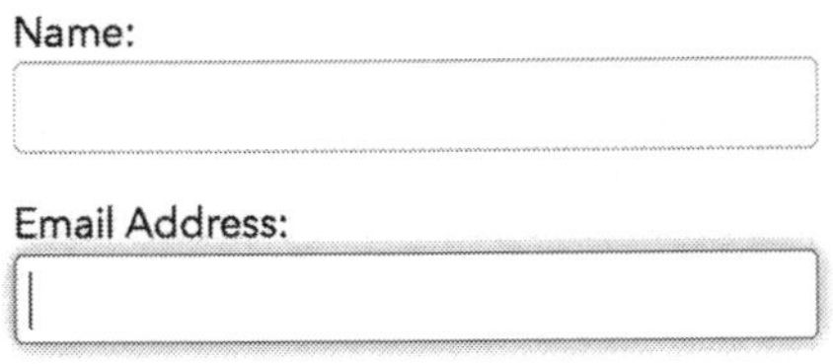

Name:

Email Address:

Figure 9-13. *A focused text input gets a different border color and a bit of a glow using box-shadow*

We have explicitly targeted the types of text-based inputs we are using in this form in the rules that we have created so far, using the `.field-text` selector. This is to avoid setting unnecessary rules for other types of input widgets, such as checkboxes. We could have gone with a list of attribute selectors instead, but as there are many possible values of the `type` attribute, a utility class name on the parent element makes the code a bit cleaner.

Adding the Rest of the Fieldsets

The rules we have created so far work equally well for other form elements such as textareas:

```
<div class="fieldset-wrapper">
  <fieldset>
    <legend>Comments</legend>
    <p class="field field-text">
      <label for="comment-text">Message:</label>
      <textarea name="comment-text" id="comment-text" cols="20" rows="10"></textarea>
    </p>
  </fieldset>
</div>
```

To adjust the appearance of the `textarea` element, we can simply add it to the list of selectors in any rules where we set properties for text inputs and labels, and get the same behavior:

```
.field-text label,
.field-text input,
.field-text textarea {
  /*...*/
}
```

Textareas will get a default height based on the `rows` attribute, but we can of course override that with `height`. When a user enters text that is longer than the visible space, the textarea will overflow and receive a scrollbar.

Many browsers will also let the user resize the textarea, so that they can see the whole text they have entered. Some browsers let the textareas resize in both width and height, and some only allow the height to resize. We can actually be explicit about this in CSS, using the `resize` property. It can be set to any of the keywords `vertical`, `horizontal`, `none`, or `both`, but shown here set to `vertical`:

```
textarea {
  height: 10em;
  resize: vertical;
}
```

Adding Radio Buttons

For the last part of the form, we are adding a radio button control, which enables the user to select only one choice out of two options. These are represented by input elements with their type set to radio. Rather than having their labels above them, these elements usually have their labels to the right (see Figure 9-14).

Figure 9-14. *Our radio buttons, with the label text to the right instead of above*

The effect of only being able to select one of these inputs is created by making the name attribute equal for these two inputs (the id attribute can still be different though):

```
<div class="fieldset-wrapper">
  <fieldset>
    <legend>Remember Me</legend>
    <p class="field">
      <label><input name="comment-remember" type="radio" value="yes" />Yes</label>
    </p>
    <p class="field">
      <label><input name="comment-remember" type="radio" value="no" checked="checked"
      />No</label>
    </p>
  </fieldset>
</div>
```

Notice that we have chosen to nest the input inside of the label in this case, instead of associating it with a for attribute and an id on the input element. This means that the display: block declaration on the label doesn't put it on a separate row from the radio button.

The last thing we'll do is add a little bit of right margin to the radio buttons, to provide some spacing between the labels:

```
input[type="radio"] {
  margin-right: .75em;
}
```

Buttons

We have one more thing to add before our form is complete. The user needs a button with which to submit the form, so the server can process it.

There are two ways of creating buttons with HTML. First, there's the input element with type set to button, reset, or submit:

```
<input type="submit" value="Post comment" />
```

Then there is the button element, which can have the same type attribute values:

```
<button type="submit">Post comment</button>
```

The button type can be used for actions initiated by JavaScript when used outside of a form, rather than actually submitting the form to the server. The reset type (not used very often these days) resets the form to its initial values. Finally, the submit value sends the form data to the URL specified in the form's action attribute, if the button is inside a form element. It is the default value when the type attribute is missing.

These two elements for buttons work the same way, and initially look the same. We recommend that you use the button element for your buttons, as you can put other elements inside them (such as spans or images) to help with styling.

Buttons have a specific default look on each platform (see Figure 9-15), as do checkboxes, radio buttons, and other form controls. As buttons are such a ubiquitous part of user interfaces, there is a big chance that you'll want to style them according to the specific look of the site you're building. Luckily, they are one of the easier form components to style with CSS.

Figure 9-15. *Unstyled button elements from Chrome on OS X, IE10 on Windows 7, Firefox on Windows 7, and Microsoft Edge on Windows 10*

We'll go for a very subtle 3D-looking edge for our button using gradients and box shadows (see Figure 9-16). Just like with the input element, messing with the border property switches the OS-specific styling off.

```
button {
  cursor: pointer;
  border: 0;
  padding: .5em 1em;
  color: #fff;
  border-radius: .25em;
  font-size: 1em;
  background-color: #173b6d;
  background-image: linear-gradient(to bottom, #1a4a8e, #173b6d);
  box-shadow: 0 .25em 0 rgba(23, 59, 109, 0.3), inset 0 1px 0 rgba(0, 0, 0, 0.3);
}
```

Figure 9-16. *Our styled button*

The pseudo-3D edge on the button is created with box-shadow rather than border properties. This allows us to leave the dimensions of the button unchanged, since the shadow doesn't affect the box model. The shadow also automatically follows the rounded corners of the button. Note that we are using two shadows. One is the outside shadow creating the edge, and one is inset, adding a subtle 1-pixel color shift to the top of the button.

We have also added a rule for the focused state of the button (see Figure 9-17), where the background is a bit lighter and a third shadow is added, giving the same slight "glow outline" effect as with the text inputs. (We'll revisit the button to animate the pressed state in Chapter 10, when we explore transforms and transitions.)

284

```
button:focus {
  background-color: #2158a9;
  background-image: linear-gradient(to bottom, #2063c0, #1d4d90);
  box-shadow: 0 .25em 0 rgba(23, 59, 109, 0.3),
              inset 0 1px 0 rgba(0, 0, 0, 0.3);
}
```

Figure 9-17. *Normal state of the button (left) and focused state (right)*

Browsers that lack support for rounded corners, gradients, and box shadows will get a flat-looking button for both states, but it will still be perfectly usable.

Clear Form Feedback and Help Texts

Poor feedback and bad error messages have long been considered some of the worst and most common design problems on the Web. When designing forms, make sure you don't just make the form controls look nice, but take care to style help and error messages too.

You can use the `placeholder` attribute to put an example of the expected input in an input field (see Figure 9-18). Browsers will show that text until you focus the field or until you start writing.

```
<input placeholder="http://example.com" name="comment-url" id="comment-url" type="url" />
```

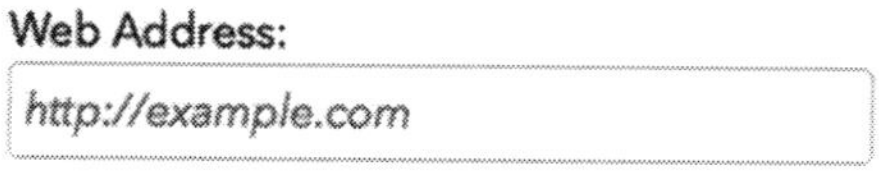

Figure 9-18. *Example input using the placeholder attribute*

We can do some limited styling of that `placeholder` attribute, for example, by making it italic. There's no standard selector for the placeholder, but different browsers offer different prefixed pseudo-elements that you can then style. Since each one is only recognized by its respective browser engine, they can't be merged into a single rule. When a browser sees an unrecognized selector, it will discard the rule as a whole, so we'll need to repeat ourselves a bit:

```
::-webkit-input-placeholder {
  font-style: italic;
}
:-ms-input-placeholder {
  font-style: italic;
}
::-moz-placeholder {
  font-style: italic;
}
```

Placeholders are meant for example input, so you must **_not_** use them as labels. After all, placeholders disappear as the user interacts with the form, so if the user loses focus (no pun intended!) for a while, they need to be able to have any instructions still present.

If a label is not enough, you can add help text next to the form control. As we want to conserve space and keep the form a bit tidier, we'll use the sibling selector to only show the extra help when the input field is being focused (see Figure 9-19).

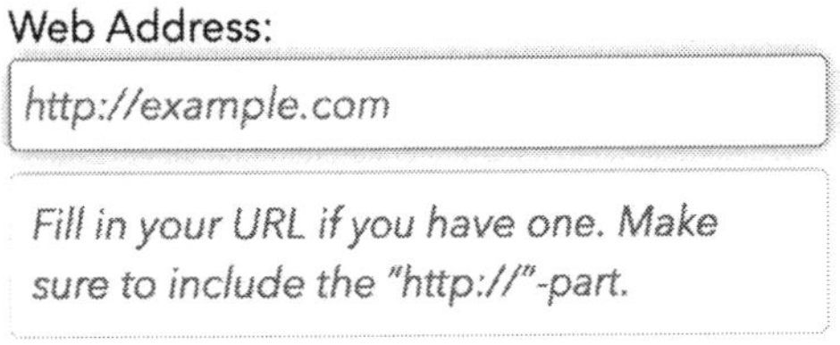

Web Address:

http://example.com

Fill in your URL if you have one. Make
sure to include the "http://"-part.

Figure 9-19. *Showing an extra help text when a field is focused*

We want to hide the text visually, but not necessarily for screen readers, even when the field is not focused. Using a combination of the `clip` property, absolute positioning, and `overflow: hidden` does the trick.

This specific combination of properties is to avoid various bugs in older browsers. A deeper discussion of this technique can be found on Jonathan Snook's blog (`http://snook.ca/archives/html_and_css/ hiding-content-for-accessibility`). These properties are then overridden when the help text is next to a focused input, using the sibling selector:

```
.form-help {
  display: block;
  /* hide the help by default,
     without hiding it from screen readers */
  position: absolute;
  overflow: hidden;
  width: 1px;
  height: 1px;
  clip: rect(0 0 0 0);
}

input:focus + .form-help {
  padding: .5em;
  margin-top: .5em;
  border: 1px solid #2a80fa;
  border-radius: .25em;
  font-style: italic;
  color: #737373;
  background-color: #fff;
  /* override the "hiding" properties: */
  position: static;
  width: auto;
  height: auto;
  crop: none;
}
```

ACCESSIBLE HIDING TECHNIQUES

The technique in the help text example uses CSS to hide something visually while keeping it accessible for screen readers. Using other techniques, like `display: none` or `visibility: hidden`, can make screen readers skip the text altogether.

When designing forms, it's quite a common pattern to see the visual design omitting a label, or using one label for multiple fields. As an example, you might have a date section split into three fields representing year, month, and date, but with just one label saying "date of birth."

Using an accessible hiding technique in this instance allows you to add a label for any field without actually displaying it on the page. The technique can, of course, be used for any element that would help the semantic structure of the page but could be unnecessary for visual users.

This makes for an ideal candidate for a "helper class" that you apply to your markup whenever this situation arises. The HTML5 Boilerplate project (`http://html5boilerplate.com/`) uses this very technique with the class name `.visuallyhidden`, for example.

The markup for our help text is simple enough, but with some added semantic richness to make sure the help is accessible:

```
<input placeholder="http://example.com" name="comment-url" aria-described-by="comment-url-
help" id="comment-url" type="url"  />
<span id="comment-url-help" role="tooltip" class="form-help">Fill in your URL if you have
one. Make sure to include the "http://"-part.</span>
```

The `aria-describedby` attribute on the `input` element should point to the `id` of the help text. This makes screen readers associate the help text with the field, and many of them will read the help text in addition to the label as the field is focused. The `role` attribute set to `tooltip` further clarifies for screen readers that this is text that appears as the user interacts with the form field.

If you do form validation either on the server or with JavaScript in the browser, any error messages in HTML can be marked up in a similar way, using `aria-describedby` to associate the message with the form control.

Modern browsers supporting HTML5 also have built-in form validation, and along with it a range of CSS pseudo-classes that help with client-side validation.

HTML5 Form Validation and CSS

As soon as you use the newer attributes of HTML5 forms, the browser will try to help you validate the value of the form fields. For example, when you use an input with `type` set to `email` and fill in something invalid and try to submit the form, the browser will show an error message (see Figure 9-20).

Figure 9-20. *Validation message in Mozilla Firefox*

Browsers supporting HTML5 validation also supply us with a number of pseudo-classes that correspond to various states in form fields. For example, we can use the following code to highlight invalid text-input fields with a red border and a red glow:

```
.field-text :invalid {
  border-color: #e72633;
  box-shadow: 0 0 .5em rgba(229, 43, 37, 0.5);
}
```

We have already seen the `:required`, `:optional`, `:valid`, and `:invalid` pseudo-classes back in Chapter 2. There are several more of them, corresponding to various states of numerical inputs, sliders, etc. Styling input fields based on these pseudo-classes is no problem, but what about the actual error messages?

Sadly, these are another example of interface elements that are mostly beyond the reach of CSS. WebKit-based browsers offer some limited possibilities to style error messages using browser-specific pseudo-elements like `::-webkit-validation-bubble`, but other than that there is no way as of yet to style their appearance.

If you need more control over these error messages, there are many JavaScript plug-ins that hook into the form events that are triggered by the browser. They override the built-in validation, and often supply you with methods to generate elements (and set the text) for error messages, as well as offer validation support for older browsers. See for example the form plug-in of the Webshim project (`http://afarkas.github.io/webshim/demos/`).

Advanced Form Styling

So far, we have kept our form styling to a very sane minimum. And for good reason: forms are rarely the place to experiment. People wanting to register a profile or pay for a product will likely appreciate clarity over any attempt to be different for the sake of it. That doesn't mean that more creative CSS techniques don't have a place in form design. In this section, we'll show a few tips to sweat the details.

Modern CSS for Form Layout

By default, most form elements display as inline blocks and thus line up in the text direction. We used the block display mode in the earlier example to make labels and input fields display as stacked on the page.

When we want more advanced form layout, some of the newer layout mechanisms really shine. Flexbox was created specifically to target things like rows or columns of buttons or other interface elements, where the space between them needs to be divided in a clever way. This is often the case with forms, so let's look at an example where we use flexbox.

Building on the styles we saw in the previous simple example, let's create a slightly more complex form, where we collect some information about job applicants. We are aiming to collect the applicant's name, e-mail address, and Twitter handle, and a list of coding languages that the applicant has mastered (see Figure 9-21).

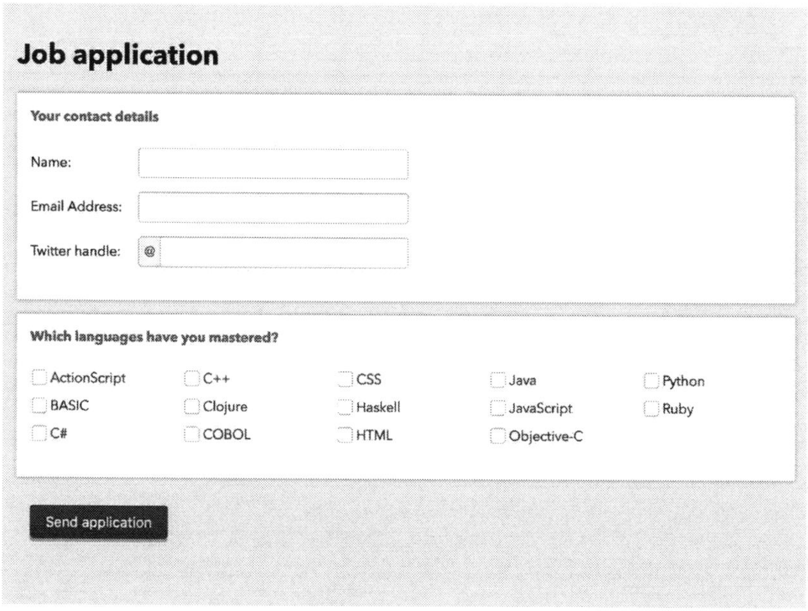

Figure 9-21. *Our applicant form*

For larger viewports, the top part of the form switches from a stacked version (where labels are stacked over the fields) to a version where the label appears on the same line as the field. There is also some guidance text prepended to the Twitter handle field, indicating that only the part after "@" needs to be filled in. Let's start with the inline fields.

We'll use flexbox to control the field layout. To detect it, we'll use the Modernizr library that we saw in Chapter 6. As a short recap, Modernizr can detect CSS features via JavaScript, and adds class names for each supported feature to the html element of your page. You can create a custom script containing only the detections that you need at https://modernizr.com. In this case, the flexbox detection adds the flexbox class to the html element.

We can now start coding our inline field solution using the .flexbox class as a selector prefix, and be confident that only browsers with support will see it.

First of all, we only want to serve the inline layout when the viewport is big enough to handle it. Around 560 pixels seems about right, which comes down to 35em:

```
@media only screen and (min-width: 35em) {
  /* the rest of the code snippets go here */
}
```

Next, our text input fields need to become a flex container in the larger viewport, where the items line up horizontally (which is the default). They also need to have a larger maximum width.

289

```
.flexbox .field-text {
  display: flex;
  max-width: 28em;
}
```

We want the labels to all have the same width (about 8em seems to do the trick) and neither shrink nor grow—that is, flex-grow and flex-shrink set to 0, with a flex-basis of 8em:

```
.flexbox .field-text label {
  flex: 0 0 8em;
}
```

As for the label text, we want to center it vertically. We could do this with line-height, but we'd be tying that to the height of the input elements. Flexbox can actually help us with this as well, without specific measurements.

To achieve this effect, we need to declare the labels themselves as being flex containers where the contents are centered. Since there are no children of the label element that we can center, we are relying on the fact that any text content inside a flex container becomes an anonymous flex item. We can then tell the container to center all its items vertically.

```
.flexbox .field-text label {
  flex: 0 0 8em;
  display: flex;
  align-items: center;
}
```

That gives us the finished field layout for larger viewports, as seen in Figure 9-22.

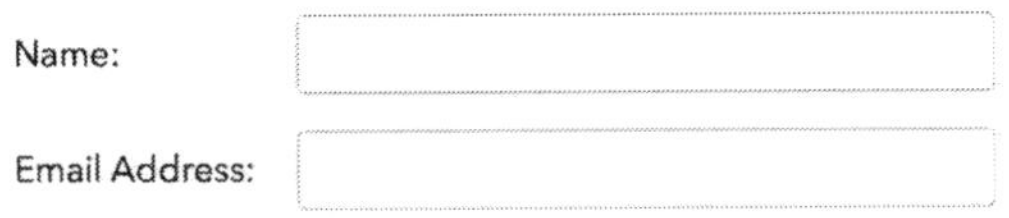

Name:

Email Address:

Figure 9-22. *The inline label/field placement for larger viewports*

As for the width of input elements, flexbox will figure them out automatically. They're already set to width: 100% from before, which will then shrink to make room for the fixed-width labels since the default flex value is 0 1 auto. Reading that value out means "base your width on the width property (auto), don't grow over that, but feel free to shrink to make room."

Prefixed Input Fields with Flexbox

When it comes to the prepended text, this is a situation that flexbox really excels at. We have some constraints that are really tricky to solve in a flexible way using any other layout technique:

- The input and the prepended text component need to be the same height.
- The prepended element needs to stay flexible in width, depending on the text inside.
- The input then needs to adjust in width so that the combination of prepended text and input field add up to the same width as the other text fields.

To target these components, we'll wrap the whole thing in a span and apply some generic class names. We'll also add relevant attributes to make the purpose of the prepended text accessible. Here's the complete markup for the field:

```
<p class="field field-text">
  <label for="applicant-twitter">Twitter handle:</label>
  <span class="field-prefixed">
    <span class="field-prefix" id="applicant-twitter-prefix" aria-label="You can omit the
    @">@</span>
    <input aria-describedby="applicant-twitter-prefix" name="applicant-twitter"
    id="applicant-twitter" type="text" />
  </span>
</p>
```

The aria-label attribute here gives the prefix element an accessible name for screen readers that explains the purpose of the prefixed text.

For the styling, we'll start by creating a fallback style for browsers that do not support flexbox. We'll keep that simple, and just offer an inline block box containing the prepended text, and make the input next to it short enough to not end up on different rows on small screens (see Figure 9-23).

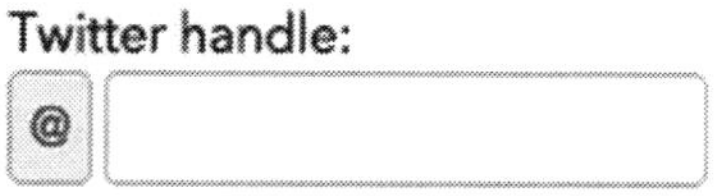

Twitter handle:

Figure 9-23. *Our baseline is just the prepended text inside a styled inline block box*

```
.field-prefix {
  display: inline-block;
  /* border and color etc omitted for brevity. */
  border-radius: .25em;
}
.field-prefixed input {
  max-width: 12em;
}
```

We will also have to complement the rule where we set the width of the inputs by adding our prepended field class name to the selectors:

```
.field-text label,
.field-text input,
.field-prefixed,
.field-text textarea {
  /* ... */
}
```

Finally we'll apply the flexbox magic, using the .flexbox class name to scope our rules. We'll make the .field-prefix wrapper into a flex container, and vertically center the contents of the prefix element. Just like with the label in the inlined field examples earlier, we create a nested flex container and align the anonymous item vertically inside. We also tweak the border to only be rounded on the outside corners of the items.

```
.flexbox .field-prefixed {
  display: flex;
}
.flexbox .field-prefix {
  border-right: 0;
  border-radius: .25em 0 0 .25em;
  display: flex;
  align-items: center;
}
```

The input will need to get its max-width reapplied. Other than that, it will automatically fill up the rest of the space.

```
.flexbox .field-prefixed input {
  max-width: 100%;
  border-radius: 0 .25em .25em 0;
}
```

Figure 9-24 shows the result. These styles provide a flexible and reusable base for prepending texts (and other controls) to text input fields while keeping them the same width as other inputs. It could easily be extended for *appending after* the field as well.

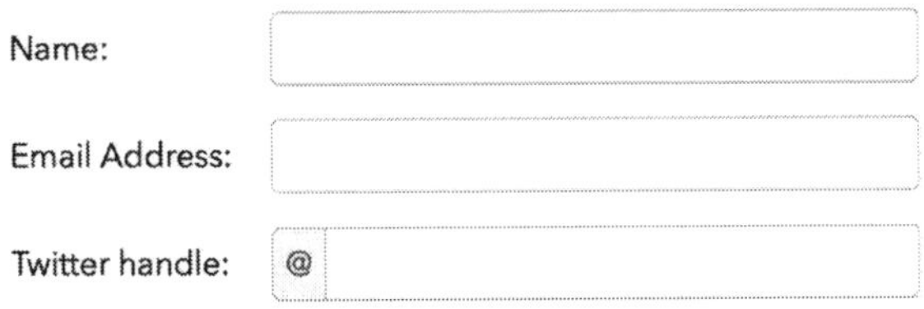

Figure 9-24. *The finished prefixed field*

Using Multi-Column Layout for Checkbox Collections

In the same way an inline field placement can save vertical space, we can save space by placing collections of checkboxes into columns. The Multi-Column Layout module is a perfect candidate for this, and falls back to the single-column layout where not supported.

Our markup is simple enough: an unordered list with a class name of checkboxes, containing the individual checkboxes and their associated labels inside each list item.

```
<ul class="checkboxes">
  <li>
    <input type="checkbox" name="lang-as" id="lang-as">
    <label for="lang-as">ActionScript</label>
  </li>
  <!-- ...and so on-->
</ul>
```

We could have nested the checkboxes inside the labels as we did with the radio buttons, but the order here will actually be used for styling purposes in the next example.

To get the checkboxes to line up in columns, we can simply tell the browser the minimum width for each column. Around 10 ems seems reasonable to allow for longish labels. Other than that, we'll just remove the list styling and tweak the margin and padding. Figure 9-25 shows the checkbox columns.

```
.checkboxes {
  list-style: none;
  padding: 0;
  column-width: 10em;
}
.checkboxes li {
  margin-bottom: .5em;
}
```

Figure 9-25. *Checkboxes in four automatically generated columns on a midsized viewport*

Styling the Unstylable: Faux Custom Checkboxes

We have seen that buttons and text inputs can be tamed by removing default styling like borders. But buttons are mostly just one flat surface with some text in it, and other form components are more complex. Checkboxes, for example, consist of the little box and the potential checkmark inside it. What does it even mean to apply padding, for example, to a checkbox? Does it go inside the graphic of the box, or outside it? Is the checkmark affected by any sizing we apply to the checkbox?

Sidestepping these issues, we can choose to replace the checkbox completely with a graphic. This is done with clever use of the label element and the pseudo-classes for form states.

Because of the order of the markup, combining the sibling selector and the :checked pseudo-class gives us a way to generate rules for the look of both the checkbox and the label, based on the state of the checkbox.

We also need to draw a line in the sand here in terms of browser support. Old browsers that don't understand selectors like :checked need to fall back to the unstyled native checkbox. To achieve this, we'll reuse the :root selector trick, which causes old browsers like IE8 to skip the whole rule:

```
:root input[type="checkbox"] + label {
  /* unchecked checkbox label */
}
:root input[type="checkbox"]:checked + label {
  /* checked checkbox label */
}
```

Next, we need to make the checkbox itself invisible while still accessible and focusable. We will use an *image* of a checkbox that we have created ourselves as the background image for the label. Figure 9-26 explains the thinking.

Figure 9-26. *The checkbox itself is hidden using CSS, and the label element has a background image showing the fake checkbox*

People using a mouse or touchscreen can click the label, which triggers the checkbox to change state and thus updates the styling. Keyboard users can still focus and interact with the checkbox, and the state will likewise be reflected in the styling of the label.

There are two crucial parts to the technique. First, the `label` needs to come right after the `input` element in the markup, and have the proper `for` attribute that associates the two. Second, the `label` needs to be hidden but still accessible. The last one is a matter of giving it the same collection of styles as the hidden help message from the earlier example:

```
:root input[type="checkbox"] {
  position: absolute;
  overflow: hidden;
  width: 1px;
  height: 1px;
  clip: rect(0 0 0 0);
}
```

Now we need to supply the rules for the images of the various states of the checkboxes, including focus states for keyboard access. We'll need four images in all: unchecked, checked, unchecked with focus, and checked with focus. Figure 9-27 shows the final result.

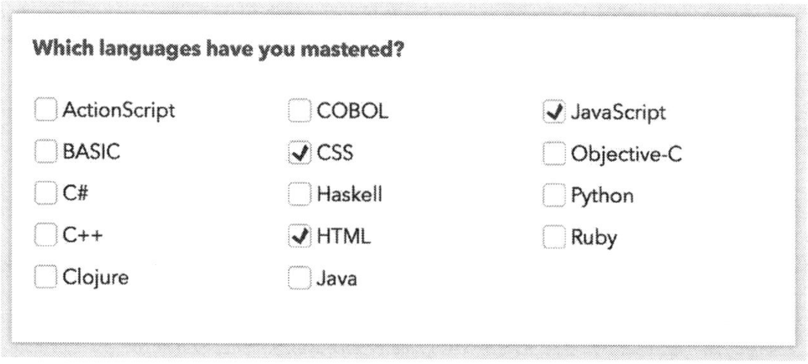

Figure 9-27. The results of our checkbox styling: our checkboxes now follow the overall color theme of our page across all modern browsers

We are using Modernizr to detect support for SVG, so our rules have a svgasimg class added to them:

▓ **Note**   The Modernizr test actually detects support for the `<image>` element in SVG, but it overlaps pretty much perfectly with the support for SVG for background images, which is otherwise undetectable, as well as SVG files used for `img` element sources (hence the class name).

```
:root.svgasimg input[type="checkbox"] + label {
  background: url(images/checkbox-unchecked.svg) .125em 50% no-repeat;
}
:root.svgasimg input[type="checkbox"]:checked + label {
  background-image: url(images/checkbox-checked.svg);
}
:root.svgasimg input[type="checkbox"]:focus + label {
  background-image: url(images/checkbox-unchecked-focus.svg);
}
:root.svgasimg input[type="checkbox"]:focus:checked + label {
  background-image: url(images/checkbox-checked-focus.svg);
}
```

In the final example files, we have also included some rules for padding and text styles of the label. We have also URL-encoded the (tiny) SVG files and placed them inline in the CSS file as data URIs, which helps bring the number of requests down.

Sadly, there are browsers that support all the selectors we've used but not SVG. To combat this, we need to use a fallback solution, where we fall back to PNG images if JavaScript is prevented from running or the browser doesn't support SVG as background images. We add the PNG-based solution before the SVG solution in our CSS:

```
:root input[type="checkbox"] + label {
  background-image: url(images/checkbox-unchecked.png);
}
:root input[type="checkbox"]:checked + label {
  background-image: url(images/checkbox-checked.png);
}
/* ...and so on. */
```

The upside is that we now have complete support for our custom checkboxes in any browser that supports the form pseudo-classes. IE8 (and older) falls back to plain native checkboxes. The exact same technique can also be used for radio buttons, and you can take it as far as you like in terms of style.

You could use other techniques for the checkbox graphic as well, including animating the action of checking and unchecking, like in the demo from Manoela Ilic (`http://tympanus.net/Development/AnimatedCheckboxes/`) shown in Figure 9-28.

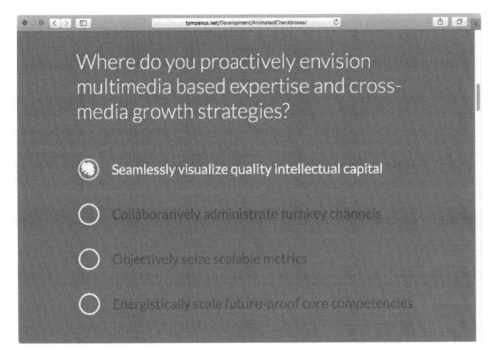

Figure 9-28. *A demo that uses animated SVG graphics to "pencil in" choices for a radio button*

The downside is that we've introduced a small dependency on JavaScript to enhance our checkbox component to its full potential, but it is a very minimal one and with a very decent fallback.

A word on Custom Form Widgets

So far, we've seen that we can successfully style input fields and buttons with CSS. We can also style checkboxes and radio buttons using CSS and image replacement techniques. The `select` element is a slightly more complex form control, consisting of the drop-down menu itself, its arrow indicator, and a list of options. There's also things like the file upload and color picker versions of the `input` element that have more complex widgets representing them.

Traditionally, these kinds of widgets have been virtually impossible to style, leading to a wealth of JavaScript-driven solutions that fake the appearance of a file picker or `select` element using regular `div`s and `span`s. While these solutions solve the problem of being able to style the widget, they often create new challenges that are much harder to get right.

These challenges include not breaking on mobile devices, using the same keyboard controls as the native version, and being performant across different devices and browsers. For example, attempting to fake and then style the options inside a select element is an especially risky thing, since the control can look drastically different on mobile devices (see Figure 9-29).

Figure 9-29. *A select element on iOS doesn't display the options underneath the select at all, but triggers a rotator-type widget at the bottom of the screen instead*

When deciding on a design, you might want to think twice about customizing these types of controls, and about whether having them match the theme of the page is worth the potential trouble.

That said, there are also plenty of developers who have tried hard to solve the problem in a thoughtful manner using JavaScript, so the option to use a third-party library is there. Most of these libraries depend on general DOM-manipulation libraries like jQuery, as the creation and handling of elements in the page quickly becomes nontrivial for these kinds of widgets.

You might want to check out any of the following libraries:

- Filament Group has published a simple select menu plug-in for jQuery, that works in a similar way to the previously described checkbox technique, but with some added JS trickery. It offers a quick way to style the select element itself, but not the list of options: `https://github.com/filamentgroup/select`. Filament Group also has a small plug-in with a similar approach for file inputs.

- Chosen (`http://harvesthq.github.io/chosen/`) and Select2 (`https://select2.github.io/`) are two of the more popular jQuery plug-ins for advanced enhancement of a select element. Options include styling the placeholder and options, searching or filtering, and better UI for multiple selection. Both of these libraries have made improvements in accessibility in recent versions, but you should know that they may still have issues.

Developer Todd Parker has made a heroic effort to find such a pure CSS solution for the simplest case of styling just the dropdown-button of the `select` element. You can see his solution at `http://filamentgroup.github.io/select-css/demo/`. At the time of writing, it is more a proof of concept than a finished technique, but it manages to style the `select` element (sans the `options`) in a majority of browsers, using no JavaScript and a single wrapper element for styling. Older browsers are filtered out with clever hacks, so they get the unstyled default select.

No matter which way you go with custom styling or advanced widgets when it comes to forms, make sure they work as well as the native elements when you use them on a live site.

Summary

In this chapter, we have looked at styling forms and tables. They are some of the more complex collections of HTML elements, but often crucial to help users interact with web pages and understand complex data.

We have looked at how to style data tables, and a simple way to make them responsive.

We created a simple form and learned how to style fieldsets, labels, text inputs, and buttons. We also looked at how to use modern CSS layout techniques to create more efficient use of space in forms, and how to get past some of the troubles of styling form components like checkboxes and radio buttons.

In the next chapter, we'll take interactivity to another level and show you how to make your web pages come alive, using transforms, transitions, and animations.

■ ■ ■

CHAPTER 10

Making It Move: Transforms, Transitions, and Animations

This chapter is all about moving things around—either through space, with transforms, or through time, using animations and transitions. Often, these two families of properties work together.

Transformation is a different concept from moving things with positioning or other layout properties. In fact, transforming an object doesn't affect the layout of the page at all. You can rotate, skew, translate, and scale elements, even in 3D!

Animating elements can be done with the CSS Animation properties. Transitions are a simplified flavor of animations. When you only have an on-off state (like with hovering over an element), transitions are there to automate the process.

Taken together, these properties give you lots of ways to breathe life into your pages. As an added bonus, they also have really good performance.

In this chapter, we will go through the following:

- Two-dimensional transformations: translating, scaling, rotating, and skewing

- Simple and advanced transition effects

- What you can and can't transition

- Keyframe animations and the animation properties

- Three-dimensional transformations and perspective

How it all Fits Together

CSS transforms allow us to move things around in space, while CSS transitions and CSS keyframe animations control how elements can change over time.

Even if those two aspects are somewhat unrelated, transforms, transitions, and keyframe animations are often lumped together conceptually. This is because they are so regularly used to complement each other. When animating something, you are changing its appearance up to 60 times per second. Transforms allow you to describe certain kinds of changes to appearance in a way that the browser can very efficiently calculate.

Transitions and keyframe animations allow you to animate those changes in a smart way. As such, these features go together hand in glove. The end result gives us the capability to do things like the animated 3D pop-up book Google created (see Figure 10-1) to showcase creative use of its products (http://creativeguidebook.appspot.com/).

© Andy Budd and Emil Björklund 2016
A. Budd and E. Björklund, *CSS Mastery*, DOI 10.1007/978-1-4302-5864-3_10

Figure 10-1. *Google created an animated 3D pop-up book to showcase creative use of its products*

Since the examples in this chapter quite literally have a lot of moving parts, it's hard to describe them on the pages of a book. We strongly recommend you try out the examples in a browser while reading, to understand what's going on. A lot of the time, JavaScript is used for interactivity—we won't go into the specifics of how the scripts work, but the examples include JS files for you to explore as well.

A Note on Browser Support

The specifications for transforms, transitions, and keyframe animations are still being worked on. Despite this, most of these features are pretty well supported across commonly used browsers, notable exceptions being Internet Explorer 8 and Opera Mini. IE9 only supports the 2D subset of transforms using the -ms- prefix, and does not support keyframe animations or transitions. Transforms, transitions and keyframe animations all require the -webkit- prefix to work in various versions of WebKit- and Blink-based browsers. The -moz- prefix is only needed if you need to cover old versions of Firefox.

2D Transforms

CSS transforms allow you to shift the rendering of an element on the page by translating, rotating, skewing, or scaling it. In addition, you can add a third dimension into the mix! In this section, we'll start with the 2D transformations, and move on to 3D later. Figure 10-2 gives an overview of what the 2D transforms do.

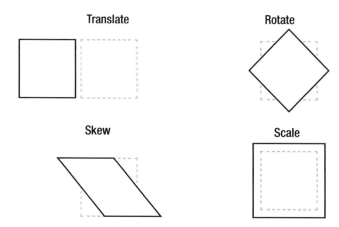

Figure 10-2. *The different types of 2D transformations illustrated*

In technical terms, transformations change the *coordinate system* of the element as it appears on the page. One way of looking at transformations is to view them as "distortion fields." Any pixel that belongs to the rendering of the transformed element is caught in the distortion field and gets teleported to a new position or size on the page. The element still remains where it was originally positioned on the page, but the resulting *image* of the element is transformed.

Imagine that you have a 100×100-pixel element with a class name of box showing on the page. The position of the element can be affected by margins, positioning, sizes of other elements in the flow of the page, and so forth. Regardless of how it ended up where it did, we can describe the position of the box by using coordinates within the viewport—for example, 200 pixels from the top of the page and 200 pixels from the left. This is the *viewport coordinate system.*

In the page, there is a 100×100-pixel space reserved for the element as it normally renders. Now let's imagine we were to transform the element by rotating it 45 degrees:

```
.box {
  transform: rotate(45deg);
}
```

Applying a transformation to an element creates what is known as a *local coordinate system* for the space where the element was originally placed. The local coordinate system is the distortion field, displacing the pixels of the element.

Since elements are represented as rectangles on the page, it's perhaps easiest to think about what happens to the four points at the corners of the box. The Firefox developer tools have a nice visualization of this when inspecting an element. In the Rules panel of the inspector, hover over the transform rule to see the resulting transformation (see Figure 10-3).

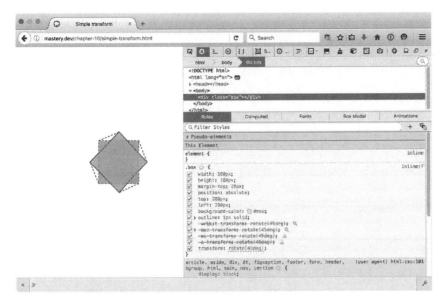

Figure 10-3. *Visualizing a 45-degree transformation in Firefox developer tools. The original box and the transformed box are shown along with arrows showing the changed position of the corners.*

The page still retains its 100×100-pixel gap where the box used to be, but any point belonging to the box is now transformed by the distortion field.

It is important to understand this technial background when applying transformations to elements in addition to other properties that affect their place on the page. What happens when we apply `margin-top: 20px` to the transformed div? Does the corner pointing upward now end up 20 pixels from the top of the original position? No: the whole local coordinate system of anything belonging to the box is rotated, including the margin, as shown in Figure 10-4.

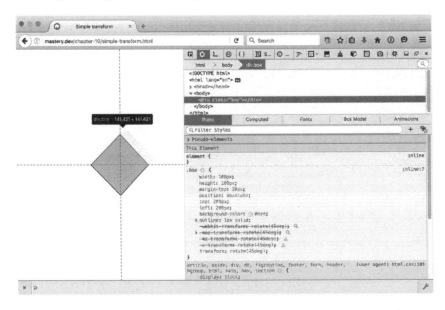

Figure 10-4. *Rotating a box includes rotating its whole coordinate system, so the top margin is also rotated*

It's also important to note that the rotated appearance in no way interferes with the layout of the rest of the page as it would appear without the transformation. If we rotate the box a full 90 degrees so that the top margin is visually poking out to the right, it doesn't push on any elements that may be sitting to the right of the box.

■ **Note** There is actually one thing on the page that can be affected by transformed elements, and that is overflow. If a transformed element ends up sticking out in the text direction of any box that has an `overflow` property that causes scrollbars, the transformed element may affect the scrollable area. In left-to-right languages, this means that you can, for example, hide things offscreen using translation upward or to the left, but not downward or to the right.

Transform Origin

By default, any transformation is calculated based on the center of the element's border box. The property responsible for controlling this is `transform-origin`. For example, we could rotate the box around a spot situated 10 pixels from the top of the box and 10 pixels from the left.

We can supply `transform-origin` with one to three values, giving coordinates for the x, y, and z axes. (The z axis is for 3D transformations; we'll get back to that later in the chapter.) If you only supply one value, the second is assumed to be the keyword `center`, just like when you set a `background-position`. The third value does not affect two-dimensional transformations, so we can safely leave it out for now.

```
.box {
  transform-origin: 10px 10px;
  transform: rotate(45deg);
}
```

This gives us a completely different result when rotating the box, as shown in Figure 10-5.

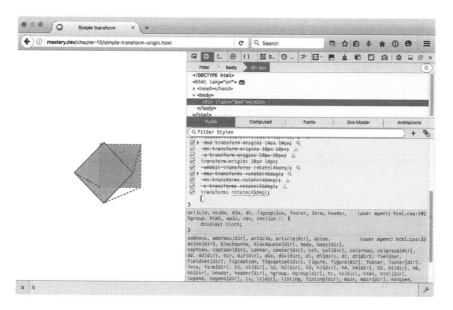

Figure 10-5. *Rotating the box around a point 10 pixels from the top and left edges*

■ **Note** Transformations work a little bit differently if you apply them to SVG elements. One example is the default value of the `transform-origin` property: it defaults to the top-left corner, not the center of the element.

Translation

Translating an element simply means moving it to a new position. You can choose to translate along a single axis using the `translateX()` and `translateY()` functions, or set both at the same time with `translate()`.

The `translate()` function works by feeding it a pair of positions representing the amount of translation on the x and y axes. This amount can be any length like pixels, ems, or percentages. It is worth noting that percentages in this context refer to the dimensions of the element itself, *not* the containing block. This allows you to translate the element to end up exactly to the right of its own original position without knowing how wide the element is (see Figure 10-6).

```
.box {
  /* equivalent to transform: translateX(100%); */
  transform: translate(100%, 0);
}
```

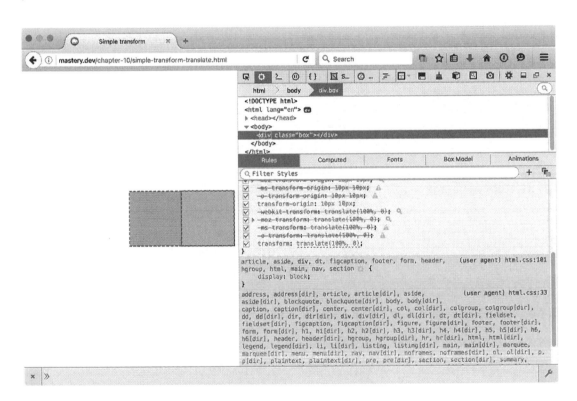

Figure 10-6. *Our box translated 100% to the right*

Multiple Transformations

It's possible to apply multiple transformations at once. The transformations are supplied as a list of space-separated values to the transform property, and are applied in the order they are declared. Let's look at an example where we do both translation and rotation.

For this example, we'll use an ordered list of rules for something called "Fight Club." We'll do some formatting of the numbered rules, and rotate them to go down the side each item in our list (see Figure 10-7). We want the list numbers to read from bottom to top, but positioned at the top of the list item.

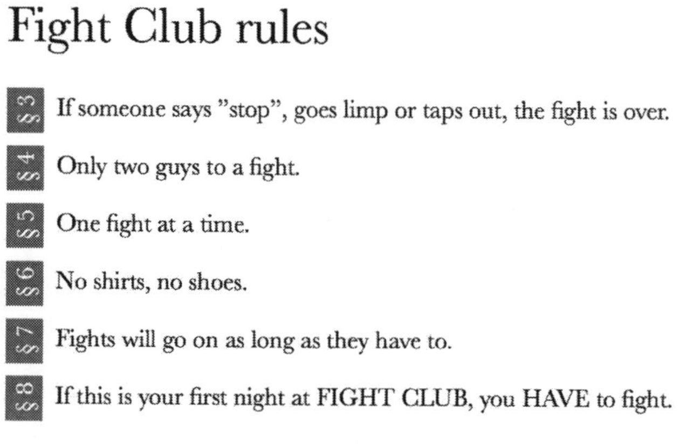

Fight Club rules

§3 If someone says "stop", goes limp or taps out, the fight is over.

§4 Only two guys to a fight.

§5 One fight at a time.

§6 No shirts, no shoes.

§7 Fights will go on as long as they have to.

§8 If this is your first night at FIGHT CLUB, you HAVE to fight.

Figure 10-7. *The list of rules, with the numbered items rotated down the side*

To begin with, we'll need an ordered list in our markup. We'll start the list with rule number three, since the first two rules have mysteriously gotten lost:

```
<ol class="rules" start="3">
  <li>If someone says "stop", goes limp or taps out, the fight is over.</li>
  <li>Only two guys to a fight.</li>
  <li>One fight at a time.</li>
  <li>No shirts, no shoes.</li>
  <li>Fights will go on as long as they have to.</li>
  <li>If this is your first night at FIGHT CLUB, you HAVE to fight.</li>
</ol>
```

By default, we can't really do much to affect the rendering of the numbers in an ordered list. The CSS Lists and Counters Module Level 3 spec describes a ::marker pseudo-element to control list marker styling, but no browsers support it at the time of writing. We'll get creative and use the well-supported counter-properties in CSS combined with pseudo-elements to work around that. Counters allow you to generate numbers by counting certain elements, which you can then insert into the page.

First off, we remove the default list style (which removes the numbers) and add a counter-reset rule. It tells the browser that this element resets the numbering on a counter we have named rulecount. This name is an arbitrary identifier that we have chosen ourselves. The number after the name tells the counter which initial value it should have.

```
.rules {
  list-style: none;
  counter-reset: rulecount 2;
}
```

305

Next, we'll tell the counter to increment the `rulecount` value for every time it encounters a list item inside the list. This means that the first item will be numbered 3, and so on, as intended.

```
.rules li {
  counter-increment: rulecount;
}
```

Finally, we inject the number from the `rulecount` counter as pseudo-elements using the `content` property, before the text of each list item. We'll insert a section sign (§) before the number. This gives us the rendered content we see in Figure 10-8.

```
.rules li:before {
  content: '§ ' counter(rulecount);
}
```

§ 3If someone says "stop", goes limp or taps out, the fight is over.
§ 4Only two guys to a fight.
§ 5One fight at a time.
§ 6No shirts, no shoes.
§ 7Fights will go on as long as they have to.
§ 8If this is your first night at FIGHT CLUB, you HAVE to fight.

Figure 10-8. *The list with the injected section signs and numbers*

It doesn't look great yet, but we now have something to grab and style instead of the default numbers. Next, we'll try and position the section numbering vertically along the side of the rule instead of inline with the text.

We don't want the list numbers to take up any space in the flow of the page, so we'll need to position them absolutely; doing so puts the section number at the top left of the item automatically. To achieve the effect of the number being rotated but anchored at the top of the list item, we'll need to think about how to translate and rotate it. We'll set the `transform-origin` at bottom right (100% 100%), translate it 100% to the left and 100% up (remember that the percentage refers to the dimensions of the transformed element) and then rotate it 90 degrees counterclockwise. Figure 10-9 shows the transformation step by step.

```
.rules li {
  counter-increment: rulecount;
  position: relative;
}
.rules li:before {
  content: '§ ' counter(rulecount);
  position: absolute;
  transform-origin: 100% 100%;
  transform: translate(-100%, -100%) rotate(-90deg);
}
```

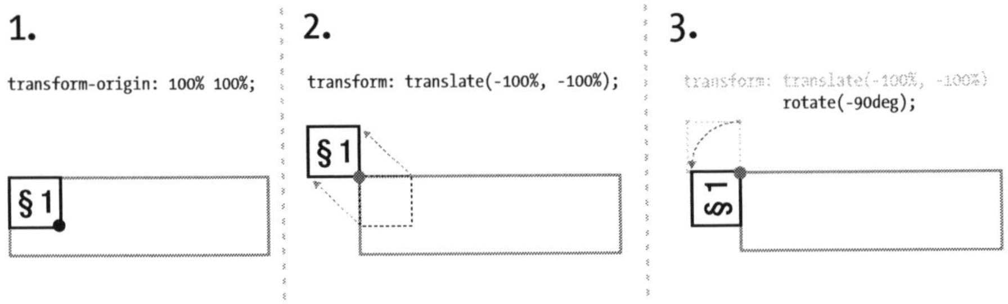

Figure 10-9. *The steps of transforming the counter so it runs from top to bottom next to the list-item text*

The order of the transformation functions is *very* important here. Had we started off by rotating the pseudo-element, the translation would have happened in relation to the rotated coordinates, and the offsets on the x and y axes would have pointed 90 degrees the wrong way! Lists of transformations add up, so you have to plan them out in advance.

CHANGING THE LIST OF TRANSFORMATIONS

When you declare a list of transformations, you cannot add to it after the fact, but only replace the whole list. For example, if you have a transformed element with a translation, and you want to also rotate it on :hover, the following will *not* work as expected:

```
.thing {
  transform: translate(0, 100px);
}
.thing:hover {
  /* CAUTION: this will remove the translation! */
  transform: rotate(45deg);
}
```

Instead, you must redeclare the whole list, but with the rotation appended:

```
.thing:hover {
  /* preserves the initial translation, and then rotates. */
  transform: translate(0, 100px) rotate(45deg);
}
```

In the finished example, we've added a gray left border to the list items that the section numbering sits on top of. The benefit of using a border here is that it will automatically stretch to the height of the list item in case the rule goes over several lines. We have also added some typographic rules and tweaked the padding a bit. For example, the generated section numbers have a tiny bit of padding at the top. But remember, that actually means padding-right since it is now rotated! (See Figure 10-10.)

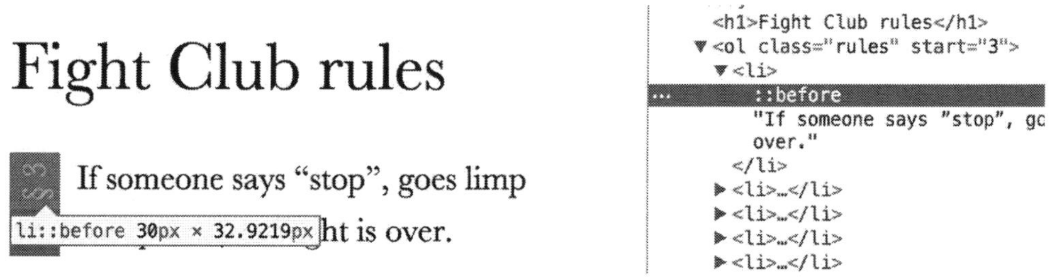

Figure 10-10. *Using a border allows us to draw the sidebar background even if lines wrap. The padding-right we add to the section number is now at the top of the rotated element.*

Scale and Skew

So far, we have explored the translate() and rotate() transform functions. Of the remaining 2D transformations, that leaves scale() and skew(). Both of these have corresponding functions for scaling and skewing on a single axis. Just like translate we have scaleX(), scaleY(), skewX() and skewY()

307

Using the scale() function is pretty straightforward. Unitless numbers are used in the scale() function. It accepts either one or two numbers. If only one is used, the element is scaled equally on both the x and y axes. A scale of 2 for both axes, for example, means that the element becomes twice as wide and twice as tall. A scale measurement of 1 means the element is unchanged.

```
.doubled {
  transform: scale(2);
  /* ...is equivalent to transform: scale(2, 2); */
  /* ...and also equivalent to transform: scaleX(2) scaleY(2); */
}
```

Only scaling one axis means that the element squashes (see Figure 10-11) or stretches out.

```
.squashed-text {
  transform: scaleX(0.5);
  /* ...equivalent to transform: scale(0.5, 1); */
}
```

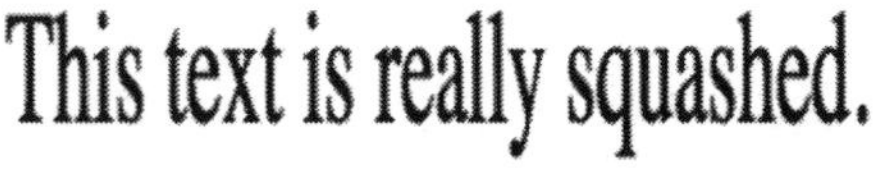

This text is really squashed.

Figure 10-11. *Text scaled to a measurement below 1 on the x axis becomes squashed*

Skewing means that the horizontal or vertical parallel edges of the element are moved in regard to each other by a certain number of degrees. It's easy to get the x axis and y axis mixed up—skewing on the x axis means that the horizontal lines are still horizontal, while the *vertical* lines are slanted. The key is to think about which axis you want the edges to move in relation to each other.

Going back to the Fight Club example, we could use skewing to create a popular "2.5D" effect, perhaps inspired by retro video games (the fancy name for it appears to be *axonometric projection*).

If we give our list items alternating background and border colors as well as alternating skew transforms, we get the appearance of an "accordion" type surface (see Figure 10-12):

```
/* some properties omitted for brevity */
.rules li {
  transform: skewX(15deg);
}
.rules li:nth-child(even) {
  transform: skewX(-15deg);
}
```

Fight Club rules

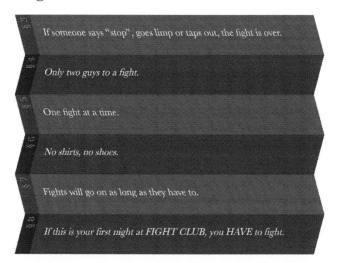

Figure 10-12. *Using skew transforms to create a "2.5D" look*

2D Matrix Transformations

As we discussed in the beginning of this section, transformations cause each point on the surface of the transformed element to go through a calculation that determines where it ends up in the local coordinate system.

When we write CSS, we think in terms like "rotate this element around its center and move it up and to the left." To the browser, all of these transformations we apply are mashed up into one mathematical structure called a *transformation matrix*. You can manipulate its values directly using the low-level matrix() function, using a combination of six different numerical values.

Now, don't worry: this is not something you would normally do by hand, as anything beyond a single scaling or translation operation requires considerable math skills.

To show you an example, the following is an application of the matrix() function that is equal to rotating an element by 45 degrees, then scaling it up to twice its size, then translating it by 100 pixels on the rotated x axis, and finally skewing it by 10 degrees on the x axis. The resulting numbers (which have been rounded somewhat to save space) have little resemblance to the original values of the individual transforms, at a glance.

```
.box {
  width: 100px;
  height: 100px;
  transform: matrix(1.41, 1.41, -1.16, 1.66, 70.7, 70.7);
  /* equivalent to:
     transform: rotate(45deg) translate(100px, 0) scale(2) skewX(10deg); */
}
```

Not exactly easy to interpret, is it?

For all intents and purposes, the transformation matrix is a "black box" that needs an input of various numbers representing the final transformation, which could be a combination of a several steps. We can precalculate these values (if we know the math) and feed them into the matrix() function, but we can't look at the values of a matrix() function and know which individual transformations went into it.

The key point is that a single matrix can succinctly represent the combination of *any number of transformations*. The main use case for the `matrix()` function is not to save space and show off math skills—but it really shines when combined with JavaScript. As a matter of fact, when you set a transformation on an element and ask for the computed style of the transformation back in a JavaScript file, you get a matrix representation.

Since matrices can be manipulated very efficiently by a script and then plugged back into the `matrix()` function, many JavaScript-based animation libraries make heavy use of it. If you're writing CSS by hand, it's a lot easier (and more readable!) to stick with the normal transformation functions.

If you want to read more about the math behind how to manipulate the CSS transformation matrix, you can find a good introduction from Zoltan Hawryluk at `http://www.useragentman.com/blog/2011/01/07/css3-matrix-transform-for-the-mathematically-challenged/`.

Transforms and performance

When the browser calculates how CSS affects elements on the page, some things are more expensive in regard to performance than others. If you change the text size, for example, the generated line boxes may become different as text wraps, and then the element can become taller. Becoming taller pushes down other elements on the page, which in turn forces the browser to do even further recalculation.

When you use CSS transforms, these calculations only affect the coordinate system of the element you are applying it to, changing neither how things are laid out internally nor how things are laid out outside the element. Furthermore, this calculation can be done pretty much independently of all the other things going on in the page (like running scripts or laying out other elements), since the transformation is unlikely to interfere with those. Most browsers also try to let the graphics processor handle these things (if one is present), since it is specially built for that kind of math.

This means that transformations are great from a performance standpoint. Any time that you want to create an effect that can be replicated with a transformation, there's a high chance that it will have better performance. Doing multiple transformations in quick succession compounds the gains, such as when animating or transitioning an element.

SOME FINAL TRANSFORMS "GOTCHAS"

Transforms have great performance and are pretty easy to work with. That said, there are a few unexpected side-effects of using transforms:

- Some browsers switch the anti-aliasing method for transformed elements. This means that things like text rendering can suddenly look different when dynamically applying a transformation. To counter this, you can experiment with applying a transformation that only uses the initial values, leaving the element in place, right as the page loads. That way, the rendering is switched even before the final transformation is applied.

- Any transform applied to an element creates a new stacking context. This means that you need to be careful in combining `z-index` and transform, as the transformed element creates its own stack—even if you set `z-index` very high on child elements inside of a transformed element, they will not sit on top of elements outside it.

- Transformed elements also establish a new containing block for fixed positioning. If a transformed element has an element inside it with `position: fixed`, it will treat the transformed element as its viewport.

Transitions

Transitions are automated animations from one state to another, such as when a button goes from its regular state to its pressed state. Normally, that change happens instantly, or at least as fast as the browser can make it. As you click or tap a button, the browser calculates the new look of the page and draws it within a few milliseconds. When you apply a transition, you tell the browser how long that change should take, and the browser will calculate what the screen should look like in the intervening time.

Transitions run automatically in both directions, so as soon as the state is reversed (like when you release a button), the animation runs in the reverse direction.

Let's take the button from the forms chapter (Chapter 9) to illustrate this, and create a smooth pressed-state animation for it. Our goal is to create the appearance of the button being pressed down by moving it a few pixels down on the page, and to decrease the offset of the shadow to further the illusion of it disappearing into the page behind it (see Figure 10-13):

```
<button>Press me!</button>
```

Figure 10-13. *Normal and :active state of a button*

Here is the basis of the button code from Chapter 9 (some properties omitted for brevity). This time we've added the transition property to the rule.

```
button {
  border: 0;
  padding: .5em 1em;
  color: #fff;
  border-radius: .25em;
  background-color: #173b6d;
  box-shadow: 0 .25em 0 rgba(23, 59, 109, 0.3), inset 0 1px 0 rgba(0, 0, 0, 0.3);
  transition: all 150ms;
}
button:active {
  box-shadow: 0 0 0 rgba(23, 59, 109, 0.3), inset 0 1px 0 rgba(0, 0, 0, 0.3);
  transform: translateY(.25em);
}
```

When the button is activated, we translate it downward the same distance as the y-axis shadow offset. At the same time, we decrease the shadow offset. By using the transform property to move the button, we avoid forcing the page to reflow.

The preceding code also tells the button to change *all* affected properties using a transition, and that the change should happen over 150 milliseconds, or 0.15 seconds. Using animation introduces us to new time-related units: ms for milliseconds and s for seconds. Most transitions in user interface components should fall below 0.3 seconds, or they will feel sluggish. Other visual effects may take longer.

The `transition` property is a shorthand that allows us to set several properties at once. Setting the duration of the transition and telling the browser to transition all properties that are changed between states could also have been done with the following:

```
button {
  transition-property: all;
  transition-duration: .15s;
}
```

If we had only wanted to specifically transition the `transform` and `box-shadow` properties while other changes (e.g., a different background color) should happen immediately, we would have had to specify individual properties instead of `all`.

We can't specify more than one property name in the shorthand for a single transition, but we can specify several transitions, separated with commas. This means that we can repeat the same values, but for different property keywords:

```
button {
  transition: box-shadow .15s, transform .15s;
}
```

Note that we now have to repeat the duration in both transitions. This repetition is a recipe for things going out of sync later. Don't Repeat Yourself (DRY for short) is a fundamental rule of writing good code. When the transition is more complex, it might be better to set the `transition-property` separately to avoid repetition:

```
button {
  /* First, specify a list of properties using transition-property */
  transition-property: transform, box-shadow;
  /* Then, set values that go for those properties. */
  transition-duration: .15s;
}
```

When you are using multiple comma-separated values in `transition` declarations, they work in a similar way to multiple background properties. The list in `transition-property` is what determines the number of transitions to apply, and if other lists are shorter, they repeat.

In the previous example, the `transition-duration` only has one value, but two transition properties are defined, so the duration value applies for both.

▓ **Note**   When you transition prefixed properties, you must target the prefixed property name as the `transition-property` as well. For example, `transition: transform .25s` usually needs to be complemented with `-webkit-transition: -webkit-transform .25s` in older WebKit-based browsers, where both transitions and transforms are prefixed.

Transition Timing Functions

By default, the rate of change in a transition is not exactly the same from frame to frame—it happens slightly slower at first, accelerates quickly, then gradually slows down before reaching its final value.

This shifting speed is known in animation terms as *easing*, and it often makes changes feel like they happen more naturally and smoothly. There are mathematical functions in charge of creating this variable change, and they are controlled using the `transition-timing-function` property.

There are keywords representing different flavors of timing functions. The default described earlier is called ease. The other are `linear`, `ease-in`, `ease-out`, and `ease-in-out`.

"Easing in" means starting out slowly and then accelerating. "Easing out" means the opposite: starting fast, then slowing down at the end. Finally, doing both gets us slow change in the beginning and in the end, but sped-up change in the middle.

It's tricky to visualize the results on the pages of a book, but the illustration in Figure 10-14 should give you an idea. It represents a rectangle where we change the background color from black to white over a period of one second.

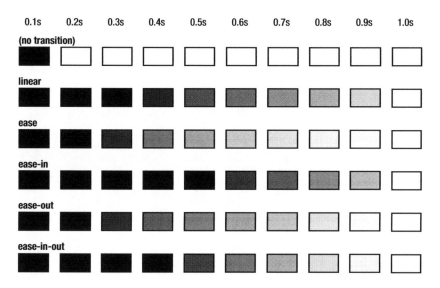

Figure 10-14. *The results at sampled stops 100 milliseconds apart in a 1-second animation*

If we wanted to change the button animation to use the `ease-in` timing function, we'd do it like this:

```
button {
  transition: all .25 ease-in;
  /* ...or we could set transition-timing-function: ease-in; */
}
```

Cubic Bézier Functions and "Bouncy" Transitions

Behind the scenes, the mathematical functions that deal with the rate of change are built on something called cubic Bézier functions. Each of the keywords are shortcuts to using these functions with specific arguments. Usually the change over time using these functions is visualized as a curved line going from intital time and initial value (bottom-left corner) to final value at the end of the duration (top-right corner), as seen in Figure 10-15.

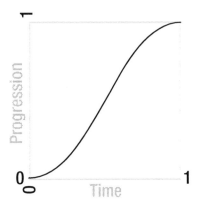

Figure 10-15. *Curve showing an ease-in-out transition timing function*

A cubic Bézier function needs four arguments to calculate the change over time, and we can use the cubic-bezier() function as an easing value in CSS transforms. This means that you can create your own timing functions by calculating and filling in these four values. The four values represent two pairs of x and y coordinates for two *control points* that shape that curve.

Just like with the matrix transformations, it's not something you would normally do by hand, since it requires advanced math skills. Luckily, there are others who have used these skills to create tools for the rest of us! Lea Verou has written one such tool specifically for CSS, available at http://cubic-bezier.com (see Figure 10-16).

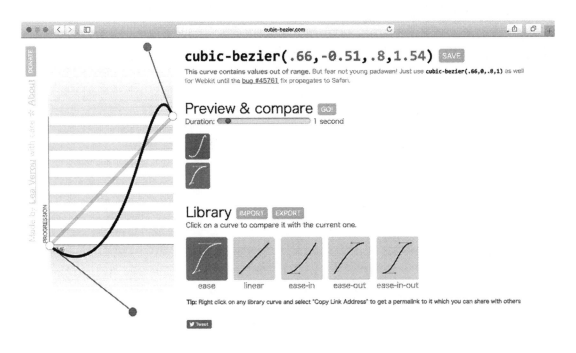

Figure 10-16. *At* http://cubic-bezier.com, *you can play with the preset values of different easings, and create your own*

One of the more interesting results of using a custom timing function is that you can change the value to go outside of the start and end values while transitioning (as seen in Figure 10-16). In practice, this means overshooting your target before finally stopping when you move something, for example. This gives you some potential to create bouncy transitions, where elements seem to be elastic or snap into place. Try playing around with the example on `http://cubic-bezier.com` to see the effects!

Step Functions

As well as specifying easing with preset keywords and `cubic-bézier()` functions, you can create transitions that happen stepwise. This is very useful for creating stop-motion animation. Imagine having an element with a background image consisting of seven different images, all in the same file. The image is positioned so that only one of them shows (see Figure 10-17).

Figure 10-17. *A stop-motion animation with seven frames using* `background-position`

As we hover over the element, we want to animate the background image by shifting the `background-position` property. If we do this using a linear or easing transition, the background image will just slide by, destroying the illusion. Instead, we need it to transition in six discrete steps:

```
.hello-box {
  width: 200px;
  height: 200px;
  transition: background-position 1s steps(6, start);
  background: url(steps-animation.png) no-repeat 0 -1200px;
}
.hello-box:hover {
  background-position: 0 0;
}
```

The `transition-timing-function` is now set to `steps(6, start)`, which translates as "divide the transition duration into six steps, and change the property at the start of each new step." All in all, we get seven different frames, including the starting state.

By default, `steps(6)` would change the property at the *end* of each step, but if you pass in `start` or `end` as the second argument, you can be explicit about this. Since we want to see the change directly as the user hovers over the element, we've opted to start the transition at the start of each step.

315

Now, there is a problem with the steps() function for transitions. When you reverse the state before the transition has completed (e.g., by removing the mouse pointer quickly), the transition will play backward. That is expected, but the unexpected part is that the reverse transition *still has six steps*. Those steps now no longer map to the carefully thought-out background positions, making our animation look bad.

Sadly, this is undefined behavior in the current version of the spec, and all browsers seem to treat step functions in this arguably poor manner. To counter this bad experience, we can use one of a couple of useful techniques for transitions, coming up in the next section.

Different Transitions for Forward and Reverse Directions

Sometimes, we want something to transition quickly in one direction and slowly in the other, or vice versa. In the stepping example earlier, we can't gracefully step backward when the hover state is aborted before the transition is finished. We could counter this by having the transition revert immediately.

To achieve this, we need to define different sets of transition properties: one for the unhovered state and one for the hovered state. The trick is to set the right one in the right place.

We give the initial transition a 0 duration, and then set the "real" transition to happen as the element is hovered. Now the hovered state triggers the animation, and as that hover is cancelled, the image snaps back.

```
.hello {
  transition: background-position 0s steps(6);
}
.hello:hover {
  transition-duration: .6s;
}
```

"Sticky" Transitions

Another trick for transitions is to have the transition not reverse at all, which is the opposite of our previous example. To make a "sticky" transition, we could use a ridiculously long transition-duration. Technically, it would still run backward when we cancel the hover, but very, *very* slowly—you would have to have the browser tab open for years and years to see any change!

```
.hello {
  transition: background-position 9999999999s steps(6);
}
.hello:hover {
  transition-duration: 0.6s;
}
```

Delayed Transitions

Usually, an element will begin its transition as soon as the state is changed—for instance, when a class name is changed by JavaScript or a button is pressed. We can choose to delay this transition using the transition-delay property. For example, we may only want to run the stop-motion animation if the user hovers the pointer over it for more than a second.

The shorthand for transition is quite forgiving in terms of the order of values, but the delay must be the second time value that appears—the first will be interpreted as the duration.

```
.hello {
  transition: background-position 0s 1s steps(6);
  /* equivalent to adding transition-delay: 1s; */
}
```

You can also use negative delays. While this sadly doesn't enable time travel, it does allow you to skip straight into partway along the transition right from the start. If you set `transition-delay: -5s` on a 10-second transition, it will immediately jump to the halfway mark as the transition is triggered.

What you can and can't Transition

So far, we've transitioned `transforms`, `box-shadow` values, and `background-position`. But not every CSS property can be animated, nor every value. Mostly, the ones that use lengths or colors are fine: borders, width, height, background colors, font sizes, etc. It's all about whether you can calculate a value in between them. You can find the middle between *100px* and *200px* as well as between *red* and *blue* (as colors are also number values behind the scenes), but not between, for example, `block` and `none` for the `display` property. There are also some exceptions to this rule.

Interpolated Values

Some properties can be animated, despite not having clear middle values. When you are using `z-index`, for example, you can't have a value of `1.5`, but `1` or `999` would be fine. For many properties, like `z-index` or `column-count` that only accept integer values, the browser will interpolate them into whole numbers along the way for you, sort of like with the steps() function earlier.

Some values that can be interpolated are a little bit surprising. For example, you can transition values of the `visibility` property, but the browser will "snap" the value to either one of the two end states as soon as the transition passes the halfway point between them.

Designer Oli Studholme has a convenient list of properties that are animatable, both from the CSS specs and properties in SVG animatable via CSS: `http://oli.jp/2010/css-animatable-properties/`.

Transitioning to Content Height

A final pitfall with transitions is that properties that *can* be transitioned, such as `height`, can only be transitioned between numeric values. This means that other keywords, like `auto`, can't be represented as one of the states to transition to.

A common pattern is to have a collapsed element that you transition to its full height when the user interacts with it, like an accordion component. The browser will not know how to transition between a length like `0` and the keyword `auto`, or even intrinsic measurement keywords like `max-content`.

In Figure 10-18, we have a restaurant menu component, initially showing the top three menu choices. As we toggle the rest of the list, it should slide down and fade in.

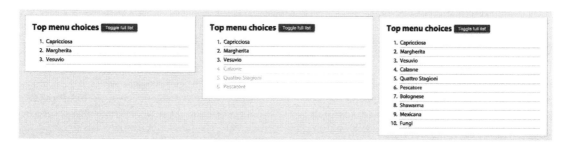

Figure 10-18. *An expanding menu list component*

In this situation, we know the approximate height of the list since it will have a total of ten items—it can still vary a bit since there may be long names with line breaks. We can now transition it with max-height instead. Using that technique, we go from the initially set measurement to a length that is sure to be taller than the expanded height of the element. In this case, we have decided to limit the rest of the "Top menu choices" to an additional seven items.

The markup of the component is based on two ordered lists, where the second list starts with number 4:

```
<div class="expando">
  <h2 class="expando-title">Top menu choices</h2>
  <ol>
    <li>Capricciosa</li>
    <li>Margherita</li>
    <li>Vesuvio</li>
  </ol>
  <ol class="expando-list" start="4" aria-label="Top menu choices, continued.">
    <li>Calzone</li>
    <!-- …and so on… -->
    <li>Fungi</li>
  </ol>
</div>
```

The markup includes an aria-label attribute on the second list, to make the purpose of the two lists clear for users of screen readers.

In order to toggle the states, we use a small snippet of JavaScript to set the scene. In the running example, you can find this script that creates a button for us, appends it to the heading, and toggles a class name of is-expanded on the container element when the button is clicked.

It also adds a class name of js to the html element. We can then base our styling on the presence of these class names, so if the JavaScript doesn't run, the user will see the full expanded list from the start.

```
.js .expando-list {
  overflow: hidden;
  transition: all .25s ease-in-out;
  max-height: 0;
  opacity: 0;
}
.js .is-expanded .expando-list {
  max-height: 24em;
  opacity: 1;
}
```

The expanded max-height is set to a value that is a quite bit more than the expected maximum height of the actual list. This is to have a safety margin: we don't want the list to be cut off by the max-height if there are a couple of unexpected line breaks inside the menu items on small screens, for example.

The small downside is that the max-height transition will still run as if the element was exactly 24 ems tall, making the easing and stopping point overshoot the full height of the list. If you play with the example, this is most noticeable as a small delay in the collapsing animation. In a more robust example, the script could initially transition to a very tall max-height, and then measure the element *after* the transition to dynamically update the max-height based on the content.

CSS Keyframe Animations

CSS transitions are *implicit* animations. We supply the browser two different states, and when an element goes from one state to the other, any property included in a transition will be animated. Sometimes, we need to do more than animate between just two states, or explicitly animate certain properties that may not be there to begin with.

The CSS Animations spec allows us to define these kinds of animations using the concept of *keyframes*. Furthermore, they allow us to control several other aspects of how and when the animation runs.

Animating the Illusion of Life

One of the benefits of using animation is to convey a message by showing, not telling. We can use it to direct attention (like a moving arrow to tell you "Look over here! This is important!"), explain what just happened (for example, when using a fade-in animation to show that a list item was added), or just to make our web pages seem a bit more alive, to make an emotional connection.

Walt Disney Studios teaches a set of 12 principles for expressing character and personality through animation. These were later collected in a book called *The Illusion of Life*. Animator Vincenzo Lodigiani created a short animated film to illustrate these principles (`https://vimeo.com/93206523`), with a little cube as the main character. Go ahead and watch it!

Inspired by that, we're going to create an animated square logo, showing some of what keyframe animations can do. The static rendering of the logo consists of a square next to the word "Boxmodel" (see Figure 10-19), which will be our fictive company name.

Figure 10-19. *The static logo*

The markup is pretty simple: a heading element with some extra `span` elements to wrap the words, and two nested `span` elements to represent the little square. Using extra empty elements for presentation is not ideal, but for reasons that will become clear, it's necessary in order to achieve what we want.

```
<h1 class="logo">
  <!-- This is the box we are animating -->
  <span class="box-outer"><span class="box-inner"></span></span>
  <span class="logo-box">Box</span><span class="logo-model">model</span>
</h1>
```

For the basic styling, we give the page a background color, give the logo some font properties, and set the dimensions and color of the square. We prepare the two `span` elements representing the square for animation by setting their display mode to `inline-block`, as it is not possible to transform an inline text element.

```
body {
  background-color: #663399;
  margin: 2em;
}
.logo {
  color: #fff;
  font-family: Helvetica Neue, Arial, sans-serif;
  font-size: 2em;
  margin: 1em 0;
}
.box-outer {
  display: inline-block;
}
.box-inner {
  display: inline-block;
  width: .74em;
  height: .74em;
  background-color: #fff;
}
```

Creating the Animation Keyframe Block

Next up, we need to create the actual animation. We want to imitate the opening sequence of the "Illusion of life" film, where the little square struggles to roll across the screen.

CSS animations are a bit of an odd bird in terms of syntax and structure. You define and name an animation sequence using a @keyframes rule, and then connect that sequence to one or more rule sets in CSS using the animation-* properties.

Here's how the first keyframe block will look:

```
@keyframes roll {
  from {
    transform: translateX(-100%);
    animation-timing-function: ease-in-out;
  }
  20% {
    transform: translateX(-100%) skewX(15deg);
  }
  28% {
    transform: translateX(-100%) skewX(0deg);
    animation-timing-function: ease-out;
  }
  45% {
    transform: translateX(-100%) skewX(-5deg) rotate(20deg) scaleY(1.1);
    animation-timing-function: ease-in-out;
  }
  50% {
    transform: translateX(-100%) rotate(45deg) scaleY(1.1);
    animation-timing-function: ease-in;
  }
  60% {
    transform: translateX(-100%) rotate(90deg);
  }
```

```
  65% {
    transform: translateX(-100%) rotate(90deg) skewY(10deg);
  }
  70% {
    transform: translateX(-100%) rotate(90deg) skewY(0deg);
  }
  to {
    transform: translateX(-100%) rotate(90deg);
  }
}
```

It's definitely a mouthful, but there is a lot of repetition in there. First up, we have named the keyframe sequence `roll`—this can be any valid identifier as long as it doesn't clash with any predefined names in CSS. We haven't decided yet how long this animation takes, so points in time inside the block are selected using *keyframe selectors*, written as percentages along the timeline.

We can also use the special keywords `from` and `to`, which are aliases for 0% and 100%, respectively. If either `from` (or 0%) or `to` (or 100%) are missing, they are constructed automatically from the initial state of the element's existing properties. The number of keyframe selectors you can have is anywhere from one to how ever many you need—you decide.

The first keyframe (at 0%) sets the `animation-timing-function` property. It works just like with transitions: use a preset keyword for easing, or a `cubic-bezier()` function. Setting the timing function here inside a keyframe selector controls the transition timing between this keyframe and the next.

We also move the starting position of the square to 100% to the left of itself using `translateX(-100%)`.

Next, we set a whole range of keyframes where various transforms are applied, as well as individual timing functions. Figure 10-20 shows how the element looks in each keyframe. Note that some keyframes are the same, for example at the end: this is to control the speed of the animation.

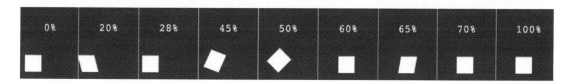

Figure 10-20. *The various keyframes of our animation*

The element will first skew a bit as if to gather momentum, then rotate and stretch, almost stopping at the 45-degree angle, to finally complete the 90-degree rotation and skew a bit on the rotated axis, making a bouncy stop. That's our first animation.

Connecting a Keyframe Block to an Element

Now that we have defined an animation keyframe sequence, we need to connect it to the square in the logo. Just as with the transition properties, there are animation properties controlling duration, delay, and timing functions, but with a few additional controls:

```
.box-inner {
  animation-name: roll;
  animation-duration: 1.5s;
  animation-delay: 1s;
```

```
  animation-iteration-count: 3;
  animation-timing-function: linear;
  transform-origin: bottom right;
}
```

We apply `animation-name` to this element to use the `roll` animation. Using `animation-duration`, we set how long each iteration is. The `animation-delay` property tells the browser to wait 1 second before running the animation. We want the box to roll over its side three times before stopping, so we set `animation-iteration-count` to 3.

We can set `animation-timing-function` inside keyframe selectors and on the element being animated. Here, the timing function is set to `linear` across the whole sequence, but we already saw how we can override that between individual keyframes.

▓ **Note**   You can apply multiple animations to the same element using the same sort of comma-separated syntax as with transitions. If two animations try to animate the same property at the same time, the animation declared last wins.

Finally, we've set the `transform-origin` property to `bottom right`, since we want the square to pivot on its bottom-right corner.

Using the shorthand `animation` property, we can boil all of the previous details down to one line, much like with transitions:

```
.box-inner {
  animation: roll 1.5s 1s 3 linear;
  transform-origin: bottom right;
}
```

But we're not done yet. So far, we have a square that repeats the rolling animation in place. We need it to move from outside the viewport to its final destination. This would have been possible using a single animation, but with a massive number of keyframes. Instead, we can apply another animation and another set of transformations on the outer `span` element. This time, the animation is much simpler. We want it to move in from the left, from a distance of three times the width of the box:

```
@keyframes shift {
  from {
    transform: translateX(-300%);
  }
}
```

Since we want to animate from something to the intial state, we can omit the `to` keyframe and just leave the `from` state.

A NOTE ON KEYFRAME BLOCKS AND PREFIXES

We are keeping to the standardized, unprefixed versions of the various properties in this chapter. The code examples have the full, prefixed code.

In browsers where the animation properties are prefixed, the keyframe rule is prefixed as well. This means you will have to write one set of keyframe rules per prefix! Thankfully, most browsers accept the unprefixed version these days, so usually you will only need to add the `-webkit-prefix`.

We can now apply the `shift` sequence to the outer `span` using a stepping timing function. There are three steps, so that each time the rolling animation finishes and reverts the square to the initial position, the stepping function moves it forward by the same amount. This is what creates the illusion of the square rolling across the screen; it's hard to illustrate, but play around with the code example to see how it works.

```
.box-outer {
  display: inline-block;
  animation: shift 4.5s 1s steps(3, start) backwards;
}
```

That last keyword, `backwards`, sets the `animation-fill-mode` property of the animation sequence. The fill mode tells the browser how to treat the animation before or after it runs. By default, the properties in the first keyframe aren't set until the animation runs. If we supply the keyword `backwards`, those values are filled backward in time, so the first keyframe properties are set straight away even if the animation is delayed or paused initially. Filling `forward` makes the last values in the sequence stick forward in time, and both does forward and backward filling.

In this instance, we want the animation to be offscreen straight away but retain the final value (since it is identical to the initial position of the box), so we fill `backwards`.

And with that, our first keyframe animation is done. When you load the example, the little square happily struggles across the screen.

Animating Along Curved Lines

Animating the position of an element between two points by definition moves it in a straight line. You could create the appearance of a curved movement by creating a large number of keyframes, changing the direction slightly every time. A better way is to move the object by means of combining rotation and translation in a specific order, like in this example by Lea Verou: `http://lea.verou.me/2012/02/moving-an-element-along-a-circle/`.

In the example files, we have included an example of a loading animation that uses this technique to illustrate files being uploaded to a server. The files "jump" from the computer to the server icon along a path in the shape of a half-circle, while shrinking a bit to fit behind the server icon (see Figure 10-21).

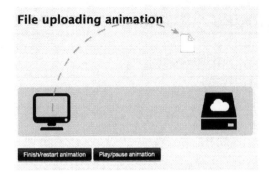

Figure 10-21. *The file icon moves to the server icon along a curved path*

Here is the keyframe block for this animation:

```
@keyframes jump {
  from {
    transform: rotate(0) translateX(-170px) rotate(0) scale(1);
  }
  70%, 100% {
    transform: rotate(175deg) translateX(-170px) rotate(-175deg) scale(.5);
  }
}
```

The initial keyframe translates the file element 170 pixels to the left (in order to start over the computer icon). The second keyframe selector rotates the element by 175 degrees, still translating it the same amount, and then rotates it back by 175 degrees in the opposite direction. Since this is done in the translated position, it serves to keep the element upright, so it doesn't turn upside down while rotating. Finally, we scale the element down to half its size.

Figure 10-22 illustrates how this particular combination of transformations works together to create movement along an arc.

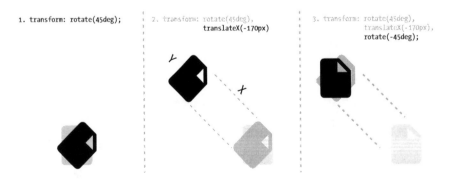

Figure 10-22. *Since the rotation is applied before translation, the icon is moved along an arc. Here's how it would look about a quarter of the way through the animation, at 45 degrees rotated.*

We then wire up this animation to the `file-icon` element, and set the duration and easing function. Since it's a loading animation, we set it to repeat indefinitely (we've all been there!), by adding the keyword `infinite` as the `animation-iteration-count` value.

```
.file-icon {
  animation: jump 2s ease-in-out infinite;
}
```

You might have noticed that the final keyframe selector targeted both the *70%* mark and the *100%* mark of the animation. This is because we want the animation to pause in the finished state for a short while before starting over.

There's no specific property to control this delay, so instead we want the states at 70% and 100% to remain the same, and we can combine keyframes that share the exact same properties in this way, just like we combine normal comma-separated selectors.

Animation Events, Play State, and Direction

At some point, the file transfer should be done, hopefully. In the full code example, we have added buttons to click to simulate finishing, restarting, and pausing the animation. Their only function is to add one of two class names to the file icon. These classes add the property `animation-play-state` to the file icon and set it to paused. There are two values for this property: by default it's set to `running`.

The stopping action is different from pausing, in that it hooks into the JavaScript events fired when animations start, stop, or initiate a new iteration. As soon as the animation finishes its current iteration, the file icon disappears and a checkmark appears next to the server icon. You can study the source code for this example to see how this works, or read more about animation events in JavaScript at MDN (`https://developer.mozilla.org/en-US/docs/Web/API/AnimationEvent`).

Finally, you can also control the direction of an animation using the `animation-direction` property. By default, it's set to `normal`, but you could run the animation backward using the `reverse` keyword, and you would have a "downloading" animation for free!

There are also the `alternate` and `alternate-reverse` keywords, which alternate the direction between animation iterations. The difference between them is that `alternate` starts in the normal direction, while `alternate-reverse` starts off as reversed.

SOME ANIMATION "GOTCHAS"

There are quite a few pitfalls and inconsistencies when using CSS keyframe animations. Here are a few that may be good to know:

- Some of the animations begin running as soon as the page loads, albeit with a small delay. This can be tricky, as some browsers have buggy behavior when it comes to running things smoothly right at the start; if you check the rolling square example in a few different browsers, you'll notice this sometimes. It's often better to trigger animations using JavaScript when everything is good and ready.

- Properties in keyframes don't have any specificity. They simply change properties on the element they are applied to. Despite this, some browsers (but not all) let you override a property set with the `!important` flag in a normal rule, from inside an animation, which can be confusing.

- Conversely, properties set inside keyframe blocks are not allowed to be set with the
  !important flag. Any declaration with that flag set inside of a keyframe block will be
  ignored.

- Versions 2 and 3 of the Android OS supports CSS animations, but only one property at a
  time! If you try to animate two or more properties, the element will disappear completely.
  To combat this, you could split up your animations into separate keyframe blocks.

3D Transforms

Now that we have used regular 2D transforms, transitions, and animations, it's time to look at perhaps the
most impressive tool in the CSS toolkit: 3D transforms.

We have already gone through the basics of transformations and coordinate systems in 2D space. When
we move to 3D, we are dealing with exactly the same concepts, but this time, we have to consider the z
dimension as well. 3D transforms allow us to take the coordinate system and rotate, skew, scale, or move it
toward or *away* from us. To achieve this effect, it's necessary to introduce the concept of perspective.

Getting some Perspective

When dealing with 3D, we need to represent transformations on three axes. The x and y axes still represent
the same thing, but z represents a line going through the screen and toward us as a viewer, so to speak (see
Figure 10-23). The surface of the screen itself is often called the *z-plane*, which is the default location on
the z axis.

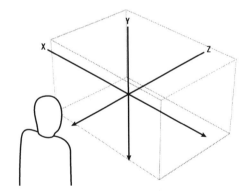

Figure 10-23. *The z axis in the 3D coordinate system*

This means that things need to appear smaller as we move them away from us (negative direction on
the z axis) and bigger as we move them toward us. Rotating something on the x or y axis will make parts of it
bigger and others smaller, etc.

Let's dive right in and try an example. We'll use our trusty 100×100-pixel box from the 2D section, and rotate it around the y axis:

```
.box {
  margin: auto;
  border: 2px solid;
  width: 100px;
  height: 100px;
  transform: rotateY(60deg);
}
```

This alone will not get you far: the box will appear narrower (which is expected when rotating on the y axis), but will lack any 3D feel at all (see the leftmost part of Figure 10-24).

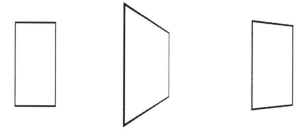

Figure 10-24. *Our rotated 100×100-pixel box with no perspective (left),* perspective: 140px *(middle), and* perspective: 800px *(right)*

The reason is that we haven't defined a *perspective*: we must choose how far from the box we should appear to be. Changes will be more pronounced the closer you are to an object, and less so when you are far away. The default perspective is basically that of being inifinitely far away, so we're not getting a very pronounced effect.

We remedy this by setting the perspective property on a parent of the element to be transformed:

```
body {
  perspective: 800px;
}
```

This measurement represents how far the viewing point is supposed to be positioned from the screen. You'll have to experiment to find the right value case by case, but somewhere around 600 to 1000 pixels is a good starting point.

Perspective Origin

By default, it is assumed that the perspective of the viewer is centered on the element that has the perspective applied to it. Technically, this means that the *vanishing point* is in the center. You can control this using the perspective-origin property. It works in a similar way to the transform-origin property: you supply it a pair of values for the x and y coordinates with keywords (top, right, bottom, left), percentages, or a length.

Figure 10-25 illustrates 3D objects with a `perspective` on the body element. All of the boxes have a 90-degree rotation on the x axis applied to them (so they are facing up), but the left and right images have different perspective origins.

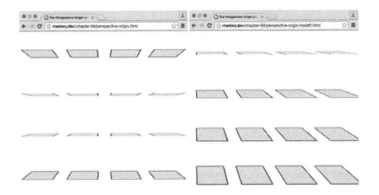

Figure 10-25. *The left browser window has a default* `perspective-origin` *(50% 50%), the right has the* `perspective-origin` *set to* `top left`

The Perspective() Transform Function

Setting the `perspective` property on a parent element makes all 3D transformations on elements inside it share the same perspective. This is usually what you want, since it makes for more realistic effects.

The `perspective()` function lets you set an individual perspective on each transformed element. A similar result to the earlier example could be achieved by the following, but the perspective wouldn't be shared among elements:

```
.box {
  transform: perspective(800px) rotateY(60deg);
}
```

Creating a 3D widget

Now that we have the recipe for moving things around and displaying them in 3D perspective, we can create something more useful. Besides using motion to add a bit of flair or explain what is going on, we can combine motion and 3D to save space and declutter the design at the same time.

Our goal is to build a 3D widget using CSS and JavaScript, where bits of the user interface are hidden on the backside of the element. We'll reuse the menu component from earlier and add options for filtering instead of expanding all items. By clicking a "Show filters" button, the element will flip 180 degrees and reveal the back panel (see Figure 10-26). Clicking "Show me pizzas!" flips it again, and in a real-world example the list of pizzas would now be filtered according to the checkbox selection.

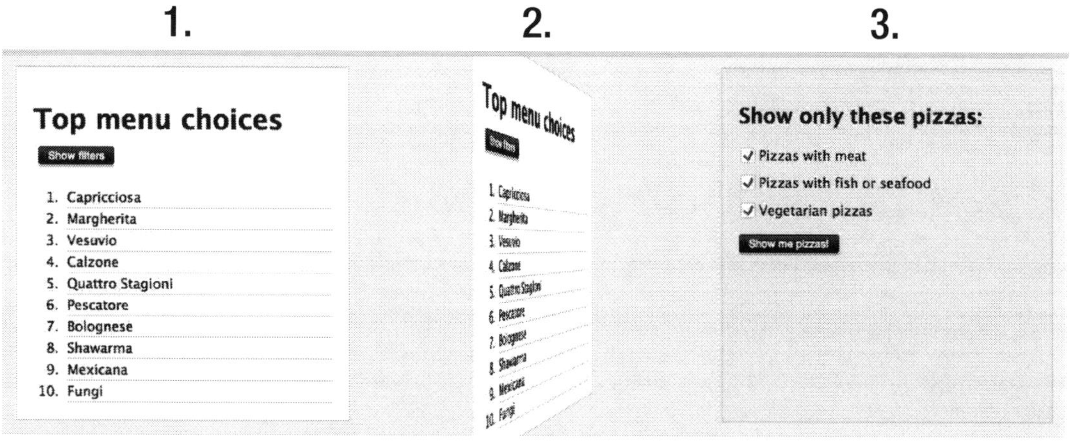

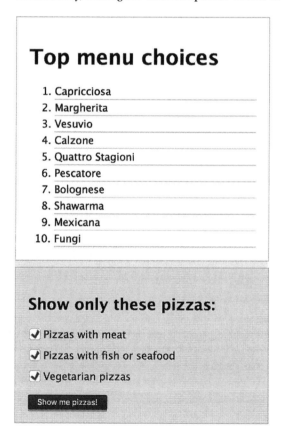

1.   2.   3.

Figure 10-26. *Our "flipable" widget*

To start off, we'll need some solid markup and a default case for browsers that don't support 3D transforms, or when the JavaScript doesn't run properly. When the browser doesn't support 3D transforms, we could just display the front and back sides after one another as blocks on the page, as shown in Figure 10-27. Theoretically, clicking the "Show me pizzas!" button would simply reload the page with the new filters applied.

Top menu choices

1. Capricciosa
2. Margherita
3. Vesuvio
4. Calzone
5. Quattro Stagioni
6. Pescatore
7. Bolognese
8. Shawarma
9. Mexicana
10. Fungi

Show only these pizzas:

☑ Pizzas with meat
☑ Pizzas with fish or seafood
☑ Vegetarian pizzas

Show me pizzas!

Figure 10-27. *The basic "2D" version shows the two sides of the widget one after another in the page*

The markup is similar to the menu from earlier in the chapter, but we've added some new class names and a wrapper to hold the whole structure.

```
<div class="flip-wrapper menu-wrapper">
  <div class="flip-a menu">
    <h1 class="menu-heading">Top menu choices</h1>
    <ol class="menu-list">
      <li>Capricciosa</li>
      <!-- ...and so on, all 10 choices -->
    </ol>
  </div>
  <div class="flip-b menu-settings">
    <!-- the form on the back of the widget goes here. -->
  </div>
</div>
```

We will use Modernizr to detect support for 3D transforms, so the rules for the enhanced widget will be "prefixed" with the class name that's added to the `html` element when CSS 3D transforms are supported.

First, we'll set the `perspective` on the body element, and make the wrapper element a positioning context for its descendants. We'll then add the transition, aiming for the `transform` property of the wrapper.

```
.csstransforms3d body {
  perspective: 1000px;
}
.csstransforms3d .flip-wrapper {
  position: relative;
  transition: transform .25s ease-in-out;
}
```

Now we'll make the content destined for the back of the widget absolutely positioned so that it covers the same space as the front side, and flip it 180 degrees on the y axis. We also want both sides to be invisible when they are flipped the wrong way, so one doesn't end up obscuring the other. We'll use the `backface-visibility` property to control this; it defaults to `visible`, but setting it to `hidden` makes the element invisible when viewed from the back.

```
.csstransforms3d .flip-b {
  position: absolute;
  top: 0;  left: 0;  right: 0;  bottom: 0;
  margin: 0;
  transform: rotateY(-180deg);
}
.csstransforms3d .flip-b,
.csstransforms3d .flip-a {
  backface-visibility: hidden;
}
```

When we rotate the widget, we want the whole thing to be rotated, including the already flipped backside. By default, any 3D transformation applied to a parent will nullify 3D transformations on child elements, flattening them. We need to create a *3D context* where transformations on children happen in the same 3D space as the parent. We do this by setting the transform-style property on the wrapper element to the value preserve-3d:

```
.csstransforms3d .flip-wrapper {
  position: relative;
  transition: all .25s ease-in-out;
  transform-style: preserve-3d; /* default is flat */
}
```

The final piece of the puzzle now is getting JavaScript to toggle a class name on the wrapper element when the buttons on the front and back are clicked. The is-flipped class name that's added triggers a 180-degree rotation on the y axis for the whole widget:

```
.csstransforms3d .flip-wrapper.is-flipped {
  transform: rotateY(180deg);
}
```

And with that, the styling is in place. But, sadly, there are real-world constraints that force us to revisit the widget to make it cross-browser compatible and accessible.

IE and the lack of preserve-3d

Internet Explorer 10 and 11 don't support the preserve-3d keyword. This means that no element can share the 3D space of a parent, which turn means that we can't flip the whole widget and have the sides follow along. We have to transition each side individually to make things work in IE.

Furthermore, IE has some severe bugs with perspective on the parent element in combination with multiple transformed elements, which means we have to resort to the perspective() function in the list of transformations instead.

The updated code sets a 0-degree initial transform on the front of the widget, a -180-degree transform on the back, and then flips both as the class name on the wrapper element is toggled. Furthermore, the perspective() function needs to be introduced first in the chain of transformations for each of these.

```
.csstransforms3d .flip-b,
.csstransforms3d .flip-a {
  transition: transform .25s ease-in-out;
}
.csstransforms3d .flip-a {
  transform: perspective(1000px) rotateY(0);
}
.csstransforms3d .flip-b {
  transform: perspective(1000px) rotateY(-180deg);
}
.csstransforms3d .flip-wrapper.is-flipped .flip-a {
  transform: perspective(1000px) rotateY(180deg);
}
.csstransforms3d .flip-wrapper.is-flipped .flip-b {
  transform: perspective(1000px) rotateY(0deg);
}
```

Safari on iOS 8 has an opposite bug where elements with a `perspective()` transform applied sometimes disappear as they start to transition. One fix is to apply the otherwise redundant `perspective` property back on the body element:

```
.csstransforms3d .flip-wrapper {
  perspective: 1000px;
}
```

Responsible Code: Adressing Keyboard Control and Accessibility

When developing components that hide things, we have seen in previous chapters that *how* you hide them matters. Simply rotating something out of view does not remove it from, for example, the tab order of the document. In the final code for the 3D widget (and the JavaScript code that goes with it), we have incorporated several other fixes to make the widget more robust:

- Besides using Modernizr to detect support for 3D transforms, we also detect support for the `classList` JavaScript API. This is used for efficient switching of class names when the widget state changes. This means that all the CSS rules in the final code are prefixed with `.csstransforms3d.classlist`.

  The support for 3D transforms and support for the `classList` API are *almost* overlapping, but we don't want any edge cases left with a broken widget. The widget will not run if these two features are not supported by the browser, and the "2D" style is then left untouched.

- When one side of the widget is hidden, it automatically has the class name `is-disabled` added to it, as well as the `aria-hidden` attribute set to `true`. The `is-disabled` class sets the `visibility` property in CSS to `hidden`.

  This prevents keyboard users from accidentally tabbing into form controls they cannot see, and screen readers from reading the content. (The `aria-hidden` attribute is there solely for screen readers, so as to not be dependant on the CSS hiding technique.) The hiding occurs first after the flip is complete, so it depends on the `transitionend` event.

- Conversely, the other side is explicitly made accessible before being shown using the class name `is-enabled`.

- When flipping the widget back, keyboard focus is moved back to the "Show filters" button.

Advanced Features of 3D Transforms

This section features parts of the 3D transforms specification that are perhaps less used in day-to-day coding, but offer some additional functionality to play around with.

The Rotate3d() Function

Apart from the individual rotation functions—rotateX(), rotateY() and rotateZ() (and its 2D equivalent rotate())—there is a function called rotate3d(). This function allows you to rotate an element around an arbitrary line going through 3D space, instead of a specified amount on each axis. Here's how using this function could look:

```
.box {
  transform: rotate3d(1, 1, 1, 45deg);
}
```

The rotate3d() function takes four arguments: three numbers representing x, y and z *vector coordinates*, and an angle. The coordinates define a line in space around which the rotation occurs. For example, if the vector coordinates are 1,1,1, the rotation will be around an imagined line that goes from the transform-origin point, through the point situated at 1 unit on the x axis (right), 1 unit on the y axis (down), and 1 unit on the z axis (toward the viewer), relative to the origin.

We don't need to specify *which* unit here, since the points are all relative to each other—if we would have used 100,100,100, we would have gotten the same result, since the line going through the element would be the same.

In effect, the 3D rotation is equivalent to *some* rotation (0 degrees or more) on each of the axes, but some quite complex math is involved in figuring out *how much* for each of them. It's much easier to see this function as a way to rotate by some angle around a line of your choosing. If you need to rotate by a specific degree on several axes at the same time, it's much easier to stick to a combination of single-axis rotations.

3D Matrix Transformations

Just as with the 2D subset of CSS transforms, there is a matrix3d() function that allows you to combine an arbitrary amount of translation, scaling, skewing, and rotation on each of the three axes.

We won't go into the details of how a 3D matrix works here, but the function itself needs 16 (!) arguments for various aspects of the final manipulation of the coordinate system. It arguably takes the prize for "most complex CSS property ever."

Just as with the 2D version, 3D matrices are not something you would normally write by hand, but they can help you create high-performance interactive experiences like games using a combination of CSS and JavaScript. For example, the Digital Creativity Guidebook example at the very beginning of the chapter (shown in Figure 10-1) uses matrix3d() heavily to calculate the transformations on all of the characters inside the animated book.

Summary

In this chapter, we got into manipulating elements in space as well as time. We looked at how transforms in 2D or 3D change the rendering of an element, but without affecting other elements on the page. We had a sneak peek at advanced transformations like the matrix() function and rotate3d().

Putting these together with animations, using CSS transitions or CSS keyframe animations, we can create either lively "delighters" like the animated logo, or more practical 3D widgets like the flipping pizza menu.

Throughout, we have seen techniques for applying these effects responsively, making every effort to not ruin the experience for users whose browsers don't support them as well as users browsing with a screenreader or navigating using only a keyboard.

CHAPTER 11

■ ■ ■

Cutting-edge Visual Effects

Coding creative designs has always been difficult using CSS alone. Until recently, the language itself has been quite restrictive in terms of the visual effects you can use. Re-creating the visual effects from graphics editing packages like Photoshop was difficult, if not impossible, and regularly required nasty hacks.

We have always been able to work around these constraints by sacrificing simplicity (extra elements purely for presentation purposes) or performance (pages too heavy on images, JavaScript to do visual effects).

In this chapter we will look at how we can achieve these effects using a variety of CSS features. Some of them are very new and have limited browser support today, while others have been around for a few years. Many have existed in SVG for a long time, but are only now bleeding into CSS—we'll see a few examples of that harmonization later in this chapter.

All of these techniques could take your designs to the next level: they are spices to lift the raw ingredients to new heights. As such, they should be used with caution, and applied with progressive enhancement in mind. You should also be aware that many of these techniques have associated bugs. So even in browsers where they are supported, they are often a work in progress.

In this chapter, we'll look at the following topics:

- CSS Shapes

- Using clipping paths and masks with CSS and via SVG

- CSS blend modes

- Filters with CSS and via SVG

In Figure 11-1, we have put together a page (describing some celestial bodies) packed full of visual effects. Just a few years ago, these effects would have been impossible to re-create in CSS. The page layout, had it been attempted at all, would have been re-created with loads of images and extra elements.

© Andy Budd and Emil Björklund 2016

A. Budd and E. Björklund, *CSS Mastery*, DOI 10.1007/978-1-4302-5864-3_11

Figure 11-1. A page using a range of visual effects

Today, these kinds of effects are actually achievable with CSS in many browsers, and where they fail, they can be made to fail gracefully. Using a large number of visual effects on the page at the same time is still something to be careful with, as they come with a performance cost; some more than others. Despite this, there are huge benefits to having these effects as part of CSS. They become less dependent on hacky markup and easier to maintain. Besides, once features are standardized in competing browsers, the performance tends to get better over time.

In the rest of this chapter, we are going to go through all of the techniques used in the "Stargazing" page example, and more.

Breaking Out of the Box: CSS Shapes

As we've said before, web layout is all about rectangles, so there's an inherent boxiness built-in. In earlier chapters, we've seen examples of how to counter this by using images and gradients to introduce a more organic feel, and by using rounded corners to create softer shapes and even circles.

CSS Shapes is a new standard to allow for a wider range of shapes in web design. Shaped elements affect the actual flow of content in the page, and not only the surface-level appearance.

Inside and Outside Shapes

CSS Shapes consists of two groups of new properties: one to set the shape that affects the content inside of a box, and another to set the outside shape that affects content flow *around* a shaped element. In Figure 11-2, an element is set to a circular shape. The left example shows how the outside shape affects content flowing around the circle, while the example on the right shows how content within the circle would be affected by the inside shape.

Figure 11-2. Outside vs. inside shapes

These two kinds of shaping methods are defined in separate levels of the CSS Shapes specification. The shape-outside property (defined in CSS Shapes Level 1) is the only one to have reached a reasonable level of maturity, and has started to find its way into browsers. We'll leave shape-inside out of this section, as it hasn't been implemented in any browsers just yet, but it is likely to start appearing soon.

The shape-outside property only works on floated elements. It works by carving out a shape that affects the flow of content outside the element, but it does not change the appearance of the element itself.

In the "Moon" section of our example, the text flows around the shape of the Moon image (see Figure 11-3) via `shape-outside` as follows:

```css
.fig-moon {
  float: right;
  max-width: 40%;
  shape-outside: circle();
}
```

Figure 11-3. *The text flows in a circular shape outside the Moon image*

Before we go into how the shaping works, it's worth noting how `shape-outside` affects the layout. The image file itself has a black background. If we change the background color of this section of the page, the effect of the shape shows more clearly (see Figure 11-4). The image itself remains a square, but the text flows *over* the image, around a circular shape inside it. In browsers that don't support CSS Shapes, the text will flow around the rectangular shape as normal.

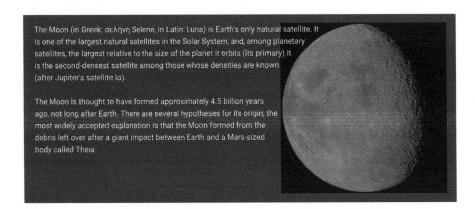

Figure 11-4. *The text flows in over the element boundaries of the shaped element*

■ **Note** As shown in Figure 11-4, the text follows the shape only on the left side of the float. You can only get a shape to affect the line boxes on one side, so even if the shape carves out space to the right of itself, the text will never flow there.

Shape Functions

The shape-outside property for the Moon image has the value circle(). There are a number of these *shape functions*: circle(), ellipse(), polygon(), and inset(). Most of these are self-explanatory, except for inset(), which means a rectangular shape inset from the box edges, optionally with rounded corners. It is basically a souped-up version of the old CSS 2.1 clip property, but with a slightly different syntax.

The syntax for circles and ellipses is similar to the syntax for sizing and positioning radial gradients that we saw in Chapter 5:

```
.shape-circle {
  /* circles take 1 radius and a position value: */
  shape-outside: circle(150px at 50%);
}
.shape-ellipse {
  /* ellipses take 2 radii and a position value: */
  shape-outside: ellipse(150px 40px at 50% 25%);
}
```

Just like gradient functions, there are some sensible defaults for circles and ellipses. The circle() value for our Moon image has no arguments supplied, which results in positioning the circle shape in the center of the element and extending the radius to the closest side.

The inset() shape works by supplying a list of lengths that represents the distance from the top, right, bottom, and left edges, a lot like the margin or padding shorthand. The same shortening rules for margins or padding apply when supplying one to three values. You can also supply values for rounded corners by adding the round keyword, followed by radii values that work the same as the border-radius property:

```
.shape-inset {
  /* shape the outside of the box 20px from
   * the top and bottom edges and 30px from
   * the left and right edges, with 10px
   * radius rounded corners.
   */
  shape-outside: inset(20px 30px round 10px);
}
```

A more complex example is using the polygon() shape function. This lets you supply a list of coordinate pairs for points on the box surface, relative to the top-left corner, and a line is drawn between them resulting in a shape. The last point listed connects to the first to close the shape. In the "Planets" section, we have created a polygon shape from the image of Saturn.

The easiest way to quickly create a polygon shape is to use the CSS Shapes Editor plug-in, available both for the Google Chrome and Opera developer tools (https://github.com/oslego/chrome-css-shapes-editor). Chrome and Opera both support Shapes, and offer a preview of the shape when inspecting an element. The plug-in adds additional tools, so that you can both visualize how a shape affects the page, and create new ones by creating and dragging control points (see Figure 11-5).

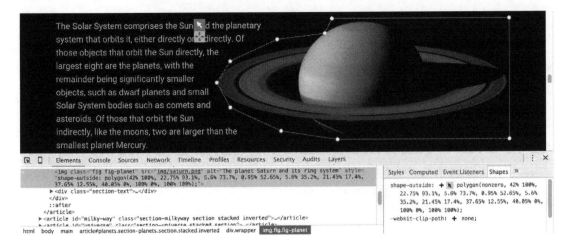

Figure 11-5. *A polygon shape drawn on the image of Saturn with the Shapes plug-in for Google Chrome*

We can now copy and paste the resulting polygon shape into our code:

```
.fig-planet {
  float: right;
  max-width: 65%;
  shape-outside: polygon(41.85% 100%, 22.75% 92.85%, 5.6% 73.3%, 0.95% 52.6%, 5.6% 35.05%,
21.45% 17.15%, 37.65% 12.35%, 40% 0, 100% 0%, 100% 100%);
}
```

The coordinates for each point on the polygon are represented as percentages here for maximum flexibility, but you can also use other lengths like pixels, ems, or even calc() expressions.

Shape Images

Creating polygons based on complex images can be tedious. Luckily, we can also create shapes directly from an image source, based on image transparency. We could create a separate image file with the desired outline shape, but the Saturn image is already a PNG with transparency, so we can use that to generate the shape. All we need to do is change the shape-outside value from a polygon() function to a url() function pointing to the image:

```
.fig-planet {
  float: right;
  max-width: 65%;
  shape-outside: url(img/saturn.png);
}
```

If we inspect the image in the Chrome Developer Tools (DevTools) now, as shown in Figure 11-6, we can see that the transparency data from the image is picked up, generating the shape.

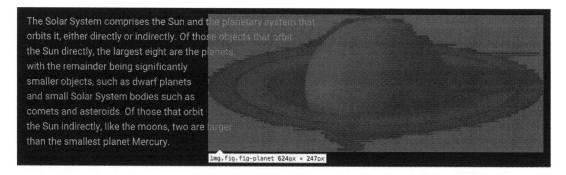

Figure 11-6. The outline of the transparent parts of the image is used to create the shape

---

■ **Tip**   If you try this example by just opening the HTML file directly in your browser, it will not work—even if the browser supports CSS Shapes. You need to fetch the page via a web server, so that the referenced image has proper HTTP headers describing it as coming from the same origin server as the CSS. This is a security trade-off that exists in some newer browsers, to prevent referenced files doing unsafe things to your computer.

By default, the shape outline will be generated from the outline of where the image becomes fully transparent, but we can change that value with the shape-image-threshold property. The default is 0.0 (fully transparent), while higher values (up toward 1.0) will mean higher opacity values are tolerated before the shape edge is created. If we change the Saturn image to use an image threshold of 0.9, for example, the semitransparent rings will not be included in the shape outline, and the text will overlap them (see Figure 11-7):

```
.fig-planet {
  float: right;
  max-width: 65%;
  shape-outside: url(img/saturn.png);
  shape-image-threshold: 0.9;
}
```

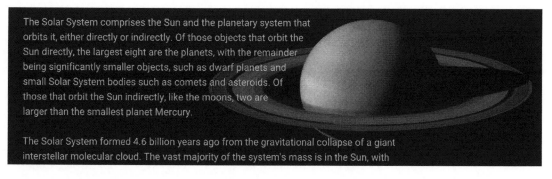

Figure 11-7. Using shape-image-threshold, semitransparent parts of the image are now ignored when generating the shape

Shaped Boxes and Margins

Instead of using a shape function or an image, we can also use the reference boxes for the element to generate the shape. This may sound strange at first, as it is the boxiness that we wanted to get away from, but the shape will also follow rounded corners.

For example, if we go back to the Moon example, we may want to change that section's background color, but at the same time get rid of the black square frame around the image, as shown in Figure 11-8. We can use border-radius on the image to create the circular shape:

```
.fig-moon {
  float: right;
  max-width: 40%;
  border-radius: 50%;
}
```

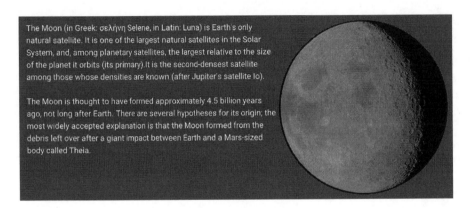

Figure 11-8. *Applying border-radius to the Moon image*

The border radius alone does not generate a shape, but we can tell the shape-outside property to use the now circular border-box as a reference for the shape:

```
.fig-moon {
  float: right;
  max-width: 40%;
  border-radius: 50%;
  shape-outside: border-box;
}
```

The outside shape is now back to a circle, following the border box of the element. The other possible reference box values for shapes are content-box, padding-box, and margin-box. We've seen reference boxes before (with properties like box-sizing and background-clip), with the exception of margin-box. Since shapes operate on the float area, they can include the margin as well, so this keyword is special to shapes—there's no box-sizing: margin-box, for example.

The margin-box on a shaped item will also follow the border radius. This means that we can use a normal margin declaration for the Moon image to create some space around it:

```
.fig-moon {
  float: right;
  max-width: 40%;
  border-radius: 50%;
  shape-outside: margin-box;
  margin: 2em;
}
```

The text will now flow around the curved margin shape. If we inspect the item in Chrome DevTools, we will see how this shape behaves, as well as the original margin (see Figure 11-9).

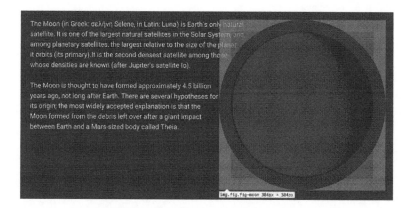

Figure 11-9. *With the margin-box as a shape reference, the margin distance follows the rounded corners*

If we wanted to add a margin to the more complex shape of the Saturn image, there's a new property called shape-margin to set a margin distance around the whole shape, regardless of the method used to create it (see Figure 11-10):

```
.fig-planet {
  max-width: 65%;
  shape-outside: url(img/saturn.png);
  shape-margin: 1em;
}
```

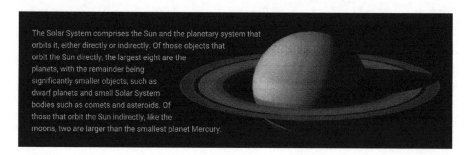

Figure 11-10. *Adding a shape-margin property on the Saturn image shape*

Browser Support for CSS Shapes

At the time of writing, CSS Shapes only work in newer WebKit- or Blink-based browsers: Google Chrome, Opera, and Safari 7.1+ (or Mobile Safari on iOS 8+).

Clipping and Masking

Where CSS Shapes lets you alter the flow of content around the shape of an element, it does not allow you to alter the appearance of the element itself. We saw that adding a border radius is one way of visually shaping the element. There are other ways to affect the shape of an element, by making parts of it transparent.

Clipping uses a path shape to define sharp edges where the element's visibility toggles fully on and off. *Masking* is slightly different, and is used to set areas of an element to be more or less transparent. Clipping also affects the hit surface of an object, whereas masking does not. For example, hover effects will be triggered only when your mouse pointer is over the visible parts of a clipped element. When you hover over a masked element, any :hover rule will become active regardless of the visibility of the portion underneath the mouse pointer.

Clipping

Clipping was first introduced in CSS 2.1, with the clip property. However it could only be used on absolutely positioned elements to clip them into a rectangular shape, using a rect() function. Boring!

Luckily, the new clip-path property allows us to clip elements in more exciting ways. It can use the same basic shape functions as CSS Shapes to define how the element should be clipped. We can also use an SVG document to clip an element, by referencing a <clipPath> element inside it via a URL.

We'll start by looking at the version using shape functions. This version only works in Blink- and WebKit-based browsers at the time of writing, and needs a -webkit- prefix in addition to the unprefixed property. In the upcoming examples, we will stick with the standard unprefixed property for brevity.

The sections in the Stargazing example page are all clipped, to give them a slight diagonal tilt (see Figure 11-11).

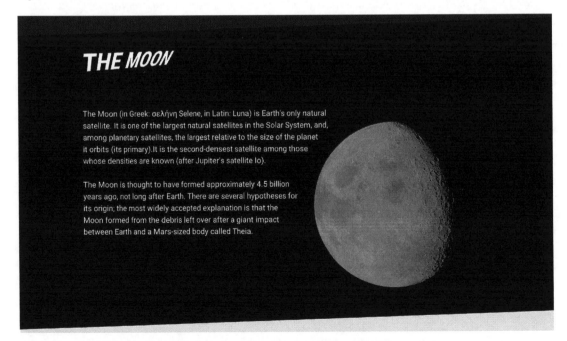

Figure 11-11. *All the sections of the page are clipped to give them a slight tilt*

Each section is given the class name `stacked`, and for this class name, we add a rule with the clipping path defined as a polygon shape:

```
.stacked {
  clip-path: polygon(0 3vw, 100% 0, 100% calc(100% - 3vw), 0% 100%);
}
```

This polygon shape is not as complex as the one for the Saturn shape earlier, and gives us a chance to dive into the syntax a bit more. Each point in the polygon is represented as a pair of space-separated values, and the points are separated with commas.

Starting at the top left, we clip from 0 on the x axis and 3vw on the y axis. We use viewport-relative units here to keep the angle relative to the viewport size. The next coordinate pair is at the top-right corner of the element, so the coordinate pair is 100% 0. The next point is 3vw from the bottom-right corner, and cannot be represented with a percentage as we start from the top. This means we need to calculate it as 100% - 3vw. Finally, we place the last point in the bottom-left corner of the element, at 0 100%.

Since the clipping paths only affect the rendered appearance of the element and not the flow of the page, the clipped elements will now have transparent gaps between them (see Figure 11-12). To fix this, we can apply a negative margin for each stacked element, slightly larger than the 3vw distance that we clip away, so that the sections overlap. We only want this negative margin in browsers that do support clip-path, which gives us an excellent opportunity to use the @supports-rule. Since these new visual effects are only implemented in very recent browsers, we can safely scope them this way.

```
@supports ((clip-path: polygon(0 0)) or
          (-webkit-clip-path: polygon(0 0))) {
    .stacked {
        margin-bottom: -3.4vw;
    }
}
```

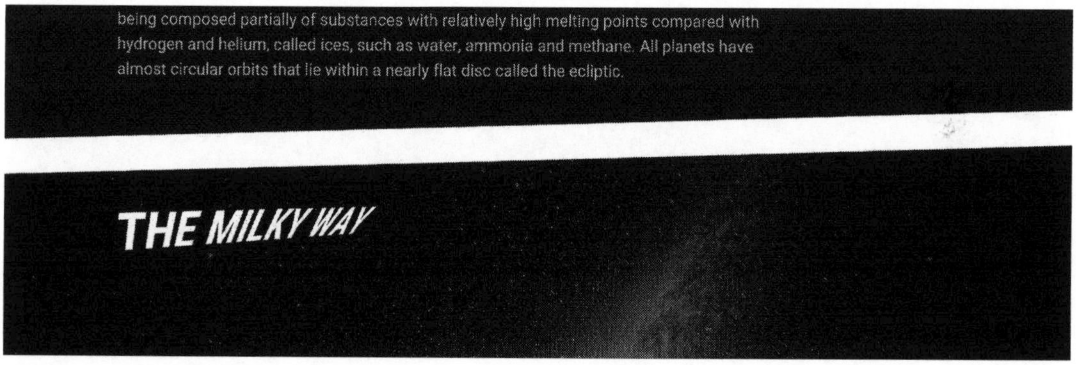

Figure 11-12. *With just the clipping, there will be gaps between sections*

In the @supports-block, we test for support of the minimum polygon shape, consisting of a single point.

With this fix, the sections stack up nicely and browsers with no support for clip-path via shapes get the normal straight sections without the overlap.

Clipping with SVG Clip Sources

You can use `polygon()`, `circle()`, `ellipse()`, and the `inset()` function to create clipping paths, just like in CSS Shapes. For more complex shapes, it's probably easier to create them using an image editor, and then use the graphic as the source of the clipping shape. This is what we have done with the shapes in the page navigation shown in Figure 11-13.

Figure 11-13. *The complex shapes in the navigation section are clipped from SVG sources*

To achieve this, we need to use SVG to create our clipping path, and then use a URL reference to this *clip source* in place of the shape function. To start with, we need to create the shape in a graphics editing program such as Illustrator, Sketch, or Inkscape. The process is not as straightforward as it could be, but doable.

The navigation itself is an unordered list containing in-page links:

```
<nav class="stacked section nav-section inverted">
  <ul class="wrapper">
    <li><a href="#moon">The Moon</a></li>
    <li><a href="#sun">The Sun</a></li>
    <li><a href="#planets">Planets</a></li>
    <li><a href="#milky-way">Galaxy</a></li>
    <li><a href="#universe">Universe</a></li>
  </ul>
</nav>
```

We'll leave the details of the navigation styling out of this example; suffice to say we're using flexbox to lay the items out horizontally, and sized them as 100×100-pixel squares at the default font size.

Next, we create an image in an SVG-capable graphics editor, Adobe Illustrator in this case. The image is also set to be 100 by 100 pixels in size (see Figure 11-14). We draw the planet by creating two black shapes: a circle and a rotated ellipsis. Next, we save the graphic as an SVG file named `clip.svg`. This process differs between different graphics editing software; we'll leave out the details of this, and focus on the general workflow.

Figure 11-14. *Creating the planet shape in Illustrator*

If we now open the SVG file in a code editor, it will look something like this:

```
<svg xmlns=http://www.w3.org/2000/svg width="100px" height="100px" viewBox="0 0 100 100">
  <circle cx="50" cy="50" r="45"/>
  <ellipse transform="matrix(-0.7553 0.6554 -0.6554 -0.7553 -12.053 54.99)" cx="50" cy="50"
rx="63.9" ry="12.8"/>
</svg>
```

In order to transform this image into a clipping path, we need to wrap the contents inside a <clipPath> element and give that element an ID:

```
<svg xmlns="http://www.w3.org/2000/svg"
    width="100px" height="100px" viewBox="0 0 100 100">
  <clipPath id="saturnclip">
    <circle cx="50" cy="50" r="40.1"/>
    <ellipse transform="matrix(0.7084 -0.7058 0.7058 0.7084 -20.7106 49.8733)" cx="50"
    cy="50" rx="62.9" ry="12.8"/>
  </clipPath>
</svg>
```

We are finally ready to reference the clipping path inside of the clip.svg file from our CSS:

```
.nav-section [href="#planets"] {
    clip-path: url(img/clip.svg#saturnclip);
}
```

Using this technique, you can keep a number of clip sources in a single SVG file, and reference them by their ID in the URL fragment.

Sadly, the current state of browsers leaves two major obstacles to overcome in order to make SVG clip sources work reliably:

- So far, only Firefox allows external clip sources applied to HTML content in CSS— other browsers are likely to follow suit eventually.

- The coordinates in the SVG <clipPath> are interpreted as pixels, so the clip shape is inflexible and will not resize with the HTML content it is applied to. Percentages in measurements are technically valid, but support is lacking.

There are solutions for these obstacles, but they require some slight reshuffling of our code.

Inline SVG Clip Sources

Browsers that do not support external clip source references *do* allow you to use SVG clipping paths, as long as the CSS, HTML, and SVG are all in the same file.

If you put the CSS inside a `<style>` element inline with the content, and also put the SVG contents inline in the same file, you can reference the `<clipPath>` element directly via the ID. This would all be in the same HTML source file:

```
<!-- Here's the element we want to clip -->
<li><a href="#planets">Planets</a></li>

<style>
/* in the same HTML file, we put the CSS for the clip-properties */
.nav-section [href="#planets"] {
  clip-path: url(img/clip.svg#saturnclip);
}
</style>
<!-- Still in the same HTML file, the clipping path inline as SVG -->
<svg xmlns=http://www.w3.org/2000/svg height="0" viewBox="0 0 100 100">
  <clipPath id="saturnclip">
    <circle cx="50" cy="50" r="40.1"/>
    <ellipse transform="matrix(0.7084 -0.7058 0.7058 0.7084 -20.7106 49.8733)" cx="50"
    cy="50" rx="62.9" ry="12.8"/>
  </clipPath>
</svg>
```

The preceding technique gives us slightly better cross-browser support, but at the cost of sacrificing the reusability of having all our clipping paths in one external SVG file, as well as not having to mess about in the HTML.

■ **Note**   WebKit-based browsers have a bug where the coordinates for the position of the clipping path start at the top left of the page instead of relative to the element. In order for them to be positioned correctly, the final example also features `transform: translate(0, 0)` on the clipped item, which does nothing visually, but fixes the problem.

Using the Object Bounding Box to Size Clipping Paths

The next problem is that the clipping path will not resize with the size of our navigation items; it has a hard-coded size of 100 by 100 pixels.

There are two coordinate systems we can use to size our clipping path. The default is called the "user space on use," meaning the coordinate system for the content the clipping path is applied to. In our case, this means that one unit inside the clipping path is interpreted as one CSS pixel in the clipped HTML content.

The other coordinate system is called "object bounding box," which uses a scale where the units are relative to the size of the content being clipped. In this scale, a value of 0 on the x axis means the left edge of the clipped content's border box, and 1 means the right edge. Similarly, 0 is the top of the box in the y axis, and 1 is the bottom.

For simpler graphics, you might get away with changing the values by hand—a value of 50 in our 100×100-pixel image would become 0.5, and so on—but for more complex graphics, this would be too error-prone. The easier solution is to resize the graphic to a 1×1-pixel size inside the image editing software, before exporting the SVG.

In the final example, we have used the objectBoundingBox value for the inline SVG clipping paths. For the Saturn clipping path, the final code looks like this:

```
<clipPath id="saturnclip" clipPathUnits="objectBoundingBox">
  <circle cx="0.5" cy="0.5" r="0.45"/>
  <ellipse transform="matrix(-0.7553 0.6554 -0.6554 -0.7553 1.2053 0.5499)" cx="0.5"
  cy="0.5" rx="0.639" ry="0.125"/>
</clipPath>
```

Browser Support for Clipping Paths

Using the inline SVG method for clipping paths, you can target most modern browsers: Chrome, Opera, Safari, and Firefox all support this version. WebKit- and Blink-based browsers also support the basic shape functions for clipping paths. Sadly, IE does not support clipping paths at all. At the time of writing, Edge was also missing support, but it is on the roadmap and likely to be added soon. External references for SVG clip sources only work in Firefox at the time of writing, but are expected to work elsewhere in a near future.

Masking

The title in the header of the "Stargazing" page appears to be behind the "atmosphere" of the Earth graphic (see Figure 11-15). This gradual transparency is achieved with masking.

Figure 11-15. *The "Stargazing" title is masked with a gradient mask image*

Safari implemented masking way back in 2008, using a nonstandard property called -webkit-mask-image. This property allowed you to take an image and use it as a source for the transparency levels of the masked element. This is based on the *alpha level* of each pixel in the mask: how transparent it is. Where the mask image is completely transparent, so will the masked element be. Conversely, completely opaque parts of the mask will make the masked element completely visible. The color values of the mask are irrelevant, so the most common approach is to use a grayscale image to do the masking.

Instead of creating an image file, we can also use CSS gradients to create the mask. This is exactly what we've done in the header:

```
.header-title {
  mask-image: radial-gradient(ellipse 90% 30% at 50% 50%,
                              rgba(0,0,0,0) 45%,
                              #000 70%);
  mask-size: 100% 200%;
}
```

You'll recognize the syntax: mask images are declared pretty much exactly as you would declare background properties. For example, the mask-image property works just like background-image syntax-wise; you can even declare multiple mask images on top of each other.

Along with picking a mask image, you can also specify sizing and position. For this example, we've opted to use twice the height of the mask image in order to place it at the bottom of the text, instead of positioning it there. If we simply moved the gradient image down, the top part of the mask image surface would be transparent, which would mask away the top part of the text. Figure 11-16 illustrates how the gradient mask is sized and positioned over the text.

Figure 11-16. *The mask image as it would look if it were an image on top of the text*

Since the original WebKit implementation, the mask properties are being standardized and expanded, as well as harmonized with the corresponding SVG effects. Yes, that's right: just like with clip-path, masking exists in SVG and is being made applicable to HTML content as well.

At the time of writing, WebKit- and Blink-based browsers offer support for the prefixed -webkit-mask-properties for alpha transparency mask images. Along with Firefox, they also support SVG <mask> sources. All except Firefox require the same inline method we saw for clipping paths.

```
.header-title {
  /* inline CSS, pointing to an inline SVG <mask> element */
  mask: url(#ellipseMask);
}
```

The SVG equivalent of the CSS gradient we created looks something like this:

```
<mask id="ellipseMask" maskUnits="objectBoundingBox" maskContentUnits="objectBoundingBox">
  <radialGradient id="radialfill" r="0.9" cy="1.1">
    <stop offset="45%" stop-color="#000"/>
    <stop offset="70%" stop-color="#fff"/>
  </radialGradient>
</mask>
```

Just like with clip-paths, we need to use the `objectBoundingBox` coordinate system from 0-1 to size the mask surface to the boundaries of the element. SVG masks also have the additional `maskContentUnits` attribute, which here sets the same coordinate system for the mask shapes.

SVG mask sources use luminance values for the mask rather than alpha. This means that the masked element will be transparent where the mask is darker, and opaque where the mask is lighter. In the preceding SVG mask example, we used a gradient from black to white.

The browser will automatically assume that you are using an alpha mask for mask image sources, and a luminance mask if pointing to an SVG source. With the proposed standard version, you can toggle between these with the `mask-type` property.

There are some further differences between the `-webkit-` prefixed version and the proposed masking standard. Refer to the MDN docs for the full list of properties and syntax for the WebKit implementation (`https://developer.mozilla.org/en-US/docs/Web/CSS/-webkit-mask`).

Transparent JPEGs with SVG Masking

The page header uses masking in two places, one of them harder to spot than the other. The title itself uses masked text, but the background image of Earth (taken from an Apollo expedition) actually has its own mask baked in.

This image is a fairly high-resolution photograph, and the header has a nice, smooth gradient background. In Figure 11-17 we have removed the text and lightened the gradient a bit so the result is more visible.

Figure 11-17. *The header with the Earth photo*

Photographic images with baked-in transparency are usually achieved with PNG images. The downside with PNGs is that they have a massive file size—the Earth image would be around 190 KB as a PNG. In this technique, we are going to use the power of SVG to apply alpha transparency to a JPEG file via masking. The resulting file will be around 24 KB instead.

Images Inside SVG

The first thing we need to do is to create the image as a normal JPEG, with the background still there, as shown in Figure 11-18.

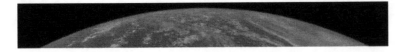

Figure 11-18. *The JPG photo*

Next, we create an SVG "wrapper" file named earth.svg that loads the bitmap image. SVG is primarily a vector format, but you can load and use bitmap images inside SVG files with the <image> element. We'll eventually use this SVG file as the header background image in CSS.

We'll size the SVG graphic to the same dimensions as the bitmap image using the viewBox, width, and height attributes. The viewBox attribute is responsible for setting up the coordinate system inside the image, and the width and height attributes are there to set the outside image dimensions. Most browsers don't need the latter, but IE has a bug which skews SVG background images if these two are missing.

The code looks something like this:

```
<svg xmlns="http://www.w3.org/2000/svg" width="1200" height="141" viewBox="0 0 1200 141"
xmlns:xlink="http://www.w3.org/1999/xlink">
  <image width="100%" height="100%" xlink:href="earth.jpg" />
</svg>
```

SVG Masking

Next, we'll need to create the mask. For this shape we can get away with a radial gradient, which we will size and position to cover Earth's horizon in the image. The radial gradient has a slight transparency at the edge. It's kind of hard to pick out the right coordinates, but we can make this easier by using a graphics editor. In Figure 11-19 we've drawn a giant semitransparent circle on top of the bitmap image inside Adobe Illustrator, to quickly be able to get some measurements. We could have drawn a path to create the mask shape as well, but the radial gradient gives us the possibility of a smoother edge. This is just a throwaway document, to come up with the right numbers.

Figure 11-19. *We've drawn a giant circle shape over the photo, to quickly pick out the mask coordinates*

It turns out that the gradient needs to have a radius of about 1224 pixels, and be positioned at 1239 pixels on the y axis and 607 pixels on the x axis. We then create an SVG <mask> element in the earth.svg file, consisting of a rectangle covering the entire SVG viewport, filled with the radial gradient.

```
<mask id="earthmask">
  <radialGradient gradientUnits="userSpaceOnUse" id="earthfill" r="1224" cx="607" cy="1239">
    <stop offset="99.5%" stop-color="#fff"/>
    <stop offset="100%" stop-color="#000"/>
  </radialGradient>
  <rect width="1200" height="141" fill="url(#earthfill)" />
</mask>
```

The gradient color stops go from white to black, with a slight feathering at the edge. Note that gradient dimensions work the opposite way from clip-paths, in that they are sized with objectBoundingBox dimensions by default. For that reason, we also need to add gradientUnits="userSpaceOnUse".

We can now point the image to use the mask we created:

```
<mask id="earthmask"><!-- mask content here --></mask>
<image width="100%" height="100%" xlink:href="earth.jpg" mask="url(#earthmask)" />
```

Inlining the Image

At this point, our file could be done, if we were to use it as a stand-alone SVG graphic. The problem is that SVG background images can't load other resources. For this reason, the final step is to convert the bitmap image (earth.jpg) into a Base64-encoded data URI. There are plenty of tools and services that let you do this, like http://duri.me—just go there and drag and drop the image file to get the text string.

Finally, we swap out the image file reference in the SVG to the encoded string:

```
<image width="100%" height="100%" mask="url(#earthmask)" xlink:href="data:image/
jpg;base64,/9j/4AAQSkZ..." />
```

Note that this string of characters can be very long. Base64 encoding increases the file size compared to the binary image file by about 30%, but as the original JPEG file is around 18KB, we land at 24 KB total.

Now we're finally ready to apply this SVG image as the header background, along with the gradient:

```
.page-header {
  background-image: url(img/earth.svg),
                    linear-gradient(to bottom, #000, #102133);
  background-repeat: no-repeat;
  background-size: 100% auto, cover;
  background-position: 50% bottom;
}
```

This technique works in almost all browsers that support SVG, the exceptions being IE9 and some older versions of Android that do not support SVG masking at all.

Automating the Technique

Creating this background image was a lot of work, but we did get the file size down to one-tenth of the size, compared with the transparent PNG. For this shape, a radial gradient did the trick of masking very well, albeit with a bit of manual work.

For more complex shapes, there's a very handy web service that does this for you, called ZorroSVG (mask, get it?). At `http://quasimondo.com/ZorroSVG/`, you can upload a transparent PNG, and it will spit back a masked SVG with a JPEG inside it. The downside is that it converts the transparency data to a bitmap mask, which takes up some additional space compared to drawing it as an SVG shape. Even so, you are still likely to gain some massive savings with this technique.

Blend Modes and Compositing

In graphics editing applications like Photoshop, Sketch, or Gimp, designers have long been able to choose how the colors mix when putting design elements on top of each other (see Figure 11-20). In CSS, we've only recently been given decent control over *alpha* blending: regular transparency in the form of transparent PNG files, rgba background colors, the opacity property, masking, etc. Needless to say, designers have wanted to see the same blend modes they are used to from graphics editing applications as part of CSS. This is finally coming, in the Compositing and Blending standard.

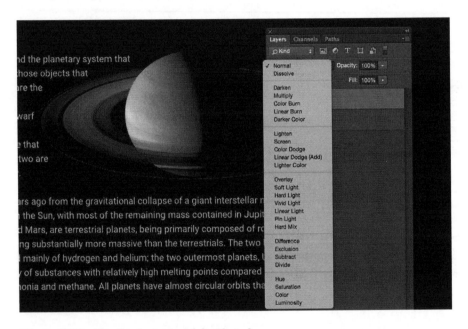

Figure 11-20. *Blending layers in Adobe Photoshop*

Compositing is the technical term for merging image layers together. Blend modes are probably the most commonly encountered aspect of compositing. If you haven't used blend modes before, or haven't thought about what they are, they all represent different mathematical ways of combining color values for of one image (called the *source*) on top of another (called the *destination*).

The simplest example is perhaps the "multiply" blend mode, where each color channel value of the source pixel is multiplied with the values of the pixel behind it, which results in a darker image. It helps to think of this in terms of a grayscale example and the color being from 0 (black) to 1 (white). If the source is 0.8 and the destination is 0.5, the resulting pixel will have a color value of $0.8 \times 0.5 = 0.4$.

Colorizing a Background Image

Another example is the "luminosity" blend mode. It takes the light-levels from the source and applies them to the hue and saturation of the destination. The "Milky Way" section in our example page has a background image with some rather vibrant blue tones. We have tweaked it slightly by applying a purplish background color and then applying `background-blend-mode: luminosity` (see Figure 11-21). This colorizes the image and gives it a more uniform color range.

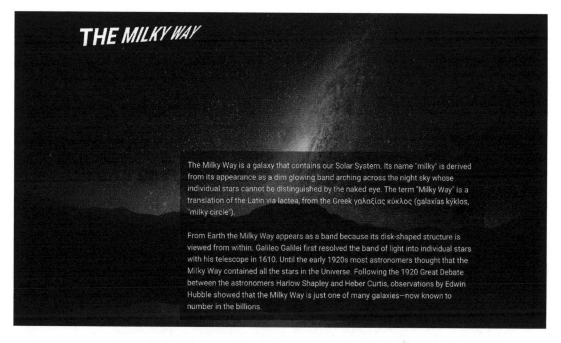

Figure 11-21. *Colorizing a background image with the* `luminosity` *blend mode*

```
.section-milkyway {
  background-image: url(img/milkyway.jpg);
  background-color: #202D53;
  background-blend-mode: luminosity;
}
```

▓ **Note**   If you are reading this in black-and-white print or on a monochrome e-reader: sorry! It's really hard to demonstrate color effects in those situations. You can find the working code in the example files from the book.

It's tricky to explain what each of the full 16 blend modes does without getting into the color math. Most of them only become useful in certain situations, like how luminosity allows you to colorize an image by mixing it with a solid color layer. In Figure 11-22 we have mixed the relatively dark blue background image with a light pink background color to show you the effects of each mode when the two layers have an exaggerated difference.

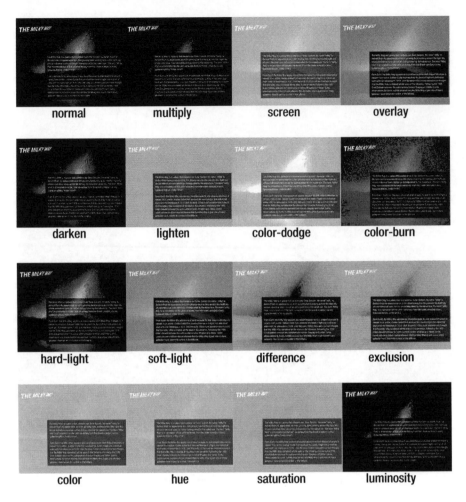

Figure 11-22. *The 16 blend modes*

If you want to dive deeper into the how each mode works, we recommend the article and video "The Ultimate Visual Guide to Understanding Blend Modes" by Pye Jirsa (`http://www.slrlounge.com/school/photoshop-blend-modes/`).

As we discussed in Chapter 5, you can have multiple background images per element, and backgrounds are stacked on top of each other in the reverse order they are declared in. The background color sits at the bottom of this stack of background layers. If you have more than one image layer, you can declare a comma-separated list of background blend modes, applied in turn between each layer and the ones below it.

Note that the background layers are not mixed with the content behind the element itself, regardless of the background transparency. You can't set a `background-blend-mode` for a single background color layer—mixing elements together is achieved via a separate property, and we'll tackle that next.

Blending Elements

Just as you can blend background layers, you can blend *elements* with their backdrop. This means either a statically positioned child element blending with its parent elements, or something like an absolutely positioned element overlapping another part of the page. The caveat is that elements that are in different stacking contexts do not blend with each other; we will examine that effect further in a moment.

The syntax is exactly the same as with its background counterpart, but the property is called `mix-blend-mode`. The Saturn image uses the `screen` blend mode to better fit in with the background color of the page section (see Figure 11-23).

Figure 11-23. *The Saturn image uses the* `screen` *blend mode to fit in better with the background*

```
.fig-planet {
  mix-blend-mode: screen;
}
```

The `screen` blend mode is another of the more immediately useful modes. It is named after projecting two images on top of another on the same screen, resulting in an overall lighter image. Where one image "shines" less light (i.e., is darker), any light from the second image shows through, and vice versa, generating an overall lighter image.

This means that white source parts will be completely opaque, but black source parts become transparent, making it useful as a masking technique. We can use this for some interesting "knock-out text" effects.

Typographic Lock-ups with Knock-Out Text

This see-through effect is exactly what we've done in the title for the "The Observable Universe" section title of the example page, shown in Figure 11-24.

The observable universe consists of the galaxies and other matter that can, in principle, be observed from Earth at the present time because light and other signals from these objects have had time to reach the Earth since the beginning of the cosmological expansion. Assuming the universe is isotropic, the distance to the edge of the observable universe is roughly the same in every direction. That is, the observable universe is a spherical volume (a ball) centered on the observer. Every location in the Universe has its own observable universe, which may or may not overlap with the one centered on Earth.

The word observable used in this sense does not depend on whether modern technology actually

Figure 11-24. *The "typographic lock-up" using* `screen` *blend mode*

The text sits on a white background positioned on top of the image. It is also part of what's sometimes called a "typographic lock-up," where the text is made to fit the container exactly, by sizing or spacing the text. CSS makes this effect a bit tricky. It will work with viewport-relative units, but even those have their drawbacks; for example, since viewport-relative units are not relative to the element itself, we will need to lock them down at a maximum breakpoint.

Instead, the example uses SVG text to achieve fluidly sizing text that is relative to the element size. The markup of the heading contains a snippet of SVG:

```
<h2 class="universe-title">
  <svg viewBox="0 0 400 120" role="presentation">
    <text>
      <tspan class="universe-span-1" x="6" dy="0.8em">The Observable</tspan>
      <tspan class="universe-span-2" x="3" dy="0.75em">Universe</tspan>
    </text>
  </svg>
</h2>
```

SVG text is a complex subject in itself, but to quickly note what the code is doing:

- SVG text is more like graphical objects, and does not flow like HTML content. Line breaks are not automatic, so each line needs to be wrapped in a `<tspan>` element and positioned by hand.

- Each `<tspan>` is positioned horizontally with the x attribute relative to the left edge of the SVG viewport.

- Text is positioned vertically from the *bottom* of the line box. If we want to keep the sizing flexible, we need to position each line vertically with an offset relative to its size, acting as a sort of line height. This is what the dy attribute is for.

- Text inside inline SVG should be perfectly accessible for screen readers—in theory. In practice, some assistive technologies have issues, but adding `role="presentation"` should maximize accessibility.

As the `<svg>` sits inline with our HTML, we can style it in our normal CSS. Note that text color in SVG is controlled with the `fill` property rather than `color`.

```
.universe-span-1 {
    font-size: 53.2px;
}
.universe-span-2 {
    font-size: 96.2px;
}
.universe-title text {
    fill: #602135;
    text-transform: uppercase;
}
```

Each `<tspan>` element is sized with pixels to exactly fill the space. What's important to note is that the pixel sizes are relative to the coordinate system of the SVG fragment, not the HTML. This means that as the SVG is resized with the page, the font size of the text follows, keeping the lock-up intact.

To keep the `<svg>` element itself sized consistently across browsers, we use the same aspect-ratio hack that we saw in Chapter 5. See the example code for the full details on this. The whole heading is then absolutely positioned on top of the image.

Finally, we add the blend mode to the title:

```
@supports (mix-blend-mode: screen) {
  .universe-title {
    mix-blend-mode: screen;
  }
    .universe-title text {
        fill: #000;
    }
}
```

The text inside the SVG was initially styled using a dark red color that goes well with the overall color of the image behind it. This works as a fallback for browsers without support for `mix-blend-mode` (see Figure 11-25). Inside the `@supports` rule, we set the blend mode, but also change the fill color of the text to black, making it fully transparent.

The observable universe consists of the galaxies and other matter that can, in principle, be observed from Earth at the present time because light and other signals from these objects have had time to reach the Earth since the beginning of the cosmological expansion. Assuming the universe is isotropic, the distance to the edge of the observable universe is roughly the same in every direction. That is, the observable universe is a spherical volume (a ball) centered on the observer. Every location in the Universe has its own observable universe, which may or may not overlap with the one centered on Earth.

The word observable used in this sense does not depend on whether modern technology actually

Figure 11-25. The heading as it appears in IE9, which does not support mix-blend-mode. *The SVG sizing works fine though, even in this older browser*

In general, blend modes are not too hard to apply with progressive enhancement in mind. The effects are mostly subtle, and where we do more drastic changes, the @supports rule is there to help. Blend modes for elements work in the latest versions of Chrome, Opera, and Firefox, as well as Safari (from 7.1 on Mac and in Mobile Safari from iOS8). Safari is however missing support for the luminosity, hue, and color blend modes. IE, Edge, Opera Mini, and Android WebKit browsers all lack support at the time of writing.

Isolation

Apart from blend modes, the other aspect of compositing we can control with CSS is *isolation*. In effect, this means creating groups of elements that blend within the group but not outside it. We mentioned earlier that elements in different stacking contexts (see Chapter 3) do not blend together.

In Figure 11-26, we have two examples of a group of items with a multiply blend mode applied. Each group sits on top of a patterned background. In the left example, the blend mode is not isolated, so the individual elements also blend with the background. In the right example, the figure has opacity: 0.999 set, which forces a new stacking context and isolates the blending.

Figure 11-26. The left group blends all the way through to the background, but the right group is isolated

```
.item {
  mix-blend-mode: multiply;
}
.group-b {
    opacity: 0.999;
}
```

The items in "group B" blend with each other, but not the background.

We can create new stacking contexts (and thus isolate groups) without hacking the `opacity`, using the new `isolation` property. The same result as above could be achieved with the following change:

```
.group-b {
    isolation: isolate;
}
```

Image Processing in CSS: Filters

The next tool for modern CSS is also straight out of image editing software: applying graphical filters to an element. Filters are applied to the whole element and its children. It's a bit like taking a screenshot of part of a page and then adjusting aspects of that image like you would in Photoshop. (In fact, this analogy is not far off from how browsers actually implement these things—we'll come back to that in Chapter 12.) Filters are available in WebKit- and Blink-based browsers like Safari, Chrome, and Opera, as well as Firefox and Edge, so support is reasonably broad. There are ten different filters available, plus the ability to define your own filters in SVG. We'll start by going through the predefined filters available in CSS.

Adjustable Color Manipulation Filters

Filters allow you to apply one or more effects to an element, in order. Some of these are more general color manipulation filters, allowing you to tweak lightness, contrast, saturation, etc. The following code snippet should be pretty self-describing (see Figure 11-27 for the results):

```
.universe-header {
  filter: grayscale(70%) brightness(0.7) contrast(2);
}
```

Figure 11-27. *The "Universe" header with a range of filters applied*

We have desaturated the element 70% of the way toward being fully grayscale, then decreased the brightness from 1 (normal brightness) to 0.7, and finally cranked up the contrast to double the normal value.

Most of the filters can take either a percentage or a number value. For values that can go both up and down like constrast(), brightness(), and saturation(), the default is 100% or 1. For grayscale(), invert(), and sepia(), the default is 0, going to 100% or 1. Any values higher than that are capped to the maximum value.

There's also an opacity() filter, which has a default of 1 (or 100%) and takes values down to 0. The difference between this filter and the opacity property is that the filter can have different results depending on where in the filter chain it is added. By contrast, the opacity property is always applied after all of the filters are applied. We will revisit the order of application later on in the chapter.

Finally, there are a few filters that work a little bit differently, and we'll examine them individually using examples from the "Stargazing" page.

Hue Rotation

The image of the Sun and its spots is actually a grayscale photo with a black background. This isn't the cheeriest of photos, and in most situations you'd pop open an image editor before even putting it on the page—as you should, as that is probably the best-performing route. For the purpose of illustrating how filters work, let's assume we don't have access to the image at all, only the CSS. Just like we colorized the background image earlier, we're going to colorize the Sun image and make it just a little brighter. Figure 11-28 shows the image without any filters applied.

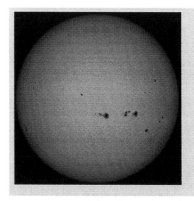

The Sun (in Greek: Helios, in Latin: Sol) is the star at the center of the Solar System and is by far the most important source of energy for life on Earth. It is a nearly perfect spherical ball of hot plasma,with internal convective motion that generates a magnetic field via a dynamo process. Its diameter is about 109 times that of Earth, and it has a mass about 330,000 times that of Earth, accounting for about 99.86% of the total mass of the Solar System.

The Sun is a G-type main-sequence star (G2V) based on spectral class and it is informally referred to as a yellow dwarf. It formed approximately 4.567 billion years ago from the gravitational collapse of matter within a region of a large molecular cloud. Most of this matter gathered in the center, whereas the rest flattened into an orbiting disk that became the

Figure 11-28. *The original astronomical photo of the Sun. Not very shiny*

The hue-rotate() filter lets us rotate all the hues of an image by a number of degrees, based on the standard color wheel. The bright yellows sit about 40 degrees (starting at the top) on this wheel, so hue-rotate(40deg) should do the trick. Problem is, the image is grayscale, so there's no hue to work with, and the hue rotation won't have any effect!

To solve this, we can use a trick involving another filter. The sepia() filter already colorizes the image with a brownish hue sitting at around 30 degrees on the color wheel. We can then chain this together with a hue rotation of about 10 degrees to arrive at the right yellow nuance. Finally, we need to lower the contrast and up the brightness a bit to make the sun shine. This needs to be done *before* the hue manipulations; otherwise the yellow becomes too washed out. Remember, filters are applied in order.

```
.fig-sun {
  filter: contrast(0.34) brightness(1.6) sepia(1) hue-rotate(10deg);
}
```

Next, we mask away the black background with the SVG masking technique we coved earlier, arriving at the result in Figure 11-29:

```
.fig-sun {
  filter: contrast(0.34) brightness(1.6) sepia(1) hue-rotate(10deg);
  mask: url(#circlemask); /* points to a circular SVG mask we created */
}
```

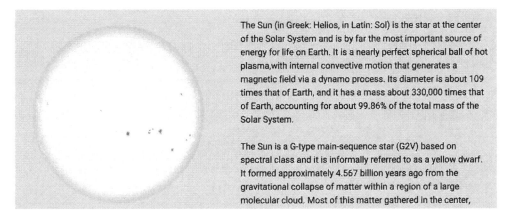

Figure 11-29. The filtered Sun image with mask applied

Drop-Shadows on Clipped Shapes

The next filter we're going to look at is `drop-shadow()`. This filter is very similar to the `box-shadow` and `text-shadow` properties, but it has some limitations as well as extra tricks up its sleeve.

Where a `box-shadow` is applied to the rectangular border-box shape of an element, the `drop-shadow()` filter applies to the transparency outline of an element. This includes things like putting shadows on images with alpha transparency and having them follow the contours of the image, or adding shadows to elements shaped with `clip-path`.

In the navigation menu of the Stargazing page, the items are clipped to different shapes and are then filtered with a `drop-shadow()` (see Figure 11-30 for the results). The syntax looks exactly like the `text-shadow` property: it includes x and y offsets, a blur radius, and a color. This means that the spread parameter that we find in `box-shadow` is missing here.

```
.nav-section li {
  filter: drop-shadow(0 0 .5em rgba(0,0,0,0.3));
}
```

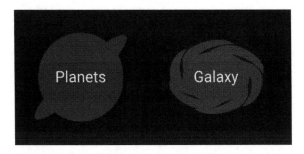

Figure 11-30. The navigation menu items have a drop-shadow effect around their clipped shapes. To the right, a hovered or focused element gets a lighter shadow, resulting in a glow effect

The CSS filter effects use the dedicated graphics chip when available. This makes the `drop-shadow()` filter surprisingly performant. For example, when animating a shadow, you may be better off to use the `filter` version rather than the `box-shadow` version. In Chapter 12, we'll dive deeper into the developer tools, and see how you can measure the impact of CSS properties of rendering. The next effect we'll cover is not so kind on performance.

The blur filter

The `blur()` filter applies a Gaussian blur to the element. You supply it with a length setting how far the blur radius spreads. In Figure 11-31, we have set a blur radius of 10px on the image of Saturn in the example page:

```
.fig-planet {
  filter: blur(10px);
}
```

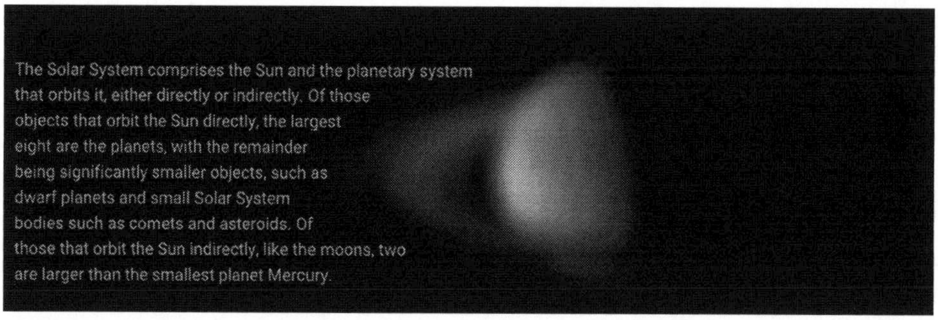

Figure 11-31. *Blurring the Saturn image*

The `blur()` filter tends to be a performance hog, at least in current implementations, so use it wisely. It's a bit of a shame, as blurring can make for some interesting animated effects. Blurring and focusing can be an effective tool when directing attention in an interface, or toning down something that's in the background.

Backdrop Filters

Speaking of backgrounds, there are a few other places where filters have snuck into CSS. In the "Milky Way" section of the example page, we have used an experimental property from the Level 2 Filter Effects spec: `backdrop-filter`.

It works exactly like the `filter` property, but it applies the filter in the compositing of the element background with the page behind it. This enables us to do some nice "frosted-glass" effects, for example (see Figure 11-32).

```
.section-milkyway .section-text {
  backdrop-filter: blur(5px);
  background-color: rgba(0,0,0,0.5);
}
```

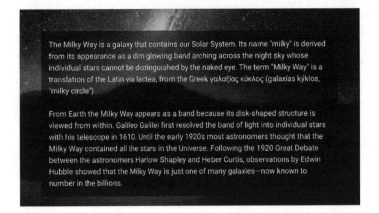

The Milky Way is a galaxy that contains our Solar System. Its name "milky" is derived from its appearance as a dim glowing band arching across the night sky whose individual stars cannot be distinguished by the naked eye. The term "Milky Way" is a translation of the Latin via lactea, from the Greek γαλαξίας κύκλος (galaxías kýklos, "milky circle").

From Earth the Milky Way appears as a band because its disk-shaped structure is viewed from within. Galileo Galilei first resolved the band of light into individual stars with his telescope in 1610. Until the early 1920s most astronomers thought that the Milky Way contained all the stars in the Universe. Following the 1920 Great Debate between the astronomers Harlow Shapley and Heber Curtis, observations by Edwin Hubble showed that the Milky Way is just one of many galaxies—now known to number in the billions.

Figure 11-32. *Applying a backdrop blur to the backdrop behind a semitransparent element*

This property so far is implemented only in very recent WebKit-based browsers like Safari 9 (as -webkit-backdrop-filter) and behind a flag in Google Chrome.

Filtered Background Images with the Image Filter Function

The Filter Effects spec also dictates that filters can be used when loading images in CSS. To filter a background image, you would run it through the filter() *function*. This function uses the same type of filter chain as the filter *property*, but does so when loading an image. The image is the first parameter, and the filter chain is the second.

For example, we can change the opacity of a background image and turn it grayscale (see Figure 11-33):

```
.figure-filtered {
  background-image: filter(url(img/saturn.png), grayscale(1) opacity(0.4));
}
```

Figure 11-33. *A component where we have changed the opacity of the background and turned it fully grayscale*

The bad news is browser support. At the time of writing, only recent experimental builds of the WebKit browser support this functionality. For some reason, all other browsers who have implemented filters have ignored the image filter function.

■ **Note**   Safari 9 does have a prefixed (and undocumented) version of the `filter()` function, but it is horribly broken, as the background cannot be resized properly. For that reason, stay away from the `-webkit-` prefix on this property.

Advanced Filters and SVG

In photo apps like Instagram, you can apply a precomposed filter to an image, often by combining color overlays and a few of the operations that we have seen in the shorthand filter functions so far. Developer and designer Una Kravets combined the Instagram filters into a small CSS library (`http://una.im/CSSgram/`), where the color overlays are created with clever use of pseudo-elements, CSS gradients, and blend modes (see Figure 11-34).

Figure 11-34. *Screenshot of a few of the filters from the CSSgram library*

One of the most powerful aspects of CSS filters is that we can use SVG to create custom filters just like these, with practically no limit to the complexity of the filter effect, and requiring less work in the CSS.

The CSS version of filters began life as filters in SVG. As with most of the other visual effects in this chapter, they started to bleed into HTML. First among the browsers was Firefox, letting us apply straight-up SVG filters to HTML content, using the same kind of techniques we've seen for clipping and masking. Then followed a specification for CSS filters in 2011—authored by Adobe, Apple, and Opera—that took the SVG filters and bundled them up into easy-to-use "shorthand" filter functions we have seen so far.

In fact, all of the CSS filter functions are defined in terms of their SVG counterparts. For example, a `filter: grayscale(100%);` declaration corresponds to this SVG filter:

```
<filter id="grayscale">
  <feColorMatrix type="matrix"
    values=".213 .715 .072 0 0
            .213 .715 .072 0 0
            .213 .715 .072 0 0
            0 0 0 1 0" />
</filter>
```

The preceding filter declaration consists of just one *filter primitive*, represented by a "Color Matrix" filter effect element (`<feColorMatrix>`). The color matrix filter is a very versatile tool, allowing you to map input colors to outputs in various ways. It's not important to know exactly what each value does, but the point is that `grayscale` itself is not a low-level thing, but the result of a general color manipulation—at least as far as SVG is concerned.

There are several other filter primitives, and most effects are the result of combining several. The `drop-shadow()` filter, for example, is composed of the filter primitives Gaussian Blur, Offset, Flood, Composite, and Merge.

Now, the interesting part is that we can author and apply our own SVG filters to HTML content. This means that we are free to create as complex filters as we like, as long as we define them in SVG and point to them as the source for our filters. This is done with the `url()` functional notation in our `filter` declarations, just like with masking and clipping. To show something slightly more complex, in Figure 11-35 we have re-created the "1977" filter from CSSgrams in SVG.

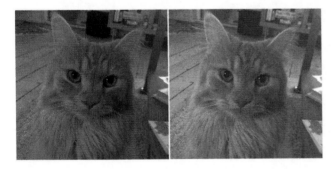

Figure 11-35. On the left the original image, on the right the filtered one

In the original code for the CSSgram version of the filter, there are three filter operations: `contrast(1.1) brightness(1.1) saturate(1.3)`. There are also a color overlay pseudo-element with a pink hue set to an `opacity` of `0.3` and a `mix-blend-mode` of `screen`. Since the filters are defined in the spec in terms of SVG, we can look up how to write them and calculate the values. It turns out we need two instances of a `feComponentTransfer` filter (for contrast and brightness) and a `feColorMatrix` filter for the saturation. We can create the color overlay with the `feFlood` filter, which creates a filter layer with a solid fill color. All of these are then merged together using an `feBlend` filter, where we set the blend mode to `screen`.

```
<filter id="filter-1977" color-interpolation-filters="sRGB">
  <feComponentTransfer result="contrastout">
    <feFuncR type="linear" slope="1.1" intercept="-0.05"/>
    <feFuncG type="linear" slope="1.1" intercept="-0.05"/>
    <feFuncB type="linear" slope="1.1" intercept="-0.05"/>
  </feComponentTransfer>
  <feComponentTransfer in="contrastout" result="brightnessout">
    <feFuncR type="linear" slope="1.1"/>
    <feFuncG type="linear" slope="1.1"/>
    <feFuncB type="linear" slope="1.1"/>
  </feComponentTransfer>
  <feColorMatrix in="brightnessout" type="saturate" values="1.3" result="img" />
  <feFlood flood-color="#F36ABC" flood-opacity="0.3" result="overlay" />
  <feBlend in="overlay" in2="img" mode="screen" />
</filter>
```

SVG filters allow you to "pipe" the results of various filters and filter primitives into each other by naming the inputs and outputs with the `in` and `result` attributes, respectively. The first filter primitive has no `in` defined, and defaults to using the source graphic as input.

We can now reference this snippet of SVG in CSS:

```
.filter-1977 {
  filter: url(#filter-1977);
}
```

SVG filters are chainable and composable. You can create noise, add lighting effects, and manipulate color channels to your heart's desire. The only limit is your imagination—and willingness to get into the somewhat arcane syntax. But beware of performance: SVG effects are not yet hardware accelerated in browsers, so use custom filters sparingly.

The same caveats apply: some browsers have restrictions on using external SVG fragment identifiers, so you may need to use the "all in one HTML file" technique for the time being.

SVG filters applied to HTML are supported everywhere that the "shorthand" CSS filters are supported, except Edge at the time of writing. Note that IE versions 10 and 11 do support filters *within* SVG, but not applied to HTML content.

Order of Application for Visual Effects

Since we could get different (and perhaps undesirable) results based on the order of clipping, masking, blending, and filtering, there is a standardized order of application for these properties.

All of clipping, masking, blending, and filtering come after any other properties (except `opacity`, which we'll get to in a second) have been set: `color`, `width`, `height`, `border`, `background` properties, etc. set the basic appearance of the element. Then comes the "post-processing" step with the advanced effects, where the element and its contents are effectively treated as a single image.

First, filters are applied in the order they are declared. Then the element is clipped, then masked. Note that since clipping and masking happen after filters are applied, we can't use the `drop-shadow()` filter directly on a clipped shape. Shadows (and the fringes of a blurred element, for example) will be clipped off. In the navigation for the Stargazing example, we have solved this by adding the clipping path to the links inside the items, but the drop-shadow to the item elements.

Finally, there's the compositing step, where blend modes are applied. They share this step with the `opacity` property, which is effectively a sort of blending in itself.

Summary

In this chapter, we have taken quite a big leap from the boring and boxy pages of yesteryear. We've explored how to shape the flow of our pages with CSS Shapes, and how to stamp out visual boundaries with clipping paths. Using masking, we can further control the visibility of the elements of our designs.

We have also taken a look at how to finally achieve the sort of blending of different layers that many designers are used to in graphics editing software, via CSS blend modes.

CSS filters are starting to add even more of the effects we have come to expect from the graphical world into the design we can actually affect in the browser.

Throughout a lot of these effects, we have seen how CSS is being harmonized with the powerful graphics editing of SVG, letting us push the envelope on what web design can be.

After this firmly visually focused chapter, we will shift to looking at CSS as software: how to write modular, readable, and maintainable code.

CHAPTER 12

▨ ▨ ▨

Code Quality and Workflow

Throughout this book, we have dealt with various techniques and the (many!) different specifications and properties of CSS. In the process, we have touched on some useful ways of thinking responsibly about these solutions. In this final chapter, we will revisit some of these approaches to dive deeper into the reasons why some are better than others.

CSS mastery is about writing markup and styles that not only work (and work well), but also have qualities like readability, portability, and maintainability. We aim to give you all the knowledge you need to address the more complex aspects of writing great CSS in this last chapter.

For the most part, we won't introduce much in the way of new standards, but will instead switch between theory and some practical examples. Toward the end of the chapter, we'll explore some tools for working efficiently with your code, as well as give you a glimpse of the future of the language.

In this chapter, we will cover the following subjects to help you write better CSS:

- How browsers go from style sheets to rendered web page

- How to use the developer tools to help optimize rendering performance

- Managing the cascade by limiting selector types and selector depth

- Naming schemes and balancing complexity in HTML vs. CSS

- Tools like linters, preprocessors, and build systems to handle complex CSS

- Future standards like custom properties, HTTP/2, and Web Components

Debugging CSS: External Code Quality

In this section, we'll explain how browsers work with HTML and CSS, and how we can use that knowledge to address problems like rendering performance.

These aspects of code are sometimes called *external* code quality—things that are noticeable for the person using the end result. A few important ones include:

- **Correctness:** Is the code working as intended? Did we type in the right property name in the CSS, and does the browser understand it?

- **Usability:** Does the code result in something that not only looks right, but can be used? Accessibility falls into this category, for example.

- **Robustness:** What happens if something goes wrong? As an example, we might declare two sets of properties, where one is a fallback for older browsers.

- **Performance:** Is the design fast to load, and do animations and scrolling work smoothly?

© Andy Budd and Emil Björklund 2016
A. Budd and E. Björklund, *CSS Mastery*, DOI 10.1007/978-1-4302-5864-3_12

Some of these qualities are a matter of having the right mindset before writing any code, and we've tried to demonstrate good principles for usability and robustness throughout this book. When coding a real-world project, you will need to think deeply about what correctness and good performance means for each unique component. This is a great place to use the developer tools built into most browsers.

We've seen in previous chapters how we can use these tools to view which properties are applied to an element or debug animations. Developer tools are constantly being improved, and we can use them for much more than this. For example, Figure 12-1 shows how we can use the developer tools in Firefox to find out exactly which font file was used, not just what the font stack declaration was.

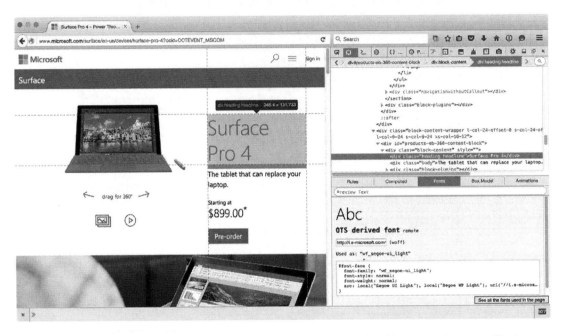

Figure 12-1. *Using the Firefox developer tools to find out exactly which font file gets used on a specific element on* http://www.microsoft.com

Digging further into the developer tools, you will find panels and buttons that let you inspect other qualities. This enables you to see not just what gets applied, but how and when. To understand those tools, it helps to know a little bit about how browsers parse CSS.

How Browsers Interpret CSS

What follows is a whirlwind tour of the process from CSS file to "pixels on screen," in order to better understand the impact of the CSS we write. The steps described in the following sections represent a simplified model of what happens every time a new page is loaded, but some (or all) of the steps may happen when the page is interacted with as well.

Parsing Files and Constructing Object Models

When you load a site, the browser receives an HTML response first of all. This response is interpreted into objects (nodes) that have relationships to each other. For example, the body node is a descendant of the html node, and p and h1 nodes might exist inside the body node. This is the DOM: the Document Object Model (see Figure 12-2).

HTML source

```
<html lang="en">
<head>
  <meta charset="UTF-8">
  <title>Test Document</title>
</head>
<body>
  <h1>This is a test</h1>
  <p>This is a paragraph</p>
  <p>This is another paragraph</p>
</body>
</html>
```

Document Object Model

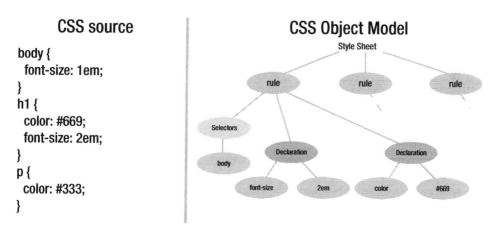

Figure 12-2. *The Document Object Model is how the browser understands the HTML internally*

When a link element pointing to a CSS file is encountered inside an HTML document, the browser will fetch and parse that file. Similar to how the HTML is turned into a DOM tree, the CSS file is parsed into something called the CSSOM: the CSS Object Model. Not just external files, but any CSS inside a `style` element or an inline `style` attribute will be parsed and added to the CSSOM. Just like the DOM, it is a tree-like structure, containing the combined hierarchy of styles for the page (see Figure 12-3).

CSS source

```
body {
  font-size: 1em;
}
h1 {
  color: #669;
  font-size: 2em;
}
p {
  color: #333;
}
```

CSS Object Model

Figure 12-3. *The CSSOM tree represents the hierarchy of styles in a style sheet*

Each DOM node is matched with the relevant CSS selectors, and the final style calculation is made (on the basis of things like cascade, inheritance, and specificity).

The DOM and CSSOM are both standardized, and are supposed to work the same across browsers. After this step, it's up to the browser how to go from the data it now has to what's shown on the screen, but all browsers follow similar steps to achieve that.

373

The Render Tree

The next step in rendering the page is constructing yet another tree structure, usually called the *render tree*. Here, each object represents something to be rendered on the screen. This structure will look somewhat like the tree for the DOM, but they are not equal. For example, visually hidden DOM nodes will not be present in the render tree, and pseudo-elements like ::before may have a render object without being in the DOM. The browser will also need to represent other aspects of the visual representation of the page, like scrolling blocks and the viewport (see Figure 12-4).

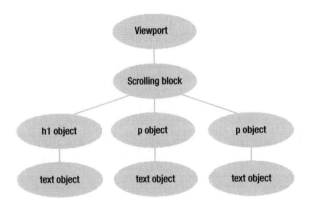

Figure 12-4. *A simplified hypothetical render tree. Elements like head,* title, *and* meta *do not have their own render objects. The same would go for elements with* display: none, *for example*

When the render tree is constructed, each object in the render tree knows what color it's supposed to be, what font any text is in, if it has an explicit width, etc.

Layout

In the next stage, the geometric properties of each render object are calculated. This is known as the *layout* or *reflow* stage. The browser will go through the render tree and try to figure out where to fit each item on the page.

Since a lot of web layout is about keeping the flow of the page, where elements "push" on other elements, this can get quite complex. Figure 12-5 is from a fascinating video (https://www.youtube.com/watch?v=dndeRnzkJDU) by programmer Satoshi Ueyama, who hacked the Gecko engine to show a visualization of the actual reflow operations that Firefox does when laying out a site.

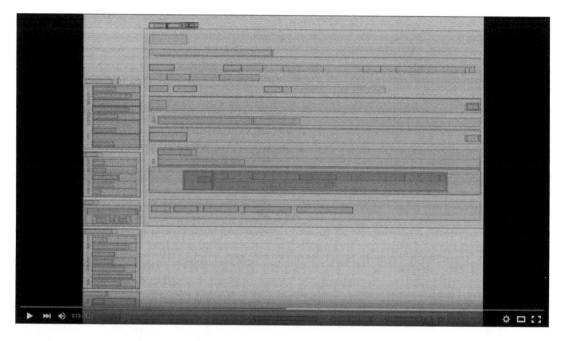

Figure 12-5. *Screenshot from a video visualizing the slowed-down reflow of* http://www.wikipedia.org *in Firefox*

Sometimes, additional rendering objects with their own rendering properties will need to be constructed at this stage. For example, a piece of text with a certain font size may generate a line break, which splits it into two anonymous line boxes. This in turn influences the final height of the parent element, and the other elements following it.

Eventually, the position of each render object will be calculated, and it's time to put them on the screen.

Painting, Compositing, and Drawing

In a very simplified model, the browser now takes everything it can learn from the render tree and puts the visual representation on screen. In reality, things are a little more complicated.

When the position and properties of every render object are determined, the browser can figure out the actual pixels that are to be shown on the screen, a process known as *painting*. But in addition to this, the browser may need to do some further work.

When the browser knows that a certain part of the final graphic representation can't influence the display of the rest of the page, it may decide to split the work of painting into different tasks, each responsible for a specific part of the page known as a *layer*.

Some things, like 3D transforms, may even be hardware accelerated by using the dedicated graphics chip. Others may have filters or blend modes applied that will determine how they mix with other layers. This task of splitting up the rendering into layers and then recombining them into the final result is called *compositing*. If the page were made of tracing paper, this would be the equivalent of drawing on different pieces and then gluing them together on top of each other.

Finally, the page is ready to be displayed (or *drawn*) on the screen. Phew!

Optimizing Rendering Performance

If anything in the page changes, the browser will need to do some of the preceding steps again. In order to keep the page appearing smoothly on the screen, it should preferably do so in under about 16 milliseconds—the amount of time between each update of the screen, providing it has standard 60hz refresh rate.

Some things are usually very cheap from a performance perspective, like scrolling: the entire final rendering is just redrawn at different positions. When something causes the styles of the page to change, things get a little more performance heavy.

If we change the `width` or `height` properties of an element in JavaScript, the browser would need to do layout, compositing, and paint. Changing only the color of text doesn't affect layout, so it triggers painting and compositing. Finally, the cheapest operation we can make is one that is entirely done by compositing.

The site `https://csstriggers.com` is a handy reference of which property maps to which rendering operations (see Figure 12-6). The site (by Paul Lewis) currently tracks rendering operations in Google Chrome, but they are likely to work similarly in most browsers.

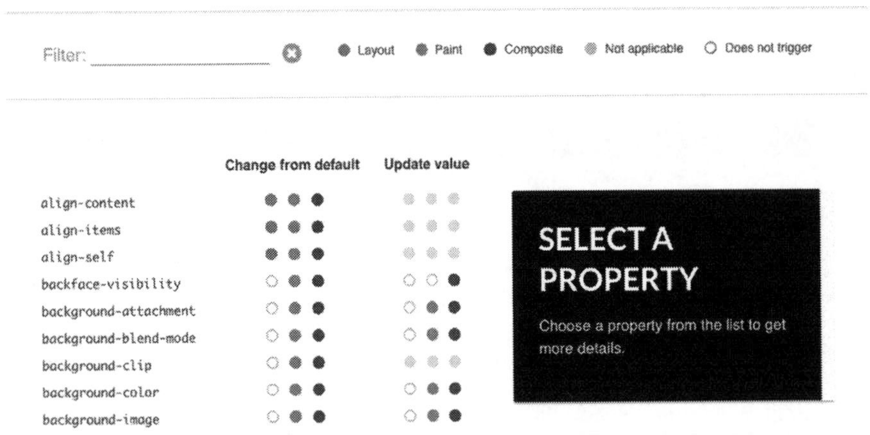

Figure 12-6. *CSS properties and how much work they trigger in the browser, from* `https://csstriggers.com`

We can use the developer tools to see when these different steps are performed, and what the resulting performance is like. By going to the Timeline panel in the Chrome DevTools, we can record as we interact with the page and track if the interactions trigger specific rendering steps. Other browsers also have timeline recording features, but the Chrome DevTools have historically been the most feature-rich. In Figure 12-7, we have recorded a 1.5-second timeline of us scrolling an example page, where a fixed header is animated into view, while scrolling.

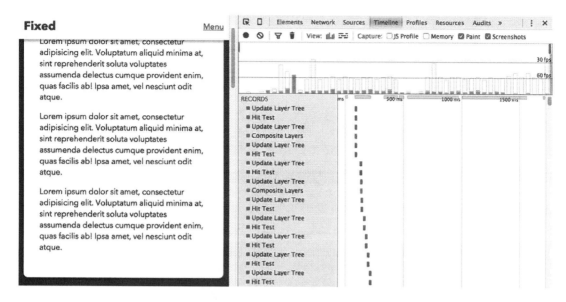

Figure 12-7. *A timeline recording in the Chrome DevTools. The recording is started and stopped by clicking the circular icon in the right-side panel*

We can zoom in to the level of individual frames, and determine what kind of operations are going on inside the browser. Each bar represents a rendered frame, and the colored bits of each bar represent a rendering operation. In this instance, green represents a paint operation. Below the timeline, each operation is listed, and we can click each row to get even more detail.

As the timeline shows, something is causing paint operations in every frame. It's not horrible, but it might prevent smooth scrolling on slower machines, and should not need to happen on scrolling. To figure out what's going on, we can turn on something called "paint flashing" in the Rendering tab. The browser will then draw a color highlight around any areas that are repainted, as we interact with the page (see Figure 12-8).

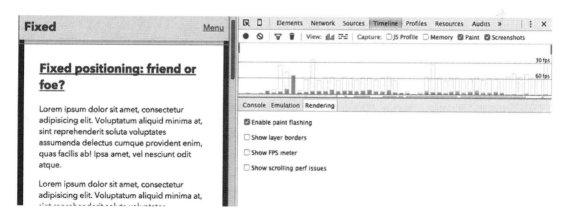

Figure 12-8. *Turning on paint flashing reveals that the fixed header is repainted as we scroll*

The fixed header is constantly repainted as we scroll, since it affects the scrolling content underneath it. Luckily, the browser optimizes the painted area, so at least it's not the entire page. But we can do even better, by forcing the browser to render the fixed part in a separate layer, and only do compositing. The current styles for the header look something like this:

```
.page-head {
    position: fixed;
    top: 0;
    left: 0;
    width: 100%;
    transition: top .25s ease-in-out;
}
.page-head-hide {
    top: -3.125em;
}
```

The .page-head-hide rule is toggled via JavaScript, and moves the header out of the viewport when we're scrolling down, and back into view as we scroll up.

The trick to avoiding paint is to force the browser to create a separate, hardware-accelerated layer for rendering the header, and then just composite it together with the rest of the page. We're going to use the will-change property to do this. This property provides a hint to the browser that this element will be updating the transform property in the future. A transform property doesn't create a new layer on its own, but animated transforms do. When the browser gets the preview hint that the header will animate in the future, it will create a new layer right from the start.

This means that we can transition the transform property rather than the top property, and kill two birds with one stone: both scrolling performance and animation performance will benefit.

The new styles look like this:

```
.page-head {
    /* some styles left out for brevity */
    transition: transform .25s ease-in-out;
    transform: translateY(0);
    will-change: transform;
}

.page-head-hide {
    transform: translateY(-100%);
}
```

Rerunning the timeline recording now shows that there is no painting going on. We can also verify that a separate layer is created, by turning on the "Show layer borders" option inside the Rendering tab. The header should now have a colored border around it (see Figure 12-9).

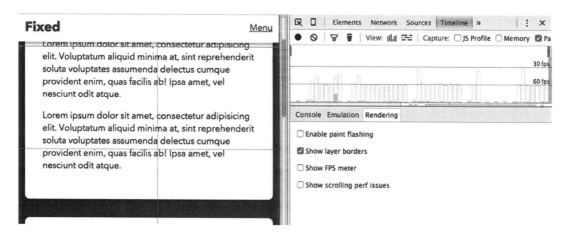

Figure 12-9. *The timeline is now showing no paint operations going on as we scroll. Turning on "Show layer borders" draws a colored outline around the header layer*

■ **Note** The `will-change` property is supported in recent versions of Firefox, Safari, Chrome, and Opera at the time of writing. For a more backward-compatible technique, you can use a 3D transform to move the header, which also forces a separate layer.

The ability to use developer tools to peek into browser internals like this hasn't been around for long, and the tools to discover exactly what's going on behind the scenes are improving in leaps and bounds. You won't have to go into this much detail for every single rule in your project, but to understand how CSS works (and why some things are more expensive than others), a grasp on browser rendering and debugging is invaluable.

CSS for Humans: Internal Code Quality

We should always consider the needs of users over the convenience of developers, so it makes sense to put a lot of effort into securing the external qualities of our code.

It might seem like a contradiction in terms, then, that some would probably argue that *internal* code qualities are even more important. To name a few internal quality markers:

- **How DRY ("Don't Repeat Yourself") is the code:** Is each unique problem solved in one place, or would you have to update lots of different places if you change one solution?

- **Readability:** Can someone understand what the code does easily when reading it?

- **Portability:** Will a piece of your code work only if combined with other parts of your codebase, or does it stand on its own?

- **Modularity:** Can you combine and reuse parts of your code into new things in a self-evident way?

The reason these qualities are so important is that they affect the person writing or changing the code. If there is a problem with the external quality (a bug) and no one can understand the source code that caused the bug, you won't know how to fix it. High external quality is usually a consequence of high internal quality, but the inverse is rarely true.

Internal code quality is also much more subjective and based on personal preference as well as the properties of each individual project. So, put your critical goggles on, and let's explore!

Understanding the Shape of CSS

CSS was constructed with several design principles in mind. One of the most important principles is simplicity: CSS is meant to be easy to learn. You shouldn't need a computer science degree to use it. As a designer you should be able to get to grips with selecting a piece of a page and applying styles to that piece. This doesn't require extensive knowledge of software construction.

Viewing CSS as Software

At the same time, CSS is *also* software. As software, it has qualities beyond just working. For a quick prototype, the quality of the code is largely irrelevant as long as it does the job. But as soon as something is made part of a living product, the quality of the code may have wide repercussions. It will affect things like how costly it is to maintain over time, how likely it is that new bugs will appear, and how easy it is to work with for new developers.

Even if the thing you are creating is a one-person project, it's healthy to assume that there are at least two people on the team: you, and the *future you*. When you're fixing some bug in a few months or years, you will likely have forgotten what the heck you were thinking when you initially crafted the code.

Bring your Own Structure

CSS is often described as a *declarative* language. In simplified terms, this means that you use it to tell a computer *what* to do, limited to a set of things that the language knows how to do. In contrast, many general-purpose programming languages are more *imperative*, meaning that you use them to tell the computer step-by-step instructions of exactly *how* (and in what order) it should go about doing things.

Many imperative programming languages are equipped with a small number of building blocks that allow for new kinds of control structures and logic, specific to your code. Not so in CSS: it has functions that you can call, like the url() function, but it lacks the building blocks that would allow you to define your own functions.

All of the CSS that gets added to a document is also sharing a global scope. If you have a rule with the selector p, it will factor into the style calculation for all paragraph elements, no matter which style sheet it originated from or how it was loaded. The selector determines the scope of each *rule*, but the connection between the style sheet and the document is always global. For example, you can't create a CSS file containing a p selector and load it in a way that only applies it to paragraphs in one part of the page. (This model *does* exist in the world of Web Components, which is a technology still in its infancy. Well get back to Web Components toward the end of the chapter.)

THE SCOPED ATTRIBUTE

There *is* one way to style a section of a page with its own isolated styles: the `scoped` attribute on a `style` element. It's a rather clumsy mechanism, and browser makers have been hesitant to implement it (so far only Firefox is on board).

The `style` element when using `scoped` is limited to apply only to the parent element or child elements within it. In the following markup, only the inner `<p>` will be red:

```
<p>I will not be red</p>
<div>
  <p>I will be red.</p>
  <style scoped>
    p { color: red; }
  </style>
</div>
```

While this is a handy concept, it will work poorly with regard to backward compatibility—nonsupporting browsers will apply the styles globally anyway.

Many programming languages have the concept of *namespaces*: isolated contexts where code is unable to influence or be influenced by the outside world, unless explicitly imported or exported. This makes it easier to manage bits of a code base without unintended consequences elsewhere.

The simpler model of the CSS language means that any structure we want to impose must come from the way we write our rules. In the next part of this chapter, we'll look at a simple example and try to derive some guidelines for writing CSS with high internal quality.

Code Quality: an Example

The alert message boxes in Figure 12-10 all look exactly the same, but they are implemented differently. When we look at the source code, we hope that some of the theoretical talk about internal code quality will become clearer.

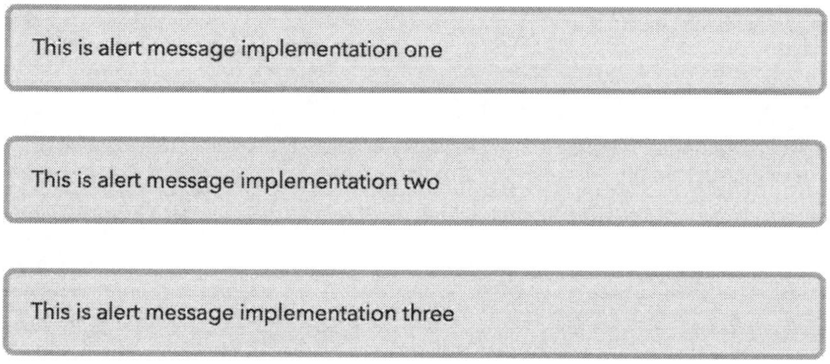

This is alert message implementation one

This is alert message implementation two

This is alert message implementation three

Figure 12-10. *An alert message box, implemented in three slightly different ways*

The first implementation uses the following markup and CSS:

```
<div id="pink-box">
   <p>This is alert message implementation one</p>
</div>
div#pink-box {
  border-radius: .5em;
  padding: 1em;
  border: .25em solid #D9C7CC;
  background-color: #FFEDED;
  color: #373334;
}
```

The first thing to note is the use of an id in the selector. This prevents the reuse of this selector anywhere else on the page, which is unnecessarily limiting. There is nothing wrong with using id attributes per se: they are great for in-page links or JavaScript hooks. There's nothing preventing you from using them as CSS selectors either, but the high specificity (as we discussed way back in Chapter 2) makes it troublesome to override any variations of the rule. Something like a message component is likely to be both overridden and repeated on the page, so in this case an ID is definitely a problem.

Furthermore, we've added a completely unnecessarily div qualifier to the selector, which does nothing but increase the specificity even more in this case. It's common to see element selectors used together with ids or classes in this way—usually it's a result of trying to override some all-too specific rule somewhere else. Often, the solution is not to escalate the specificity "arms race" but to rethink your naming strategy.

Another thing to note is the id attribute name: #pink-box is describing a specific property of the alert message box. We could decide to change the warning message to a white box with a red icon inside instead, and the class name would no longer make sense.

In terms of the style declarations, there's nothing wrong with them per se: there's font-relative sizing for the border, padding, and border-radius properties, and some colors for text, border, and background. We can do better though, and looking at the second implementation, we will highlight some clear differences:

```
<div class="warning-message">
  <p>This is alert message implementation two</p>
</div>
.warning-message {
  border-radius: .5em;
  padding: 1em;
  border: .25em solid rgba(0, 0, 0, 0.15);
  background-color: #FFEDED;
  color: rgba(0, 0, 0, 0.8);
}
```

Here, the class name is much clearer in purpose: it is a warning message component, and the implementation details are left out of the name. The colors are defined differently: the different shades of the text and border are both generated using a semitransparent black when mixed with the pink background. This means that we could change only the background color and get the other two shades for free—one less place to update the code.

But the name is still kind of specific to one style of message box. If we had a success message box rule where we wanted to override the color, it wouldn't make sense for it to also have a class name starting with warning in the markup. The third example fixes this:

```
<div class="message message-warning">
  <p>This is alert message implementation three</p>
</div>
.message {
  border-radius: .5em;
  padding: 1em;
  border: .25em solid rgba(0, 0, 0, 0.15);
  background-color: #ffffed;
  color: rgba(0, 0, 0, 0.8);
}
.message-warning {
  background-color: #FFEDED;
}
```

At first sight, this example uses more code to do the same thing. The trick is that the .message rule is actually a neutral message style with a faint yellow color. The .message-warning rule turns the generic message into a warning message by changing the one thing that's different—the background color.

We can easily create other types of message rules by deciding on other names, like a green .message-success rule (see Figure 12-11):

```
.message-success {
  background-color: #edffed;
}
```

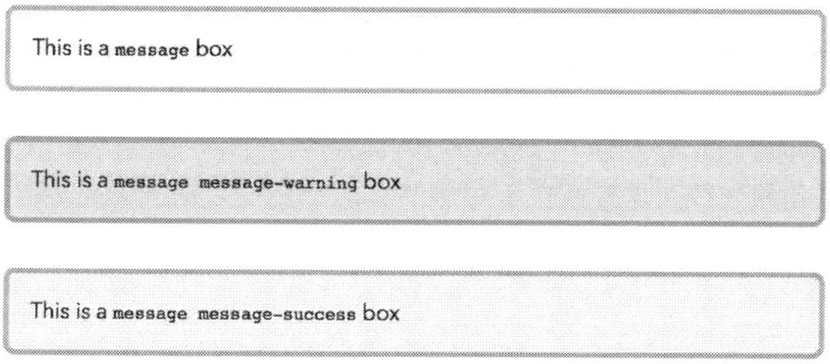

Figure 12-11. *A smart structure allows us to quickly create other flavors of message boxes*

By structuring the code this way, we get a number of benefits:

- The semitransparent text and borders allow us to create new variations with just a single declaration.

- The name message is related to the functionality of this component rather than the end result (a box of a certain color scheme). Hopefully, the name is also clear in its purpose to people who are new to the code.

- By starting the class names for variations of the component with the base name (.message in this case) and keeping them together in the CSS file, it becomes easier to visually scan the file and recognize the purpose of these rules.

The initial three variations of the message box were perfectly valid and externally equivalent in terms of how they looked in a browser. By structuring the code, giving it a different set of names, and carefully choosing how to apply the properties, the final implementation differed substantially in terms of quality. For the remainder of this part of the chapter we will dive deeper into some of the common patterns, methods, and tools for writing high-quality CSS.

Managing the Cascade

We can begin to extract a few principles from the previous message example to help improve the quality of our code:

- Use class names as the primary styling hook

- Make class names readable and clear

- Avoid unnecessary repetition by breaking out single-purpose rules

- Avoid tying the type of element to the style rule

All of these have one thing in common: they limit the effects of the cascade, mostly by managing specificity.

Why this focus on limiting the use of one of the most powerful features of the language? To some extent, the question answers itself, as any power tool needs to come with safety instructions—"aim away from body when using." But the cascade was also invented for a specific purpose: allowing a mix of style rule sources (user agent defaults, author rules, and user rules) to determine the final presentation of a document.

We use the word "document" here for a reason—at the time when CSS was invented, the Web was predominantly seen as a technology for sharing text documents. CSS allowed an elegant way to promote consistency through cascading and inheritance. It also brought concepts like user style sheets: if the user is more comfortable reading web pages with a high-contrast style sheet, they can override the author styles.

While the Web still has the underlying architecture of a document model, it is now being used to create more advanced visual designs and user interfaces. In practice, this has meant a shift in importance toward the author styles. As these become more complex, there has been a movement toward compartmentalizing them, making them more portable, self-contained, and predictable. The principles listed earlier are a starting point for achieving that purpose. In the next section, we will look at CSS from a slightly different angle, working out how we can take these principles even further.

Structured Naming Schemes and CSS Methodologies

In the message example earlier, we started the class names with `.message-`. This idea of a "prefix" not only makes the code more readable, but also organizes the code in a way resembling the namespace idea.

There are several people and organizations that have taken on the task of coming up with methodologies that encapsulate the quality principles outlined so far, often coupled with this kind of structured naming scheme, as a way to guide CSS authors. You may have stumbled upon names like OOCSS, SMACSS, or BEM, as they have been immensely popular for a few years now.

OOCSS

OOCSS stands for Object Oriented CSS, and it is an approach to writing CSS created by Nicole Sullivan in 2009. It was in many ways the starting point of a wave of exploring how to write CSS from the perspective of maintainable software. With OOCSS, Nicole used metaphors from object-oriented programming, where reusable class names associated with well-defined rule sets in CSS act as a way to create hierarchies of objects.

In OOCSS, class names are used (on top of a foundation of semantically correct HTML) as the primary mechanism to explain what the purpose of the component is in the UI. Nicole calls this "visual semantics."

Perhaps the most famous example from the OOCSS mindset is the "media object" that we encountered first in Chapter 3—a common pattern of an image, video, or other media sitting next to a block of text (see Figure 12-12). By extracting this pattern to a single object and sprinkling the class names where needed, Nicole showed that a lot of repetition could be cut from your CSS.

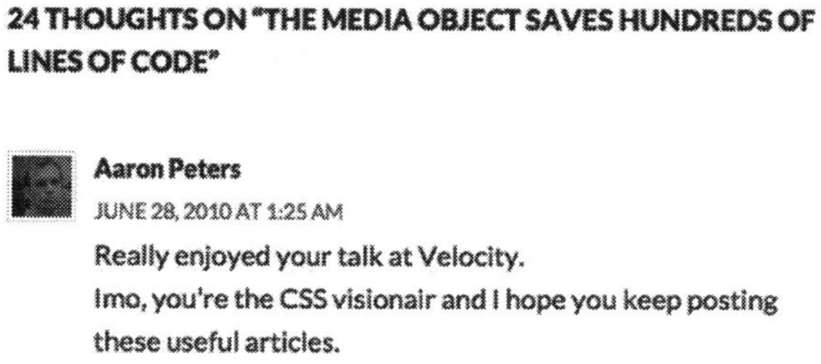

24 THOUGHTS ON "THE MEDIA OBJECT SAVES HUNDREDS OF LINES OF CODE"

 Aaron Peters
JUNE 28, 2010 AT 1:25 AM
Really enjoyed your talk at Velocity.
Imo, you're the CSS visionair and I hope you keep posting these useful articles.

Figure 12-12. Screenshot from the comment section of Nicole Sullivan's article on the "media object," where each comment actually illustrates the principle of the pattern

OOCSS includes the advice to separate "skin from structure" and "container from content." Separating skin from structure means that you should try to avoid writing rules that do things like typography and colors (skin) as well as positioning, floats, etc. (structure). In those cases, you might be better off creating a separate rule and class name for each aspect. For example, the "media object" takes care of the layout of a floated image and the associated text, while the colors and typography are attached to the component itself. The following markup for a blog post teaser illustrates the combination of classes in the markup:

```
<article class="media-block post-teaser">
    <div class="media-body post-teaser-body">
        <h2 class="post-title">Media object</h2>
        <p>Article text goes here…</p>
    </div>
    <img class="media-fig" src="" alt="">
</article>
```

The post- classes could represent the "skin" of this component, and the media object pattern has its own class names.

The separation of "container from content" can be seen in the grid strategy we saw in Chapter 7. By applying the styles for how the component fits into the layout of the page to a technically redundant outer element (.col), we eliminate the risk of collision with the styles of the component itself:

```
<div class="row row-trio">
  <div class="col">
    <article class="media-block post-teaser">
      <div class="media-body post-teaser-body">
        <h2 class="post-title">Post teaser heading</h2>
        <p>Article text goes here...</p>
      </div>
      <img class="media-fig post-fig" src="" alt="">
    </article>
  </div>
  <!-- ..and so on, more post-teasers here.
</div>
```

SMACSS

Scalable and Modular Architecture for CSS, or SMACSS for short, is an approach created by Jonathan Snook while working at Yahoo. It has a lot of similarities to OOCSS, like advocating class names and component-focused rule sets as the primary mechanism to create a hierarchy of UI elements, as well as avoiding specificity clashes. Jonathan focuses the SMACSS thinking a little differently, by introducing a categorization of rules:

- Base styles, giving a default style to HTML elements as well as variations based on element attributes.

- Layout styles, handling grid systems and other layout helpers, similar to the abstractions we saw in Chapter 6 ("rows," "columns," etc.).

- Module styles, consisting of all rules that make up the components specific to the site you're building: products and product lists, site headers, etc. This is where the bulk of your styles are likely to end up.

- States, which are overrides that change the appearance of existing modules. For example, a menu item can be active or inactive.

In adhering to this classification of rules, SMACSS encourages you to think about how you name things, and where they fit. These rules should normally be included in your style sheet in the order described, so that they go from most generic to most specific. This is another part of avoiding specificity battles, and using the cascade in a sensible way.

Apart from the categorization of styles, the SMACSS methodology also advocates using prefixes to some of your class names in order to more clearly signal the intended purpose. In Chapter 6 we talked about layout helpers, and used names like .row and .col. SMACSS recommends that you prefix such classes with something that communicates their nature, like .l- for Layout:

```
.l-row { /* row container */ }
.l-row-trio { /* row with three equally weighted "columns"  */ }
.l-col { /* column container */ }
/* ...etc */
```

Similarly, you can clarify state prefixes with `is-`, so a component named `.productlist` in a disabled state could be targeted with something like `.is-productlist-disabled` or `.productlist-is-disabled`. Components themselves use no specific prefix, but the name of the component itself can act as a prefix for any subcomponents:

```
.productlist { /* styles for the product list container */ }
.productlist-item { /* item container in the list */ }
.productlist-itemimage { /* image inside a product list item */ }
```

BEM

Where OOCSS and SMACSS can be seen as a more of frameworks for thinking about structured CSS combined with some handy rules of thumb, BEM is a much more rigid system for how to author and name your styles.

BEM is originally an application development methodology from the search engine company Yandex. It includes several conventions, libraries, and tools for how to structure UI in large-scale web applications. The naming convention used in these applications has become synonymous with the word BEM in the context of HTML and CSS.

The acronym BEM stands for *Block, Element, Modifier*. The block is the top-level abstraction, comparable to a module in SMACSS or an object in OOCSS. Anything remotely self-contained can be described as a block. Elements are subcomponents of a block—not to be confused with pure HTML elements. Finally, modifiers are different states or variations of a block or element.

Blocks, elements, and modifiers in BEM are written in lowercase with dashes separating multiword items:

```
.product-list { /* this is a block name */ }
```

Elements inside blocks are separated with two underscores:

```
.product-list__item { /* this is the item element inside the product list */ }
```

Modifiers are added with single underscores, and can modify either blocks or elements:

```
.product-list_featured { /* product list variation */ }
.product-list_featured__item { /* item inside featured product list */ }
.product-list__item_sold-out { /* Sold out item inside normal product list */ }
```

There are also several variations of this syntax. Developer Harry Roberts uses a variation where modifiers are delimited with double dashes instead of a single underscore:

```
.product-list__item--sold-out {}
```

Harry has also written extensively on his website (`http://csswizardry.com`) about how to work with these types of naming schemes, including various ways of combining BEM syntax with prefixes. (He has also written a comprehensive resource on writing high-quality CSS, including how to structure and name things, available at `http://cssguidelin.es`.)

Regardless of which syntax you choose, the main idea of BEM is to be immediately able to identify the type of rule associated with a certain class name, as long as you know the naming scheme used. This also helps to keep the code focused. If a single class gets too many responsibilities, it will start to clash with the explicit purpose of the name. This acts as a signal to rethink the abstraction. There is nothing stopping you from breaking out a complex part of a block into its own nested block, which in turn invites further reusability.

Managing Complexity

The bottom line for all of the guidelines and methodologies we have described so far can be summarized as aiming to *manage complexity*. Anything beyond a trivial piece of code gets complex fast, so we can either dramatically limit the scope (by only allowing a much simpler design) or break the complex parts down into simpler chunks.

Using naming schemes and class names that represent UI behavior makes the CSS easier to understand, but it doesn't make the overall complexity go away. Instead, it shifts some of the complexity over to the HTML. It may do so in varying degrees, and for different parts of a web page or site, but it always does. To understand why this is, we need to backtrack a bit, to when CSS was introduced.

Separation of Concerns

As the Web moved from a soup of `<font>` and `<center>` tags to a model were CSS dictated the presentation, there was a huge push for companies to start using CSS and to keep HTML pure, free from any mention of how the document was to be presented.

Sites like CSS Zen Garden (`http://www.csszengarden.com/`; see Figure 12-13) did a great deal to convince designers and developers of the value of semantic markup and the power of CSS. Viewing the presentation as independent from the markup of the underlying document is a good illustration of the software design principle of *separation of concerns* (SoC): markup should not include presentation nor be dependent on the presentation layer, and the two layers should have as little intermingling as possible. This is something built into the Web itself: the basic representation of a web page should make sense even if the CSS (or JavaScript, for that matter) is not there.

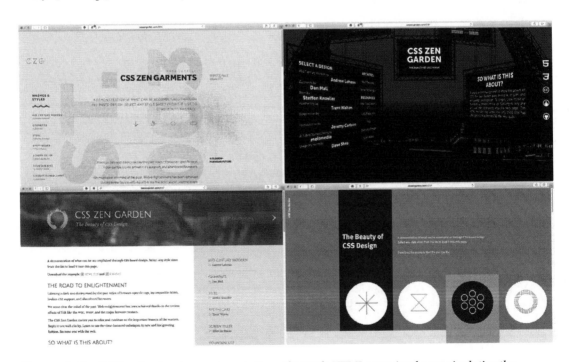

Figure 12-13. *CSS Zen Garden showcases variations of a single HTML page, just by manipulating the CSS—sometimes with very clever use of pseudo-content*

The separation into distinct areas of responsibility helps both how the end users experience a website and how we build them. The end user should be able to consume the content represented in the HTML regardless of ability or if the CSS for some reason fails to load. As developers, we should be able to focus on the CSS files and not update each HTML element specifically when we want to update the design.

Now, consider the case of using a class name that only deals with a specific presentational aspect, like row and col for horizontal layout structures (that we used in Chapter 7):

```
.row {
  margin: 0 -.9%;
  padding: 0;
}
.row:after {
  content: '';
  display: block;
  clear: both;
}
.col {
  float: left;
  box-sizing: border-box;
  margin: 0 .9% 1.375em;
}
```

Even if we rename them to something less visually telling like group and block, they are still there for one purpose, which is to create presentational hooks. We have put presentational information in the HTML, no two ways about it. This goes against the SoC, so why would it be acceptable?

The SoC principle itself is much older than the Web. It was coined by legendary computer scientist Edsger Dijkstra in 1974 (https://www.cs.utexas.edu/users/EWD/transcriptions/EWD04xx/EWD447.html), in an essay where he reasoned about how to advance the field of software engineering.

The way to face increasing complexity, to summarize Dijkstra's essay, was "focusing one's attention upon some aspect" rather than "tackling these various aspects simultaneously." Since we may need to work on both HTML and CSS at the same time, we are violating this principle in one place.

Here's the thing: we are free to apply the "separation of concerns" principle on any level of our code, and it may be beneficial to sacrifice the theoretical purity of one part in order to benefit another.

The single purpose of a rule like .row is an example of the type of focus that Dijkstra talks about. When we solve the general problem of column-based layout in one place, it stays solved: when we find a better way, we don't have to update everywhere we've repeated the same solution in the CSS.

The trade-off is that we need to update the HTML when the name changes, or a specific part of the code does not use the solution any longer. Proponents of using these kinds of naming hooks tend to argue that it's easier to find and replace where we have used the class name in HTML than it is to refactor a messy CSS file.

HTML Semantics vs. Class Semantics

Here's what the HTML specification has to say on the subject of class names:

> *There are no additional restrictions on the tokens authors can use in the* class *attribute, but authors are encouraged to use values that describe the nature of the content, rather than values that describe the desired presentation of the content.*

When it comes to CSS, the CSS 2.1 specification has the following to say about class names:

> *CSS gives so much power to the "class" attribute, that authors could conceivably design their own "document language" based on elements with almost no associated presentation (such as DIV and SPAN in HTML) and assigning style information through the "class" attribute. Authors should avoid this practice since the structural elements of a document language often have recognized and accepted meanings and author-defined classes may not.*

First of all, we should note the language used in the last sentence: "encouraged," "should," "often," "may." Using a class name that could be considered presentational is not forbidden: it will not cause validation errors, and it has no effect in itself on the structural semantics or accessibility of the document. Class names and other identifiers are mostly there for the sake of developers, not users. We should therefore make a clear distinction: the semantics of HTML and its attributes is distinct from the semantics of author-defined values like classes.

The part about designing your own "document language" is important: there is a huge difference between something that looks like a button, using markup like `<span class="myButton" onclick="myFunction()">Click me!</span>`, and using `<button>Click me!</button>`. The `<button>` tag creates an element that is focusable and accessible, which is styled according to the OS conventions by default, and is potentially associated with a form. The same principle goes for any element or attribute with semantic meaning in HTML—use them responsibly.

What the specification *doesn't say* is that we can't use classes as an extension to the correct use of these elements, or augment the document with a few extra semantically meaningless elements to aid presentation.

Developer Nicolas Gallagher made the argument for re-evaluating the semantics of class names in an influential article titled "About HTML semantics and front-end architecture" (`http://nicolasgallagher.com/about-html-semantics-front-end-architecture/`), published in 2012. It nicely summarizes the thinking behind seeing presentational class names as a valid (if not always preferable) tool rather than a forbidden anti-pattern.

Finding the Right Balance

Minimizing the intermingling of style and structure via names that don't relate to presentation is obviously a good place to aim. But even when the class names represent the "visual semantics," we can try to keep the presentational nature at a minimum.

If you go down the route of allowing presentational class names, it might be tempting to decide that `arial-green-text` is a good one. Maybe you find that a reusable rule is beneficial for this font and color combination, since it's part of the brand guidelines. *If* you create such a rule, try to leave the implementation details out of the name—perhaps `brand-primary-text` would be a better choice? That way, you are at least protected from changes in color and font guidelines, if not fully from which parts use this particular style.

We must also remember that no matter how we name our classes or structure our rules, we don't have to make a binary choice. Any element could have class names describing the content, *in addition to* names describing their function as part of the UI.

Similarly, we can completely back off from expecting class names on some parts of the markup, especially where non-developers work with it. The markup in bits of application UI is likely to be authored with full control over the attributes, whereas the content of a blog post is probably just pure HTML spat out from a content management system.

If you set sensible rules for base typography and avoid styling too much based on context (in effect, more heavily based on class names where applicable), these situations will sort themselves out. On the other hand, the people who will make use of a collection of code you write may be more or less comfortable with the markup complexity.

In the blog post "Code refactoring for America" (`https://adactio.com/journal/7276`), Jeremy Keith writes about how he and Anna Debenham had to back away slightly from a heavy use of class names in the Code for America pattern library project. In short, the people who created pages based on the pattern library weren't necessarily people who wrote CSS or understood the naming conventions used. Thus, they benefitted from more readable and short HTML rather than CSS.

Code is for People

At the end of the day, the verdict on whether a specific way of writing CSS and HTML is good or bad comes down to the situation and the people involved, as long as it's technically sound and accessible. If you or the team of people you are working with find that certain ways of doing things decrease complexity in the grand scheme of things: go for it. If they hinder more than help, you should consider avoiding them.

Tooling and Workflow

As we start to treat CSS as software and impose greater demands on how we write and optimize it, we often look for better tools to manage our workflows. There has been an explosion of things like preprocessors and build systems in recent years, to the point where it is very easy to get lost in the buzzword jungle. In this section, we'll briefly present some options to beef up your toolkit.

Preprocessors and Sass

As we mentioned at the start of the chapter, CSS is intentionally designed without many of the building blocks that you'd expect in a general-purpose programming language. Things like loops, functions, lists, and variables are not available. As we've already concluded, there are good reasons for keeping them out of CSS, but on the flipside there are good reasons why people with programming experience miss them when writing CSS. They allow you to more easily create reusable bits of code, hopefully lowering the overall effort to create and maintain your styles.

People have created other languages, known as *preprocessors*, where these building blocks exist, that in turn output CSS. There are several flavors available—Sass, Less, Stylus, PostCSS, etc. At the time of writing, the most popular is Sass—Syntactically Awesome Style Sheets. We're going to look at a brief example of how this particular flavor of preprocessor works.

The most common way of writing Sass is using a superset of CSS syntax called SCSS, meaning you can write anything that is already valid in CSS, plus the extra Sass functionality you choose to use.

INSTALLING AND RUNNING SASS

The Sass compiler exists in various flavors, either as a stand-alone program or as a plug-in to many popular code editors. You can often set up your editor so that when you save a `.scss` file, it automatically updates a corresponding CSS file.

If you go to the Sass language installation page (`http://sass-lang.com/install`) you can find instructions to install on various platforms, as well as links to several editors and plug-ins with built-in support.

Following are snippets from two files where a whole host of Sass features are used. This is far from the full range of what Sass can do, but it's a taste of how the syntax looks and what various language features are used for. Don't worry if it doesn't immediately make sense to you.

First, the file named library.scss:

```scss
$primary-color: #333;

$secondary-color: #fff;

@mixin font-smoothing($subpixel: false) {
    @if $subpixel {
        -webkit-font-smoothing: subpixel-antialiased;
        -moz-osx-font-smoothing: auto;
    }
    @else {
        -webkit-font-smoothing: antialiased;
        -moz-osx-font-smoothing: grayscale;
    }
}
```

Next, the main.scss file:

```scss
@import 'library';

body {
    color: $primary-color;
    background-color: darken($secondary-color, 10%);
}
.page-header {
  color: $secondary-color;
  background-color: $primary-color;
  @include font-smoothing;
}
.page-footer {
    @extend .page-header;
    background-color: #14203B;
    a {
        color: #fff;
    }
}
```

Browsers will have no use for this code, so SCSS files are always run through a preprocessor that outputs normal CSS. Here's the result:

```css
body {
  color: #333;
  background-color: #e6e6e6;
}
.page-header,
.page-footer {
  color: #fff;
  background-color: #333;
```

392

```
  -webkit-font-smoothing: antialiased;
  -moz-osx-font-smoothing: greyscale;
}
.page-footer {
  background-color: #14203B;
}
.page-footer a {
  color: #fff;
}
```

A lot of the main.scss file is probably familiar to you: there's the same syntax for selectors, rule sets, property/value-pairs, etc. The library.scss file is imported into the main file, using a regular @import statement. For the Sass compiler, this means that the file is included into the output. In this case, the library file doesn't actually contain anything to output, but rather a collection of supporting material.

For example, Sass allows us to define *variables*, which we can then reuse in multiple places. The $primary-color and $secondary-color variables can then be used to set background and text colors, for example.

The library.scss file also contains a *mixin*, which is a collection of reusable CSS we can output anywhere. The font-smoothing mixin that we've defined allows us to toggle the browser-specific properties that keep track of which antialiasing method is used for text.

Inside the main.scss file we have used this mixin to include the font-smoothing properties as part of the .page-header rule. Mixins are called on using the @include syntax.

The .page-footer rule in turn uses another language feature—the @extend syntax. This means that its selector is added to that of the one it extends, in this case meaning that .page-footer is sharing styles with .page-header.

Finally, there's *nesting*: inside the .page-footer rule there is a selector for the a elements inside it. By writing the rules this way:

```
.page-footer {
  /* rules for page footer here */
  a {
    /* rules for links in footer here */
  }
}
```

...the Sass compiler automatically creates two sets of rules like this:

```
.page-footer {}
```

```
.page-footer a {}
```

While nesting saves us from having to type the full selector, nesting selectors can go too far. It might be tempting to nest all rules for a specific component inside each other for some sort of visual neatness, but the output will suffer in terms of overly specific rules:

```
.my-component {
  /*...rules here */
  .subcomponent {
    /*...rules here */
    .nested-subcomponent {
```

```
      /*...rules here */
      h3 { /*...rules here */ }
    }
  }
}
/* ...will output... */
.my-component { /* ...rules here... */ }
.my-component .subcomponent { /* ...rules here... */ }
.my-component .subcomponent .nested-subcomponent { /* ...rules here... */ }
.my-component .subcomponent .nested-subcomponent h3 { /* ...rules here... */ }
```

It's a good idea to check your output CSS often, so that you are not inadvertently creating bloated style sheets.

The Case for Preprocessors

Preprocessors can have a big effect on how you write CSS. When the code starts getting large and complex, preprocessors can help you achieve consistency and structure in your code, as well as speed up development.

When you're comfortable using a preprocessor, even smaller projects can benefit; especially as you start to build up an arsenal of conventions, mixins, and functions that you can share among projects.

..and the Case Against

But there are also things to consider before choosing to use a preprocessor. There is a definite hurdle in learning to use one, and using it right. If you write code that others are then going to maintain or collaborate on, you also commit to their knowing how to write in the preprocessor language you have chosen. It is also a bet on that language sticking around and being supported in the long run.

Looking back to the initial section on code quality, we saw that the main enemy of good code is complexity. The same rule applies here: don't assume that preprocessors always make your code easier to handle, but don't hesitate to try using them if they seem to help you write better code.

There are other tools that help you keep check of your code in different ways. In the next section, we'll look at some of them.

Workflow Tools

Regardless of whether you use CSS or a preprocessor language, there are usually tasks you need to do over and over again when developing. Luckily, computers are excellent at handling boring and repetitive stuff. In this section, we'll take a brief look at some tools that can be helpful.

Static Analysis and Linters

In terms of the correctness of your code, a lot of code editors have built-in syntax checkers that will highlight any selector or style declaration that doesn't look right. This kind of error checking is often referred to as "static analysis"—fancy programmer talk for trying to find problems in your code before it's even run.

If you want to beef up the static analysis of your code, there are tools that you can configure to check for issues that even go beyond syntax errors. Known as *linters*, these tools focus on finding "lint"—bits of cruft that aren't supposed to be there. For CSS, there's CSS Lint (http://csslint.net) and Stylelint (http://stylelint.io/). These tools check both for syntax errors and patterns in your selectors and declarations that may be undesirable (see Figure 12-14). Both are configurable and you can even write your own rules.

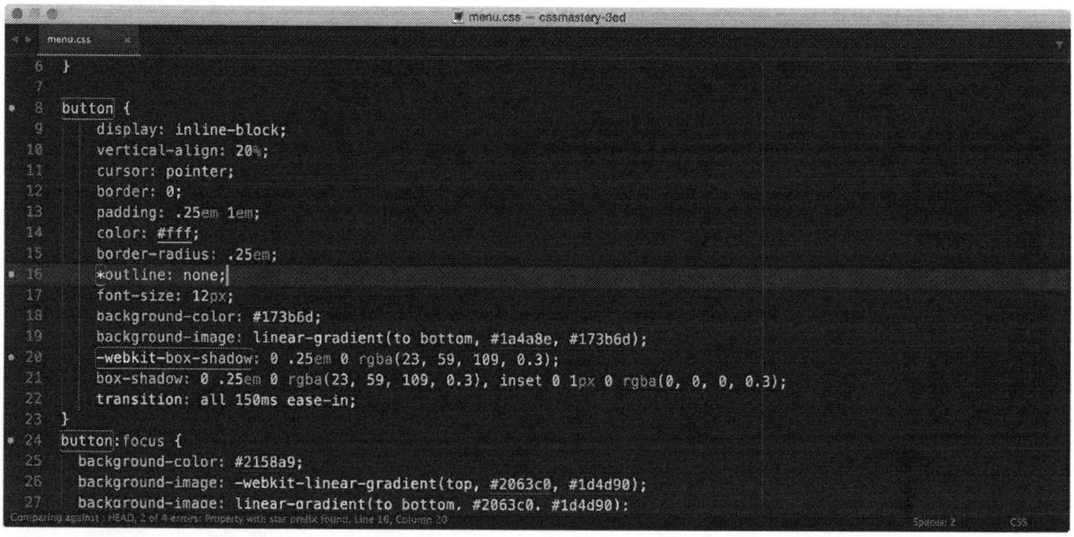

Figure 12-14. *Using CSS Lint in the Sublime Text editor. Dots in the left gutter indicate potential problems, and the explanation message is printed on the bottom bar*

Build Tools

Apart from linting, there are a lot of tasks outside of the editor that we may need to do over and over again while developing a site:

- Preprocessing CSS

- Concatenating CSS files together, if working in multiple shorter files

- Minifying CSS, removing comments and so forth to save space

- Optimizing images referenced in the CSS

- Running a development server

- Reloading one or more browsers to inspect our changes

Luckily, there are numerous tools that help you do these tasks automatically in a project. They range from more advanced tools run from the command line, to more simple setups that you can manage in a graphical user interface, like Koala (see Figure 12-15).

Figure 12-15. Koala is a build tool GUI available for Windows, Mac, and Linux

There are also lots of apps available that allow you to configure your build system entirely in code. This typically requires a bit more setup, but since the configuration can then be shared among developers and projects, it can help keep development environments consistent and quick to set up.

Setting up a CSS Build Workflow with Node and Gulp

Node is a flavor of JavaScript that you can run outside of a browser and use for any type of programming task. Since Node came about, a lot of the tooling for front-end development is based on JavaScript, as people who already knew it could scratch their own itch, so to speak.

For front-end build workflows, there are lots of Node applications like Grunt, Gulp, and Broccoli (yes, those are the actual names) that specialize in managing build tasks. They help by configuring and chaining together the output from separate tasks, each responsible for one part of the workflow.

For our example workflow, we are going to use Gulp, which is in turn handled via NPM, a utility program that comes with Node. NPM is a command-line tool, so all of the commands in the example are run inside a terminal window.

■ **Note**   If you need a crash course in how to use the command line, go to `http://learnpythonthehardway.org/book/appendix-a-cli/introduction.html` and work through some examples. It can be a daunting task, but you will learn invaluable skills for managing your computer and taking advantage of more advanced tools.

First things first: you'll need to install Node. Go to https://nodejs.org to download and run the installer for your platform. Next, navigate to the workflow-project folder inside the Chapter 12 examples in the code accompanying the book.

This folder has a file called package.json, which is the file that keeps track of what's needed to run the project. These dependencies are stored in a central code repository on https://www.npmjs.com, where hundreds of thousands of free code libraries are shared. Normally, you'd create your own package file by invoking the command npm init and answer a few questions about your project, but this time we've gone down the TV-chef route and prepared one ahead of time.

To install the dependencies listed in the package file, run the command npm install. This will download and install the following small applications, locally in your project folder:

- **Gulp:** The task runner that puts the rest of the programs together.

- **Gulp-sass:** A version of the Sass preprocessor library.

- **Browser-sync:** A tool to run a lightweight development server, and synchronize the reloading of and interacting with web pages across browsers. Also includes a debugger, so you can debug for example on mobile devices.

- **Autoprefixer:** An immensely useful library that inspects your CSS and adds the relevant prefixes and alternate syntaxes for CSS properties, based on a list of browsers that you want to support.

- **Gulp-postcss:** A version of the PostCSS preprocessor, which is needed to run Autoprefixer.

These applications will put their files in a folder called node_modules inside the project directory. If you use any kind of version control for your files, you will probably want to tell it to ignore this folder: there will be thousands of tiny files inside, and you can re-create them at any time using the package file.

The next ingredient is the file gulpfile.js, which contains instructions for how to use the installed packages together. We won't go into all the details of how this works, but as an example, here's the part that handles the preprocessing of CSS:

```
gulp.task('styles', function(){
  var processors = [autoprefixer()];
  gulp.src(['*.scss'])
    .pipe(sass())
    .pipe(postcss(processors))
    .pipe(gulp.dest('./'))
    .pipe(browserSync.reload({stream:true}))
});
```

When the gulp program is told to run the styles task, any .scss file in the same directory is picked up. It is then run through the Sass preprocessor. After that, it runs through the PostCSS processor, where Autoprefixer appends the necessary prefixes. It does so by going to http://caniuse.com and figuring out which prefixes and syntax changes to use. By default it covers the latest two versions of all major browsers, plus browsers with an approximate market share of over 1%, but this setting is highly configurable. Finally, the CSS is saved to disk and the browser-sync program is signaled to reload any connected browser windows.

To run tasks, we use NPM. The `package.json` file contains a mapping of commands that target the applications that we installed. When we now run `npm run gulp`, the default set of tasks is run, and continues to rerun automatically whenever we save a file, until we stop it.

The default browser on our machine also launches in a new tab, where the `index.html` file in the current directory is served. As soon as the CSS file changes, the browser (and any other browser you point at the same address) reloads.

It's easy to get lost when setting up task runners and workflows. The win comes when you have it on file, and it's ready to reuse across projects or share. A new collaborator would only need to install Node and run `npm install` before they had the exact same setup on their machine. Although wrestling with development tools is probably the least fun part of building websites for most people, it is often a type of "set it and forget it" task that can save lots of time in the long perspective, once you are up and running. If you need a slightly more detailed introduction (using the Grunt task runner rather than Gulp), we recommend Chris Coyier's article "Grunt for People Who Think Things Like Grunt are Weird and Hard" (`https://24ways.org/2013/grunt-is-not-weird-and-hard/`).

The Future of CSS Syntax and Structure

Throughout this book, we have been using CSS features with various levels of browser support. We have repeated the mantra of progressive enhancement in applying new features—meaning you can use a lot of them today, as long as you have a sensible alternative lined up when they aren't yet supported. This works for a lot of things, but not all.

There are some fundamental proposed changes to how we write CSS on the horizon. Some of these are experimentally supported already, but as they are hard to apply in a progressive way, it's likely that it will be a few years before we'll be able to use all of them in our day-to-day workflows. Nevertheless, it is useful to keep an eye out for where CSS is headed.

Custom Properties—Variables in CSS

The addition of variables to CSS has been one of the most-requested features for a long time. A spec has been in the works for several years, and only recently became a Candidate Recommendation. As this book is being written, Chrome and Safari are on the verge of releasing versions with support. Firefox has already supported variables for quite a while.

The technically correct name for these variables is *custom properties*: they look an awful lot like how variables work in, for example, Sass, but are slightly different.

A custom property is declared using syntax much like a vendor-prefixed property, except the vendor name is empty, resulting in two initial dashes. To define a variable that is to be available globally, you can add it to the `:root` selector. You can also define (or redefine) a variable to have a specific value in a specific selector context.

```
:root {
  --my-color: red;
}
.myThing {
  --my-color: blue;
}
```

We can access the value of a custom property anywhere that the value has cascaded. The `var()` functional notation pulls the custom property value out, with the option of a fallback value if the property is undefined or invalid. In the following snippet, the `color` declaration will be set to `blue`, since the previous example set it on the `.myThing` ancestor:

```
.myThing .myInnerThing {
  /* second (optional) argument is the fallback */
  color: var(--my-color, purple);
}
```

Custom properties can be used with `var()` not just as the entire value, but as part of another subvalue:

```
:root {
  --max-columns: 3;
}
.myThing {
  columns: var(--max-columns, 2) 12em;
}
```

Since preprocessors like Sass have variables built in, why would we choose to do this work on the client rather than beforehand via a build script or server process? Well, since custom properties are calculated in the browser and not beforehand, they have access to the live DOM tree and the whole cascade. If something changes, the styles can be recalculated. If we use JavaScript to set the `--my-color` variable for the `html` element after the page has loaded, every element that depends on that color value updates its color instantly.

It's tricky to start using custom properties for any significant parts of your code before a wide range of browsers supports them. Any fallbacks to regular values would necessarily result in a lot of duplicated declarations. Nevertheless, they are no doubt a powerful addition to CSS.

HTTP/2 and Server Push

A lot of the performance-related patterns we use today are related to how HTTP works. More specifically, we try to counter the fact that the current version, HTTP/1.1, is relatively slow when it comes to fetching multiple things at once, so we mash together all of our styles into one file, and avoid external requests like the plague.

In HTTP/2, the underlying protocol is optimized for delivering many small assets at once. A single connection can carry multiple files, reducing a lot of the overhead for making new requests. There's also some smart thinking in HTTP/2 with regard to how web pages are delivered. Using something called "Server Push," the server can automatically deliver a single response containing both HTML and CSS, unless the request signals that the browser already has the CSS file in its cache.

These new advances may help us get rid of patterns like inlining styles, or making image sprites. The `@import` statement, which has been an anti-pattern of sorts for a long time, can get a new lease on life, allowing us to split up files as we like, without worrying about the extra request overhead.

HTTP/2 is supported in a lot of places already, and can be used today, as it falls back to the old behavior when unsupported in a browser. It does require that the web server you are using supports it, however. As with many infrastructure changes, this means that it will take some time before it's truly mainstream and built into our tools.

Web Components

Web Components is a name for a range of standards that allow web developers to package up HTML, CSS, and JavaScript into truly self-contained and easily reusable components, almost as if they were native elements. When using a Web Component, you should be able to drop it right into your project, without worrying about naming collisions between your styles (or scripts) and those belonging to the component.

If we had created a hypothetical Web Component for including thumbnail previews from the Internet Movie Database (`http://www.imdb.com`), we would use a JavaScript file to tell the browser that we intended to use a custom `imdb-preview` element in our markup. This element could then be invoked like this in HTML:

```
<imdb-preview>
  <a href="http://www.imdb.com/title/tt0118715/>The Big Lebowski</a>
</imdb-preview>
```

On the page, the result could be something like that shown in Figure 12-16, with several parts.

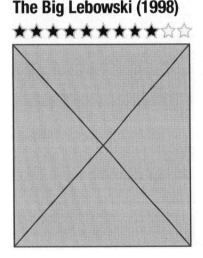

The Big Lebowski (1998)
★★★★★★★★★★☆☆

Figure 12-16. *The hypothetical result of invoking our* `<imdb-preview>` *element*

Behind the scenes, this custom element could fetch data based on the URL of the link, and replace its contents with its own hidden DOM fragment, known as the Shadow DOM. The title, review score, and image will all have their own elements in that fragment. In a sense, it's a bit like an `iframe`—the contents are shielded from the regular DOM tree of the page, and they use separate contexts for scripting and styling.

Inside a Shadow DOM fragment, `style` elements automatically have a scope limited to the web component's root element, just like if we were using the `scoped` attribute. Styles from the parent document do not bleed into the element either, so the component styles are completely encapsulated. The trick is that custom properties *can* cascade into the component—so the component author can specify exactly which properties you are allowed to override. With this mechanism, things like typography and color schemes can safely be changed to match the site where the component is used.

A lot of the proposed Web Component standards are unsupported as of yet, but the encapsulation into Shadow DOM is already happening in browsers with elements like `<video src="..."></video>`. Even if the element is empty in the markup, it has hidden elements for things like the video controls—you can activate the "Show user agent Shadow DOM" option in the Chrome DevTools, for example, to see it in action (see Figure 12-17).

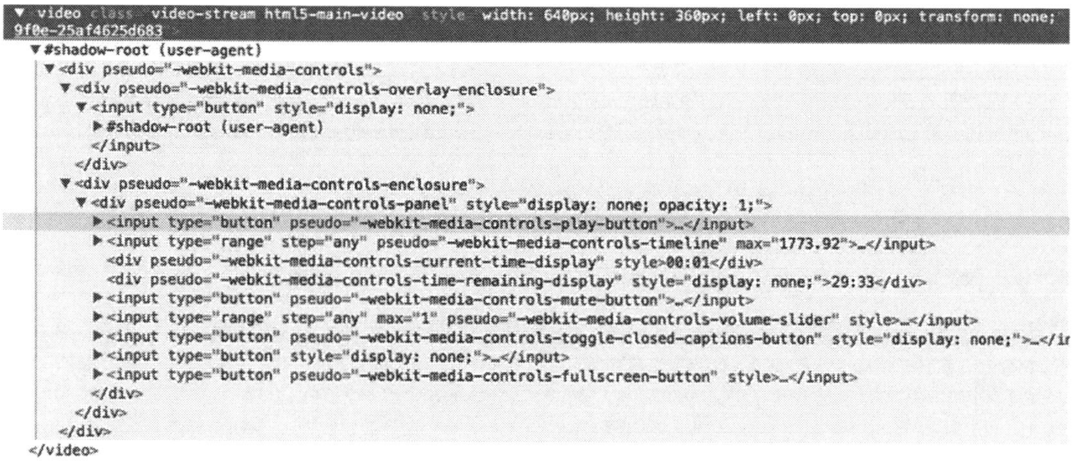

```
▼ video class video-stream html5-main-video style width: 640px; height: 360px; left: 0px; top: 0px; transform: none;
9f0e-25af4625d683
  ▼ #shadow-root (user-agent)
    ▼ <div pseudo="-webkit-media-controls">
      ▼ <div pseudo="-webkit-media-controls-overlay-enclosure">
        ▼ <input type="button" style="display: none;">
          ▶ #shadow-root (user-agent)
          </input>
        </div>
      ▼ <div pseudo="-webkit-media-controls-enclosure">
        ▼ <div pseudo="-webkit-media-controls-panel" style="display: none; opacity: 1;">
          ▶ <input type="button" pseudo="-webkit-media-controls-play-button">…</input>
          ▶ <input type="range" step="any" pseudo="-webkit-media-controls-timeline" max="1773.92">…</input>
            <div pseudo="-webkit-media-controls-current-time-display" style=00:01</div>
            <div pseudo="-webkit-media-controls-time-remaining-display" style="display: none;">29:33</div>
          ▶ <input type="button" pseudo="-webkit-media-controls-mute-button">…</input>
          ▶ <input type="range" step="any" max="1" pseudo="-webkit-media-controls-volume-slider" style>…</input>
          ▶ <input type="button" pseudo="-webkit-media-controls-toggle-closed-captions-button" style="display: none;">…</in
          ▶ <input type="button" style="display: none;">…</input>
          ▶ <input type="button" pseudo="-webkit-media-controls-fullscreen-button" style>…</input>
          </div>
        </div>
      </div>
    </div>
  </video>
```

Figure 12-17. If we turn on Shadow DOM inspection and inspect a `<video>`, we see that it's composed of lots of other elements—volume controls and player buttons, for example

In the Web Component mindset, we get a lot of the modularity and composability that other methodologies strive for—not just in CSS, but in HTML, CSS, and JavaScript together. All of the major browser vendors are on board with implementing Web Components, but there's still disagreement about exactly which feature sets and syntaxes should be used.

How much they will influence how we write CSS is still too early to tell. Maybe they will change how we construct websites all together, and maybe they'll just be another way of doing things that we bump into now and then.

CSS and the Extensible Web

One of the ideas behind Web Components is that they can be used as a testing ground of sorts for new native functionality. If a certain component becomes the de facto way to create a certain type of widget or content, and is used across millions of websites, then maybe that element should be part of the HTML standard?

The idea of creating standards based on what developers actually use is not new. For example, the jQuery JavaScript library used a CSS selector approach to select DOM elements, and became hugely popular. Nowadays, we have the `querySelector` API in native JavaScript, which works in a very similar way:

```
// jQuery code:
jQuery('.myThing p');
// Standardized way:
document.querySelectorAll('.myThing p');
```

In the same way, things like preprocessors influence how CSS is going to look in the future. There are suggestions for CSS standards covering native `@extend` directives, native nesting, custom named media queries, and more.

There is a document, signed by a range of people in the web community, called "The Extensible Web Manifesto" (`https://extensiblewebmanifesto.org/`) that pushes the idea that standards need to go in a direction that gives developers better access to lower levels of browser internals, so they may explore new ways of building. The solutions they come up with then become fed back to the standards organizations for more high-level building blocks to standardize.

This model is a step away from the current situation, where browser makers and other industry stakeholders come up with proposed high-level standards, which developers only get to try out once implemented in a browser.

For CSS, the Extensible Web idea doesn't necessarily mean that the language will become encumbered with low-level features. Instead, JavaScript APIs will, hopefully, be opened up to things like rendering and custom syntax, so that any proposed new CSS features can be implemented as scripted polyfills the moment they are conceived. If this succeeds, the rate of innovation in CSS will only increase. We'd better get ready.

Summary

In this final chapter, we've covered everything from how browsers interpret your CSS, to how authors can write flexible and maintainable code that any front-end developer worth their salt could understand. Even if the CSS you write is bug-free, nicely packaged up, and maintainable, development can still be a chore. Power tools like preprocessors and build scripts can help you along the way, but don't let them become overwhelmingly complex in themselves. With great power comes great responsibility, after all.

Finally, we've looked at some of the things on the horizon for CSS and how we can plan for the future. There are many developments ahead of us, too many for one book to cover in detail. Concepts that once felt universal and immutable when the first version of this book was written, have become more nuanced and complex as the language (and what's asked of it) matures.

The best CSS authors always have one eye on the present and another eye on the future, constantly questioning how the trends of today may become the bottlenecks of tomorrow. Rather than throwing your weight behind a particular tool or technique, put time and effort into understanding the underlying principles. That's the true route to CSS mastery.

Index

Get the eBook for only $5!

Why limit yourself?

Now you can take the weightless companion with you wherever you go and access your content on your PC, phone, tablet, or reader.

Since you've purchased this print book, we're happy to offer you the eBook in all 3 formats for just $5.

Convenient and fully searchable, the PDF version enables you to easily find and copy code—or perform examples by quickly toggling between instructions and applications. The MOBI format is ideal for your Kindle, while the ePUB can be utilized on a variety of mobile devices.

To learn more, go to www.apress.com/companion or contact support@apress.com.

Made in the USA
Lexington, KY
02 February 2017